The Energy Book

A RÉSUMÉ OF PRESENT KNOWLEDGE AND RESEARCH

BYGGFORSKNINGSRÅDET
The Swedish Council for Building Research

Editors: Hans E B Andersson and Åsa Klevard Setterwall

Design: Dagmar Forsberg

Diagrams drawn by: Karin Berg Mont & Rit

Cover: Ivar Arosenius, "Lillan",
Photo: Nationalmuseum, SKM, Stockholm.

T6:1996
ISBN 91-540-5744-2
Swedish Council for Building Research,
Stockholm, Sweden.

PREFACE

The most important reason for the State investing money in sector research is that society has an interest in change in the sector concerned, and that this change cannot be brought about without State participation in the acquisition of knowledge and competence. This is very much the case in the energy sector. Requirements in respect of changes to the Swedish energy system are based primarily on the realisation that finite natural resources must not be totally worked out, that a good living environment for the earth's organic life must be maintained and that our needs for a good indoor environment must be met.

At present, our energy system does not meet these overall requirements, which has been pointed out on many occasions, including the Rio Declaration. Technology and methods for utilisation of new energy sources, and for conservation of energy in use, are therefore being developed. At the same time, there is growing awareness that more attention must be paid to the indoor climate than has previously been the case.

All State work of sector research character starts from objectives formulated in general terms. In the work that it performs on development of energy systems in the built environment, the Swedish Council for Building Research (BFR) can start partly from the general objectives for its activities, and partly from the more specific objectives for the Government's energy policy and energy research. The Council's overall objectives in this context are to:

■ encourage establishment of the right conditions for a good living environment and quality of life in our residential and working areas,

■ ensure go on from here sustainable development through greater consideration of environmental requirements, health aspects and user requirements, in planning, construction and use of buildings, as well as in improvement of the efficiency of energy and electricity use in the built environment.

In addition, the Government's and Parliament's decisions on energy policy, and therefore also on energy research, have set out the following guidelines.

■ To stimulate technical and other measures intended to reduce the need for energy through conservation and improvements in its efficiency of use.

■ To stimulate greater use of renewable energy sources based on sun, wind and water.

■ To stimulate a substitution of fossil fuels preferably to biofuels, or to natural gas as a second choice.

■ To develop and improve combustion processes for all types of fuels.

■ To encourage the use of CHP instead of cold condensing power production.

■ To develop and encourage a change to a transport system causing considerably less emission of pollution than our present transport system.

In addition, Parliament's decision to phase out nuclear power before 2010 still applies, putting this and other activities in an important time perspective.

In any and all discussion of meeting the energy requirements of the built environment, whether in respect of supply or use, it is important to attempt to apply a genuine system perspective. This applies to all levels of the system: for example, what may be in itself a brilliant technical solution may remain unused if it is not suitable for use in or with the process of change by which it is intended to replace older and poorer technology. The same applies for public guide measures if they have not been drafted with a knowledge of the process where they are to work. The whole aim of this book is that it should be the system perspective that determines presentation.

The book presents a broad presentation of our state of knowledge and of the need for further knowledge development in the energy sector of the built environment. The presentation extends beyond the Council's area of responsibility for research and development, as we feel that it is important to maintain the system view and to attempt to present an overall picture. We also want to illustrate the favourable potentials for achieving more efficient use of energy in the built environment, while at the same time having a positive effect on the indoor and outdoor climates and environments.

As with earlier energy status reviews from the Council, the book is based on reports from research workers and other experts in the energy field or adjacent fields. A total of more than 40 persons have contributed to the book: brief notes on the authors or contributors are given after each chapter. In addition, in order to present as rounded a picture as possible, views on the whole material have also been obtained by sending drafts out for comment. The Council would hereby like to present its thanks to all those who have assisted.

In the majority of areas, knowledge is uncontested and there is general agreement on the need for continued acquisition of knowledge. However, this is not the case in all areas: in some, there are different views, and it has been our intention that this should be apparent. Final presentation and preparation of the material has been carried out by the Council, through a working party consisting of Jan Lagerström (Chairman), Hans E. B. Andersson, Heatecon (Secretary), Conny Rolén, Björn Sellberg and Gabrielle Waldén.

We hope that this book can serve as a basis not only for overall energy policy decisions and research strategy decisions, but also for individuals' decisions on matters concerning improvements in the efficiency of energy use.

Bertil Pettersson
Director-General, Swedish Council for Building Research

CONTENTS

WHAT'S IN THE ENERGY BOOK ...

Over the last 25 years, Sweden's energy use in the built environment has not increased, despite the fact that the country's gross heated floor area has increased by more than 40 %. In addition, there are still substantial potentials for improvement in the efficiency of energy use and for application of more forms of renewable energy that have not yet been utilised. Effort properly applied to these areas today can give us a better environment tomorrow, both locally and globally. In this context, life cycle analyses are important tools.

Ever since the first Swedish energy conservation standards were introduced in 1978, energy conservation in residential buildings has been directed predominantly by normative standards and mortgage rules. A characteristic of the Building Regulations is that they have specified requirements only in respect of buildings' heat requirements, and not at all in respect of electricity use in residential buildings.

Between 1970 and 1994, specific gross energy use for space heating and domestic hot water production has fallen from about 340 kWh/m^2 to about 220 kWh/m^2. For Sweden as a whole, this means that total final gross energy use has remained unchanged at about 150 TWh/year, while the heated area of the country's building stock has increased from about 430 million m^2 to about 630 million m^2. This means that energy use is more than 50 TWh/year less than what it would have been without the energy conservation measures that have been implemented. In terms of consumers' money, this is worth about 2500 million crowns/year.

Between 1970 and 1994, electricity use for domestic hot water, space heating, domestic appliances and building services systems has increased from about 15 TWh/year to about 35 TWh/year, while conversion losses at the point of use have fallen from about 34 TWh/year to about 19 TWh/year. This reduction in losses is due partly to improvements in efficiency of the use of boilers etc., and partly to a change to electricity or district heating, mainly from oil.

The greater use of electricity in buildings needs to be appreciated, both in respect of improvements in the efficiency of its use and for consideration of dealing with surplus heat. Residential buildings and commercial premises use more than half of the electricity used in Sweden, and so the potential savings resulting from improvements in efficiency and changes to other forms of energy carriers in this sector are very large.

Several of the renewable energy sources have excellent potentials for development. This includes bioenergy, solar heating and the use of heat pumps in more applications. However, there is insufficient information available for a comprehensive discussion of the economic and market factors required for success of the various methods, or for a discussion of how the present system of public regulations and support for renewable energy should be drafted within possible future scenarios. Long-term political decisions concerning the country's overall environmental and energy policy are vital in determining if, how and when these potentials can be realised.

The effects of air pollution on man and the environment are complex problems, about which insufficient is known. Caution bids us go forward with care. There is a two-way connection between the built environment and local climate, in that the climate affects energy requirements, while the built environment affects the local climate. Not enough work has been done on investigating how these effects occur and how the establishment and development of areas and traffic planning interact.

During the last decade, major improvements have been effected in reducing the environmental impact of stationary energy plant, while transport systems have expanded largely unchecked, with little consideration of their environmental effects. Some work has been done on investigating how traffic reduction measures and other restrictions affect the siting of developed areas, and thus the need for transport. The establishment and development of built-up areas also strongly affects the need for transport.

Life cycle analyses are an effective tool for determining the total energy and material flows associated with improvements in the efficiency of both production and use of energy. The method is suitable for comparative analyses and assessments of the environmental effects of use of a material or product. However, only a few such analyses have been performed for the building sector in Sweden. Some examples are roofing materials, flooring materials, solar energy technology, heat pumps and energy stores. We need further knowledge in these and associated areas, while linking the knowledge to planning, construction and building administrative/operational processes. Life cycle analyses for building materials and building designs should be widely employed.

Good indoor climate conditions can very well be combined with good energy conservation practice. Performance requirements, i.e. in respect of parameters such as temperature, clean air and lack of noise, must determine the physical systems used to create and control the indoor climate. This imposes substantial requirements on the knowledge and quality control procedures of the building sector.

The term 'good indoor climate' can be interpreted in many ways. The physical systems that control the indoor climate are artificial ones, while the humans who occupy the indoor climate are biological beings with subjective impressions. To this must be added the socio-cultural links that affect our being and our actions. Although the problem is very complex, we can nevertheless specify requirements in respect of temperature, light, humidity, clean air and absence of noise, i.e. parameters that can affect our health.

We need better to learn to identify relevant factors needed to describe the indoor environment and to express and quantify them in respect of building performances. These performance requirements must be so formulated that it is possible to convert them to technical solutions that operate well. Conscious pursuit of this theme should lay the basis for continued development of everything from formulation of performance requirements to reliable technical designs.

Many complicated health aspects are today related to buildings. There are clear links between different types of physiological problems and indoor air quality. What there are not, however, are direct relationships between energy conservation and building-related health problems. Investigations have shown that there are major differences in health problems experienced by those living in houses built before and after 1960. Development during the 1960s and 70s resulted in construction methods that are less resistant to design or constructional faults than were older methods. In turn, this imposes requirements on quality control of the building process and on the knowledge of the effects of incorrect application of new technology as possessed by the parties involved.

On the one hand, a building is a spatial system of everything from structural elements to shape and colour. On the other hand, this same system must fulfil the objective of providing a good indoor climate and good hygienic conditions. Today, we are experiencing an imbalance in competence and organisation of handling these two aspects of the system. Our ability to deal with and/or control the climatic/hygiene system is not up to the requirements associated with the task of providing a good indoor environment in a building in combination with substantial resource conservation. We need to augment research and training within this sector.

The slow rate of renewal of the built environment necessitates long-term objectives and keeping to decisions once they have been made. Deregulation of the electricity market reduces the State's short-term influence, but makes the long-term decisions even more important. In an internationalised electricity market, power conservation will be as important as energy conservation.

In recent years, energy policy has become increasingly market-orientated. The importance of price as a controlling measure has increased. However, several researchers doubt that market forces are capable of driving development in the desired direction without the support of a rules framework. The State's guide measures should have long-term acceptability, and be designed so that the necessary energy and environmental policy measures are commercially viable.

Market forces can be employed to spread energy-efficient products. Many customers need improved means of being made aware of, understanding and trusting new technology. More knowledge of the practical aspects of marketing energy efficiency improvements is needed, as is knowledge of how the State's efficiency improvement programme can make better use of market mechanisms by working with them.

There are major potentials for improvement in the efficiency of electricity use, but several investigations, whether of systems or of behavioural aspects, have shown that improvements in the efficiency of electricity use do not necessarily lead to a reduction in electricity use. Unless the price of electricity is extremely high, the money saved may be spent on further electricity use for new purposes.

In the short term, it is likely that deregulation of the electricity market will result in a reduction in electricity prices. Over the next few years, the demand for electricity can be expected to increase relatively rapidly as a result of these reductions and of the general upturn in the economy. In the longer term, integration in EU may result in Swedish electricity prices (bulk power, excluding taxes etc.) approaching prices in the rest of Europe. In due course, favourable markets for the export of electricity to the continent may arise. The structure of our electricity production system may also result in differentiation of electricity prices, during the day and during the year. If so, this will result in power conservation becoming an important part of the general programme of improvement in efficiency. If the energy systems have been suitably designed, and if appropriate operating strategies are employed, it should be possible to meet the energy requirements of buildings mainly through cheap night-time electricity, which would have

the dual effect of reducing costs for the consumer and reducing pressure for new production capacity.

We need to investigate price structures on the energy markets, financing arrangements for total heating systems, the decision-making process at various levels and the interaction between various guide measures. The side-effects of these guide measures on other areas, such as health and environment or competition and productivity, need to be analysed. Public energy planning needs to consider total process cycles on a freer energy market. Planning tools for urban planning and public regional planning need to be developed and made user-friendly.

In the long term, greater use of renewable energy sources that directly or indirectly use the sun for energy production is a prerequisite for a sustainable energy supply. Biofuels and wind power are competitive in situations where new capacity is required.

About a fifth of the country's single-family houses' heating requirements are met by log firing, unfortunately often in equipment not really suited for it. Pre-processing of the fuel, and improvement in combustion methods, could substantially increase the proportion of energy supplied by biofuels without adverse environmental effects. There is good potential for further development of combustion technology: the application of low-pollution technology should be stimulated through requirements for low emission levels.

Swedish large-scale solar heating technology is among the most cost-effective available. Its commercial niches are in replacing or assisting oil-fired group heating plants and smaller district heating systems. In recent years, small-scale solar heating for individual houses has been developed as a result of growing interest in self-build activities, often combined with the use of biofuels. An expanded advisory service would encourage technical and commercial development. The efficiencies of both solar collectors and overall heating systems could be further improved.

Interest in wind power is expressed primarily by companies and individuals. A modest environmental bonus would make local wind power financially viable for cooperatively-owned installations or distribution companies having their own production capacity. There is a need for development of both the technical aspects of wind power production and of factors relating to its use.

Small-scale CHP technologies exist, although very little use is made of them in Sweden. CHP employing Stirling engines, gas turbines or steam turbines as their prime movers offer both energy and environmental benefits, and are therefore worthy of continued development. However, small-scale CHP is commercially hampered in Sweden today by the country's low electricity prices. More knowledge is needed of the operating conditions for small-scale CHP.

Distribution technology has become simpler and more efficient, and district cooling is a new technology on the march. This is an area in which surprisingly little research resources are being invested in proportion to capital investment in plant. Development of heat distribution technology should be concentrated on repair, maintenance and improvement of the efficiency of existing systems.

Today, several different types of heat stores are at various stages of development. Several of these are commercially available, e.g. aquifer heat stores for both heating and cooling. Borehole heat stores need further development to suit them for solar heating applications.

Heat pumps have improved in efficiency and become easier to look after. In terms of numbers, the market is dominated by small heat pumps. The weak links now are to be found in the ancillary equipment and systems around the heat pumps, and further development is needed of the overall systems.

Applications for solar power today seem to be in isolated installations at a long distance from public electricity supplies. The State is adopting a relatively passive attitude. Development in the field of solar power should be concentrated both on thin-film cells and on pricing methods.

In the built environment, natural gas is primarily used for space heating: other applications are insignificant. Much more use could be made of energy gas in the built environment if the trunk mains for its distribution were extended. Development is needed primarily in tailoring system designs to suit Swedish conditions and in monitoring international developments.

Many technically advanced energy-efficient solutions that have been evaluated in experimental installations exist today. However, in many cases, the interaction effects between buildings and building services systems and the large-scale energy system have been inadequately investigated.

Building designs exist that can halve energy use relative to that of buildings complying with the present Building Regulations, but they are employed to only a slight extent. Such buildings can be both simple and easily run. However, the general situation is that energy-efficient buildings tend to become complicated and difficult to run. The new building services systems technology is demanding of both designers and builders, as well as of occupants and building operators. Considerable effort is often needed in order to achieve the actual low energy use performance that was intended.

In many cases, interaction effects between buildings and building services systems have been inadequately investigated. Major energy savings could probably be achieved if building technology and building services systems technology could be brought closer together. There are substantial gains to be made from improving the efficiency of ventilation, employing new lighting technology and improved domestic electronic equipment. In general, residential buildings require only heating, while commercial premises often have substantial cooling requirements. Greater use of comfort cooling can substantially increase electricity demand, although this is an area that is suitable for the use of energy storage techniques, thus avoiding compressor-powered cooling.

The building as an energy system forms part of a supply system with varying characteristics throughout the day and year, and where tariffs have a considerable effect. Analysis of the total system requires more extensive description of the building as part of the energy system than is available today.

Although there is substantial scope for energy conservation, financial aspects dictate that conservation effort needs to be differentiated in respect of the type of built environment and the type of heating. Analyses show that, in areas where district heating is available, it is only the cheapest energy conservation measures that are financially viable, while single-family houses with direct electric heating, beyond the reach of district heating systems can often support relatively expensive conservation measures. Development of Sweden's energy system towards a greater amount of CHP production would enhance this effect. Calculations of the technical conservation potentials can result in totally opposing conclusions in respect of where the improvements should be applied.

Research and development are needed if available knowledge is to be incorporated in the planning, building and administration processes. It is also important that there should be a strategy for further development of those involved in the building sector. The feedback of experience to the early planning stages must be improved, and knowledge must reach those involved in the building sector and the actual occupants. Operational, care and maintenance routines need to be improved, while diagnostic methods of commissioning and performance monitoring need to be developed.

In future, the value of properties will be affected by how operation and maintenance work. Attempts to fulfil the changed requirements will be decisive for a future good environment, satisfied occupants and good long-term cost conditions. New requirements, together with rising energy prices, will affect development towards more efficient operation of energy systems. From this starting point, it will be important to distinguish and investigate several non-technical factors.

Greater attention must be paid to training, competence and status of operating personnel than is now the case. Property maintenance must be preventive and long-term. The views and experience of operating personnel are very important at the planning stage. Experience needs to be fed back, with user needs and requirements being brought out in structured dialogues. Communication between all parties, ranging from planners to users, must be improved. At present, problems or questions often fall between different disciplines. We need an overall view of the Building-Indoor climate-Occupiers.

BUILDING AND ENERGY RESEARCH

*The importance of an overall view in achieving
a balance between buildings' two systems*

Photographer: Lars Säfström, Mira

THE IMPORTANCE OF AN OVERALL VIEW IN ACHIEVING A BALANCE BETWEEN BUILDINGS' TWO SYSTEMS

SUMMARY

Each individual house, or group of houses, can be regarded as two interwoven systems. One is the geometric-spatial--visual system, consisting of rooms and openings towards the surroundings, lighting, textures, shape, colour, external design etc. This system needs a greater or lesser extent of maintenance in order to operate. The second system - the climate/occupational system - consists of the same physical parts, with the addition of heating and ventilation systems, electrical systems, water and drainage systems etc. This system needs not only maintenance but also continuous operation, in order to fulfil its purpose in real time.

The two systems have been developed separately, and sometimes with only weak links between them. A review of developments from the 18th century to today indicates that there has been a constant imbalance in competence and organisation within the building sector in respect of the two systems that form a complete, ready-to-use building.

Our ability to control the climate/-occupational system does not match the requirements imposed by the need to combine good indoor conditions with extensive resource conservation, particularly in respect of energy. In order to create a balance, more resources are needed for research and training in the climate/occupational field.

It is generally assumed that houses were originally built to provide protection against cold, wind and rain, animals, evil spirits and robbers. As time passed, other factors were included, such as symbolising the owner's position in society, fulfilling aesthetic aims etc. When built close together, houses became elements in the perspectives of public streets and squares. They grew in size and complexity, and began to require the services of professionals both for building and for operation and maintenance. During the latter half of the 20th century, fantasies have been raised concerning enormous structures that are both house and town at one and the same time.

If we wish to look back at the history of the built environment and attempt to separate elements connected with energy use and the indoor environment, it is helpful to regard the house (or groups of houses) as two interwoven systems:

■ A geometric-spatial-visual system of rooms and linking elements, openings to the outside world, lighting, textures, shapes and colours, external design etc., in the form of floors, walls and roof, foundations, structural elements, floor/ceiling structures, windows, doors, furnishings and visible parts of service systems. This system as a whole needs maintenance to a greater or lesser degree.

■ A climate/occupational system, consisting of the same physical parts, with the addition of heating and ventilation systems, electrical systems, water and drainage systems. This requires both maintenance and continuous use/operation to ensure that it continues to operate properly, keep rooms warm and habitable etc.

It is not, in other words, a matter of two separate systems. When we think of two separate systems, we see the house *as if* it was one or the other. The physical components are largely the same in both systems, but with different duties. The exterior walls, for example, are structural and bounding in the geometrical-spatial-visual system, while in the climate/occupational system the same walls act as climate screens, heat stores, absorbers and emitters of chemical substances to the indoor air etc. Apart from lighting, there are only few elements of the building services systems that form part of the geometrical-spatial-visual system, but they play an important but generally unseen part in the climate/-occupational system.

The building's two systems also have separate links with the external systems to which the building is connected and with which it interacts at higher and more complex system levels. It is as a climate/-occupational system that the building interacts with, or forms part of, the energy system, the water and sanitation system, the refuse system, the surrounding environmental system etc. The need to be able to deal with these types of system relationship links is one reason for creating this concept of a theoretical division into two separate systems. The other reason is the need to improve our understanding of the internal operations of buildings.

With our present awareness of re-use and recycling, the materials flows involved in constructing a building are attracting considerable interest. These run from the original extraction of the raw materials, through materials manufacture and construction to dealing with residual products from the constructional phase and, finally, demolition. From this point of view, it is not equally clear that a building should be regarded as belonging to one or other of the two systems. If we nevertheless must make a distinction, it is probably best to regard the building as a geometrical-spatial-visual system.

Children froze to death

Historically, the two systems have developed along separate paths and sometimes with only tenuous links between them. If we take a glance at history during Sweden's imperialistic era, we can alight on Skokloster Castle, which is a magnificent building in terms of its architectonic design and as a geometrical-spatial-visual system, but so primitive in terms of its climate/-occupational system that even some of its owner's children froze to death during the winters. At least the land-owning portion of the peasant population were probably better off from a climate/occupational viewpoint in their small and externally very unpretentious timber cottages.

During the late 18th century, Sweden felt that it was facing a threatening energy crisis. A Royal Commission was set up to develop the technical aspects of housing design so that they might be less demanding of energy resources, i.e. of forest timber. The Commission

proposed substantial changes in the climate/occupational system aspect of houses. The Swedish tiled stove made its first appearance, with its complicated but energy-efficient system of internal ducts. Coupled windows and other features for improved draught-proofing and insulation were introduced throughout the country's housing stock. Rooms no longer extended all the way up into pitched roofs, but were bounded upwards by ceilings.

The energy crisis never actually occurred: it is difficult to say whether this was due to the improvements suggested by the Commission or as a result of a fall in demand for charcoal due to new technology in the iron and steel industry, or simply to the fact that the threat of a crisis had been founded on inadequate forest ecology knowledge and had thus simply been exaggerated.

Unhealthy smell

Parish records from Fredsberg parish in Västergötland from the beginning of the 19th century record unhealthy smells in the farmers' cottages since they had been draught-proofed in accordance with the advice and instructions spread over the country since the end of the 18th century. The 'technicians' of the time, who were competent within their respective areas, had evidently solved their energy problems without allowing for, or without sufficient knowledge of, the hygienic effects of eliminating ventilation.

By the end of the century, the picture is almost completely different. Doctors had learnt what the major health epidemics had been caused by, and hygienic countermeasures were being applied to stop them. Water and sewerage systems were being built in the towns. Houses were being improved, at least for those who could afford to pay. In 1881, Professor E. Heyman, Professor of Health Science at the Karolinska Hospital in Stockholm, published his work 'Concerning the Air in our Homes'. Comfort and convenience had become important elements in the new, pleasantly-situated middle-class residences, together with external status and internal atmosphere. This was a building style that had made its appearance in the stately homes and mansions of Sweden and in the homes of the exploited, and which had now achieved its urban form, with its climatic/occupational and geometrical-spatial-visual systems in mutual balance.

During the 1900s, the number of slums and the general housing shortage grew, until modern housing policy was formulated and began to change conditions during the 1930s. Photographer: A. Malmström, Stockholm City Museum

Filthy Sweden

In 1938, Lubbe Nordström wrote a series of articles on travels through the country, to which he gave the name 'Filthy Sweden'. These showed that conditions for the average family in rural areas were still extremely poor. In towns and urban areas, living conditions of the working class were squalid. Slums and housing shortages continued to increase until modern housing policy was formulated and began to have an effect during the 1930s. Nevertheless, a reasonable hygienic living standard was not available to the majority until after the Second World War. Medical and hygienic requirements and knowledge therefore remained central elements of building practices that were developed during the first half of the century, and were reflected by building legislation. However, when the problem had finally been mastered in its old, classical forms, the resulting success was such that hygienic awareness almost disappeared from the building sector over a few subsequent decades.

During the Second World War, the blockade on importation of coal and oil meant that wood again had to be used for heating. At times, fuel shortages were serious, despite the fact that substantial numbers of the country's military service intake were deployed to cut wood in the forests. Indoor temperatures fell and hot water was rationed. Little new building was being done, and so there was no particular interest in discussing improved building technology. The situation was regarded as temporary. To what extent lowered indoor temperatures and hot water rationing adversely affected health is not known, as general health was improved at the same time through a reduction in overeating.

New housing increases

After the end of the war an offensive to raise housing standards started with an increase in the amount of new building. In the small apartments of three or four rooms that were standard, it was necessary to make the best possible use of the limited floor area, right out to the exterior walls and windows. Thermal insulation and other aspects were therefore reviewed, in order to improve comfort and attempt to keep down energy costs. Energy was still expensive, relative to the lows that would be reached during the 1960s.

The Government was also worried about availability of, and dependence on, oil. With the memories of the war still fresh, the 1951 Fuels Commission specifically warned of the danger of excessive dependence on oil. In its interim report, the Commission proposed extensive energy conservation, with improved thermal insulation and heat pumps. There were proposals to develop wind power, and the importance of indigenous fuels was emphasised. However, when the final report was published in 1956, these conservation proposals had disappeared. The entire emphasis now was on solving problems on the supply side. On the general political plane, the struggle for planning measures had created substantial reservations in the face of the type of restrictions on free consumption that energy conserva-tion was regarded as involving. Oil prices had begun to fall, and on the horizon there was the possibility of developing Swedish nuclear power in order to reduce dependence on oil. Behind the scenes, too, there was also a link between the national nuclear power programme and the then still unresolved question of Swedish nuclear weapons.

The 1960s and oil

Time moved on to the 1960s. Nuclear power was developed, but only very slowly. The world's major oil companies (the Seven Sisters) pursued a policy in respect of the producer countries that resulted in substantial price drops throughout the world. Oil firing became the major method of heating, and was seen as both cheap and modern. Apart from comfort considerations, the cost of heating ceased to be of interest in the building sector. Cheap oil allowed anything to be built anywhere: finally, heating costs were so low that it began to be thought that water and drainage costs would soon overtake heating costs in a normal rent. Water conservation therefore became of interest. The fact that the oil companies' price policy was creating fertile soil for the oil cartel, OPEC, to grow in, and for the production countries to stage a revolt against exploitation, appeared not to be seen or considered.

In the residential sector, interest in the climate/-occupational system was pushed to the background. When the rate of new construction reached its peak during the Million New Homes programme of the 1960s, it was other aspects that dominated. Building services systems were seen as a building site problem, as ducts and channels required physical space and took up time in the overall work. Typically, it was the new Ministry of

Industry that appointed the Building Services Systems Sector Commission.

Awareness of the external environment

Instead, it was the new awareness of the external environment that began to make its appearance. The first ecological housing project was submitted to the Swedish Council for Building Research. The proposal was to build a small estate in Uppsala, using composting toilets instead of conventional water sanitation. The Council was interested, but specified that hygiene experts should be involved in the plan, something which those responsible for the project felt was unjustified and an unnecessary additional complication: so far had awareness of the hygienic aspects fallen on the building side.

However, interest in the quality of the external environment grew rapidly among those at work. Discussions on the quality of the built environment tended to crystallise around the climate/occupational system aspects. This was due to the growing numbers of inadequate ventilation systems, which were often poorer in performance the newer and more technically complicated they were. Large south-facing windows resulted in extremely uncomfortable excessive temperatures in schools, offices and similar premises. Problems with formaldehyde from particle board began to appear.

By the end of the 1960s and the beginning of the 1970s, the unions had taken up these matters and were on the offensive. Researchers and scientists in the building sector were engaged on a wide cross-spectrum of problems associated with the industry's working environments. However, the main roles were being played by the Factory Inspectorate, the Work Environment Fund, trades unions and health and safety representatives. On the whole, environmental problems encountered at work were not regarded as really belonging to the building sector, or being its responsibility in the same way as applied for residential buildings and living environments.

On the energy side, the 1970s started off with the same optimistic view of development as during the 1960s. In his 1972 terms of reference to the Energy Commission, Cabinet Minister Rune Johansson wrote: "High energy consumption both characterises and is a condition of the present industrial society". The first forecasts that were produced by the Commission before the oil crisis were also based on levels that, seen from a present-day viewpoint, were totally unreasonable. The high alternatives were twice as high as present-day levels, while electricity use alone was approaching the figure of total energy turnover for the 1990s.

The oil crisis

The 1973 oil crisis arrived as a total shock for the western world. Oil prices rose dramatically, and the entire western world felt itself under threat. Petrol rationing was introduced in Sweden for a few months. Nevertheless, the cost of oil during the first crisis did not rise to more than the 1959 cost, expressed in equivalent cost levels. It was not until the second oil crisis, at the end of the 1970s, that prices rose more dramatically.

Nevertheless, the effects were substantial. A Commission was appointed to review the status of the country's energy research. BFR was one of the few institutions that had been, in some respect, looking to the future in the energy sector. In its work on the first comprehensive non-specific programme, published in April 1972, the Council had identified energy matters as a major working area during the 1970s, and had started to establish an energy group within its structure. There was therefore never any discussion of who should be responsible for energy research in the building sector. The Council's group was involved in the work of the Commission, and the Council was subsequently given overall responsibility for distributing research funding assigned for energy in the built environment.

New energy policy

The results of this and other Commissions formed the basis for the 1975 Parliament decision on a new Swedish energy policy. However, the decision was not reached without a struggle: one of the aspects questioned was the feasibility of improving efficiency on the supply side, which appeared to be a threat to the positions that had been won in the 1950s. It was in this context that BFR's then Director-General presented what was probably the first futures scenario that demonstrated the possibility of a substantial reduction in energy use in the built environment.

What won the case, however, was the necessity of limiting the use of energy in order to reduce dependence on oil. The sky-high forecasts from the 1960s and 1970s were scrapped: instead, a target was set of maintaining energy use unchanged at a level slightly above that of 1975. Mechanisms were set in train in order to reduce dependence on oil. Nuclear power was to be expanded, while trials of other energy sources started - indigenous fuels, solar heating, wind power etc.

The debate on nuclear power also started. Expansion was no longer uncontroversial, despite the fact that the use of nuclear weapons had been struck from the political agenda. However, the pressure to escape from the grip of the oil producers, which Sweden shared with the entire western world, won the day. The time was still not ripe seriously to question nuclear power. The nuclear power debate was only one side of the growing interest in the environment. The building sector was more concerned with the onward march of ecological housing. The first initiatives came from scientists at Chalmers University of Technology: in due course, the result took shape as the Tuggelite ecological housing development in Karlstad.

Concrete measures

Almost everyone could now support the objective to reduce dependence on oil. 1950s resistance to conservation planning had almost disappeared. Measures were realised: both administrative requirements and subsidies were employed. These attitudes were perhaps most clearly expressed in the major energy research programme, modelled on the Ministry of Industry's and the Swedish Board's for Technical Development pattern of purchasers/suppliers. The programme bodies 'ordered' research from those who performed it, who were seen almost as suppliers or contractors. This was a somewhat unfamiliar method of working for BFR, both in terms of general policy and administrative method.

Within the building sector, there was an acceptance of hands-on State direction, even in parts of the industry that were otherwise opposed to such direction. The Royal Swedish Academy of Engineering Sciences (IVA) actively propagated that 1970s Man was an irresponsible wastrel who needed to be taken firmly in hand. This was particularly the case, went the message, for those who lived in apartment buildings and did not pay their own energy bills directly*. This gave rise to fruitless debates and trials of energy metering and other methods that partly impeded other, more important work.

---

* Heating and electricity are normally included in the rent of apartments.

There was also heavy political pressure behind bold experiments in the use of solar energy. This led to a number of full-scale trials that were not really ready, and of which the results were therefore not entirely successful. In the case of solar heating, this resulted in at least a decade of work to repair the damage. The use of passive solar heating, too, was pushed too hard. The large south-facing windows, which had been a characteristic problem of the 60s in office and similar environments, were simply reclassified as passive solar collectors, with scientists calculating the kilowatt-hours that they collected instead of noting the accompanying environmental problems.

Gradually, and in due course, the Government's Energy Conservation Plan, based on the results of research and of investigations performed by the National Board of Physical Planning and Building, brought more order to the sector.

Harrisburg

The next phase in the country's energy policy was ushered in by the Harrisburg nuclear accident and Sweden's national referendum on nuclear power's continuation or phase-out. Energy use was essentially steady, and dependence on oil was rapidly falling. This gave room to decide to restrict the number of nuclear power reactors to twelve and to phase out nuclear power production by 2010. The decision marked the start of a phase characterised by strong conflicts and opposed interests. The electricity utilities, the strongest party in the sector, who had provided a major impetus in reducing the use of oil, now became more or less open opponents of the country's official energy policy.

In this situation, a strong policy, setting out clear guidelines, was needed far more than it was during the unity of the 1970s. But instead, in the general liberalisation attitude of the 1980s, positive direction was progressively reduced. Energy research, which right from the start had been heavily concentrated on administrative methods, was subjected to strong criticism from the academic world. Only to a limited extent was this criticism directed against the actual results: instead, it was mainly based on the 1980s' general debate on autonomy of the universities and research in the universities of technology. The result was that energy research, which had been heavy-handedly directed when such direction was hardly needed, was now set free and handed over to the whims

of the academic world just at a time when energy policy had become controversial and there really was need of firm direction.

Another result of the currents of the 1980s, in combination with ownership interests in the energy sector, was that it was a long time before efforts were made to concentrate on more efficient use of electricity. Proposals from the electricity use committee (ELAK), intended to limit the use of direct electric heating, were 'lost' after pressure from strong lobby groups. Instead, work continued on heat conservation in the built environment at the price of a substantial increase in electricity use even in areas that were heated by waste heat for which there was no real alternative use.

The 1990 energy compromise

It was not until the major political energy compromise occurred in the years around 1990 that any real change of direction occurred. Efforts to improve the efficiency of electricity use, which were an essential element in any serious plan to phase out nuclear power, were started a decade too late. However, at the same time, the question of deregulating the entire electricity sector was raised. This resulted in considerable uncertainty on how any strategy for improving the efficiency of electricity use could be incorporated as part of a plan to phase out nuclear power.

In parallel with these efforts to reduce energy use by seeing housing as climate/occupational systems, new medical/hygienic problems appeared on the scene. Mildew in houses and sick buildings, which of course had previously occurred to a lesser extent, now began to make themselves felt. A number of spectacular cases kick-started the debate and political activity. The Allergy Commission, which had been set up and was engaged in work entirely outside the building sector, also helped to break the wall of silence that had previously surrounded the problem.

The fact that these problems became so clearly identified and visible just during a period that coincided with energy conservation awareness and the introduction of more stringent requirements in respect of airtightness and thermal insulation was often interpreted as a direct cause-and-effect relationship. In the eyes of many, it was energy conservation that was responsible for the sick buildings. However, things were not quite so simple. The basic problem was - and is - that the building sector had neglected hygiene aspects for decades, in the belief that there was no longer any need to consider them. Building methods that made their appearance during the Million New Homes programme period from 1965 to 1974 were quite simply badly thought out and carelessly applied. New materials and methods of construction, shorter building times with incomplete drying-out, heavy-handed sealing, poor ventilation systems and so on were already unfortunate elements of building construction before the major energy conservation programme started. All that happened after the oil crisis was that these problems suddenly became visible and significant.

Healthy buildings

This resulted in a strange response. The construction of healthy buildings established itself as an autonomous line of development within the building sector: it is hardly possible to illustrate the building sector's alienated relationship to fundamental hygienic aspects more clearly. Creating hygienically sound and risk-free indoor environments ought to be a key part of all technological development and in all building work. Yet in the middle of the 1990s, ten years after the problems with sick buildings became fully apparent, this is still regarded by the building sector as a special interest area.

This special status has quite a lot in common with ecological construction and ecological housing developments in the building sector. The two specialisms often occur together. At housing fairs, healthy houses are often ecological houses, or at least houses that are presented as ecological. There are, admittedly, a number of common links. However, this interrelationship will probably result in the position of ecological building as a contrast to mainstream building affecting the construction of healthy houses. As a result, what should be an obvious part of mainstream building will remain in an extended experimental situation instead of becoming widespread and general good practice.

How, then, is the historical development that we have briefly described here reflected in the inner circumstances of the building sector, in the self-impressions and roles of the leading professions and in the training of those involved in the building sector?

In the latter years of the 19th century, with the two

systems in reasonable harmony, leading architects also concerned themselves with the climate/occupational system. They incorporated ventilation ducts, warm air heating systems, lighting systems etc.

The start of specialisation

However, at that time, heating technology began to go its own way. With the introduction of central heating, with all that it involved in the way of pipes, radiators and boilers, it became the mechanical engineers who took over. As the 20th century progressed, this trend expanded, with specialisation throughout the sector. Groups of specialist engineers began to deal with structural engineering. New trades categories appeared on building sites: plumbers, installers of various types of systems. In the Tayloristic times at the beginning of the century, the way forward could be seen only in terms of more and more specialisation. That was the ethos of the era, and the building sector did its best to keep up.

In due course, new professions arose that looked after the various building services systems. Gradually, they took over responsibility for the climate/occupational system, while the architects and building engineers concentrated increasingly exclusively on the geometrical-spatial-visual system. However, it did not extend quite to a complete divorce between the two: thermal insulation, for example, has remained within the remit of architects and civil engineers. 1930s' functionalism placed considerable emphasis on the hygienic requirements in respect of sunlight, light and air. However, it is typical of the emerging specialisation of that time that this interest manifested itself within the geometrical-spatial-visual system, i.e. in urban planning, in orientation of buildings in relation to the sun, in large windows and so on.

There were many factors that contributed to continued development and enhancement of this trend up to recent times. An important factor was that housing construction had long been seen as the sector's flag fleet, setting the tone and giving the direction. The very flagship itself was a narrow three-storey apartment building with natural draught ventilation, central heating from a group heating plant and a simple water and sanitary installation. Slightly more complicated climate/occupational aspects had little or no place in this context. All this had a significant effect on the structure of the central institutions such as those concerned with building research, building training and government authorities.

Power in the sector

Power and ownership conditions also played their parts. Architects and civil engineers were the leading professions in the building sector, and could therefore largely pick and choose the areas of interest that they retained for themselves and those that they passed on to others. Here, the differences in principle between the two systems played a not unimportant part in the positions that were selected.

The geometrical-spatial-visual system receives essentially all its characteristics when the house is built. The sizes and relationships of rooms and spaces are determined. The building itself is made sufficiently strong to withstand all the loads that it is expected to encounter. Properly built, a house will continue to stand without being significantly changed. All that is needed is cleaning and a modicum of maintenance so that the surfaces retain their characters and characteristics. Over the years, a certain amount of modernisation may be carried out. However, in all essential features, this system is given its characteristics on the drawing-board through the work of architects and engineers.

For the architects, who seldom play a part in the process other than overall design, this effectively means selection of their favourite systems. However, even for the engineers, the work of design plays a more important part than the actual physical building and construction. For the supervisory building authorities, too, legislation restricts the part that they play to inspecting the project and performing inspection during the actual building phase. All these are methods or ways of working that can most easily be combined with the basic character of the geometrical-spatial-visual system.

Things are different, however, for the climate/-occupational system, for which only the basic features are determined during design and construction. Over the years that follow, it must operate under a wide range of varying external conditions - from sun and heat to rain, sleet and cold. Internal loadings vary throughout the day, the week and the year. The active technical components mostly handle flowing media. Technically, therefore, it is far more difficult to design such systems than the fairly simple components that merely support or separate.

A clear man/machine system

The key difference, however, is that the climate/-occupational system will not operate at all without a constant, active operational organisation. Here, maintenance alone is insufficient. The building must be cleaned and it must be habitable. Dampers and valves must be correctly set to suit the particular conditions, fans must run, boilers must fire, energy must be supplied, waste products be removed and so on. It is, in other words, very much a man/machine system, and can be understood and handled only as such. Nor is there any difference in principle between a family-owned detached house, where the family looks after these aspects itself, and a large apartment building with a professional janitorial organisation.

For such a system, it is hardly possible to attempt to cover all aspects of responsibility from the drawing-board. Rules and regulations may prescribe that certain technical components must be incorporated, but they have no control over how they are actually used in day-to-day operation. Type approval procedures for technical items can hardly be effective when it is not known in what man/machine system the items are to be installed and used. Operating instructions are meaningless if they are written only to consider the technical items themselves, without knowing anything about the organisation that will be responsible for the building as a whole etc. Many more examples can be given.

Turning a blind eye

For a long time, the main strategy of the building sector and the leading professions in dealing with problems of these types was to pretend that they did not exist. Blind eyes were turned, and problems dismissed, so that those concerned could peacefully get on with what they felt they could control, namely the geometrical-spatial-visual system. This does not mean that they disregarded the man/machine relationship, but it was a different relationship that they had in mind: users and their requirements, requests and demand for characteristics. It was not long before the relationship between users and the built environment became an area of research of its own. Surveys of living habits and the functional performance of buildinga as a whole investigated human aspects such as space and accessibility patterns and requirements, space requirements for various working tasks, furnishing and domestic equipment requirements and so on. Although all this gave worthwhile, important results, it is worth noting that research of this type dealt almost exclusively with such human requirements as could be related to the geometrical-spatial-visual system and the feasibility of determining the long-term characteristics of the system at the drawing-board stage. Determining and meeting users' needs and requirements in respect of the climate/occupational system were instead passed over to the engineering disciplines that had been assigned to look after the climate/occupational system. In this way, criteria for various types of climate comfort, as well as hygienic limit values for health risks etc. came to be dealt with outside the leading building professions and building institutions. The Swedish Institute for Building Research and, in due course, the School of Form and Environment at the Royal Institute of Technology, were excepted from this rule.

Lack of interest

But not even the heating and ventilating engineers seemed particularly interested in treating the climate/occupational system as a man/machine system. This is probably due to the fact that they played a subordinate role in relation to the dominating professions with which they worked at the design stage. They disregarded, or were forced to disregard, the fact that it was a man/machine system with which they were dealing, with living characteristics that were created each instant. These characteristics are shaped by the operational organisation and the technical components in the building in a constant interaction with the outdoor climate and interior loading. This shortsighted view sometimes resulted in grotesque misdesigns of the technical components, in poor overall system performance and not infrequently in health and other problems for the building occupiers, while energy use and costs were unnecessarily high.

In the early years of the 1970s, BFR started to concern itself actively with the establishment of R&D into building administration matters in general and operation and maintenance aspects in particular. In the final years of the Million New Homes programme, there was little interest in such initiatives. It was not until the rundown of residential building and the start of the Repair, Conversion and Extension programme (ROT)

and the oil crisis that interest began to increase.

At that time, conditions were unfavourable. There was no research into building administration at the universities of technology or at the Swedish Institute for Building Research. This lack of interest therefore resulted in the establishment of a research group within the School of Business Economics at the University of Stockholm, which is still in existence.

Things were almost as bad on the technical side. There was only one Professor of Heating and Ventilation in the whole country: in some years, he had had few or no students. As far as lighting was concerned, there was no permanent teaching post at all. At the same time, there were over 40 professors concerned with various aspects of the geometrical-spatial-visual system. The response was a plan to establish five new professorships in climate control or building services engineering. This was met by substantial resistance, and it was not until the energy crisis illustrated the need and a new Minister of Energy could be persuaded of the urgency in 1976 that a decision could be got through Parliament.

The 1990s - much has happened

Now, 20 years on, much has happened or is starting to happen. The architecture profession has developed a new interest in taking overall responsibility for houses' both systems, much as things were a century ago. Ecological houses and communities are clear expressions of this new line: experiments in the development of healthy houses are also a manifestation.

This is matched by a corresponding development of holistic interest on the part of the specialised engineering disciplines, manifested in a certain amount of experimental building activity. There are also clear indications of energy research programmes being started by several of the schools within the universities of technology: research is being established, for example, into life cycle analyses of building materials.

Building services engineering is established as a subject within the schools of architecture or civil engineering at Stockholm and Gothenburg, although there is still only limited interest in operational aspects. A number of commercial engineering companies started to engage themselves actively in this area in the early 1970s, but no significant research was started or has left lasting results. Instead, much interest has been devoted to creating automatically controlled systems that are less dependent on the human operating organisations.

Another interesting alternative is discussion of a return to extremely simple systems, in the form of minimalistic designs based on natural ventilation and airing by opening windows.

Recently, the automation approach has developed into an interest in what are usually called intelligent buildings. This is an area driven by the IT industry and is one for which the time is ripe. However, it is not difficult to see it as a manifestation of the engineering professions' classical attempts to be able to determine and control reality from the drawing-board. Information technology appears to be promising that it will be possible to create buildings that incorporate all the technology that the sector can provide, and which at the same time control and operate themselves more or less independently of partial or uncontrollable human factors.

A warning against over-confidence

Without being opposed to IT, there is good reason to warn against over-confidence on such IT design solutions. Experience from various fields indicates that IT cannot replace human participation, but that sound combinations of IT and organisation can substantially improve efficiency. No amount of automatic controls can compensate if the basic functions fail to work, or have not been provided, whether due to an original misunderstanding of the intended method of operation, poor design or poor constructional workmanship and maintenance. If anything, it can be assumed that if full benefit is to be made of IT's ability to combine performance with economy of resources (a healthy indoor climate with reduced energy demand), there must be extremely careful design of the building as a climate/occupational system.

The importance of this is emphasised by the fact that, if anything, problems of the indoor environment seem to have become worse. The number of sick buildings is still far too high, and was still rising at the end of the 1980s. Nor can we dismiss the possibility that the indoor environment may be playing a part in the growing frequency of allergies in society.

It is not possible either to seek simple solutions to these hygiene problems that necessitate increased use of energy. On the contrary, we must expect that the Rio Declarations on the environment and natural resources will increase the pressure for improvements in the efficiency of energy use. These requirements may result in drastic reductions in energy use, apart from those cases in which the heat source is low-grade waste heat for which there is no alternative use.

Resources are needed to create a balance

Summarising, this sweep through development up to the 1990s shows that there is a fundamental imbalance within the building sector in competence and organisation for handling the two systems that form a complete ready-to-use building, commercial premises, home etc. Our ability to handle what has been called the building as a climate/occupational system is not capable of meeting the requirements imposed by the duty of combining good indoor environment with substantial resource conservation, primarily of energy.

It will probably require severe measures to change conditions that are so deeply rooted in tradition as those in today's building sector. The unified responsibility of all the parties for the indoor environment, and its consequences for users, must be increased. In addition, this responsibility must be clarified in a wholly new manner. Changes in building regulations are a step in the direction towards placing the responsibility squarely on the property-owner. Further pressure is being brought to bear on property-owners by the large mortgage institutions showing a new-found interest in securing their loans by selective lending, avoiding properties for which there is a risk of poor quality. As purchasers of the work, the property-owners must therefore make new demands in respect of responsibility of the consultants and contractors working on new buildings or conversions of existing buildings.

The lack of balance between the two systems must result in effects on research and training within the building sector, even if this is at the cost of the traditionally established sectors and concentrations on what has been referred to in this chapter as the geometrical-spatial-visual system. Overall R&D effort can be regarded only as insufficient, and so more resources need to be made available to create a balance.

This chapter is based on material by Professor Olof Eriksson.

NATIONAL ENERGY POLICY
– FROM PLANNING TO DIRECTION

SUMMARY

The motives for, and the thrust of, State work and intervention in the energy field have varied with time. During the 1970s, there were serious fears that energy resources would run out, while the 1980s saw the growth of an awareness that, in the long term, environment, nature and climate could not withstand the loading to which our present energy system is subjecting them.

The view of the role played by the State has also changed. During the first years of the first Energy Research and Development Programme, which started in 1975, the State took responsibility for planning upon itself, while in recent years it is regulation of the energy markets that has come to the fore.

At the same time, the assumptions that were presented to the parties involved in energy research during the earlier stages of the programme were very different from those under which they had to work during later stages. During the first part of the 1980s, there were express expectations that the real price of oil would increase. We now know that the price of oil fell: the price of electricity, too, fell in real terms during the 1980s.

Post-war Swedish energy policy was dominated by electricity. The State's research and development was concentrated primarily on the Swedish nuclear power programme. Yet during this period, and despite the Suez crisis of 1956, oil was permitted to become the dominant primary source of energy in Sweden. There was a certain amount of public research, e.g. at the Peat Research Institute and at the oil shale installation in Kvarntorp. All this work was concentrated on the supply side: the main point was to ensure a supply of sufficiently cheap energy to Swedish society, and the State felt that it was responsible for making this possible. Building research was concerned to only a very limited extent with energy matters[1]. One result of the 1973-1974 oil crisis was the establishment of energy conservation information campaigns and public investment support for industry and the built environment.

From 1975 to 1978, the objective of energy research was to provide data and a decision-making basis for the authorities and to facilitate the effective implementation of political decisions[2][3]. The work had the character of a crisis programme. Wide-ranging investigations covering the feasibility of changes to the country's energy supply system were carried out. The rate of growth of total energy use was to fall from 4.5 % per annum to 2 % per annum over a period to 1985. This was to be made possible by such means as a rapid reduction in energy use for residential space heating[4]. The Energy Conservation Programme had begun. Funding was made available in the form of loans and grants for Research, Development and Demonstration (EFUD) of new energy technologies for energy conservation and new energy sources.

In 1976,[5] a decision by the Swedish Parliament increased the amount of funding available for loans and grants for energy conservation in residential buildings and commercial premises. The State provided funding for local authority energy advisory services and started a survey of the energy characteristics of the country's building stock. Behind these decisions were the results of research, which indicated that the potentials for improvement in the efficiency of energy use were greater than had previously been thought.

However, oil still dominated the country's energy supply, and increases in the price of oil resulted in a general uncertainty on future energy supply. Research into nuclear power generation was still receiving a significant proportion of the programme's funding[6].

Industrial and commercial policy and oil substitution - 1978 to 1981

Industrial policy objectives for the programme were introduced, new technology was to be developed and research activities would contribute to improving the international competitiveness of Swedish industry. The Three Mile Island accident resulted in a political debate on nuclear power, with the decision to phase out nuclear power generation by 2010 being taken in 1980.

In an Energy Conservation Plan Bill[7] for the existing built environment, which was subsequently adopted by the Swedish Parliament, the objective of reducing energy requirements for space heating and domestic hot water in residential buildings and commercial premises by 25-30 % over a ten-year period was established.

In the second three-year period of the Energy Research and Development Programme[8], the Council's R&D work in the field of heat pumps, solar heating systems and energy storage was expanded to special sub-programme elements. The following year[9] saw essential completion of earlier intentions relating to the energy research programme. The very substantial increases in the solar heating sector resulted in a corresponding increase in the activities of the Council. The Sol-85 programme made funding available for work to be completed by 1985 on assessment of the potentials of this new technology for the country's future energy system. Research, development and experimental building were to be employed in developing solar heating and energy storage systems.

Financial support for experimental building was introduced in 1978, while support for prototype and demonstration activities in the field of oil substitution were introduced in 1980.

Energy research - part of industrial policy - 1981 to 1984

During this period[10] the emphasis was on oil substitution and on lines of development that could be expected to contribute to energy supply in the short and medium-long terms. Investment programmes were established for stimulation of areas such as low-pollution solid fuel firing, heat pumps, electric boilers, district heating and solar heating. Development work that was close to the marketing stage was regarded as a force for change in the energy system, and close cooperation was to be established with industry in such cases. Knowledge and competence were to be developed in the long term.

In respect of the built environment, it was emphasised how expansion of district heating systems and a reduction of temperature requirements in buildings connected to them would facilitate the introduction of heat pumps, the use of waste heat and solar heat in such systems. The lower temperature would also increase the size of the heat sink for future CHP systems. Oil demand was to be reduced from 27 Mtoe (millions of tonnes of oil equivalent) in 1979 to 15 Mtoe in 1990. This was to be achieved by such means as continued energy conservation and the use of solid fuels and electricity.

Support for research, development and demonstration activities was at its greatest during this period.

Long-term scientific and technical research - 1984 to 1987

In its 1984 review of the coming three-year period[11], the Swedish Parliament shifted the emphasis towards fundamental research and long-term R&D to secure long-term establishment of knowledge within a diminishing funding framework. However, the formulated objectives concerning technological development were retained. As far as the Council was concerned, funding was relatively unchanged within the 'Energy Conservation in the Built Environment' sector, although there was some cutback of resources in the 'New Energy Systems' sector.

During 1983 and 1984, the Council - on behalf of the Government - performed an overall evaluation of the results of the research, development and experimental building work of the previous years. This report, with the title Energy 85[12], contained the following conclusions:

■ Gross energy use for space heating and domestic hot water production in residential buildings and commercial premises has fallen from about 120 TWh in 1978 to about 98 TWh in 1983. Half of the target reduction of 43 TWh has thus been achieved during half the time period planned for it.

■ This reduction in energy use that has been achieved depends primarily on simple measures such as weatherproofing, additional insulation of roof spaces and adjustment of heating systems. More extensive measures, also requiring greater investment, such as insulation of building facades, upgrading of windows and replacement of heating systems, will be needed in order to achieve the rest of the conservation objective.

■ The remaining potential for energy conservation in residential buildings and commercial premises is estimated as amounting to 23 TWh/year. It should be possible to achieve the 43 TWh/year objective, but the time for doing so needs to be extended from 1988 to a few years into the 1990s, as greater investments will be needed in order to achieve this saving.

■ Concentration on new energy technology has demonstrated its success. This applies particularly to heat pumps, although in the longer term, solar heating systems and heat stores are also expected to become financially competitive.

■ The aggregated effect of energy conservation and the introduction of new technology are expected to be able to result in a halving of energy requirements in the built environment by the beginning of the next century.

The price of oil fell in the spring of 1986. The capital investment programmes and the oil substitution programme were terminated. A new programme for encouragement of development and introduction of new technology (the Technology Development Programme) was introduced.

The National Energy Administration[13] performed an evaluation of the effects of Government guide measures.

The nuclear power phase-out and environmental recognition - 1987 to 1990

During this period, energy research acquired a more long-term character, based on the need to accommodate the phase-out of nuclear power and recognition of environmental effects. There was a further shift towards fundamental research and applied research. Money from energy research was to be used to finance research posts and non-specific grants to the various departments within the institutes of technology. As part of the

Government's ten-point programme for phase-out of nuclear power production, the Technology Development Programme was converted into the Energy Technology Fund.

The power industry established Svensk Energiutveckling AB (Swedish Energy Development Limited) for development and commercialisation of new energy technology. The nuclear accident at Chernobyl resulted in a decision to bring forward the shutdown date for a number of reactors. A special technology procurement programme for improving the efficiency of electricity use was established[14]. As far as the Council was concerned, the Research Bill[15] repeated the importance of research-related experimental building projects in order to convert the results of research and development into practical application. Social science research was included for the first time, and the environmental effects of energy sources and energy use were emphasised.

In an evaluation from 1987, the Council summarised the state of development of energy supply to the built environment in a number of points.[16]

■ Technical improvements to building structures and building services systems can significantly reduce power and energy demands in the built environment.

■ New technologies for heat supply - heat pumps, solar heating systems, seasonal storage of energy and heat distribution - have good development potentials.

■ Localisation, guide measures and user aspects are all important. The growing transport energy requirement is strongly affected by the siting of new residential development and new working areas. Local authorities' role as responsible for striking a balance between energy use and energy supply is important in planning.

■ Although the reduction in energy use for space heating and domestic hot water production in the built environment since the 1970s is significant, there are signs of incipient stagnation in this reduction, despite good prospects for further reduction in its use. Annual energy use could be reduced by up to a further 20 TWh/year using known and proven technology.

■ Dependence of the built environment on electricity is a serious, growing problem. Reduction in power demand is an increasingly important matter to be addressed in connection with the phase-out of nuclear power production.

The Swedish decision to phase-out nuclear power was taken in 1980. The Chernobyl accident in 1986 resulted in a decision to bring forward the phase-out of some reactors. Photographer: Gerry Johansson, Bildhuset

In a complementary publication[17], seven scientists presented their views on what could be done to achieve successful energy conservation. They pointed out that analysis of the built environment's future energy requirements had revealed a significant technical and financial potential for energy conservation, even on the basis of the electricity and oil prices of 1987. Applying such improvements would virtually halve the heating requirements of the built environment at the time. This would require an energy conservation programme based on the assumption that it is technically and financially possible to produce such savings. Market forces alone were not regarded as capable of achieving this energy conservation. Incentives were needed, but they would be awarded only to those who could demonstrate good results. Financial support should be linked to performance, and not to particular types of technical/-physical improvements. The final result was regarded as depending not only on the technical system: equipment also required trained persons to operate it. A long-term personnel and rewards policy was needed.

Climate considerations and long-term research at the focus - 1990 to 1993

During this period, attention was focused on effects on climate, with the objectives for the period including the reduction of emission of greenhouse gases. The programme was concentrated on fundamental research and long-term applied research. The State was no longer regarded as having the main responsibility for development, demonstration and market introduction of new technologies: these duties were to be transferred to other parties closer to the market, such as the power utilities. This tendency was partly offset by support for new energy technology and technology procurement in order to achieve short-term objectives. Public funding for energy research had been halved over a ten-year period.

The Research Bill[18] discussed experimental building work as a specific method of working for building research. "Loans enable experiments to be carried out, even where there are substantial financial risks, and have shown themselves to be a valuable element in the overall R&D chain. Experimental building work is an integral part of the R&D process. ... In this respect, it differs from more purely demonstration projects in other areas." Further on, the text discusses certain drawbacks in the

present system of financial support, resulting in a proposal that the loan system in operation at the time should be replaced by grants, allowing more flexible use of funding. A new name was introduced: Support for Experimental Building Work.

In an Energy Policy Bill in 1990/91[19], a proposal was made to expand the Energy Technology Fund. Greater priority would be given to the development of large-scale wind power and the use of motor alcohols. In addition, funding could also be used for programme-orientated activities and group research. The forms of financial assistance available were to be grants, conditional grants, loans and loan guarantees.

In addition, special development assistance for biofuels, solar heating and wind power were introduced, in the form of investment funding

The same scientists who had published the previous Energisvar[17] now published Energiansvar[20]. In it, they claimed that the potential for improving the efficiency of energy use in the built environment was still considerable, but that the knowledge available was not being applied. An example of this was to be found in sick buildings, for which there was really no excuse. Correctly selected and correctly applied measures could achieve both low energy requirements and good indoor climate. They emphasised that successful energy conservation requires all parties concerned to take an overall view of energy use in the built environment.

The 1990/91 Environment Bill[21] can be summarised as follows: "Emission limits for sulphur will be generally reduced, starting in the larger towns and in southern Sweden in 1993. These stricter limits will be in place throughout the country by not later than 1997. Emissions from new, large combustion plant should be well below the general requirements.

Guidelines for NO_X emissions from large combustion plant will be substantially reduced. It is important to investigate the feasibility of reducing emissions from domestic boilers. This includes analysis of the feasibility of introducing positive environmental declarations, consideration of systems of obligatory type approval, systems with emission declarations and measures intended to result in improved operation and maintenance. It is the responsibility of the Environmental Protection Agency, working with other appropriate authorities, to ensure that this work is carried out.

It is important to utilise the favourable conditions for wind power that exist in Sweden. More detailed regulations and factors governing location of large-scale wind power generation facilities should be considered in local authorities' physical planning."

Market responsibility and continued environmental attention - 1993 to 1996

The 1992/93 Research Bill[22] confirmed what had been set out in earlier energy policy documents: "In the short and long terms, the objectives of energy policy are to ensure the availability of electricity and other energy on competitive terms. Energy policy must be based on what nature and the environment can support."

The Bill also drew a distinction between the State's and industry's areas of responsibility. "The programme should be concentrated on fundamental energy-related research and long-term establishment of knowledge in the fields of basic technologies in the energy sector, as well as on energy system studies, while the power industry and other organisations involved in the energy system should accept greater responsibility for sector-related research and development and demonstration activities."

As far as the Swedish Council for Building Research (BFR) was concerned, the Bill noted that the priorities that the Council had put forward in its application for funding were regarded as appropriate, and should be the guiding theme in the Council's R&D work. The emphasis should continue to be on long-term consolidation of knowledge. The increase in joint financing should continue. The financial framework for experimental building funding was reduced.

In the 1992/93 Energy Policy Bill[23], the programme period for the More Efficient Use of Energy programme was extended to and including the 1997/98 budget year. The same Bill also announced support for CHP production using biofuels, available up to and including the 1996/97 budget year. Funding was also set aside for investment support for wind power and solar heating installations. In addition, the Bill announced an expansion in advisory services for the installation of wind power, amounting to a full-time consultancy post.

Special funding was also made available for the development of large-scale solar heating technology.

In the Industry Committee report (1993/94:NU17[24]), the committee proposed establishment of a Parliamentary Commission to "... review the current energy policy programme for restructuring and development of the energy system, and analyse the need for changes and further measures". It was also proposed that the commission should be asked to put forward proposals for the programme, with checkpoint dates for completion of changes to the energy system.

The 1994 Budget Bill[25] said that "The energy policy programmes are running essentially as planned, with the results to date appearing to fulfil the objectives of the 1991 energy policy decision. ... The programme for the more efficient use of energy should continue with its present extent and objectives."

As far as energy policy was concerned, the 1994 statement of Government intentions referred to the recently appointed Energy Commission[26]: "Its duties shall include analysis without delay of the public economic, environmental and energy policy effects of shutdown of one or more nuclear power reactors during the 1990s. The Government intends to fulfil its agreements in respect of this area of energy policy. Agreement and a long-term view of energy policy are of great value for the country."

The 1995 Budget Bill[27] included the following: "The overall objectives of the Energy Research programme are to enable the universities, institutes of technology and industry to acquire scientific and technical knowledge and competence for the development and restructuring of the country's energy system in accordance with the Swedish Parliament's guidelines for energy policy. ... The direction and extent of energy research is now being reviewed by the Energy Commission. Financial undertakings committing expenditure after the current 1995/96 budget year should be entered into with high restrictivity."

This chapter is based on material by Associate Professor Hans E. B. Andersson, HEATECON.

REFERENCES

1 *Energi i byggd miljö - 90-talets möjligheter* (Energy in the built environment - the way forward to the 1990s. BFR G16:1988.) BFR G17:1987

2 *Energiforskningens mål och medel* (Objectives and funding of energy research.) The Energy Research Group, Ministry of Commerce, Ds 1992:122.

3 *Energiforskningens mål och medel; ett perspektiv inför 2000-talet* (Objectives and funding of energy research; a perspective of the 21st century). The Energy Research Group, Ds 1993:13.

4 Government Bill 1975:30, *Energihushållning m.m.* (Energy conservation etc.)

5 Government Bill 1976/77:107, *Hushållning med energi i byggnader m.m.* (Energy conservation in buildings etc).

6 *Energi för kommande generationer. Energiforskning 1976-1992. Statliga satsningar, ambitioner och resultat* (Energy for Future Generations. Energy Research 1975-1992. Government measures, ambitions and results). IVA-M277, 1992.

7 Government Bill 1977/78:76, *Energisparplan för befintlig bebyggelse* (An energy conservation plan for the existing built environment).

8 Government Bill 1977/78:110, *Energiforskning. Program för forskning och utveckling inom energiområdet m.m.* (Energy Research: a programme for research and development in the energy sector etc).

9 Government Bill 1978/79:115, *Riktlinjer för energipolitiken* (Guidelines for Energy Policy).

10 Government Bill 1980/81:90, *Riktlinjer för energipolitiken* (Guidelines for Energy Policy).

11 Government Bill 1983/84:107, *Om forskning* (On research).

12 *Energi 85, Energianvändning i bebyggelsen* (Energy 85, Energy use in the built environment). BFR G26:1984.

13 *Energihushållningsprogrammets effekter. En analys av de statliga styrmedlens effekter på energihushållningen* (The effects of the energy conservation programme. An analysis of the effects of public guide measures on energy conservation). The National Energy Administration, 1984:2.

14 Government Bill 1987/88:90, *Energipolitik inför 90-talet* (Energy policy for the 1990s).

15 Government Bill 1986/87:80, *Om forskning* (On research).

16 *Energi i byggd miljö - 90-talets möjligheter* (Energy in the built environment - the way forward to the 1990s. BFR G16:1988.) BFR G17:1987

17 *Energisvar 87, Frågor och svar om energihushållning i byggnader* (Energy answers 87, Questions and answers concerning energy conservation in buildings). BFR G17:1987.

18 Government Bill 1989/90:90, *Om forskning* (On research).

19 Government Bill 1990/91:88, *Energipolitiken* (Energy policy).

20 *Energiansvar. Sju experter om effektiv energianvändning i bebyggelse* (Energy responsibility. Seven experts on efficient use of energy in the built environment). BFR T29:1992.

21 Government Bill 1990/91:90, *En god livsmiljö* (A good living environment).

22 Government Bill 1992/93:170, *Forskning för kunskap och framsteg* (Research for knowledge and advancement).

23 Government Bill 1992/93:100, Appendix 13, Ministry of Industry.

24 1993/94:NU17, *Näringsutskottets betänkande* (Report of the Industry Committee 1993/94:NU17, Energy policy).

25 Government Bill 1993/94:100, Appendix 13, Ministry of Industry.

26 Statement of Government Intentions. Stockholm 1994.

27 Government Bill 1994/95:100, Appendix 13.

NATURAL RESOURCES, CLIMATE AND THE ENVIRONMENT

The energy system
- natural resources, climate and the environment impose requirements

Life cycle assessment for the recycling approach

Environmental evaluation of buildings for resource conservation

Photographer: Thomas Wester, Bildhuset

THE ENERGY SYSTEM - NATURAL RESOURCES, CLIMATE AND THE ENVIRONMENT IMPOSE REQUIREMENTS

SUMMARY

The effects of air pollution on man and the environment are inadequately known, although it is generally accepted that critical load limits for the deposition of acidic substances are being exceeded in large parts of Europe, and that carbon dioxide concentration has increased.

Agenda 21 points out that the methods by which much of the world's energy are now obtained and used are not sustainable. Two ways of remodelling the energy system have been identified: more efficient use of energy and the use of renewable energy sources. Measures to improve the efficiency of energy use can be applied within four areas:

- in energy conversion
- in transmission and distribution
- in final use in existing installations
- in use in new installations, machines, buildings and plants.

As far as the first two areas are concerned, there is already an essentially operating market. This is not the case for the third and fourth possibilities, due to a number of facts, including:

- energy costs for the individual are often comparatively small,
- energy efficiency is seldom an important competitive point for equipment or system manufacturers,
- the price of energy does not generally reflect its total cost.

Renewable energy sources that make direct or indirect use of solar radiation for energy production have a major development potential, and their utilisation is a prerequisite for sustainable energy supply in the long term. Biofuels and wind power are already competitive in situations where new capacity is required. The lead times for technological development are long, and much work is needed now if large-scale use is to be a reality within a few decades.

The most important requirement on the energy system in the long term is that it should reduce its impact on the environment and climate to an acceptable level. This means that we need to ask ourselves what resulting requirements are imposed on our choice of energy sources and structure of the future energy system. Restructuring requirements are based not only on the environmental effects of the energy sector, but also on factors in the resource and safety areas. One thing is clear, and that is that the energy system is facing a comprehensive restructuring, both nationally and globally, if the established objectives in the environmental sector are to be realised.

Abstraction, transport and conversion of fuels and final use of energy all give rise to many different types of environmental impact. These range from effects on the world's climate to poor indoor air quality, from global-scale effects to local-scale effects and from the present to decades into the future.

In order to illustrate the character and extent of the pressures for change of the energy system resulting from their environmental effects, we shall concentrate on air quality, acidification and climate of urban areas. In the majority of countries, acidification, urban air quality and emission of greenhouse gases have been regarded as sufficiently serious to justify government intervention. In modern times, it can be said that such intervention started with work on reducing the smog episodes and local sulphur dioxide concentrations in the 1940s and

1950s, while in more recent years it has resulted in international conventions on the limitation of emissions.

The effects of air pollution on man and the environment are insufficiently known. They are also complex and non-linear, with the situation being further complicated by interaction effects between various pollutants that can exacerbate their effects. Increasing knowledge of the health and environment effects of emissions from combustion processes have resulted in stricter requirements in respect of emissions of traditional pollutants such as oxides of sulphur and nitrogen, carbon monoxide and particles.

Urban air quality: a severe problem

Globally, the air environment in urban areas is a major problem. All the many and growing megalopolis have air quality that is substantially poorer than the guidelines set by the World Health Organisation. Most of the pollution comes from the transport sector. Classification of air quality by measured values varies from country to country, and requirements tend to be tightened up in step with increasing knowledge. This applies in Sweden, too, where 10 % of the population are exposed to NOx concentrations that exceed the limit values proposed by the Institute of Environmental Medicine. The growing interest in organic substances in the air is linked to the fact that many of these substances are known to affect the central nervous system and to be carcinogens. Measured concentrations are significantly over the low-risk levels: no guidelines have yet been issued[1].

In California, where air conditions are very much poorer than specified values, requirements for reductions in emission have resulted in legislation that ultra-low emission and zero-emission vehicles must constitute a certain percentage of new vehicle sales from the end of the 1990s. The American government is running a substantial development programme, in conjunction with the major vehicle manufacturers, aimed at development of vehicles with greatly improved energy

All over the world, air pollution in urban areas is a major problem. Air quality in virtually all large towns is significantly poorer than the WHO guidelines.
Photographer: Bruno Ehrs, Bildhuset

efficiency relative to present-day vehicles.

Acidification has attracted considerable interest[2]. Damage to the environment, sometimes serious, has been noted in large parts of Europe, North and South America and Asia. The concept of critical loading has been introduced in order to assess the necessary reductions in the deposition of acidic substances. This provides a quantitative estimate of the exposure level, based on present-day knowledge levels, below which no significant adverse effects are caused. The actual magnitude of the critical loading varies from case to case, depending on the buffer capacity of the ground, i.e. the ability of the ground to withstand or neutralise an input of acidic substances. Fears have been raised that the concept of critical loading does not sufficiently allow for a flip-flop mechanism in nature. This would mean that the buffer capacity is exceeded, with no ability for the ground to return to its original state, i.e. that, at a particular loading, the biological-chemical system is totally overwhelmed in its ability to withstand the loading.

Critical loading levels are exceeded

There are concrete environmental objectives in the regional conventions concerning cross-border air pollution that Sweden has ratified, and also in the Climate Convention. Briefly, these objectives state that emissions of oxides of sulphur and nitrogen will be substantially reduced, and emissions of carbon dioxide will not be allowed to increase.

The critical loading level is being exceeded in large parts of Europe. If the best known emission cleaning technology could immediately be brought into use throughout Europe, pollution levels would drop below the critical loading limit in 95 % of all areas, but the costs would be extreme. This means that other methods are needed in order to achieve environmental objectives. We need to look for solutions at system level, and to include more efficient use of energy and forms of energy or energy carriers that do not give rise to the emission of acidifying substances.

Measurements of ice cores from the Greenland ice have shown us that rapid and major climatic changes have occurred during previous stages of the earth's history. This knowledge has started a debate of the possibility of similar changes being triggered by increasing concentrations of greenhouse gases, with

resultant increased heating of the atmosphere.
Several gases in the atmosphere absorb outward thermal radiation from the earth, which reduces cooling of the globe to space. As a result, the equilibrium temperature of the atmosphere is higher than it otherwise would be. The greatest effect in reducing this outward radiation is that caused by the natural concentration of water vapour in the air.

Carbon dioxide concentration has increased

Of anthropogenic emissions, carbon dioxide is the most important greenhouse gas. Systematic measurements indicate that carbon dioxide concentration in the atmosphere has increased from a previously essentially constant level of less than 280 ppm to about 360 ppm at present. The effects on climate have been evaluated by the Intergovernmental Panel on Climate Change (IPCC). Carbon dioxide now accounts for somewhat more than half of the anthropogenic effect on outward radiation absorption. The main source of this carbon dioxide is the use of fossil fuels, although the felling of large areas of forest, e.g. in South America, is also another cause for the increasing carbon dioxide emissions.

IPCC has estimated that emissions would need to be reduced by at least 60 % in order to stabilise the atmospheric carbon dioxide concentration. However, as a result of system inertia, a reduction in carbon dioxide concentration would not immediately stabilise the climate. Increases in atmospheric carbon dioxide concentration that have already occurred will continue to affect it for some time. Most of the system inertia is due to the fact that it takes a long time for the upper layer of the oceans, which is some hundreds of metres deep, to warm up.

Another problem is the distribution of reductions in emissions between countries of the world. A world-wide reduction in emissions would need to be apportioned so that the industrial countries accept a greater share, in order to leave some capacity for development and growing populations in the developing countries.

The IPCC study resulted in the signing of a Climate Convention at the Rio Conference. Discussions are now in progress on how the various signatories can agree to reduce their emissions. IPCC is also preparing a second status report, which will be published in the autumn of 1995.

Links between energy and security

Energy is linked to national security policies through the western world's dependence on oil from the Persian Gulf, as was clearly demonstrated during the 1970s' oil crises and now most recently during the Iraq/Kuwait crisis, as well as through the link between the use of nuclear power and the risks of proliferation of nuclear weapons. In both cases, there is no other long-term solution than using less of the particular form of energy.

Security policy considerations in respect of supplies of oil from the Middle East, where most of the world's reserves are situated, have already resulted in military actions. The risks of the spread of nuclear weapons, associated with the increasing production of plutonium in civil reactors and, to an even greater extent, the reprocessing of spent nuclear fuel in order to recover its plutonium, are now attracting growing international attention.

These environmental problems have become more serious in step with the increasing use of energy in the world. Over the last 100 years, world energy use has grown by about 3 % per annum, reaching 8.8 x 109 toe in 1990. Coal, oil and natural gas accounted for 26 %, 32 % and 19 % respectively, i.e. 77 % of the world's energy use is based on fossil fuels. The World Energy Council reference scenario for 2020 foresees an energy use of 13.4 x 109 toe. Such an increase in world energy use would greatly exacerbate already serious environmental problems.

Agenda 21

Agenda 21 notes that the way in which much of the world's energy is now obtained and used is not sustainable with unchanged technology, particularly if the quantity was substantially to increase. The need to reduce emissions of greenhouse gases and other substances is resulting in a growing need of improved efficiency of production, transmission, distribution and use of energy, together with greater use of environmentally innocuous energy systems, and particularly of new and renewable energy sources.

In its raw or 'unused' forms, such as coal or crude oil, electricity or liquid or gaseous fuels, energy is of no direct use. Energy supply is about creating energy services, i.e. the benefit resulting from the use of energy. This use may be in the form of lighting, comfortable indoor environments, transport, materials, apparatus etc.

The structure of the energy system therefore involves all these stages, ranging from the original extraction/-collection of primary energy, through processing to high-quality energy carriers such as liquid or gaseous fuels or electricity, and finally to its end use in order to provide the desired energy services. The question to be addressed is how the desired energy services can be provided at the lowest cost and within the framework of environmental and security considerations.

Agenda 21 has identified two ways of changing the energy system. Briefly, there are potentials and limitations within the areas of more efficient use of energy and use of renewable energy sources.

More efficient use of energy

The UN Commission for Development and the Environment (the Brundtland Commission) (1987) has proposed such a concentrated effort in improving the efficiency of energy use that, despite continued economic growth, the industrialised countries could approximately halve their energy use. This would provide leeway for the developing countries, so that (provided that energy-efficient technology was employed) energy would no longer set a limit on development. It would also reduce the problems within other areas that result from energy supply.

Measures to improve the efficiency of energy use can be applied both in existing apparatus and installations as well as in new ones. What is needed is:

1. more efficient conversion of energy, e.g. in power plants,
2. more efficient transmission and distribution of energy,
3. more efficient final use of energy in **existing** installations, by means of measures such as improved operation and maintenance and replacement of certain components,
4. more efficient final use of energy in **new** installations, machinery, buildings and plant, through systematic application of energy-efficient technology.

More efficient use of energy can be progressively introduced in step with the replacement and/or augmentation of existing apparatus and plant by new apparatus etc. Substantial improvements can be made when investing in new equipment, e.g. within the transport and recycling sectors by introducing new systems of providing the required services.

As far as areas 1 and 2 above are concerned, there is already a market that essentially operates. Energy service companies are working in this direction. This is not the case within sectors 3 and 4, which hold out the prospect of the greatest potential improvements in the efficiency of energy use, although a number of promising activities have started. There are several important reasons for the same interest not automatically focusing on these potentials, i.e.:

■ The cost of energy for individual users is often low.
■ Energy efficiency is seldom an important competitive factor in the eyes of manufacturers.
■ The price of energy generally fails to reflect its true (= total) cost, i.e. all direct and indirect costs (including environmental costs).

Energy use can be reduced

In comparison with average energy use by existing apparatus and plant, technology already exists that can competitively provide the same benefit (energy service) for a reduced level of energy use. The potential savings are large, often amounting to 50-80 % of the average energy use of existing equipment.

Economic growth and development result in an increase in the demand for energy services, i.e. for the value or benefit provided by the use of energy. This means that society's total energy use will not be reduced by a corresponding amount. Analyses of potentials up to 2020 indicate that the industrialised countries could reduce their energy use by about 50 %, while the developing countries could achieve a material standard equivalent to that of western Europe in the 1970s with essentially unchanged per-capita energy use[3].

A common feature of all these projections is that the proportion of electricity making up the total energy use is expected to increase substantially. In the IPCC 'Accelerated Policies' energy scenario, world economic activity is expected to increase by a factor of eight by 2050, while the use of fuels is expected to increase by only 30 %, with the use of electricity increasing by 265 %[4][5].

Substantial improvement in the efficiency of energy use alone is not sufficient. In the analysis presented in the World Energy Council's Energy for Tomorrow's

World[6], it is stated that, using the most energy-efficient technology that is known and financially viable, the world could obtain all the energy services required by continued development and economic growth with only a modest increase in total energy use.

Some reduction in emissions can be achieved by using those fossil fuels that produce less carbon dioxide. Of the fossil fuels, coal produces the most carbon dioxide and natural gas produces the least per unit of energy released. However, the possible effects are limited: even if the use of natural gas was tripled, carbon dioxide emissions would not be reduced by more than 10 %. In order to reduce emissions to levels that can be tolerated from a climate point of view, it is therefore also necessary to make significant changes in our energy sources and energy carriers.

Renewable energy sources

Renewable energy sources make use of real-time energy flows on the earth that link incident solar energy with final rejection of heat from the earth to space. The amount of incident solar energy is far greater than mankind's present and forecast future uses of energy, and so there should be no limitations on this resource. These energy flows occur in various forms; as direct and indirect solar radiation, as wind, as the hydrological cycle, as waves and as biomass. Hydro power is already well established: in Norway, for example, it meets the country's entire electricity needs, while in Sweden it meets 50 % of the country's electricity needs.

Development during the 1980s in several of these technology sectors that are of interest in this context has resulted in technologies now existing - or being in advanced stages of development - for financially viable utilisation of these energy flows to produce fuels and electricity. This technical development is based on advances that have been made in other areas of technology, including gasification of coal, development of military jet engines, fuel cells, electronics and data processing.

In principle, renewable energy sources, which utilise solar energy either directly or indirectly to produce energy carriers, open the way to energy supply systems with little or no environmental problems. A prerequisite is naturally that environmental aspects should be considered when constructing the systems. However, apart from the use of hydro power, technology that is today available for very large-scale energy production is relatively undeveloped, and produces energy only at a very high cost. In this respect, it is particularly the use of solar cells in desert areas that is of interest.

Other forms of renewable energy produce energy more cheaply. At present, bio energy sources account for about 15 % of the world's energy supply. Hydro power supplies about 5 % of the world's electricity. Utilisation of bio energy, hydro power and wind power can be substantially increased, as can the efficiency of producing energy from biofuels in particular. However, in comparison with the world's forecast energy requirements, these forms of energy production have limitations. The availability of fertile land and suitable sites for the construction of dams are limited.

The costs of wind power have fallen

In the case of wind power, for example, the costs of electricity production have fallen by a factor of about 10 to a level that is now clearly competitive with electricity from new coal-fired power plant. Gasification of biofuels seems to be capable of producing electricity at costs that are comparable with those of electricity production from gasification of coal, but without the drawback of making a net contribution of carbon dioxide to the atmosphere. Fuel cells in vehicles appear to be a promising way of improving energy efficiency and reducing emissions to the zero-emission level required in California and several other American states. Solar heating is beginning to make an impact on district heating systems[7].

In a global scenario for renewable energy sources that has been developed as part of the IPCC scenario on the use side, half of the world's primary energy could be produced by renewable energy sources by 2050[8].

Much work needed

Although the renewable energy resources are sufficient, the necessary technology to utilise them on a greatly enhanced global scale is several decades away. The lead times for technical development are long, and if we are to increase such energy use, much work is required now.

The latest IPCC study estimates that emissions of carbon dioxide can be reduced by about 75 % from the present level by the end of the next century.

Acidification problems and air conditions in urban areas could be radically improved. Concentration on development of efficient energy systems, based on the use of renewable energy sources, would constitute a consistent approach to energy and environmental problems.

In a global context, Sweden naturally plays only a small part. However, as a highly developed industrialised country, we need both to adjust ourselves to the global limiting conditions that apply to one and all, and to help to develop and apply strategies for assisting the world as a whole to start to overcome its problems. This applies even in situations with 'good availability' of energy (e.g. electricity). Energy conservation and export of electricity are attractive alternatives to the inefficient use of electricity, as they result in reduced need for fossil-based power production in other countries.

Renewable energy sources present a major potential, although in several cases the technology for utilising them at reasonable costs is still under development. However, the efficiency of energy use can already today be improved using known and cost-effective technology. This is not simply technically and financially beneficial, but is also essential if we are to have a chance of overcoming the environmental, development and security problems associated with the use of energy.

Create viable markets

Work is needed in particular to create living markets. This applies both for renewable energy and for improvements in the efficiency of energy use.

- Remove all subsidies for conventional energy forms, i.e. particularly for fossil fuels and nuclear power.
- Incorporate environmental costs in the price of energy.
- Use temporary subsidies to assist the introduction of new energy technology.
- Construct fixed cost elements of tariffs to obtain the least cost for electricity and gas services.

This chapter is based on material by Professor Thomas B. Johansson, Department of Environmental and Energy Systems, Lund University.

REFERENCES

1   Nilsson L. J. and Johansson T. B., Environmental Challenges to the Energy Industries. Presented at the Workshop on Sustainable Development and the Energy Industries, Implementation and Impacts of Environmental Legislation, The Royal Institute of International Affairs, November 19th 1993, London, UK.

2   See Nilsson and Johansson (1993).

3   Goldemberg J., Johansson T. B., Reddy A. K. N., Williams R. H., *Energi för en värld i utveckling* (Energy for a World in Development). Studentlitteratur, Lund, 1990.

4   Johansson T. B., Kelly H., Reddy A. K. N. and Williams R. H., *Renewable Energy - Sources for Fuels and Electricity*. Island Press, Washington, 1993.

5   IPCC Second Assessment Report, Working Group IIa, manuscript, 1995.

6   World Energy Council, Energy for Tomorrow's World, 1993.

7   See Johansson et al. (1993).

8   See Johansson et al. (1993) and IPCC (1995).

OTHER LITERATURE

Energi och miljö (Energy and the environment). An input report to the Environmental Protection Agency's Environment 93 action programme. The Swedish Environmental Protection Agency Report No. 4204, 1993.

Energisystemen i morgondagens ekologiska samhälle. Teknisk och ekonomisk analys (Energy systems in tomorrow's ecological society. Technical and economic analysis). Platell, O. B. BFR, R45:1993.

Energiteknik för en bärkraftig utveckling i Norden (Energy technology for sustainable development in the Nordic countries). Report from a feasibility study performed on behalf of the Energy and Environment Group of the Nordic Council of Ministers' Standing Committee for Energy Aspects. IVA Report 387, 1990.

Klimatrapporten (The climate report). NUTEK R 1994:64.

Åtgärder mot klimatförändringar (Actions to prevent climate changes). SNV Report 4120, 1993.

Balansering av energisystem till lägsta kostnad (Balancing energy systems at the lowest cost). Pedersen, L. Sweden's Technical Attachés, Overseas Report USA 9104, 1991.

Det svenska energisystemets utsläpp till luft 1970-1990. Vad hade utsläppen till luft blivit vid en kärnkraftsavveckling? En analys av verkligt utfall och avvecklingsalternativ (Airborne emissions from the Swedish energy system, 1970-1990. What would emissions have been like if nuclear power had been phased out? An analysis of actual figures and phase-out alternatives). Boström, C-Å., Grennfelt, P., Johansson, M. and Lövblad, G. IVL Report B1159, 1994.

Ekologiska utgångspunkter för planering och byggande (Ecological starting points for planning and building). Malbert, B. (edited). BFR T35:1992.

Resursteoretiska principer för en bärkraftig utveckling (Resource theory principles for sustainable development). Holmberg, J. Department of Physical Resource Theory, Chalmers University of Technology, 1992.

LIFE CYCLE ASSESSMENT FOR THE RECYCLING APPROACH

SUMMARY

When considering the environmental impact of products, life cycle assessment (LCA) is the most important method of analysing the energy and material flows involved. Life cycle assessment can be developed into an exceedingly powerful tool for quantitative analysis of environmental consequences, although it is at present hampered by the fact that the necessary data acquisition is demanding in terms of resources and the results are difficult to interpret.

LCA and similar methods have been used since the beginning of the 1970s, although it is only in recent years that they have begun to acquire the characteristics of a scientific discipline. Swedish workers and Swedish industry are well to the fore, although other countries are now also starting to invest considerable sums in R&D in this sector. In the long term, there is a risk that the comparative advantages that have been achieved by Sweden can be under threat.

There are two methods of working. One, which is described here, starts from the materials and products and makes detailed analyses. The other method, which is described in the chapter entitled 'Environmental Evaluation of Buildings for Resource Conservation', starts from the whole with the objective of developing low-environmental-impact building concepts.

Only a few life cycle assessments have been performed within the building sector in Sweden. Two examples of thorough life cycle assessments are those relating to roof covering materials and flooring materials. The environmental effects of new, building-related energy technology have been analysed for solar energy, heat pumps and heat stores.

There is a close link between energy use and environmental impact, particularly in respect of large-scale environmental effects such as the greenhouse effect, depletion of the ozone layer and acidification. A comparison of the energy use of different buildings thus also serves as a rough comparison of their environmental impacts. However, a more detailed analysis, taking a broader view of a building's total energy system and considering both supply and conservation, can give different results. This would also include the effects of material used, which means that such aspects as emissions from the original mining and processing of environmentally hazardous materials such as copper, chromium and nickel would also be considered, as would the feasibility of re-use or recycling of the materials.

Energy use that can be linked to buildings can be seen in several different perspectives. Usually we are most concerned with the need for energy input to maintain a comfortable indoor climate, i.e. energy for space heating, ventilation and domestic hot water. This particular energy requirement has been reduced through improvements in insulation standards, controlled ventilation and appliances intended to use less water. At the same time, the demand for electricity for other purposes has increased substantially, for such applications as refrigerators, food preparation, domestic appliances, computers, communication equipment and other apparatus. All this energy is finally converted to heat, although for various reasons it cannot all be offset against a corresponding reduction in other heat input. In the worst cases, some of the waste heat from appliances and equipment must be mechanically removed, requiring a further input of energy.

A different type of energy use is represented by the energy bound up in the various materials used in the building. This bound energy consists partly of energy that was used in manufacture, and partly of chemical energy in the material itself that could be released by combustion. In the case of a wooden building, for example, it is this latter form of energy that predominates, while for a material such as mineral wool it is the former category. Energy is invested in original construction of the building, and also in any subsequent conversion, repair or maintenance, all of which must be charged against the total life of the building or part of the building. A short life therefore results in a higher specific load than a longer life. Previous analyses[1][2] have shown that, when spread over the normal long life of a building, the invested energy is small in comparison with the energy for running the building. However, this conclusion should be looked at more closely, partly because energy needs for space heating have been reduced through the use of more energy-demanding insulating materials, and partly because true lives of buildings have tended to be reduced as a result of changes in requirements, new building services systems, fashion trends etc. To this must be added the fact that the quantity of energy-intensive material has increased, primarily for various building services systems, for energy conservation and for activities such as cleaning, associated with running the building.

Four quality levels for energy

The question of energy quality also needs to be considered in the perspective of energy use. A number of different requirement levels can be discerned on the basis of the final user's need for energy quality. Platell[3] assumes that there are only four such levels, namely:

- Energy use that can only be in the form of electricity, e.g. electronic equipment, electrical domestic appliances, fans and pumps, manufacture of aluminium.
- Mechanical energy in mobile, self-contained units: motor vehicles, motor cycles.
- Heat at high temperature (> 50 °C): food preparation, dish washing, drying.
- Heat at low temperature (< 50 °C): space heating.

Energy use in a building is required in all these groups, with motor vehicle transport coming into the picture as part of the production system for the materials and products included in the building. Efficient utilisation of resources involves optimisation of energy supply for each of these quality levels and always using energy of the lowest possible category capable of doing the work. In addition, as far as possible, 'used' energy from one level should be supplied to the next lower level. However, this obvious structure has still not been reflected in any form of pricing or in comparative analyses of different energy concepts. If, for example, we wish to evaluate the financial and environmental benefits of increased thermal insulation relative to a higher input of space heating energy, we find that most of the energy use for the insulation is within the three highest quality levels, while the replaced energy is at the lowest level. In other words, such comparisons need to be interpreted with a certain degree of care.

Siting, life, recyclability

Other questions of relevance for the total energy and environmental loading of a building are its geographical siting, its life and the recyclability of its various parts and materials, together with the effects associated with its use. Geographical siting has an immediate effect on the building's energy balance with its surroundings through exposure to sun and wind and other local climate factors. Siting can also be seen in relation to the infrastructure that supplies the building with water, transport, telecommunications, electricity etc., thus weaving it into a societal pattern of technical and social aspects. As far as length of life and recyclability/re-use of parts of the building are concerned, it seems to be an obvious conclusion that longer life results in a lower total load and energy use during the manufacturing phase. However, what complicates the picture is the fact that the technology, organisation and market for future recycling cannot be foreseen at the planning stage, and nor can technical developments that may occur during this time. New materials, new methods of building or new energy systems can render some present-day materials uninteresting or even directly unsuitable for recycling. Today, for example, hardly anyone would consider re-using old sawdust as insulation in a new house.

As far as user aspects of importance for the environment and energy conservation are concerned, we can consider the example of differences in cleaning requirements and protection against wear and tear. Measures that result in subjectively poorer comfort will probably result in compensation in some other respect. This may, for example, manifest itself in the form of higher electricity demand for lighting if the admission of light is reduced by small, low-energy windows, or by more manual airing in houses that are regarded as being too airtight or too protected from their surroundings.

The different functions of a building

We can therefore see that there is a very broad definition of what should be regarded as energy conservation or as energy-conserving materials in buildings. If we wish to compare different types of energy systems, or to analyse the results of some measure, we need to be aware of how the analysed system relates to others around it, and of which secondary effects we chose to ignore. Table 1[4] lists the various functions of a building, and can therefore help in determining the relevant effects:

Life cycle assessment (LCA) for systematic environmental evaluation

When attempting to determine the environmental effects of products, life cycle assessment (LCA) is the most important method of analysing energy and materials flows. Similar methods can be employed for other investigations. Life cycle assessment can be developed into an extremely powerful tool for integrating environmental consideration into decision-making processes and for the development of more environmentally benign products. The method is suitable for comparative analyses and assessments of the environmental impact of a product, process or activity throughout its entire life cycle, from mining or otherwise obtaining the original raw materials, through production processes, distribution, use, recycling/re-use and final disposal as some form of waste or refuse. The process considers both consumption of resources and emissions of pollution. One problem with LCA today is that data acquisition demands substantial resources, and that the results can be difficult to interpret. One line of development is therefore concentrated on calculation tools that can provide rapid results, based on general data. The Swedish EPS system, developed by the Swedish Environmental Research Institute (IVL) as part of the work of the Product Technology project, falls into this category, and today constitutes one of the largest concentrated areas of work within this particular field.

Table 1.   The functions of a building.

The building in the landscape	Natural and cultural aspects.
The building as a structure	This includes permanent materials in the main body of the building, insulation, windows, doors etc., surface cladding and fixed installations.
The building as a store	Furniture, equipment, books etc. that are more or less permanently stored in the building without being significantly changed.
The building as a terminal	Short-term storage of items, materials etc. that are subsequently used/degraded, e.g. cleaning chemicals, food stuffs, packaging and fuels.
The building as a process converter	Immediate use (quality degradation) of energy and materials flows, e.g. heat, air, light, electricity, water.
The building as an activity zone	User activities for various purposes, e.g. dwelling, trade, education, health care.

Time is an important factor. Buildings or parts of buildings with short lives result in higher environmental loadings. Life cycle analysis can become a powerful tool in including environmental consideration in decision-making processes and in assisting the development of less polluting products. Photographer: Mikael Andersson, Mira

LCA and similar methods have been employed since the beginning of the 1970s, but it is only in recent years that it has achieved the character of a scientific discipline, both internationally and in Sweden. The subject is cross-disciplinary. With the awakening of scientific interest, much work has been put into developing the method and research is expanding rapidly, not only in Europe but also in the USA and Japan. At present, Swedish scientists and industry are well to the fore, but other countries are now starting to invest massive sums in R&D; in relative terms, more than has been invested in Sweden. Denmark is an example. In the longer term there is a risk that the comparative advantages that Sweden has achieved may be under threat.

LCA is an iterative process

Life cycle assessment is an iterative process, which is today structured into the following elements (see Figure 1):

- Goal definition, which determines the objective and extent of the investigation.
- Inventory analysis, which is an analysis of the consumption of resources and emission of pollution together termed the environmental impact, caused by the technical system that comprises the life cycle of the analysed product.
- Impact assessment, consisting of an analysis of the effects of environmental impact, together with an overall evaluation of the environmental effects of the product.
- Improvement analysis.

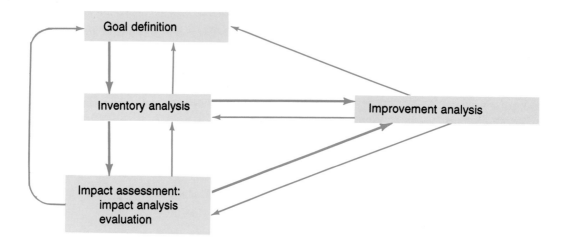

Figure 1. Life cycle assessment structure. The thick arrows indicate the main direction of working: the thin arrows indicate the iterative nature of the method.

The Society of Environmental Toxicology and Chemistry (SETAC) issued a Code of Practice[5] in May 1993, which established an international terminology concept for LCA and set out overall guidelines for practical projects. At the same time, the Society attempted to indicate how far method development had reached in various sectors, as follows:

Goal definition and scoping	Defined
Inventory analysis	Defined and understood; needs some further work.
Impact assessment	
- Classification	Defined. Needs further work.
- Characterization	Conceptually defined and partly developed.
- Valuation	Conceptually defined; different methods and approaches currently being used.
Improvement analysis	Not yet documented.

Intensive work on developing the weak elements of LCA methodology is being carried out in many institutions throughout the world. In Sweden, research and development of LCA is being carried out primarily by the Division of Technical Environmental Planning at Chalmers University of Technology and by the LCA groups at Chalmers Industriteknik and at the Environmental Research Institute. Extensive work has also been performed by a number of Swedish industrial companies in conjunction with the above institutions as part of the Product Technology project. Within the building materials sector, life cycle research is also being carried out by the Department of Building Materials Science at the Royal Institute of Technology in Stockholm.

LCA answers several questions

Energy analyses of materials and components in buildings and for other applications became popular during the 1970s as result of the energy crisis. These analyses partly formed the foundation for subsequent development of environmental analysis in the form of various methods, including LCA, which in itself includes calculation of the energy flows involved during the life cycle. LCA is a tool that can be used to obtain answers to specific questions, although at the present stage of development, only questions which relate to comparisons, rather than absolute values, are meaningful. Such questions can, for example, be of the type:

■ Is product A better than product B?
■ Would it be beneficial to change the raw material or production process involved in a product?
■ What is the effect of various degrees of recycling?

The formulation of the question affects how the life cycle is defined, the choice of data and of method of evaluation and, at the answer stage, the result arrived at. However, this potential for manipulation can be an invitation to misuse, and certain studies have justifiably been criticised for having been conducted only with the object of confirming existing decisions or of being used to justify maintenance of the *status quo*. However, this is not the fault of the LCA method as such, but rather a reflection of the complexity of the reality that the analysis attempts to investigate together with a conscious or unconscious lack of objectivity in application. In order to be able to assess the results from applied LCA projects, it is therefore important that the factors and conditions are clearly described and that the data used is consistent.

Within the building sector, and specifically for energy-conserving materials, only a few LCA studies or similar have been performed in Sweden to date. Internationally, considerably more have been carried out, although in many cases the reports are difficult to obtain. Nor are case studies from other countries always relevant for Swedish conditions, bearing in mind the effects of differences in legislation, energy systems and transport.

Quality assessed by an expert group

The Swedish Council for Building Research's Environmental Impact Group[6][7] has evaluated the environmental effects of new energy technology employed in the building sector. These particular areas are solar energy, heat pumps and heat stores in the first report, while the second report also includes methods of passive energy conservation in the form of additional thermal insulation, improved windows and passive heat storage in massive building structures. These investigations are

not complete life cycle assessments, but are based largely on qualitative assessments by an expert group. However, the presentation follows the same structure as for LCA investigations, with a clear distinction between inventory analysis and environmental impact, analysis of potential environmental effects and a final aggregation and valuation. The investigations include consideration of the consequences of materials use for various energy systems.

Solar energy - much energy used by aluminium

A common design of Swedish solar collector, having an aluminium case, weighs about 14 kg/m^2. Most of the material in the collector is glass or aluminium. After these, the materials most used are copper (in the pipes) and various types of insulation material, such as mineral wool and expanded polyurethane. Concrete is used in solar collector 'farms' as a foundation material. Acrylic plastics are used in certain cases instead of glass for the cover sheet. Other plastics are used in small quantities, including Teflon™ and EPDM rubber. Finally, there will be some form of antifreeze liquid - or, in some cases, air - as the heat transfer medium. The liquid can consist, for example, of a glycol/water mixture or a silicone oil.

In the long term, the most significant environmental impact of the use of these materials is that associated with aluminium production, with the emission of fluorides from smelters constituting a serious problem. Even at very low concentrations, these fluorides can damage vegetation.

Aluminium manufacture also requires a very large amount of energy (mainly in the form of electricity), with resulting environmental effects due to electricity production and fuel firing. In the case of a solar collector system incorporating a total of 5 kg of aluminium per m^2, almost 140 kWh of electricity will have been used for producing the aluminium. This is equivalent to 350 kWh of fuel energy in a cold condensing power station having an efficiency of 40 %. Other materials in the collector require an energy input of about 20 kWh. It can be seen that the collector requires about 370 kWh/m^2, expressed as fuel energy. In central Sweden, the amount of energy collected by a collector of this type amounts to about 330 kWh/m^2, year. This means that the energy for manufacturing the collector is equivalent to the energy that it captures during a year. In modern, roof-integrated solar collector designs, the quantity of aluminium amounts to only about 1.6-2.2 kg per m², and the collector also replaces the ordinary roof cladding. In such a case, the energy required for manufacture (expressed as fuel) is collected by the collector in about 3-6 months.

Solar cells for electricity production can be produced from various materials with differing characteristics. The best-proven type, constructed from crystalline silicon, is relatively energy-demanding in production. With present-day manufacturing methods, solar cell modules of this type take about six years to repay the energy used in their manufacture. Various sources indicate that it should be possible to reduce this payback time to about three - four years with more efficient methods of manufacture.

Solar cells of the thin film type require less energy to produce, but contain rare and/or hazardous metals such as cadmium and indium, although the use of cadmium is being phased out. Manufacture of CIS cells has sometimes employed the extremely poisonous gas, selenium hydride (SeH_2), although its use is normally avoided.

Energy stores and heat pumps leak CFCs

Heat pumps and energy stores contain relatively less material than solar energy devices. The materials in them are mainly steel, plastic (PE, PVC) and, to some extent, copper, together with the various working media and heat transport media required for operation.

Quantitatively, the problems should stand in relation to the quantities of materials incorporated in the systems. In the case of a medium-sized heat pump, for example, operating for 5000 h/year and using groundwater as its heat source, the specific weight of the unit is about 4 g/kWh, year. This can be compared with the amount of aluminium in the commonest designs of Swedish solar collectors, which amounts to about 15 g/kWh, year. In terms of energy, the materials used are therefore of lesser importance. Instead, it is the specific environmental aspects associated with the process that present the greatest potential environmental impact, primarily leakage of CFCs. The global risks of CFC emission have been regarded so seriously that they have resulted in international agreements with the objective of phasing out the manufacture and use of CFCs by around the turn of the century. This has presented an enormous challenge to the refrigeration and heat pump sector, which is now required to find an alternative to CFC that can meet all requirements in respect of performance, safety and low environmental impact - all in a very short time.

Large areas required

A common feature of solar energy, heat pump and heat storage technologies is that they utilise or result in low-intensity heat flows in nature. On the other hand, this means that it is necessary to use correspondingly large areas, that are affected in various ways to greater or lesser extents. From an energy viewpoint, this means that they take up land areas that could otherwise be alternatively employed to capture solar energy biologically in high-energy plant materials that could then either be eaten or burnt. Figure 2 is a direct comparison between land use requirements for various applications. It can be seen from the figure that heat pumps, heat stores and solar collector arrays occupy between 5 and 50 m² per MWh, year, while hydro power with reservoirs for evening out the annual inflow require areas of the order of 100 m²/MWh, year. However, if we allow for the higher energy quality of electricity from hydro power, the land area requirements of the various technologies are roughly of the same order of magnitude. Nevertheless, there is considerably greater

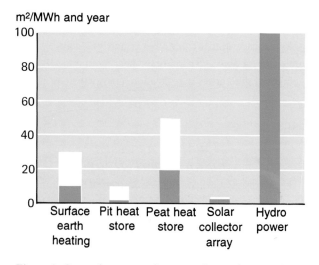

Figure 2. Ground area requirements for surface earth heat pumps, heat stores, solar collector arrays and hydro power reservoirs. The light areas represent variations within each group.

potential for making joint use of the ground for biological production in conjunction with solar and natural heating technologies than in conjunction with hydro power.

For comparison, we can consider that intensive biomass production, e.g. in the form of energy forests, produces about 55 MWh/year and hectare in fuel value. With an assumed combustion efficiency of 90 %, this is equivalent to a land area requirement of 200 m²/MWh and year.

Insulating materials

The manufacture of glass wool and mineral wool insulating materials results in the emission of substances such as phenols, formaldehyde and ammonia[8]. Mineral wool, in particular, produces large quantities of waste materials. For mineral wool, energy use during manufacture amounts to 3.9 kWh/kg, of which about 0.5 kWh is in the form of oil and 0.6 kWh in the form of electricity, with the rest consisting of coke. For glass wool, specific energy use per kg is approximately the

same, consisting of equal parts of electricity and LPG. However, glass wool insulation weighs only about two-thirds of what mineral wool insulation weighs for the same thermal insulating performance.

New insulating material, based on cellulose fibre, is being manufactured from recycled waste paper which is pulped together with borax salts in a cold process. Process energy requirement for the material amounts to about 0.17 kWh/kg, although this includes only the energy input for the actual mixing/beating process and does not include (for example) the energy required for collection. The raw material - the waste paper - has an energy content of about 4.4 kWh/kg, which could otherwise be used for heat production in a refuse incineration plant.

When assessing the environmental impact of greater insulation thickness, we can compare the environmental impact of its manufacture with the lifetime saving in environmental impact of the building as a result of reduced heating energy requirements. For such a comparison, the simplest case is that between energy input needed to produce the material and the energy

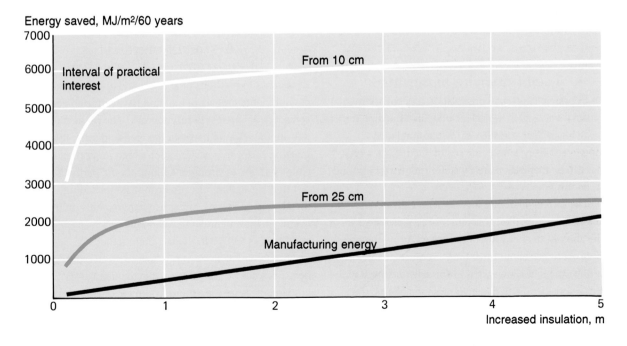

Figure 3. Energy saving resulting from increasing the thickness of thermal insulation in a wall from initial thicknesses of 10 and 25 cm, with an assumed life of 60 years and a surface area of 1 m². The graph also shows the energy requirement for producing the corresponding quantity of mineral wool.

saved during the lifetime of the building. Figure 3 shows the results of such a comparison for mineral wool.

Figure 3 shows that it is not until we reach unrealistically large thicknesses of insulation that the manufacturing energy exceeds the saving in heating energy. Similar results are obtained for emission parameters such as carbon dioxide, sulphur dioxide and oxides of nitrogen if compared with corresponding emissions from local combustion-based heating. Emissions that do increase, however, with increasing thickness of insulation are those of substances associated with manufacture, but not related to combustion. These include phenols, formaldehyde, ammonia and waste.

In the case of insulation materials, work on establishing criteria for a Nordic environmental declaration scheme is in progress within the Swedish Standards Commission. The draft proposal (3rd October, 1993) is based on a life cycle assessment with weighting of the most important environmental parameters, combined with maximum permissible emission criteria for various types of emissions or chemicals. Evaluation of the life cycle inventory is being performed using a points system that has been developed specifically for this particular product, and is not based on the methods used for LCA on an international plane.

LCA of roofing and flooring materials

In principle, energy conservation and environmental impact involve all materials included in a building if their entire life cycle is considered. Two examples of completed life cycle assessments of building materials that can be mentioned are those for roof coverings[9] and for flooring materials[10].

The roofing materials investigation considered sintered clay roof tiles, concrete roof tiles and steel sheet. The amount of energy used in manufacturing the metal roof covering is about three times as much as that used for the others, if allowance is also made for length of life. When considering all the environmental effects, the result is more varied, depending on the method of evaluation used. If we use a method based on environmental policy objectives, the metal roof is the best and that covered with concrete tiles is the worst, while employment of the EPS method, which is based on environmental cost assessments, puts the metal roof last and the sintered clay tile roof first. In this case, life

cycle assessment does not produce any clear indication of which is the best alternative from an environmental point of view. However, if we look more closely at the analysis, it does give a clear insight into how the composition and production processes of the products could be modified to reduce their environmental impacts.

The flooring study compared linoleum, PVC flooring and a solid pine floor for use in dwellings. Energy use for producing the flooring materials did not vary widely; from 0.44 kWh/m^2 for the wooden floor to 0.78 kWh/m^2 for PVC. The weighted environmental impact considerations showed clearly that the wooden floor had the lowest environmental impact, with the results for the two types of sheet covering differing, depending on the method of evaluation used. The investigation demonstrates the difficulties of obtaining reliable data, particularly for manufacture of products outside Sweden, together with a number of unresolved working method questions related to aspects such as the environmental effects of landfill disposal of waste and dealing with risk factors. Bearing such aspects in mind, the final results should be interpreted with care and be presented in such a way as clearly to indicate the working method, assumptions and uncertainties.

A growing interest in environmental research

Research into methods of analysis and of reducing the environmental impact of building have attracted very considerable interest in recent years. The reasons for this are to be found partly in the realisation that it is the building sector that accounts for a high proportion of a country's total environmental impact, and partly in the fact that legislation in several countries (including Sweden) is beginning to impose requirements on the overall environmental impact and life cycle aspects of buildings, as well as in the fact that methods of environmental analysis of products are now starting to become available. Ultimately, it is naturally users' growing pressure for a more healthy and less polluting way of life that is the driving force. The environmental impact of the building sector can be illustrated by the fact that it accounts for about 50 % of total energy use[11], and by the fact that waste from demolition of buildings and from normal building production constitutes a very large proportion of the total quantity of waste materials collected.

Environmental declarations and environmental criteria

We need to consider the overall environmental impact of building materials and building methods at all stages of the building process, and aids for doing so are progressively being introduced. This applies, for example, to environmental declarations[12] of certain building materials such as particle board and insulating materials, or environmental criteria for entire buildings, such as the British BREAAM system (Building Research Establishment Environmental Assessment Method). To some extent, reference guides such as the American Institute of Architects' Environmental Resource Guide[13], and Bjørn Berge's book 'The Ecology of Building Materials'[14] can serve to provide data for architects and designers. However, this is far from sufficient to cover the wide variation in materials, design of building details, general building design and use.

Two methods of working

Current research into the overall environmental impacts of buildings (including their energy aspects) has been presented at two international conferences, in Cambridge in 1992 and in London in 1994. A lasting impression of these conferences was that the problem is being attacked from two directions. One group is working on individual materials, products or methods, and is preparing detailed environmental or energy analyses of them. Another group is starting from the whole, and is attempting to develop low-environmental-impact building concepts based on simple criteria or principles. These two approaches can be said to complement each other, although at present there is far too great a divide between them to allow effective communication of results. The detail investigations need to be extended to include the majority of important parts of a building and to answer questions raised by the new whole-building approaches.

A Swedish programme for research within the field of 'Environmental effects - Building materials in use cycles' has recently been drafted by Chalmers Industriteknik on behalf of the building industry's Building Materials Group and the Swedish Council for Building Research. The programme is based on existing research environments and links well with the views put forward above. Two concrete objectives of the programme are to result in:

- A reliable, general method of making environmental comparisons between different technical designs.
- Concrete advice on how to consider environmental aspects during the initial design phase.

Important research and knowledge requirements

At present, the most important gaps in our research and knowledge that need to be filled are:

- The need to consider the overall environmental impact of building materials and building methods at all stages of the building process.
- The need to produce knowledge summaries of processes and materials.
- The need for detailed environmental or energy analyses of materials, products or methods.
- Development of low-environmental-impact building concepts for the whole, based on simple criteria or principles.
- Methods for determining environmental impact and effects during the life of a building must be developed.
- The effects of waste disposal and use of resources must be analysed.
- Knowledge of environmental characteristics must be linked to the building process.
- Environmental data must be made easily available for the building process, e.g. in the form of a database of the environmental characteristics of building materials.

This chapter is based on material by Assistant Professor Torbjörn Svensson, Department of Technology, Karlstad Institute of Technology.

REFERENCES

1 J. Dinesen (1992): *Det nordiske samarbejde og SBI-projektområdet: Miljøpåvirkninger fra byggeri* (Nordic cooperation and the SBI project area: Environmental impact of building). Danish Council for Building Research, Copenhagen, SBI Notice 93.

2 S. Fossdal (1992): *Energi og miljøregnskap for bygg. Vugge till grav analyse* (Energy and life cycle assessment of buildings: A cradle to grave analysis). SINTEF, Oslo, STF62 A93005.

3 O. Platell (1993): *Energisystemen i morgondagens ekologiska samhälle* (Energy systems in tomorrow's ecological societies). Swedish Council for Building Research, Stockholm, R45:1993.

4 See also the chapter entitled 'Environmental Evaluation of Buildings for Resource Conservation'.

5 SETAC (Society of Environmental Toxicology and Chemistry), Brussels (1993); Guidelines for Life Cycle Assessment: A Code of Practice.

6 T. Svensson et al. (1990); *Miljökonsekvenser av ny energiteknik. Solvärme, värmelager, värmepumpar* (Environmental effects of new energy technology. Solar heating, heat stores, heat pumps). Swedish Council for Building Research, Stockholm, T21:1990.

7 A-M. Tillman, T. Svensson et al. (1993); *Miljökonsekvenser av ny energiteknik. Solcellsteknik, absorptionsvärmepumpar, passiv energihushållning i byggnader* (Environmental effects of new energy technology. Solar cell technology, absorption heat pumps, passive energy conservation in buildings). Swedish Council for Building Research, Stockholm, T4:1993.

8 See Tillman, Svensson (1993).

9 M. Erlandsson, Å. Jönsson (1993); *Jämförande livscykelanalys av betongpannor, tegelpannor och takplåt* (Comparative life cycle assessments of concrete roof tiles, sintered clay roof tiles and metallic roof covering). Royal Institute of Technology, TRITA:BYMA 1993:2.

10 Å. Jönsson, A-M. Tillman, T. Svensson (1994); *Livscykelanalys av golvmaterial* (A life cycle assessment of flooring materials). Swedish Council for Building Research, Stockholm, R30:1994.

11 See Dineson (1992).

12 See next chapter, 'Environmental Evaluation of Buildings for Resource Conservation'.

13 AIA (1992); Environmental Resource Guide. The American Institute of Architects, Washington DC, 1992.

14 B. Berge (1992); Bygningsmaterialens ekologi (The Ecology of Building Materials) Universitetforlaget, Oslo, 1992.

OTHER LITERATURE

Byggandet i kretsloppet - miljöeffekter, kostnader och konsekvenser (Building for recycling - environmental effects, costs and consequences). Lundquist, B., Asplund, E., Danielsson, U. and Moström, L. REFORSK R&D Report 100, 1994.

Energi för att bygga, bruka, riva småhus, Bo92 (Energy for building, using and demolishing single-family houses, Bo92). Adalberth, K. Lund Institute of Technology, Department of Building Physics. Report TVBH-3024, 1994.

ENVIRONMENTAL EVALUATION OF BUILDINGS FOR RESOURCE CONSERVATION

SUMMARY

The problems that are usually considered in any environmental evaluation procedure can be divided up into those on three planes: global effects, local effects and those relating to the building and its indoor environment. The building's environmental problems can relate to aspects such as radon, daylight lighting, ventilation, surface emissions and the use or presence of renewable, recyclable and/or low-emitting materials. A fundamental aspect is that the building and its parts must be environmentally assessed over a period of time, i.e. from a life cycle perspective.

Two methods of approach apply for life cycle research. One, which was considered in the last chapter, starts from the materials and products used and makes detailed environmental analyses. The other, which is described here, starts from consideration of the whole, and is concentrated on the development of low-environmental-impact buildings.

Methods for environmental evaluation of buildings are aimed at identifying building-related environmental problems in order to make it easier for designers, developers and users to select a reduced level of environmental impact in conjunction with new building, refurbishment or operation of buildings. As yet, there are no good methods for overall assessments of the indoor environment, although such methods are being developed in a number of countries and international cooperation within this sector has started to be established.

The most important areas for research and the acquisition of greater knowledge are associated with the actual performance of life cycle assessments of building materials and entire buildings, the acquisition of data on energy use and emissions associated with raw materials extraction, manufacture, demolition and disposal of building materials, developing emission data and threshold values for health-hazardous substances in the indoor environment, obtaining and developing information for assessing the efficacy of ventilation and indoor climate and, finally, to collating and systematising knowledge concerning the environmental effects of the built environment.

The concept of Environment is defined as '... external conditions that affect all forms of life'. As far as man is concerned, this basic content covers not only physical, but also social and cultural conditions. However, when we talk of environmental destruction, we often refer only to adverse changes in the physical environment, i.e. emissions of substances to the air, ground or water that adversely affect various forms of life. Indirectly, we include also anthropogenic damage, with an implied comparison with conditions that applied before the major, global changes that, at an accelerated rate, resulted from industrialisation. The number of aspects of the real content of the concept of environment to be included in any method of environmental assessment of buildings is an open question.

The problems usually considered in an environmental assessment can be categorised as global effects, local effects and those concerned with the building and its indoor environment.

The global **environmental effects** can include, for example, emission of gases that contribute to the greenhouse effect and to acidification. These have a direct relationship with energy use through combustion processes. The type of energy, energy quantities and effects can all serve as the basis for an evaluation.

Emissions are the ultimate object of the work, although it is easy to approach them via energy use. The global effects also include the consequences of the use of CFCs that deplete the ozone layer, together with the use of finite resources such as metals and tropical hardwoods.

Examples of **local environmental** effects include

noise, sunlight, distance from high-voltage lines, flooding and waste disposal.

The actual building environmental problems can include factors such as radon, daylighting, ventilation and surface finishes, as well as the use of renewable, recyclable and/or low-emission materials.

An important objective of an environmental evaluation is that it should provide guidance for the selection of building materials that do not adversely affect human health. However, this is an area in which there is often a lack of knowledge, both of the actual emissions themselves and of their effect on human health. Work is in progress on these aspects in many places. In Denmark, for example, a system of 'indoor climate declarations for building materials' is being developed, with the intention that it could be incorporated directly into environmental evaluation techniques[1].

Must be seen from a life cycle perspective

A fundamental aspect is that the environmental assessment of a building and its parts must be made over a long period of time, i.e. from a life cycle perspective. This means that evaluations must consider energy use and emissions of/from everything from obtaining the original raw material until the building is demolished and the waste recycled or disposed of. Experience and knowledge of this aspect is being obtained from those concerned with life cycle assessments of building materials[2].

National and international systems for environmental labelling of products are being increasingly rapidly developed. For environmental evaluation of entire buildings, it is logical to employ the environmental classifications used within the building sector. In attempting to develop an environmental evaluation system, there is important experience to be obtained from work on environmental labelling of products. These considerations include, for example, factors such as environmental labels being easily understood, positive, relative and time-limited. The easily understood criterion means that there must be clear, defined rules for the criteria. The positive aspect means that it is qualities that must be quantified, not defects and shortcomings. Relativity means that it must be possible to compare different products of the same type. These criteria must be reviewed at intervals in order to

accommodate experience and new knowledge. It is most important that the status of environmental labels should be high, and so it is better to have high requirements, with few approved products, than the opposite.

Both environmental requirements and performance requirements

The criteria for environmental labelling of products normally include both environmental requirements and performance requirements. The performance requirements mean that labelled products should not, if possible, have poorer performance, or be more difficult to use, than other products. This obvious consideration leads to the question as to whether environmental declarations of entire buildings should also contain some form of performance requirement, i.e. that they should consider more than simply matters relating to pollution. It is clear that a product that has excellent environmental properties, but which does not perform its intended purpose well, is of no interest to a purchaser.

It is possible that environmental testing of buildings could be considerably more useful if it contained some form of testing of suitability for purpose. This has partly been done in other countries when considering aspects such as daylight, noise, exposure to wind etc., which have no direct connection with pollution but still affect the use of a building and its surroundings[3].

Impartial consumer information

The quantity and magnitude of the adverse environmental effects that can be linked to a building depend closely on the users and on the care that the building receives. For example, it not uncommon to find, in a group of similar detached houses, that one household uses twice as much energy as another. Although this can be due to different sizes of households, it is user habits that usually have much more effect[4]. However, environmental evaluation can concern itself only with the built-in factors, i.e. with the physical factors of the building. The important work of influencing lifestyle and user habits in order to make the best use of these potentials must lie with parties such as local authorities, property-owners, residential associations and society.

Environmental evaluation of buildings should be

concerned only with physical characteristics that can be expected to be unambiguous and unaltered, as long as no physical changes are carried out. Characteristics that would probably be valued differently by different persons, or which are strongly characteristic of their times, e.g. the use of colours or architectonic design, should not be included. Environmental assessment should not be regarded as a pointer to what persons should think: it must be a neutral statement of consumer information, with its focus concentrated on environmental aspects in a broad meaning.

Half of carbon dioxide emissions in the EU originate from the built environment

The design, quality of workmanship, use and operation of buildings have a considerable effect upon both the local and global environments. Most of these effects are invisible to us: we do not see, for example, either the kilowatt-hours or the pollution that their production causes. Nor do we see polluted indoor air or radon. Methods of environmentally evaluating buildings are aimed at revealing building-related environmental problems in order to make it easier for designers, developers and users to reduce the environmental impact associated with new building, conversion/refurbishing and operation of properties.

It has been estimated that, in the EU states, building activities account for over 4 % of society's total energy use. About 15 % of this is energy used for the production of materials. It is also estimated that about half of all carbon dioxide emissions within the EU states originate from the built environment. In Finland, investigations have been performed of the effect of built environment design on costs, energy use and the production of pollution. In the case of residential buildings, the average per-capita energy use for space heating and transport, together with the associated emissions, over a 40-year period amounted to 685 MWh of energy, 160 tonnes of carbon dioxide, 520 kg of carbon monoxide, 150 kg of sulphur dioxide, 310 kg of NOx, 570 kg of hydrocarbons and the emission of 30 kg of particles to the air[5]. The environmental effects are probably much the same in Sweden, although the proportions of emissions from a particular area are naturally strongly dependent on the overall design of the area, the types of energy carriers used, energy efficiencies of equipment and installations, effluent and

emission treatment equipment etc. However, the basis of emission problems is nevertheless always the same, i.e. an excessively high use of energy, with the combustion of fossil fuels as a dominant element.

Every reduction in energy production results in an improvement of the environment, as all energy sources involve varying degrees of safety and waste problems. However, it is not necessarily the case that every reduction in energy use results in improvement of the environment. In a life cycle perspective, new technology and new systems can result in new environmental problems.

The extraction of raw materials and the production and transport of building materials require large quantities of energy. The Finnish investigation calculated that about 140 tonnes of raw material per capita were used for the erection and operation of the built environment over a 40-year period. Of this, two thirds was used for the building materials and the remainder was fuel. It is only materials based on biofibres, e.g. wood products, that are renewable: other materials must be re-used or disposed of in landfill after demolition.

Low degree of recycling in Sweden

If we assume that local authorities deal with about half of all the building and demolition waste in Sweden, the total per-capita quantity over a 40-year period is over 10 tonnes. Of the waste dealt with by the local authorities, over 90 %[6] is disposed of in landfill. The rest is burnt or recycled in approximately equal parts. Other building waste is used mainly as a fill material. Today's demolition waste contains only about 10 % of wooden materials. The amount of recycling in Sweden is low in comparison with that of, say, Germany or Holland, where there are recycling targets of over 70 %[7].

Some building materials contain hazardous substances that are released either in the building or when the materials become waste products, e.g. cadmium, lead, mercury, PCBs and CFCs. However, the quantities of such substances are usually low. Nevertheless, despite the fact that the quantities are small, it is important to localise them when demolishing a building and to deal with as much as possible. Buildings also contain less hazardous metals, such as copper and zinc which, in the long term, should be re-used or used less. This is because these two metals

Sweden produces about 250 kg of building and demolition waste per person and year. The proportion recovered is low: 90 % ends up as landfill. Germany and Holland have recycling targets of over 70 %.
Photographer: Bengt Olof Olsson, Bildhuset

have high 'future contamination factors' i.e. a large quantity has accumulated in the biosphere in comparison with natural conditions[8].

Over a period of 40 years, the average present-day flow of materials through the built environment amounts to about 25 tonnes per capita. Most of this is organic material that can be biologically degraded. In terms of weight, almost half consists of water (in sludge etc.). By reducing the quantities of water and of packaging, as well as by developing technology and equipment for local breakdown (composting etc.), there is considerable potential for reducing these waste quantities even further in the long term.

Finally, we have indoor environment problems in the

form of the sick building syndrome. Over 100 000 dwellings in Sweden have been estimated as having radon concentrations above the threshold value. It has been estimated that, as a result of emission of gases and particles from materials, mould, poor ventilation etc., between 600 000 and 900 000 persons in Sweden are exposed to indoor climates that can adversely affect their health and well-being[9].

Evaluation methods must provide comparable overall assessments

As environmental evaluation methods are intended to provide a means of helping us to request and select good solutions, it is important that they provide comparable overall assessments when the consumer needs to refer to them in order to choose between two or more alternatives. The simplest form of overall assessment consists of a single scale to which all partial assessments are related. This type of evaluation is illustrated by the UK Building Research Establishment Environmental Assessment Method (BREEAM)[10]. Such a system is easy for anyone to understand but is, at the same time, an extremely blunt and imprecise measure, as the result is arrived at by 'adding' individual evaluations of very varying types. It is difficult to avoid factors being overestimated or underestimated.

If, on the other hand, assessment points are divided up among a number of areas, such as energy, indoor environment, outdoor environment etc., the evaluation within each area becomes more precise but the difficulty of attempting to arrive at an overall assessment is simply transferred to the user. It is also possible to refrain entirely from adding the evaluations of individual factors, and instead simply to use several evaluation profiles that are mutually compared. This gives a more nuanced result, but makes it even more difficult for the user to choose. Regardless of the aggregation level selected, the component assessments and their importance for the overall evaluation must be clearly indicated, so that the user can make his/her own decisions as dictated by his/her own knowledge and interests.

It is obvious, not least after looking at the evaluated aspects employed by BRE, that certain factors are more important for the environment than others. The answer to this might be to weight the resulting factors when

attempting to produce an overall evaluation: how the weighting is to be done then becomes a delicate matter that requires careful consideration.

Canada has launched a system that can be said to be a further development of BREEAM, employing a weighted evaluation in five different sectors. The Canadian system, which is known as BEPAC, has thus become considerably more complicated that the British system[11].

Who are the users?

The structure of any environmental evaluation method for buildings must consider who is primarily expected to use it - whether it is users, designers, contractors or developers. If it is the user to whom the results are primarily directed, it is necessary to provide clear and easily understood consumer information. If consultants are the target, then application and presentation can be more sophisticated and can contain computer or other calculations. If the method is aimed at builders, the emphasis should perhaps be placed on the actual construction of buildings, e.g. materials handling, avoidance of wet building methods, dealing with waste products etc. Finally, if it is developers who are the main target, the profile of the presentation and its results will probably be more important than the details and the criteria.

Existing areas of responsibility may change as the new awareness of the need for sustainability becomes more common and is reflected in manufacturer's liability legislation and environmental labelling. When manufacturer's liability is imposed on property-owners, the result may be that they will be required to undertake clean-ups at a particular time or in connection with demolition. Liabilities may arise due to characteristics of the building of which the owner has not even been aware. In this perspective, it will become even more important for a developer or purchaser to ensure that a property does not give unpleasant surprises in later years. In the same way, mortgage and insurance companies may be forced to take more interest in the quality or shortcomings of a property before lending money on it or insuring it.

Vulnerability to damage, e.g. as a result of interruptions in the supply of public utility systems, may also be taken into account in such evaluations. An environmental evaluation could be seen as constituting a form of quality control in many contexts.

The BREEAM system

This method has been developed by the Building Research Establishment in the UK, in conjunction with consultants and environmental interests. It is based on awarding points for solutions or designs that are known to produce less environmental impact than the standard design or minimum requirements in the Building Regulations. Points can be assigned on the basis of information shown in drawings or descriptions, which means that they can be quantified at the design stage. This contributes to increasing designers' and developers' awareness of environmental aspects. The intention is that, by publishing point levels and awarding assessment certificates, developers will be encouraged to construct better buildings than would otherwise be the case. The procedure, in other words, is entirely voluntary; based on developers regarding this as a good sales argument. It has operated well in the UK and is under constant development.

There are several objections that can be raised against the method. In order to be able to award points, there must be defined limit values. However, many environmental effects are unclear, and it is difficult to formulate limit values. Even when it is known, for example, that a substance has adverse environmental effects, the effects can be unclear and the threshold value uncertain. The relative significance of different environmental impacts are often unclear.

Other work

Methods similar to BREEAM are now being developed in several other places. A typical element for them is that they are voluntary: it is not the public authorities who determine requirements, but instead market competition for a good environment on equal terms.

Work on environmental evaluation of buildings has started in the Nordic countries, in Europe, in North America and in New Zealand. The international building organisation, CIB, has a working party in the sector.

Examples of factors that are included in a number of existing evaluation methods

BREEAM, UK	Building	Energy use Health/Legionella, smoking, humidity Material emissions Lighting/daylight Ventilation Air quality Water conservation Recycling/re-use of materials
	Local	Noise Land re-use Waste handling/disposal Wind exposure Shading
	Global	Greenhouse effect CFCs in equipment and materials Timber sustainability
The Green Builder Programme, USA	Building	Water use Recycling Sick building syndrome Natural ventilation/thermal circulation
	Local	Land use Encouragement of the local economy Pollutants

	Global	Energy use
		Pollutants
EMICUS, Finland	Building	Electricity use
		Use of fuels
		Materials
	Local	Electricity use
		Transport
	Global	Sulphur dioxide emission
		Carbon dioxide, carbon monoxide
		Methane
		NO_X
		Particles
Life cycle based building design, Denmark	Building	Materials
		Fuels
		Energy
		Building construction
		Operation
		Maintenance
		Demolition
		Re-use/recycling
	Global	Sulphur dioxide
		Carbon dioxide
BEPAC	Building	Electricity conservation
		Peak load lopping (electricity)
		Airtightness
		Insulation
		Ventilation-performance/air inlet/discharge
		Operational supervision
		Lighting and electricity system
		Domestic hot water system
		Indoor relative humidity
		Mineral fibres
		Emissions from surfaces
		Radon
		Daylight
		Noise
		Re-use/building materials
		Waste
		Building materials from residual products
		Renewable materials
		Low-water-consumption appliances and apparatus
		Refuse sorting/storage
	Landscape	Retention of virgin ground
		Local infiltration of surface water
		Land treatment

	Footpaths and traffic
	Wind/rain protection
	Sunlight and light
	Car parking
	Cycle paths and cycle storage
Global	Use of CFCs
	Carbon monoxide emission
	Sulphur, nitrogen and carbon dioxide emissions

Work in progress in several countries, such as Denmark[12] and Norway, is concentrated more on employing life cycle assessments for evaluations. Materials and components are investigated from cradle to grave, i.e. from the original extraction of the raw materials to re-cycling or disposal of residual waste products. The environmental effects at each stage of the life cycle, primarily energy use and associated emissions, are added, so that the total for an entire building becomes a measure of its environmental impact.

Ranking with respect to environment

There are very considerable potentials for improving the effect of the built environment on indoor climate and on the local and global environment. Greater use should be made of these potentials in connection with refurbishment, new building and operation and maintenance than is done at present. However, the environmental impacts are of so many different types, and have such widely varying effects, that it is impossible for, say, a designer concerned with a specific project to consider them all. The building sector has no methodology for dealing with environmental aspects.

Today, there is widespread interest among property-owners, developers and designers in giving the built environment good environmental characteristics. The environment has become an important competitive element. The thought behind the system of environmental evaluation or entire buildings is aimed at the acquisition of expert knowledge within the various fields of environmental problems in order to create a method for ranking buildings in respect of their environmental characteristics. Ideally, it would be possible to consider all known environmental aspects through the application of appropriate weighting in accordance with their relative importance, so that the environmental impact of each building could be summarised by a single total quantifier. However, this is impossible in practice, as our knowledge of environmental effects will always be incomplete and because it is difficult to sum effects of widely differing types.

However, it is possible to go some way towards achieving this objective if the emphasis is placed on applicability and some shortcomings are accepted. As our knowledge of many direct and indirect environmental effects is incomplete, and will remain so during the foreseeable future, there will never be any totally 'fair' or 'objective' environmental evaluation. Every method reflects the knowledge of its times and the views of those who have developed it. Correspondingly, each and every attempt will be incomplete and open to criticism. However, if a method is regarded essentially as able to contribute actively to systematic application of contemporary knowledge, in order to accelerate progress towards building with reduced environmental impact, it can also be defended as such. Application results in awareness of environmental aspects and in new knowledge within the building sector.

In addition to acceptance by the scientist, it is also necessary that the heavyweight parties in the market should be interested in applying a proposed method and should essentially support its creation. A successful environmental evaluation method can be expected to be a compromise between what can be accepted, what is simple to apply and what constitutes a good measure of the environmental effects. It must constantly be modified in step with changes in knowledge and values.

Cross-disciplinary knowledge needed to develop the methodology

Developing a system of environmental evaluation of buildings is, to a large extent, a cross-disciplinary task. It requires contributions from technicians with knowledge of the technical characteristics of energy systems and of their potentials for efficiency improvement and reduction of emissions to the air, ground and water. It is also technicians/scientists who need to develop methods of measurement and data for various types of emissions. In addition, input is needed from medical specialists and scientist in order to develop criteria and threshold values. Planners and social scientists are needed in order to formulate needs and wishes and to test the application. Finally, the building sector, represented by designers, administrators, developers etc., must be involved if the system is to be given a content and a profile that will ensure that it is employed. We describe below a few examples of R&D problems that need to be tackled in order to allow further development of methodology for environmental evaluation of buildings.

As mentioned above, it is the life cycle perspective that forms the whole foundation of environmental evaluations. Life cycle assessments of varying contents and levels of difficulty have been developed, and are being further developed for a range of product groups. Research within this sector relating to building materials and building designs is extremely important as a platform for environmental evaluation.

We need more data, knowledge, research and development

A major problem in connection with the development of methods of environmental evaluation is a shortage of data and poor data quality. In the case of life cycle calculations, for example, there is often little data on energy use or emissions for the extraction and manufacture of building materials, or for demolition and landfill disposal. In other cases, data may be available, but varies so widely in its quantitative aspects that it must be suspected of being unreliable or non-representative. Research and development are therefore needed, aimed at clarifying and describing energy use and emissions throughout the entire chain from abstraction of raw materials for building materials,

their production, use, operation of the building and its final demolition.

Another important area of knowledge that is used in performing environmental evaluations is that of emissions to the indoor environment. What are needed here is emission data and threshold values for various health-hazardous substances, together with possible synergy effects and effects on persons. The designer needs a means of ranking building materials in respect of their indoor environment qualities.

Ventilation is another aspect of indoor climate that is difficult to evaluate. Research is needed here that can provide a basis for assessing the efficacy of ventilation and indoor climate.

Finally, it is important that someone should be concerned with collation and systemisation of all aspects of knowledge concerning the environmental effects of the built environment. Such work would provide the basis for further development and formulation of new methods of environmental evaluation. The practical and economic consequences of various proposals must be evaluated in order to provide knowledge concerning the appropriate application factors.

This chapter is based on material by Dr. Mauritz Glaumann, Department of the Built Environment, Royal Institute of Technology, Gävle campus.

REFERENCES

1   Nielsen P. A., Wolkoff P. *Indeklimamærkning av byggevarer.* Del 1 og 2. (Indoor climate declarations of building products. Parts 1 and 2.) SBI Reports 232 and 233. Danish Institute for Building Research, 1993. Denmark.

2   See also the chapter entitled 'Life cycle assessment for the recycling approach' by Torbjörn Svensson.

3   Eriksson J. *Bostadens värden* (Dwelling values). Swedish Institute for Building Research, 1993.

4   Gaunt L. *Bostadsvanor och energi* - om vardagsrutinernas inverkan på energiförbrukning i elvärmda småhus (User habits and energy - The effects of day-to-day routines on energy use in electrically heated detached houses). Meddelande M85:14 (Notice M85:14). Swedish Institute for Building Research. Gävle, 1985.

5   Harmaajärvil, The ecological balance of a residential area. Conference contribution. NBS Infrastructure, 1994.

6   Bahr J. *Goda kretsloppslösningar för byggande, förvaltning och rivning* (Good recycling solutions for building, operation and demolition). Documentation, Planning and Building Days, 4-5 May 1994. Ministry of Planning and Building, Stockholm.

7   Sigfrid L. *Bygg- och rivningsavfall i Holland, Tyskland och Danmark* (Building and demolition waste in Holland, Germany and Denmark). Department of Building Economics, Lund Institute of Technology, 1993.

8   Wallgren B. *Natur och retur - Utgångspunkter för kretsloppssamhället* (Nature and recycled products - Starting points for the sustainable society). The Environmental Advisory Council Report, 1992:4.

9   Norlén U., Andersson K. *Bostadsbeståndets inneklimat* (Indoor climate in the country's housing stock). ELIB Report No. 7. Swedish Institute for Building Research, D10:1993.

10 a) BREEAM. An environmental assessment for new office designs. Version 1/93. Building Research Establishment Report. England.

    b) BREEAM. An environmental assessment for new superstores and supermarkets. Version 2/91. Building Research Establishment Report. England.

    c) BREEAM New homes. Version 3/91. Building Research Establishment Report. England.

11 BEPAC. Building Environmental Performance Assessment Criteria. Version 1. Office Buildings. Environmental Research Group. School of Architecture. University of British Colombia, 1993. Canada.

12 Østergaard Andersen, Dinesen J., Hjort Knudsen and Willendrup A. *Livscyklus-baseret byggningsprojektering. Energi- og miljøanalysmodel, beregningsværktøj og databas* (Life cycle based building design. An energy and environmental analysis model, design tool and database). SBI Report 224. Danish Council for Building Research, 1993.

THE BUILDING AND ITS OCCUPANTS

Indoor climate is important for health
Planning, performance requirements and quality assurance for
good indoor climate
Occupants before technology
Attitudes and lifestyle affect energy use

Photographer: Bruno Ehrs, Bildhuset

INDOOR CLIMATE IS IMPORTANT FOR HEALTH

SUMMARY

We spend about 90 % of our time indoors. Several health effects have been suspected - and in several cases, have been shown - as being connected with indoor air quality. The prescribed minimum ventilation air flow rate of about 0.5 air changes per hour, as specified in the Building Regulations, is not achieved in the majority of the country's detached houses or in about half of its apartment buildings. In 1993, only half of the country's schools, child day-care centres and health care premises had ventilation systems that operated in an approved manner.

Indoor air pollution can originate from many sources, e.g. the occupants themselves, their activities, combustion processes, micro-organisms, various materials and products in the building, pollutants in the outdoor air or the ground beneath the building. The most important health effects caused by indoor air pollution are effects on the body's airways, allergies, cancer, effects on the skin and mucous membranes in the eyes, nose and throat and effects on the senses organs. Almost 40 % of Sweden's schoolchildren have, or have had, some form of allergic affliction.

Both efficient energy use and attention to ensuring good indoor conditions are important requirements that must be fulfilled together in all new building and refurbishment work. However, there are several possible areas of conflict between these two requirements. Research workers in the field of building hygiene throughout the world are agreed that the effects on indoor air quality must always be carefully considered before applying any energy conservation measures. If such consideration shows that the consequences are likely to be unacceptable, the conservation measures should not be applied.

The prime purpose of buildings is to provide their occupants with a safe, healthy and comfortable environment in which to live and work. We spend about 90 % of our time indoors, and so it is important that the quality of the indoor environment should be such that we can occupy it without problems, discomfort or health risks. It is especially important that children's environments in homes, child day-care centres and schools are healthy. It is particularly serious that so many children today are suffering from suspected building-related allergies and other hypersensitivities. Indoor environments need to maintain a comfortable and healthy temperature, enjoy a suitable supply of fresh air, be free of smells, draughts and pollutants and be quiet and well lit. A comfortable indoor environment is dependent to a considerable degree on the use of energy for lighting, ventilation, heating and/or cooling.

The indoor environment has attracted considerable attention in recent years. Several different health effects have been suspected as - and in several cases have been shown as - being connected with indoor air quality. This is linked in turn to the location of the building, its design, building materials, interior furnishings and fittings, operation, maintenance and use. Excessively short building times, with short drying-out times, moisture damage, the use of new, unproven materials, insufficient ventilation, inadequate operation and maintenance routines for ventilation systems etc., are just some of the causes of sick buildings[1].

When buildings and other premises are improved, so that even those suffering from allergies and other hypersensitivities can use them, the health of other users also improves.

Many buildings that have been constructed or refurbished during the last 30 years have shortcomings that adversely affect the health of those who use them. Tiredness and headaches are common symptoms of those in sick buildings, as are mucous membrane symptoms in the eyes, nose, throat and airways. Some persons suffer from dry, itching, reddened skin on the face or hands. It is typical of the symptoms to occur after some period of exposure to a given environment and for them to disappear in due course after leaving the building. Almost half a million persons in Sweden (out of a population of about nine million) have health symptoms that can be related to the building in which they live or work[2]. Between a quarter and a half of all office workers in Västerbotten suffer from at least one symptom that they relate to the indoor climate at their workplaces[3].

Poor air quality costs enormous sums

The potential costs to society of poor indoor air quality are high, and have been estimated as amounting to hundreds of thousands of million crowns in Europe[4]. These costs include those of medical care and loss of income during illness and a greater number of days lost due to illness and poor working performance. An investigation in Norway arrived at the conclusion that the costs of medical care alone, arising from poor indoor air quality, amounted to 10 000-15 000 million crowns per year[5]. It should be noted that salary costs per m[2] of office area are considerably higher than the corresponding cost for energy and environmental control[6]. In the USA, the loss in productivity per employee as a result of indoor air quality problems has been estimated as amounting to 3 %, with 0.6 extra days of absence due to sickness per year[7]. In Sweden, the costs to society for just one of the health problems that is suspected largely to be building-related, namely allergy, has been estimated as amounting to about 5600 million crowns/year[8]. From a purely cost point of view, measures to ensure good indoor air quality are probably cost-effective, even though they may necessitate relatively expensive conversion/rebuilding.

Indoor air quality depends on the balance between emission of pollutants to the air, their separation from the air and the supply of outdoor air. By far the best way of reducing the need for air change (and thus reducing the need for energy) is control at source, i.e. to remove or restrict all unnecessary sources of pollution.

Energy losses through leakage of heat or air can be reduced by insulating and weatherproofing the envelope of the building. However, when weatherproofing, care must be taken to ensure that the required ventilation air change rate remains adequate. As long as the outdoor air quality is better than the indoor air quality, any reduction in the supply of outdoor air will inevitably result in an increase in the concentration of pollutants in the indoor air, thus degrading the indoor air quality.

Poor ventilation equipment

Unfortunately, there are no generally accepted values of the magnitude of the minimum effective air change rate. An international review of recommendations for office premises reveals outdoor air flow rates ranging from 0.8 to 3.2 l/s and m[2], depending on the quality ambition levels and on the organisation making the recommendations[9]. The Swedish Building Regulations prescribe an outdoor air flow rate of not less than 0.35 l/s and m[2] [10]. In practice, a typical value for Swedish office premises is about 1.3 l/s, m[2] [11]. However, the Building Regulations' prescribed minimum ventilation air flow rate, equivalent to about 0.5 air changes/h, is not reached in the majority of the country's detached houses or in about half of its apartment buildings[12]. Only half of the country's schools, child day-care centres and health care premises had ventilation systems that operated properly in 1993[13].

Users' requirements in respect of ventilation air change rate, heating and cooling are all affected by physiological, psychological, sociological and cultural factors. There are large differences from one person to another. It is important to design buildings so that the needs of the great majority of their users are satisfied, and not just the needs of the average user. The more the individual user can control his/her indoor environment conditions (through control devices or by opening windows), the more satisfied he/she will be. Opening windows is an effective way of quickly improving air quality. Calculations show that opening windows can result in an additional air change rate of between 0.1 and 0.8 air changes/h[14]. If a mechanical ventilation system can be individually controlled in response to demand, there will be less need to open windows, which will thus improve conditions for, say, heat recovery.

Many sources of indoor air pollution

The quality of indoor air depends on its concentration of pollutants. Some of these pollutants can have serious health effects, e.g. carbon monoxide and radon. Others have no effect on health at all, but adversely affect comfort and subjective air quality, e.g. bodily odours. Indoor air pollution can arise from many sources, e.g.:

- The occupants themselves.
- The occupants' activities.
- Different materials and products in the building and its ventilation system.
- Combustion processes.
- Micro-organisms, e.g. dust mites and mildew.
- Pollution from the outdoor air.
- The ground beneath the building.

We still do not know enough about the sources of indoor air pollution, or of the load/effect that they have on the indoor environment. In general, the effect of pollutants is linked to their concentration in the indoor air and to occupants' exposure and sensitivity. We also know too little concerning factors that affect the emission of pollutants from their sources (temperature, moisture, air velocity etc.), and the maximum concentrations of pollutants and mixtures that can be accepted from health or comfort viewpoints. Any assessment must therefore be based on a combination of scientific fact and proven experience.

Indoor environment requirements - not hazardous, but comfortable

The occupants/users of a building have two basic requirements in respect of their indoor environment. Firstly, there must be negligible health risk: second, the indoor environment must be pleasant and comfortable. User requirements can vary widely from person to person, for such reasons as differing sensitivities to indoor conditions and differing lengths of exposure to various environments.

Exposure to pollutants in indoor air can cause health effects which may develop either quickly or only after a longer period of time. The most important health effects are:

- effects on the airways,
- allergies,
- cancer,
- effects on the skin and mucous membranes of the eyes, nose and throat, and
- effects on the senses organs.

Each of these effects requires consideration of all available relevant knowledge, such as which are the most important pollutants and what their sources are, what are the relationships between the effects and indoor air pollutants, which user groups are particularly sensitive, what the significance of the health effects is in a broad population perspective, what assessment methods are available and which areas need further research and investigation.

For certain health effects, international research has demonstrated unequivocal links with exposure to pollutants in the indoor air[15 16]. These include afflictions of the airways (particularly in children), allergies (particularly to dust mites) and irritation of the mucous membranes (particularly by formaldehyde). Many persons suffer from these health effects.

Tobacco and radon increase lung cancer risks

An increased risk of developing lung cancer has been demonstrated in connection with the presence of tobacco smoke in indoor air and with the decay products of radon. Lung cancer is a disease with a high mortality rate. In Sweden, radon concentrations are estimated to be higher than maximum permissible levels in about 140 000 single-family houses and 70 000 apartments in apartment buildings[17]. About 400 cases/year of lung cancer are estimated to be linked to radon exposure[18].

Almost 40 % of schoolchildren have suffered from allergies

Allergies and other hypersensitivities are disease conditions that result in certain persons reacting to contact with everyday substances to which most persons do not react through various symptoms, e.g. in the airways (including asthma), mucous membranes or the skin. Asthma is a chronic inflammatory condition of the airways, causing varying degrees of blockage. It often results in greater sensitivities of the airways to many different types of irritants.

The number of allergies and other hypersensitivities is high, and has increased significantly in recent decades[19]. Swedish investigations have shown that asthma occurs in about 5-7 % of schoolchildren, with allergic responses from the eyes and nose, together with allergic eczema, in about 10 % of them. Almost 40 % of the country's schoolchildren have, or have had, some form of allergic problem.

Allergic problems in children and young persons are generally due to a combination of inherited factors and environment. However, the rapid increase in allergies shows that the inherited factors probably play only a minor part in the present problems. In addition, as exposure to the most important allergens (pollen and fur-bearing animals) has not increased in recent years, it is possible (although not yet proven) that exposure to some other type of substance (including chemical substances in the indoor air) has increased. Clear links have already been demonstrated between asthma, passive smoking, early exposure to domestic animals, dust mites and damp buildings[20].

All fur-bearing animals and birds spread allergens from such sources as their skin, fur, saliva and urine. The allergens are carried and spread in clothes and hair. Dust mites are microscopically small arachnids that thrive in warm moist conditions, particularly in beds. The commonest symptoms of dust mite allergy are asthma, eczema, running nose and running eyes. To remove dust mites requires good ventilation and low relative humidity. High relative humidity indoors during the winter increases the risk of dust mite allergy, as well as the growth of micro-organisms such as mildew and bacteria. Every third child suffering from asthma reacts to mildew. Certain types of micro-organisms can grow in air humidification equipment and cause severe pulmonary inflammation (Legionnaires' disease) or sauna-takers disease.

Passive smoking is the greatest risk factor

Children exposed to tobacco smoke from other persons suffer from more, and more severe, infections of the airways, more asthma, more allergies and other hypersensitivities. Passive smoking is the greatest risk factor associated with the development of severe airways infections and asthmatic problems. Other risk factors include emissions from vehicles and industry, damp buildings, poorly ventilated buildings and severe cold. Additional factors that can increase the risk of allergic reactions are stress, worry and poor physical condition. The risk is greatest during the first years of life: children are more sensitive than adults and react more quickly.

Outdoor air is used to ventilate buildings, and so its quality also affects indoor air quality. Present-day outdoor air is often far from pollution-free, at any rate in urban areas. Emissions from traffic, industry and heating systems increase the risk of problems, especially in those suffering from asthma and other airways afflictions. There is a greater risk of allergies in towns than in rural areas, and this 'urban area factor' is suspected to be air pollution[21]. Those who already suffer from allergies or other hypersensitivities often demonstrate symptoms in response to pollution levels that are below the recommended maximum guide levels[22].

Many senses respond to the indoor climate

Between 5 and 15 % of the residents of Swedish apartment buildings experience comfort problems such as draughts, low temperatures, stale or dry air, noise and dust[23].

We experience and judge the indoor climate with many senses: sense of smell, chemical irritation, temperature, hearing and sight. Our sense of smell is situated in the nose cavity and is sensitive to a large number of chemical substances in the air. Our chemical irritation sense is located in all parts of the mucous membranes of the nose and eyes, and is sensitive to a large number of airborne substances. A common symptom of poor indoor environment is a sense of dryness which can be caused not only by low relative humidity but also, and which is perhaps more common, by the presence of irritants in the air.

It is the combined impressions from the smell and irritation senses that determine whether indoor air is experienced as fresh and pleasant or as stale, stuffy and irritating. It is important to realise that the effects of air pollution on our senses are not necessarily related to the toxicity of the substances. Several health-hazardous substances, e.g. carbon monoxide and radon, do not trigger the senses at all. Although subjective air quality is an important measure of indoor air quality, it is not an exclusively valid indicator of the presence or absence of health risks.

It is most important that children's environments in homes, child day-care centres and schools are healthy. It is particularly worrying that so many children today suffer from suspected building-related allergies and other hypersensitivities. Photographer: Ole Christiansen, Bildhuset

Thermal balance is important

If an occupant of a building is to experience the thermal climate as comfortable in the long term, he/she must be in thermal balance. This occurs when the body's heat production equals its heat losses to its surroundings. Balance is achieved by modifying behaviour, e.g. by altering the amount of clothes or choosing a suitable level of activity, and/or by adjusting the surrounding environment to suit requirements, e.g. by changing the air temperature or the temperatures of surrounding surfaces, changing air currents or the relative humidity of the air. In addition, the person's own thermal control system attempts to maintain a thermal balance by controlling skin temperature and sweating.

Local thermal discomfort can be caused by draughts, e.g. if there is too great a vertical temperature difference between head level and foot level, or if the floor or surrounding surfaces are too cold or too warm. High indoor temperatures can also increase the health and/or comfort effects of volatile organic compounds in the indoor air and affect the subjective experience of indoor air quality.

Health and comfort can also be affected by lighting and noise conditions, which are also linked to energy use in the building. A number of measures intended primarily to improve the efficiency of energy use can also have a beneficial effect on the acoustic environment, e.g. upgrading of windows can reduce traffic noise.

Efficient use of energy and good indoor environment

Both efficient use of energy and attention to establishing good indoor conditions are important requirements that need to be fulfilled together in all new building and refurbishing work. However, there are several aspects in which these two requirements conflict. Research workers in the field of building hygiene throughout the world are agreed that the effects on indoor air quality must always be carefully considered before applying any energy conservation measures. If such consideration shows that the consequences are likely to be unacceptable, the conservation measures should not be applied.

Pollutants indoors should preferably be stopped at source, i.e. before they start to spread through the air in the building, using passive measures as far as possible. The natural driving forces in the building should be utilised, and in any case certainly not opposed. Smoking results in a waste of energy, as ventilation requirements have to be dramatically increased in order to maintain an acceptable indoor air quality.

When planning and designing a building and its services systems, it is necessary to consider the risks of the occupants operating systems incorrectly or simply neglecting to operate them at all. Building services should either be extremely simple and self-explanatory, or should be so automated that there is practically no need of maintenance or control. Ventilation is intended primarily to ensure good air quality and the comfort of the occupants, and secondarily to protect the building, its services systems and its fittings.

The following strategy is recommended for refurbishment of existing buildings, with the object of ensuring that both air quality and energy use are the best possible simultaneously[24].

- Keep sources of pollution and energy demand under control by suitable choice of materials, enclosures, local extractions etc.
- Base the choice of ventilation strategy and design of ventilation systems on energy-efficient and passive methods if possible.
- Design energy systems on the basis of the required ventilation air change rate.
- Design air quality and energy systems so that the building caretakers and users really can operate them properly in practice.
- Design systems so that they can easily be inspected, maintained and controlled.

Improving indoor air quality is generally regarded as cost-effective. Much knowledge is already available, but it needs to be better used. Those who design and build or refurbish property should make more effort to find and apply information and to coordinate the work of energy conservation and air quality improvement.

Effective operation and control of systems, good maintenance and good general care of the properties are important factors in reducing the risk of conflicts between energy efficiency and good indoor air quality. Suitable strategies need to be developed, and research is needed into the development of good instruments and methods for simultaneous analysis of both energy efficiency and air quality.

This chapter is based on material by Professor Thomas Lindvall, Department of Environmental Medicine, Karolinska Institute, Stockholm.

REFERENCES

1   ECA (European Collaborative Action): *Indoor Air Quality and Its Impact on Man. Indoor Air Quality and the Use of Energy in Buildings.* Luxembourg: Office for Publications of the European Communities, 1995 (accepted for publication).

2   Norlén, U. & Andersson, K. *Bostadsbeståndets inneklimat* (Indoor Climate in Residential Building Stock). Gävle, Swedish Institute for Building Research, ELIB Report No. 7, 1993.

3   Sundell, J. & Kjellman, M. *Luften vi andas inomhus. Inomhusmiljöns betydelse för allergi och annan överkänslighet* (The air we breathe indoors: The importance of the indoor environment for allergies and other hypersensitivities). Stockholm, Institute of Public Health, 1994.

4   See ECA, 1995.

5   Skåret, E. *Innemiljø og ekonomi* (Indoor environment and costs). Oslo: Norwegian Institute for Building Research, Project N 6405, 1992.

6   US EPA. Report to Congress on Indoor Air Quality: Executive Summary and Recommendations. Washington, DC: Environmental Protection Agency, EPA/400/1-98/001A, 1989.

7   Brooks, B. O. & Davis, W.F. *Understanding indoor air quality.* Boca Raton, Florida: CRC Press, 1992.

8   Persson, U., Svarvar, P. et al.: *Samhällsekonomiska kostnader avseende allergiska besvär för barn/vuxna i Sverige 1983-1993* (The cost to society of allergy problems in children/adults in Sweden, 1983-1993). Stockholm, Institute of Public Health, 1994.

9   See ECA, 1995.

10 The National Board of Housing, Building and Planning, Building Regulations, BBR 94. Stockholm: Fritzes, BFS 1993:57, 1993.

11 Sundell, J., Lindvall, T., Stenberg, B. & Wall, S. *Sick Building Syndrome (SBS) in office workers and facial skin symptoms among VDT-workers in relation to building and room characteristics: Two case-referent studies.* Indoor Air, 4, 83-94, 1994.

12 See Norlén & Andersson, 1993.

13 Sävenstrand Rådö, I. et al.: *Byggnadsrelaterade hälsofrågor* (Building-related health problems). Stockholm: Swedish Council for Building Research, G4:1995.

14 IEA. *Inhabitants' behaviour with regard to ventilation. Energy conservation in buildings and community systems - Annex VIII. Summary Document. Coventry* (UK): International Energy Agency - Air Infiltration and Ventilation Centre, 1988.

15 ECA (European Concerted Action 'Indoor Air Quality and Its Impact on Man'). Effects of Indoor Air Pollution on Human Health. Luxembourg: Office for Publications of the European Communities, Report No. 10, 1991.

16 See Sundell & Kjellman, 1994.

17 See Norlén & Andersson, 1993.

18 Pershagen, G., Åkerblom, G. et al. *Residential radon exposure and lung cancer in Sweden.* New England Journal of Medicine, 330, 159-164, 1994.

19 Formgren, H. *Omfattningen av allergi och annan överkänslighet* (The extent of allergies and other hypersensitivities). Stockholm: Institute of Public Health, 1994.

20 See Sundell & Kjellman, 1994.

21 Björkstén, B. *Allergies - many risk factors involved.* Enviro, 18, 10-13, 1994.

22 Bylin, G. & Boström, C-E. *Luften vi andas utomhus. Utomhusmiljöns betydelse för allergi och annan överkänslighet* (The air we breathe outdoors: The importance of the outdoor environment for allergies and other hypersensitivities). Stockholm: Institute of Public Health, 1994.

23 See Norlén & Andersson, 1993.

24 ECA (European Collaborative Action): *Indoor Air Quality and Its Impact on Man. Indoor Air Quality and the Use of Energy in Buildings. Luxembourg:* Office for Publications of the European Communities, 1995 (accepted for publication).

OTHER LITERATURE

Luften vi andas inomhus. Inomhusmiljöns betydelse för allergi och annan överkänslighet. Vetenskaplig kunskapssammanställning (The air we breathe indoors. The importance of the indoor environment for allergies and other hypersensitivities. A scientific collation of knowledge). Sundell, J. and Kjellman, M. Institute of Public Health. Report 1994:16.

PLANNING, PERFORMANCE REQUIREMENTS AND QUALITY ASSURANCE FOR GOOD INDOOR CLIMATE

SUMMARY

Today, health problems related to buildings are widespread. There are clear links between hypersensitivity and indoor air quality. Allergies have doubled during the last decade and are still increasing at a worrying rate.

Investigations have shown that there are major differences in health problems of occupants, depending on when their homes were built. Problems with nasal irritation, hoarseness/dry throats and irritation of the eyes are twice as high in properties built since 1960 as in those built prior to 1960. During the Million New Homes programme of the 1960s and 1970s the building process, building technology, building services systems, building materials and user habits all underwent rapid change, and we now know that present-day building technology is less tolerant of poor workmanship or incorrect design than was older technology.

A reasonable starting point in any discussion on good indoor climate is that all occupants should regard the indoor climate as good. The target of at least 80 % satisfied is a realistic objective. In order to improve indoor climate, we need to:

■ continue to develop methods and routines for the formulation of overall performance requirements in respect of the characteristics needed by the indoor climate,

■ consciously monitor the performance of all new building work in order to provide information for continued development of performance requirements and means of fulfilling them,

■ improve and increase our knowledge of air quality and the chemical composition of indoor air that gives rise to health problems,

■ work on quality assurance.

A good indoor climate is one that the occupants of the building experience as good, or at least as acceptable. The building must not give rise to health problems among its occupants or users.

This starting point may seen elementary. However, the fact is that today health problems related to buildings are widespread. The ELIB investigation[1] provides the following approximate estimates of the extent of the problem:

1. *Between 200 000 and 400 000 persons live in dwellings (mainly detached houses) with radon gas concentrations in excess of 400 Bq/m³, which is the limit set by the National Board of Health and Welfare for Existing Buildings[2]. This exposes them to an increased risk of lung cancer. (In new buildings for which planning permission is required, the permissible limit is 200 Bq/m³.)[3]*

2. *Between 400 000 and 500 000 persons exhibit health symptoms resulting from exposure to indoor climate.*

In the spring of 1994, the National Institute of Public Health allergy programme published a scientific review document entitled 'The air we breathe indoors'[4]. The report indicates that there are clear links between hypersensitivity problems and indoor air quality, not least among children. More than one person in three, and 40 % of schoolchildren, have or have had some form of allergy or other hypersensitivity. Allergies have doubled during the last decade, and are continuing to increase at a worrying rate.

It is only during the last few decades that occupants' experience of indoor climate and health began to be studied seriously. Unfortunately, we cannot today say with certainty how we ought to build in order to produce a healthy, good quality indoor climate. However, our knowledge is steadily increasing, and developers who consciously impose clear requirements in respect of quality, performance checking, monitoring and careful operation and maintenance can achieve considerable improvements in respect of thermal comfort, noise and lighting conditions, as well as in air quality. Nevertheless, it is necessary for both the designers and contractors to understand the factors in the local environment, in the building itself and in the room that interact to produce a good, healthy indoor climate.

New technology is more vulnerable

During the 1980s, we have increasingly come to realise that building methods that are used today are more vulnerable than older methods, and that incorrect design, constructional workmanship or care of our buildings can result in real health problems. This has resulted in a tightening-up of legislation, e.g. the law concerning building guarantees and the requirements for regular inspection of ventilation equipment. Another result of this increasing awareness is the country-wide House and Health campaign which the Swedish Council for Building Research and the National Board of Housing, Building and Planning conducted some years ago on behalf of the Government.

Development of technical methods of measurement has not reached the stage that such measurements can reliably give an indication of whether a particular building is suffering from problems or not. Instead, the definition of sick buildings is based on occupants' experiences - an abnormally high frequency of problems associated with the building. It is still the situation that the causes of sick building problems are difficult to identify in individual cases by means of performance checks and technical measurements. This has meant that questionnaires to those using such buildings have been developed as a means of identifying problem buildings and as a complement to physical measurements and performance checks when attempting to find explanations for the problems.

A number of larger questionnaire investigations have been carried out in recent years, with the aim of establishing occupants' views on the indoor climate in buildings[5][6][7]. Two of these were for the home environment. The results are relatively consistent. We therefore have today a good picture of how occupants experience their indoor climate. One of the main objectives of the House and Health investigation in Stockholm (the Stockholm investigation)[8] was to identify the number of buildings having a high frequency of health problems among their occupants. The results are based on questionnaires to occupants in about 7000 apartments in apartment buildings.

High problem frequencies in properties built after 1960

An important objective of the Stockholm investigation was to ascertain the number of buildings of which the occupants exhibited a high frequency of health problems. The questionnaires therefore contain a substantial number of questions relating to the health of the occupants. The results present the average frequency of various types of problems regarded as having weaker or stronger links to the sick building concept.

The most important result from the investigation is the major difference in frequency of health problems between properties built before and after 1960. The frequency of nasal irritation, hoarseness/dry throats and eye irritation is twice as high in properties built after 1960 as in those built before 1960. It is also so that the proportion who associate these problems with their residence is approximately three times as high in the properties built since 1960. A positive factor in the overall picture is that it is possible to see a somewhat reduced frequency of problems for the majority of symptoms in properties built since 1985, relative to the frequency of symptoms in properties built during the previous decades.

Further processing of the material from the Stockholm investigation has employed the double average frequency of various health symptoms as an indication of the presence of serious health-related problems in the property. Properties from different building periods and having different types of ventilation systems have been investigated.

The results show that 2-4 out of ten properties built since 1960 exhibit problem frequencies for these symptoms in excess of this level. Within the various building periods, it is particularly properties with balanced ventilation systems, built since 1985, that stand

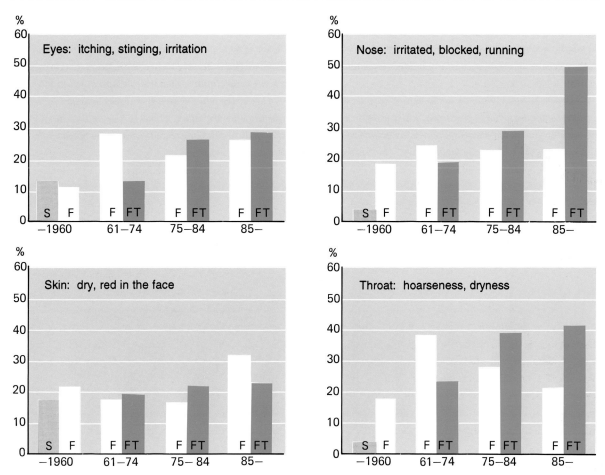

Figure 1. Proportion of properties, classified by year of construction and type of ventilation system, in which more than 16 % of the occupants (or 20 % for nasal irritation) frequently suffer from various mucous membrane symptoms. S = natural ventilation, F = mechanical exhaust ventilation, FT = balanced ventilation.

out in respect of problems due to irritated, blocked or running noses, hoarseness and dry throats. It is twice as common for these properties to have more than twice the average frequency of symptoms as for properties built during the same period but having only mechanical exhaust ventilation (Figure 1). It is worth noting that the numbers of properties having mechanical exhaust ventilation and those having balanced ventilation are approximately the same for the 1975-84 building period and the post-1985 building period.

Compared with the Västerbotten investigation[9] and the ELIB investigation[10], the Stockholm investigation reveals a higher frequency of problems even in the properties built during the 1960s. In the two other investigations, it is 1975 that marks the beginning of the period for properties having the highest frequencies of health problems and links with the buildings.

Few scientifically confirmed links

Many attempts have been made to clarify the relationships between indoor environment and allergies and other hypersensitivities. The 'Air we breathe indoors' report from the National Institute of Public Health[11] provides a thorough summary of the present state of knowledge. However, the report also points out that there are still major gaps in our knowledge.

"The clearest relationship that has been scientifically

demonstrated between health problems and building hygiene is that between inadequate ventilation, high relative humidity, infestation by dust mites and asthma. Ventilation rate in the dwelling, and particularly in the bedroom, is of decisive importance.

Condensation on windows, damp patches on interior surfaces, standing water in basements, water leaks, visible or ill-smelling growth of a microbial nature are examples of criteria employed to define damp buildings. There is a clear link between occupation of such buildings and bronchial problems.

There is no clear boundary between sick buildings and healthy buildings. Among the technical factors that are most important in determining how their occupants feel in them are the age of the building (whether it was built or refurbished after the middle of the 1970s), outdoor air ventilation flow rates, moisture problems, the presence of copiers and low cleaning level."

The Stockholm investigation shows that six out of ten buildings in Sweden meet the objective that at least 80% of the occupants should regard thermal comfort, noise and daylight conditions as good or acceptable.
Photographer: Ann Eriksson, Mira

A reasonable starting point in any discussion on good indoor climate is that all the occupants should experience the indoor climate as good. This is, for example, the starting premise in the Building Regulations, where the requirement is expressed that air quality in dwellings must be experienced as good. In practice, it is presumably impossible to ensure that everyone experiences the indoor climate as good, as a result of variations in the circumstances and wishes of different individuals. In the 'Energy-efficient healthy apartment buildings - new buildings' project[12] programme, as employed in Stockholm, the minimum requirement for approved indoor climate conditions has been expressed by specifying that the building should not result in an abnormally high frequency of health symptoms, and that at least 80 % of the occupants should regard the indoor climate as good or acceptable.

At least 80 % satisfied

The Stockholm investigation shows that six out of ten existing buildings meet this 80 % objective in respect of thermal comfort, noise and daylight conditions. If only properties having balanced ventilation, and built since 1985, are considered, then eight out of ten properties meet the criterion.

As far as air quality is concerned, no less than eight out of ten existing buildings meet the 80 % objective. It is interesting to relate the alarming figures concerning health problems in properties built in recent years to the fact that it is in only 20 % of these new buildings that the air quality is regarded as being unacceptable. Serious ill-health and unacceptable air quality are therefore concentrated mainly in about one-fifth of the stock of modern apartment buildings. This means that it cannot be said that all newly built properties are, in general, poorer than older properties built prior to 1960.

The conclusion must also be that it is perfectly realistic to set an 80 % satisfaction level in respect of air quality (and also of thermal comfort) as an objective for newly-built properties.

Apart from some interesting exceptions (Figure 2), there are no clear differences in the occupants' experience of indoor climate between properties with different types of ventilation systems.

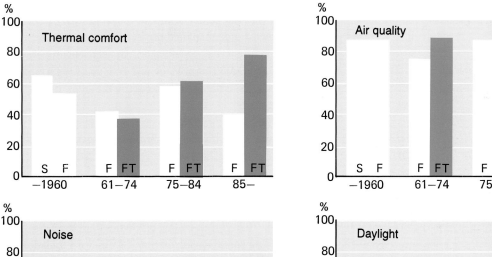

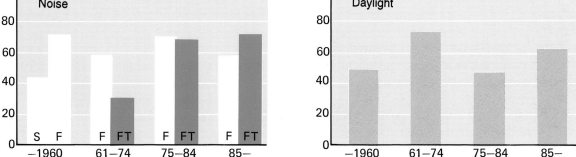

Figure 2. Proportion of properties, classified by year of construction and type of ventilation system, in which more than 80 % of the occupants are essentially satisfied with heating, ventilation, noise and lighting. S = natural draught ventilation, F = mechanical exhaust ventilation, FT = balanced ventilation.

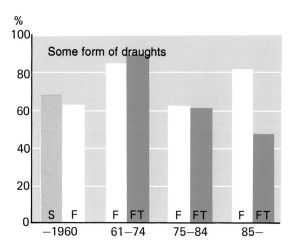
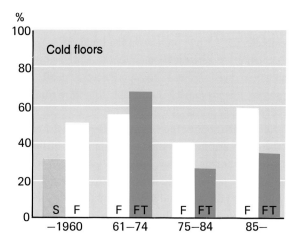

Figure 3. Proportion of properties, classified by year of construction and type of ventilation system, in which more than 40 % of the occupants suffer from draughts and cold floors. S = natural draught ventilation, F = mechanical exhaust ventilation, FT = balanced ventilation.

■ Properties built since 1985, and having balanced ventilation, show the best results in terms of subjective thermal comfort.

■ Properties built between 1961 and 1974, and having balanced ventilation, exhibit the most noise problems.

■ In properties built since 1976, those having mechanical exhaust ventilation exhibit better results in terms of subjective air quality than those having balanced ventilation.

Draughts and cold floors are common

Problems with draughts and cold floors are common reasons for the occupants experiencing thermal comfort as poor. Draughts are common in all ages of properties, although they are greatest in properties built between 1961 and 1974 and in those built since 1985 with mechanical exhaust ventilation. More than 40 % of the occupants in eight out of ten houses in these groups experience problems with draughts. Problems with cold floors are also greatest in these groups (Figure 3).

'Dry air' and 'odour' are common problems in modern houses

Of the various parameters that the occupants can judge in respect of air quality, it is 'dry air' and odour ('musty', 'pungent, 'cooking smells', 'mildew', 'stuffy', 'fumes') that have the highest responses.

That occupants experience air as 'dry' is very common in properties built at any time after 1960. The difference between such properties and those built prior to 1960 is very marked. Those living in properties with balanced ventilation all classify the air as 'dry' to a greater degree than do those living in properties with mechanical exhaust ventilation. In nearly all properties having balanced ventilation and built since 1985, more than 40 % of the occupants classify the air as 'dry' (Figure 4).

Problems due to occupants complaining about various types of smells are greatest in properties built between 1975 and 1984. In about five out of ten properties, more than 40 % of the occupants complain about smells indoors. Properties with balanced ventilation all have somewhat less of a problem with smells than corresponding properties from the same building period having mechanical exhaust ventilation.

Modern housing stock includes both good and poor buildings

From the results described above, it might seem as if the choice lies between constructing new properties with balanced ventilation systems and which are regarded as having acceptable thermal comfort or those with mechanical exhaust ventilation systems which reduce the risk of occupants suffering from health problems. However, this is not the case: in each and every group,

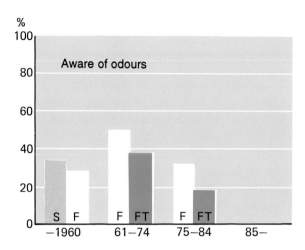 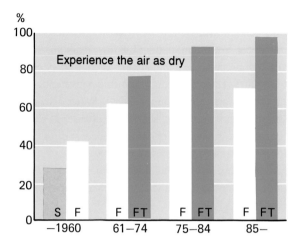

Figure 4. Proportion of properties, classified by year of construction and type of ventilation system, in which more than 40 % of the occupants notice smells (cooking, mildew, pungent smell etc.) and dry air. S = natural draught ventilation, F = mechanical exhaust ventilation, FT = balanced ventilation.

categorised either by building period or by type of ventilation system, there are both good and poor buildings.

Among buildings constructed since 1985, we have looked particularly at those with the best and worst results in respect of health effects among both those with balanced ventilation and those with mechanical exhaust ventilation. The results show that it is possible to build properties with either type of ventilation system, having good, healthy indoor climates, and that it is equally possible to fail to do so, regardless of the type of ventilation system.

The most extensive physical investigation of indoor climate parameters in recent years was that performed by the Swedish Institute for Building Research (SIB) within the framework of the ELIB investigation[13]. The results from this investigation provide an interesting background to the discussion of indoor climate problems in our residential buildings.

Indoor temperatures have increased by half a degree during the last decade

The ELIB report points out that the average indoor temperature in apartment buildings is considerably higher than in detached houses, at 22.2 °C as compared with 20.9 °C. In the apartment building group, the average indoor temperature is lowest in buildings dating from before 1940. These higher indoor temperatures could provide part of the explanation for the fact that many of those living in the more modern properties suffer from dry air. ELIB estimates that indoor temperature has increased by about 0.5 °C during the last decade.

The average ventilation rate, expressed in $l/s,m^2$, is less than the minimum level of 0.35 $l/s,m^2$ specified in the Building Regulations for all age groups of detached houses and for apartment buildings built between 1941 - 1960 and 1976 - 1988. In all cases, ventilation in apartment buildings is better then in detached houses.

Higher humidity in detached houses than in apartment buildings

The ELIB investigation shows that the average measured relative humidity in detached houses was 39 %, while in apartment buildings it was 32 %. Average humidity is highest in properties having natural draught ventilation, followed by those with mechanical exhaust ventilation, and is lowest in those with balanced ventilation systems, i.e. the higher the ventilation air flow rate, the lower the relative humidity. This, as with the case of higher indoor temperatures in apartment buildings, provides an interesting starting point for further analysis of the problem of dry air in properties with balanced ventilation systems.

10 % of all properties have moisture damage

Moisture damage is very common in Swedish residential buildings. According to the ELIB investigation, over 10 % of properties exhibit damage of such an extent that it requires remedial action (not including water damage in utility rooms and bathrooms etc.). Water damage can be found in roofs, roof spaces, living areas and basements, in the form of damp, mildew and rot. The moisture itself comes from all possible sources - precipitation, residual building moisture, damp from the ground, moisture from the air and leakage from piping systems.

Moisture damage in bathrooms and utility rooms is also very common. Over 15 % of detached houses have moisture, mildew or rot problems in their bathrooms. In apartment buildings, 10 % of the apartments are affected. The ELIB report estimates that most of the problems in bathrooms and utility rooms are harmless and easy to deal with.

Rapid changes have affected the indoor climate

Over several centuries, house-building in Sweden followed a line in which small developments in a traditional skill progressively improved designs in a number of respects. After the Second World War, this trend was replaced by a more industrialised method of building. Development was driven by the need for more rapidly and cost-effectively satisfying a strongly growing demand for homes and commercial premises. The real breakthrough for modern rational building methods came during the 1960s, and was seen as a means of solving the acute housing shortage through the Million New Homes programme. The oil crises of the 1970s introduced a new factor, with the need to reduce the amount of heat wasted from buildings.

During the 1960s and 1970s, it was difficult to say what the radical changes in building methods would mean for the indoor climate. However, today we are in a position to conduct such a discussion. We need to study the various stages of changes in building and building services systems methods, the building process and user habits, in order to enable us to analyse their effects in terms of system changes of importance for the indoor climate.

The following pages do not attempt to provide an all-round picture, but should be seen as examples of changes that could have affected the indoor climate. They can provide a basis for starting a debate on, and research into, this relatively unresearched area.

Increased specialisation

The trend towards building larger numbers of units and towards the use of prefabricated elements has also meant that individual projects have become more extensive. Many small building companies could not survive the competition and new, larger companies appeared. This also resulted in increased specialisation. The purchasing function, design and construction were all divided up into several different areas of expertise.

Over the last decades, the actual building process itself has changed, in such ways as the pressure for shorter building times and construction at all times of the year.

Changes in building materials

Developments in building can also be illustrated by changes in the market for building materials. At the beginning of the century there were about 50 different product lines of building materials available: today there are over 40 000. The major change occurred in the 1960s, with such factors as the use of plastic beginning to replace more traditional building materials, particularly for cladding, and when the use of additives started in order to modify the characteristics of materials. Emissions from building materials indoors became a new factor to allow for.

An important step in development occurred with the introduction of reinforced concrete to allow a change in structural designs so that transverse walls and gables became load-bearing. The load-bearing capacity of reinforced concrete meant that floor/ceiling structures could be supported on only two or three sides: a load-bearing exterior wall was no longer necessary. Load-bearing by the outer walls and heart walls had been replaced by load-bearing by transverse separating walls of concrete. This also enabled light infill walls to be used for the facade walls of multi-storey buildings.

The use of these non-load-bearing exterior walls in multi-storey buildings opened up the way to specialisation of material functions. In such walls wooden panels, for example, provided rain protection, building paper provided wind protection, mineral wool gave insulation, plastic film was a vapour barrier and particle board provided the surface for final internal wall covering, which could be woven glass fibre painted with plastic paint. Specialisation also made it possible progressively to increase the performance demanded of the wall, e.g. in terms of thermal insulation.

New, unproven design features, such as flat roofs and slab foundations with insulation above them, became common during the 1960s and increased the risks of moisture damage.

Other ventilation systems

Building services engineering features developed in parallel with these changes in building methods. During the 1960s, mechanical exhaust ventilation became the dominant ventilation principle in apartment buildings. One of the objectives of the introduction of mechanical ventilation was to ensure a sufficient flow of ventilation air to all rooms and apartments throughout the building. At the same time, the system meant that there was no longer a need to provide space for the bulky natural-draught ventilation flues, and room heights could be reduced. During the 1970s, mechanical exhaust ventilation was replaced by balanced ventilation with heat recovery systems, intended to ensure necessary air change rates with greater security. Preheating of the supply air also reduced problems with draughts and simplified problems of heat recovery.

Both the trend towards mechanical ventilation systems and increasing awareness during the 1970s of the need to conserve heat and improve thermal comfort resulted in more stringent requirements in respect of the airtightness of buildings. Good airtightness is essential in order to ensure that the air to mechanically ventilated rooms enters where it is intended to do so. Mineral wool had better insulation performance than materials previously used. In order to avoid moisture damage in walls incorporating mineral wool, it was necessary to employ a special design to prevent the wall elements from becoming damp. To avoid condensation caused by the diffusion of water vapour from the room, the use of a vapour barrier, usually of coated impregnated building paper, became standard during the 1960s. In the 1970s, vapour barriers made of plastic film with sealed joints became common.

Changes in living habits, the use of laundry and drying equipment in the apartments etc. had also resulted in increased moisture loading. In addition, the amount of cleaning done in homes, schools and public premises has tended to decline over the last few decades.

It can be seen that the building process, building methods, building services, building materials and user habits all underwent very rapid changes over a period of essentially two decades. Most of the driving forces were economic, and the objective was to provide good homes for all. However, overall knowledge of how these changes affected indoor climate was inadequate: indeed, this aspect was not at the centre of discussion in any case.

It should be emphasised that energy conservation in itself has not given rise to the sick building syndrome, although if indoor climate is not considered during the planning stage there is a risk that solutions intended to deal with other problems, such as minimising energy use, might be employed that are less suitable from a health viewpoint.

Good indoor climate requires early planning

What we learnt during the 1980s is that present-day building methods are less forgiving in respect of unsuitable designs than older methods, and that defects easily arise in workmanship or coordination of the many specialised elements, or in the operating stage. Building properties that will have good indoor climates can be done only if the indoor climate is considered right from the start of the planning stage and if indoor climate requirements are formulated. Retaining good indoor climate conditions requires good care of the property, not least of the ventilation system.

A prerequisite for achieving our objective of building houses with good indoor climates that do not give rise to health problems is that we can clearly formulate the indoor climate objectives, which must also be capable of being monitored. In an attempt to formulate such monitorable indoor climate and health requirements, the overall objective of health safety has been broken down into a number of physically measurable components such as requirements in respect of the minimum acceptable ventilation air flow rate. The public Building Regulations and inspection of building works have been based on such operational objectives and detailed requirements in respect of different parts of the building.

This hierarchy of standards conceals a fundamental danger as long as we do not know with certainty that the various detailed technical requirements will together result in achieving the overall objective. By breaking everything down into detailed operations, the efforts of the building sector are being focused on satisfying the various partial objectives, instead of solving the underlying problem of building healthy buildings. The problems with health and indoor climate in properties built since 1960 show that we have not been particularly successful in specifying requirements in such a way as to guarantee a good, healthy indoor climate.

Formulate overall performance requirements

An alternative to drafting standards based on detailed requirements and performance requirements for individual parameters or parts of the building is to formulate overall performance requirements for the required characteristics of the building and to monitor them in the completed building. This model is being applied today in Stockholm's 'Healthy Energy-efficient Apartment Buildings - New Building' programme[14]. A similar programme for refurbishment work is being prepared.

The following overall performance requirements for indoor climate and health have been formulated within the programme:

- **Health safety** is approved if the frequency of symptoms of the occupants does not exceed predetermined reference values and if radon gas concentrations do not exceed the permissible concentrations (maximum 200 Bq/m^2).
- **Thermal comfort** is approved if at least 80 % of the occupants regard it as good or acceptable.
- **Air quality** is approved if at least 80 % of the occupants regard it as good or acceptable.

In the building planning application, the developer has to describe the physical performance requirements and technical features that have been selected in order to meet these overall objectives, and the quality system that will be applied in order to ensure compliance with the requirements in the completed building. After the second heating season, indoor climate and health are monitored through the use of a standard questionnaire method. The results from the questionnaire show whether the requirements have been achieved or not.

Against this method, it can be claimed that the developer cannot know with certainty whether a design feature that he selects will meet the overall performance requirements. Indirectly, this can be said to be the objective of the method. If we do not have sufficient knowledge today to ensure that houses that we build will provide an acceptable indoor climate and not cause health problems for their occupants, we must increase our knowledge. The only way of achieving this is consciously to attempt to acquire such knowledge. By employing the concept of overall performance requirements to focus the interest of the entire building sector on the desired characteristics of the building, this process will be accelerated.

More and continuous monitoring is required

Today, monitoring of indoor climate conditions and health is performed on only a small scale and often in the form of research projects at arm's length from those who originally ordered, designed, built and administered the properties. Continuous monitoring of all new building in accordance with the model described above will result in extensive accumulation of knowledge on the part of developers, consultants, administrators and local authorities. The extent of follow-up also makes it possible to link the results with the technical descriptions that were submitted in connection with the application for planning approval.

The new legislation that has accompanied the changes in the Planning and Building Act has placed greater responsibility on the developers for ensuring that the building is healthy, i.e. on those who order the building. It is therefore important that they should make best use of the knowledge that does exist on how to build healthy buildings. During the next few years, most building work will probably be concentrated on refurbishment projects. A working party within the National Institute of Public Health's allergy programme has developed a programme of how attention can be concentrated on the indoor climate, and how it can be quality-assured, when refurbishing schools and child day-care centres[15]. Most of the model can also be used in connection with refurbishment of other types of buildings. It comprises six stages, with associated aids, for integration of indoor climate aspects in planning and activities. These aids include a technical checklist for quality assurance of the building process, together with an activities-based checklist for day-to-day operation to ensure maintenance of a good, low-allergy indoor climate in the completed building. These six stages are listed below.

Six stages of quality assurance

1. **Establish a refurbishment group with a wide range of skills**

   ■ Cross-disciplinary composition.

   ■ Make use of current research results.

2. **Analyse the situation**

   ■ Obtain details of the subjective indoor environment, health and occurrence of allergies using a questionnaire.

   ■ Perform an allergy survey. These surveys have hitherto been carried out in schools and child day-care centres, and have involved the environmental representative and the school nurse interviewing those such as the kitchen and cleaning staff to find out what they do protect persons suffering from allergy problems.

   ■ Go through technical documentation on the building (Ordinance Concerning Obligatory Inspection of Ventilation Systems [OVK] forms etc.)

   ■ Make any necessary complementary measurements.

3. **Establish objectives for the refurbishment**

   ■ Formulate health objectives.

   ■ Draft a performance specification for the indoor environment.

4. **Quality assurance work**

   ■ Draw up a checklist for the building stage (including operation and maintenance preparations).

   ■ Enter into a quality assurance agreement with designers and contractors.

5. **Monitor the indoor climate in the completed building**

   ■ Use a questionnaire of the same type as before refurbishment in order to check that objectives have been achieved.

   ■ Check fulfilment of the terms of the performance specification for the indoor climate.

   ■ Allow time for commissioning and feedback of experience.

6. **Monitor the indoor climate while the building is in use**

   ■ Conduct a yearly allergy survey (see the description in 2 above).

   ■ Train personnel.

This chapter is based on material by Marie Hult, Architect, Stockholm Konsult ByggA, and Per-Anders Hedkvist, MSc. Eng., Stockholm City Council Real Estate, Streets and Traffic Department.

REFERENCES

1 Andersson K., Norlén U. *Bostadsbeståndets inomhusklimat* (Indoor climate in the country's residential building stock). Swedish Institute for Building Research. ELIB Report No. 7 (TN:30), 1993, Gävle.

2 SOSFS 1993:25.

3 National Board of Housing, Building and Planning Building Regulations 1994, BFS 1993:57.

4 Kjellman M., Sundell J. *Luften vi andas inomhus - inomhusmiljöns betydelse för allergi och annan överkänslighet. En vetenskaplig kunskapssammanställning* (The air we breathe indoors - the part played by the indoor environment in allergy and other hypersensitivity, a scientific presentation of knowledge). The National Institute of Public Health, 1994.

5 Andersson K. et al. *Inomhusklimatet i 3000 svenska bostäder* (Indoor climate in 3000 Swedish dwellings). Swedish Institute for Building Research, ELIB Report No. 3 (TN:26), 1991, Gävle.

6 Engvall K., Norrby Ch. *Upplevt inomhusklimat i Stockholms bostadsbestånd* (Subjective indoor climate experience in Stockholm's residential building stock). Stockholm City Council Investigation and Statistics Office, Report No. 1992:4.

7 Stenberg B. et al. *Inomhusmiljö och hälsa bland kontorsarbetare i Västerbotten - en enkätstudie av upplevd hälsa samt exponeringsförhållanden i arbete och bostad* (Indoor environment and health of office workers in Västerbotten - a questionnaire investigation of subjective health and exposure conditions at work and at home). The Work Environment Institute's Report Series 1991:11.

8 See Engvall et al. (1992).

9 See Stenberg et al. (1991).

10 See Andersson and Norlén (1993).

11 See Kjellman and Sundell (1994).

12 See Stockholm City Council ... (1993).

13 See Andersson and Norlén (1993).

14 Stockholm City Council, *Energieffektiva sunda flerbostadshus - Nybyggnadsprogram 1993* (Healthy, energy-efficient apartment buildings - New building programme, 1993)

15 The National Institute of Public Health, *Allergiprogrammet. Allergianpassning vid renovering och drift av daghem och skolor* (The allergy programme. Allergy considerations when refurbishing and operating child day-care centres and schools). 1994, Stockholm.

OTHER LITERATURE

Att uppleva inneklimat i energisnåla hus. En jämförande studie av de boendes upplevelser av inneklimat i sex energisnåla experimenthus samt ett ordinärt nybyggt hus (The indoor climate in low-energy buildings. A comparative investigation of occupants' impressions of the indoor climate in six low-energy experimental buildings and in an ordinary newly-built house). Engvall, K. USK Investigation Report 1989:9.

Hus och hälsa. Inneklimat och effektiv energianvändning (House and health. Indoor climate and efficient energy use). Summary. BFR T19:1991.

Inneklimat och energihushållning (Indoor climate and energy conservation). Government Report. BFR G5:1990.

OCCUPANTS BEFORE TECHNOLOGY

SUMMARY

In future, the value of properties will be affected by how their operation and maintenance systems are working. Attempts to fulfil changed requirements will be decisive for future good environmental conditions, satisfied tenants and good long-term financial return. New requirements, coupled with rising energy prices, will tilt development towards more efficient operation of energy systems. Bearing this in mind, it will not be the technology that will be at the fore, but the following factors that will be important:

Improved communication between different parties. Communication between all parties, ranging from planners to users, must operate if the result is to be a good indoor climate. All too often, questions fall between disciplines. There needs to be an overall view of the building/indoor climate/occupier. **Training, competence and status for operating personnel.** Clear operational management and well-motivated operating personnel, with carefully defined areas of responsibility and means of accepting responsibility, are

prerequisites for good operating results. **Operational organisation.** Maintenance is often neglected. Poor maintenance results in serious long-term problems. The operating personnel's views and experience are very important, right from the planning stage. **Means of formal monitoring.** Experience needs to be fed back, user needs and requirements brought out in structured dialogues and important information collected in a service book. Methods for controlling energy systems need to be developed.

A case example from reality

An apartment building, built in Stockholm in 1984, has balanced ventilation with heat exchange. Together with five other apartment buildings erected at approximately the same time, it was part of a large demonstration and evaluation project. Among the points to be evaluated were the effects of enhanced quality management and control. Employees were trained and the amount of inspection performed by those doing the work was increased.

Operational performance of the building was evaluated by a group of scientists from the Royal Institute of Technology in Stockholm. This was accompanied by a sociological investigation into how the indoor climate was experienced. After some years' operation, measurements showed that energy use in the building was too high in comparison with the design calculations. At the same time, the occupants complained that thermal comfort was poor. Among the defects identified, it was found that the total air flow rate

through the ventilation units was approximately twice the design values.

The firm responsible for managing the building was contacted and the various defects were pointed out, including the high air flow rates. The managing company, which naturally compared the new building with the other buildings for which it was responsible, could not see that the energy use was high: instead, it felt that the building's energy performance was excellent. As far as the high air flow rates were concerned, there were the inspection records, clearly filled in, from the work of setting up the ventilation system that was carried out in connection with handover of the property by the contractor.

The evaluation group stood its ground and maintained that something must be done. Eventually, the owner of the property (in the same group of companies as the managing company) decided to perform its own additional investigation of the building. This revealed such serious shortcomings in installation of the ventilation ducting system that it was obvious that the system had never been adjusted, despite the fact that the adjustment records claimed this. The building owners then adjusted the ventilation system under their own control. After this, measurements of the total air flow rate through the fans indicated the expected values. Peace and quiet were restored, and evaluation of the performance of the building could continue and be concluded.

In due course, the Ordinance Concerning Obligatory Inspection of Ventilation Systems (OVK) was issued in 1991. The resulting OVK inspection of the building in 1994 found that the air flow rate in several apartments was very low or practically non-existent. There were also complaints from the tenants concerning stale air etc. The property-owner was now forced, as an initial measure, to clean the duct system and the ventilation unit. The system was then re-adjusted, not entirely without difficulty. One of the problems was that it was difficult to obtain data on certain parts of the ventilation system, that were important for correct adjustment, from the manufacturers.

The system had also been designed so that it is practically impossible to measure supply air flow rates at the room air inlets. Adjustment this time found that the previous adjustment had been performed on the basis of incorrect initial values. Incorrect data concerning the means of adjustment incorporated in the system had probably been received from the manufacturer. The result was that the adjusted ventilation air flow rate to individual air inlets was about half of that intended. After a few years' accumulation of dirt in the system, these air flow rates were virtually non-existent.

This particular building had been the subject of much attention, both during the time of construction and subsequently. Nevertheless, it was nearly ten years before its ventilation system was properly adjusted so that it could perform its purpose in an acceptable manner. One of the fundamental underlying ideas during the building period had been enhanced quality control ...

*

Today, there is a great amount of knowledge of various systems and their performances, of technical performance and of how various performances and functions are experienced by the occupants of the buildings. The building construction and building management sectors try various ways of disseminating the available knowledge: running courses on quality systems, quality development, quality management, latest developments etc. The question is why all this knowledge is not actually applied in the day-to-day operation of buildings. Why do we keep discovering, time and time again, that so much is failing to work when it reaches the user stage?

Doubtless, all parties understand the need for making use of new knowledge in an overall perspective. However, if this knowledge is to reach all the way along the chain to the operating personnel and those who use the building, greater attention needs to be paid to the interfaces between costs, design and technology to the user for whom the system has been designed.

The organisation that is created in order to look after operation and maintenance is often based on the needs of technical systems and the ability to monitor them, rather than on the needs of the user and the ability of the operating personnel to understand these needs and to do something about them. Present-day organisations are often hierarchical, with several levels where not only knowledge but also management's motivation need to reach out to operating personnel and users. However, if motivation and knowledge are to reach out, the system needs to employ clearly delegated responsibility and coordination in order to achieve the prescribed objectives for efficient operation.

Two property management philosophies

We can today discern two philosophies in terms of property management, and particularly of operation of heating, ventilation and sanitary installations. One of these philosophies favours competitive procurement, purchasing not only equipment but also operational services, while the other places greater emphasis on the local administration level. Competitive procurement can result in strategic contact with users being lost, and create a crisis of confidence between users and administrators. If greater responsibility is imposed on the operating personnel, they must also be given correspondingly increased abilities to accept this responsibility.

There is also an important relationship between small-scale and large-scale performance in a particular property. Each unit is a part of this larger system. How the occupants of an office room or apartment set their radiators, radiator valves, opening of windows, sunshading, doors etc. has an affect on the performance of the building as a whole. Naturally, users must be able to do what they want in such respects, but they need to be informed of how the system is thereby affected. Some points are obvious, others are not. Complaints, for example, that air quality is poor in a room that is being used by more persons than the number for which it was designed illustrate a common example of failure of information to reach the users.

Good performance presupposes that the user understands the building, knows the main features of its operational systems and what to look for in order to spot any faults. In general, operating personnel need to accept some of the responsibility for performance of the building and act as a link between users and technology.

Requirements imposed on the various parties in the property sector have increased, while operation and maintenance are often looked after by personnel with little training and status. The caretaker's or maintenance technician's ability to influence design of the energy system has been slight. Increasingly complicated properties increase the need for knowledge and quality.

In future, the value of a property will be influenced by how operation and maintenance work. Discussions have included consideration of whether insurance premiums should be reduced for properties that are well managed and work well. In the next stage, mortgage interest rates could be dependent on building condition and status. This would require some form of classification.

Technology is not the most important aspect

Attempts to fulfil the changed requirements will be decisive for future good environmental conditions, satisfied tenants and good long-term financial return. New requirements, coupled with rising energy prices, will tilt development towards more efficient operation of energy systems. Bearing this in mind, it will not be the technology that will be at the fore, but the following factors that will be important:

- ■ Improved communication between different parties.
- ■ Training, competence and status for operating personnel.
- ■ Operational organisation.
- ■ Means of formal monitoring.

Improved communication between different parties

If building services systems in buildings are to operate as efficiently as possible, it is essential that communication works at all levels. Quality and performance requirements must be complied with throughout the building and operational process. Problems often fall between the remits of different disciplines. An overall view of the building/indoor climate/occupants is required: if not, there is otherwise a risk that essentially good ideas and technical designs will not operate as intended or, in the worst case, will cause damage or undesirable effects.

Information and knowledge are needed if this communication is to result in correct adjustment and use. When different parties and disciplines are involved and required to work together, jargon and even their use of language can result in misunderstandings that may be difficult to detect. Documents from one discipline must be comprehensible to those involved in other disciplines. Improved communication between parties is essential in order to arrive good quality buildings, good indoor climate conditions and low energy use.

Training, competence, status

The picture that appears is gloomy. Although a relatively wide range of courses in building management is offered, the general knowledge level is low. An extensive questionnaire survey of 42 property companies that was carried out by the Real Estate Sector Training Council - FABUR - found that about only 6 % of caretakers, and only about 40 % of equipment operators, had high school education. The average age was over 40, and few replacements were coming forward.

The caretakers - who have the lowest level of training - make up no less than 45 % of the operating personnel corps, while the system operators - who have the highest training - make up less than 10 % of it. It should also be pointed out that, in practice, the various different categories often perform the same tasks. At the same time, the requirements on them are increasing. The introduction of new technology, such as computerisation and control technology,[12] in several working areas will require major training effort over the next ten years and will have a substantial effect on the work performed by operating personnel.

Despite a relatively wide range of courses in property management, general knowledge levels are low. Only about 6 % of caretakers and about 40 % of plant operators received higher secondary education.
Photographer: Kjell Johansson, Bildhuset

The new energy line at high school level includes streams for heating, ventilation and sanitation, marine engineering and energy, with the energy stream being least in demand. Training of operators and technicians at institute of technology level in Stockholm and Kalmar is to be discontinued. An investigation carried out by the Swedish Association of Heating and Air-conditioning Engineers[3] pointed out the lack of suitable training for electricity and energy efficiency as a problem of the 1990s.

Behavioural science knowledge needed

In addition to the purely technical aspects, there is a major need for better understanding of user requirements, viewpoints, expectations and questions concerning indoor climate. All too often, complaints from users are ignored. The results of questionnaires are regarded as unscientific and lacking in objectivity. If an occupant complains that his/her apartment is cold, and measurements of the indoor temperature show +22 °C, he/she is often simply regarded as a troublemaker, even if there are draughts and the floor temperature is low.

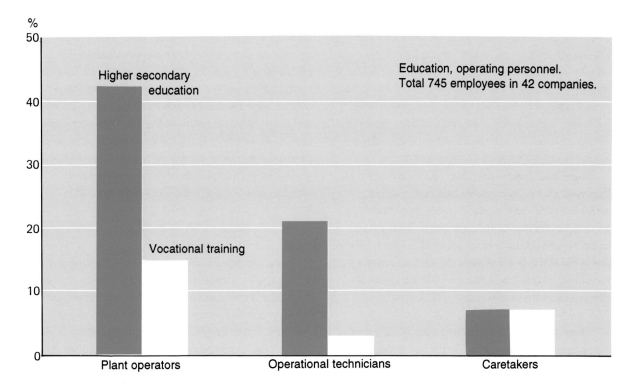

Figure 1. Education of property management operating personnel (Property Sector Training Council, 1995).

Nor can the operating personnel make full use of the sensitive instrument that is the human body. Technical training needs to be complemented with behavioural science and humanistics. Expansion of training in this direction could also result in attracting more women into technical training and property care.

Training also needs to suit the requirements and levels appropriate to each item or property company. As the educational/training level of individual caretakers varies, although is generally low, training needs to be more or less tailor-made. Building management companies need to note personnel competence and need of training, and make appropriate allowance for this when assessing necessary measures and investments.

In the longer term, basic training and recruiting should naturally be matched to the need. Another way would be to offer additional training courses, similar to those of the high schools, for those already employed. It is also important to start research in the operational and maintenance sector: there is a gap between this sector and the research world, partly due to a lack of interest by institutes of technology and politicians.

SEK 95 000 million per year

Feedback is another important aspect: listening to employees and keeping them informed of results and measures. In a large organisation, or where the building services cannot be handled entirely by the operating personnel, someone could be appointed responsible for energy aspects. It can be beneficial to be able to see energy aspects in a broader perspective.

The annual cost for operation and maintenance of the country's total administered rental real estate area of about 395 million m^2 (which excludes single-family houses, second homes and agriculture), amounts to about SEK 95 000 million[4], or about SEK 240/m^2. Today, about 180 000 persons work in the field of property administration, of whom about 50 000 are caretakers. On average, each caretaker is responsible for about 8000 m^2 of building floor area.

Major variations in energy use occur in each sector, despite similar needs and building services systems. Operating personnel and organisational factors have a decisive effect in determining the efficiency of energy use.

It can be seen from Figure 3 that operation and maintenance costs vary substantially. The relatively high costs of planned maintenance are offset by reduced costs of heating and energy, satisfied tenants and higher property values.

Maintenance is often neglected

The extent and quality of property maintenance varies substantially. Unfortunately, maintenance is often neglected. One result of such neglect was the need to introduce legislation requiring obligatory inspection of ventilation systems (OVK) in 1991. The commonest form of maintenance is acute maintenance, in response to an alarm or an actual breakdown. This is a cheap, short-sighted solution that requires a minimum of personnel.

In the longer perspective, preventive maintenance and long-term planned maintenance are naturally preferable. However, if the future of a property is uncertain, this is often reflected in maintenance, which is reduced to acute maintenance. We can naturally expect to see many examples of this policy in the wake of the property speculation of the boom years at the end of the 1980s.

Within the field of maintenance, computerisation does not have the same leverage effect as it does on operational monitoring. Each company's strategic planning needs to be clearly determined, with allowance for life cycle costs and resources in the longer term. Manual methods need to work, starting from personnel competence and ambition. Here, too, the training of caretakers within the company or on site is an important element, not least in the light of the present competence levels. As a result, personnel responsibilities will increase, which will in turn affect the organisation.

A service log with each property

Tomorrow's operational organisations must have a wide span, with skilled technicians, accountants and market analysts. Tenants must be at the centre. Better information, in a number of directions, will be required. Tenants must be kept informed of inspections that have been carried out, planned maintenance, new tenants, refurbishing etc. It is only when tenants have been told

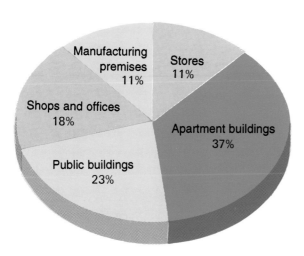

Figure 2. Classification of total building floor area by application in the Swedish building stock.

Figure 3. Operating and maintenance costs in offices during 1994 (Repab Program AB, 1994)[5].

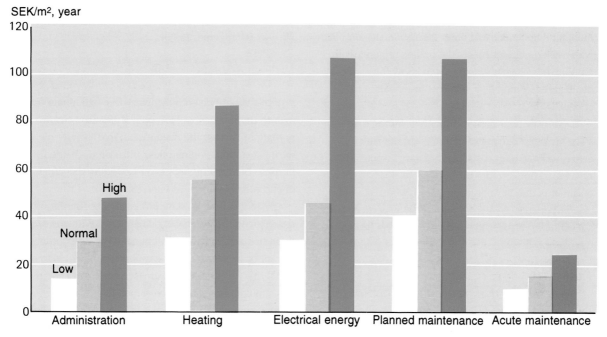

of their rights that they can present their own demands at the right level. The property-owner, on the other hand, needs information concerning the present state of the property, both in marketing terms and in respect of its physical condition and performance. Documentation of work carried out, energy statistics etc. needs to be improved. One way in which this could be done is in the form of a log book, which remains with the property throughout its life. This log book would contain all important information on the property, the results of inspections, refurbishment, acute faults, alarms, annual energy statistics etc.

Targeted monitoring of the various functions of a building needs to be prepared with the assistance of active commissioning. The right conditions for efficient operation need to be created at an early stage. The foundations for a good system design, suitable for monitoring and maintenance, are laid at the initial idea stage. It is not unusual for the designer of a new system not to know enough about the capabilities of the operational organisation to look after the system, which naturally complicates both commissioning and operation. Operational experience needs to be fed back to the purchaser of new plants and to the designers.

Feedback of experience is essential

Feedback of the views and experience of operational personnel is most important at this early stage. Unfortunately, it very seldom occurs, despite the fact that concepts such as 'experience feedback' have been buzzwords for several decades. It can be difficult for individual designers to see the overall performance of a system in a longer perspective. It is easy for the work to concentrate on the purely technical aspects, which in any case can be sufficiently complicated and troublesome on their own.

There are, admittedly, rules in the 1994 Building Regulations[6], although they are not comprehensive and are not always followed. Naturally, the designer needs to be familiar with current rules, although it is ultimately the developer who is responsible for ensuring that the Building Regulations and other legislation are complied with. The purchaser makes the outline requirements, but it is the designer who needs to know the applicable detailed requirements, including those relating to energy.

Defects or poor designs that occur during the design stage are often difficult to detect, and can result in extensive long-term costs. An ordinary inspection does not reveal shortcomings of this type, as it is based on the documents that have been produced, with the emphasis on components. Nor can a traditional inspection, lasting a few hours, consider the underlying system design or dynamic processes.

70 % of defects caused by the human factor

Evaluation of the causes of defects in the new building of six apartment buildings and an office (the Stockholm project)[7] found that by far the greatest proportion of defects - over 70 % - resulted from the human factor. Only about 30 % were material or component defects. In addition, special measurement and analysis work was needed to find faults originating from the design or construction stages.

The purchaser should really, at the procurement stage, specify activity-related and cost requirements in respect of the building services systems, and how these are to be monitored. Unfortunately, this is not always done, which means that these matters are passed to the designer or contractor. There is a substantial risk of energy and other aspects failing to be considered.

It has to be accepted that a property and its building

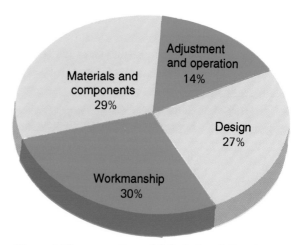

Figure 4. The proportion of defects in relation to causes in building services systems in the Stockholm Project (Wånggren, 1990).

services will not be entirely defect-free when handed over to the purchaser. However, if all parties were prepared to accept the need to 'run in' the systems during a commissioning phase, this serves the dual purpose of revealing defects and avoiding the situation of everyone blaming everyone else.

System commissioning procedures need to be described in the purchasing documents, with costs for them being included in the budget. The descriptions can set out what is to be measured and how it is to be done. If a physical supervisory system is incorporated, this should be used as much as possible. Tests of various operating modes can and should be described.

Structured dialogue with the user

Planned monitoring enables a structured and documented dialogue with the user to be established. By giving the user a structured set of questions, various functions and their use and operation can be checked off and finally used for an overall assessment of how the systems are working and how the indoor environment is experienced. For this information to be of value, it is also necessary to be able to link the replies to different parts of the property and to different systems and functions.

For this purpose, a form of measurement such as that offered by a structured questionnaire can have many benefits. It can provide a picture of how the apartments/offices in the property are being used, i.e. how often windows are opened, filters cleaned etc. The questionee is also able to note important observations, such as the presence of moisture and mildew, leakage etc. However, above all, the questionnaire can indicate how the premises are experienced in terms of indoor climate, thus providing an overall picture of how the various system functions are working together. By repeating the questionnaire at intervals, information is also obtained on how users experience improvements or deteriorations.

Today, as a result of the major survey of indoor climate in the Stockholm housing stock that was carried out in connection with the House and Health Project, we have good reference quantifiers for subjective indoor climate and health[8]. These reference quantifiers are today used systematically in questionnaire surveys to occupants in connection with guarantee inspections. User opinions are sought in order to:

- Reveal system defects related to the particular system design by comparison with reference values for other newly-built apartment buildings in Stockholm.
- Reveal system defects related to poor building workmanship in individual properties by comparing the quantifiers for that property with the average for the area as a whole.
- Test given hypotheses concerning suspected system defects indicated by visual inspection.
- Provide a systematic means of directing discussions with contractors concerning further inspection measurements and direct measures.

Two types of measurement

As far as operational analysis in concerned, there are two main types of measurement that are normally used. One is long-term monitoring of energy statistics, while the other involves real-time measurements during commissioning and subsequent inspections of the system. Both types are essential, but require different working methods and instruments.

Today's technical methods of measurement are sophisticated, available in a wide range and meet essentially most requirements. Development is rapid, and the capabilities of available measurement technology greatly exceed the resources for processing the subsequent data. A good guide to deciding on the appropriate method of measurement is carefully to go through in advance how the measured data is to be used.

The debiting meters that are normally used for metering electricity and heat can be read manually or by data-loggers. This provides a good basis for assessing system performance in response to various operating modes and when changing from one mode to another.

To obtain a more detailed breakdown, electric power to various sub-loads can be measured by clip-on meters. Temperatures in different parts of a building can be measured with temperature sensors integrated with data-loggers in order to avoid awkward and time-consuming cable-running. Air change rates, air flow rates and efficacy of air exchange can all be measured using tracer gas methods.

Operational monitoring of energy use is an important element in arriving at efficient operation. Relatively simple means provide an overall view of system performance. Complemented by manual meter-reading and reporting routines, this provides a good basis for assessing the effects of major changes to the system.

Inspection methods need to be developed and standardised

Within the field of operational monitoring, there are no defined methods for detailed monitoring and analysis of the performance of building services systems. Attempting to track changes in operational statistics is not sufficient, as some changes do not reveal themselves in this sort of overall monitoring. Air flow rates, for example, could be reduced, and temperatures increased with a resultant deterioration in the indoor climate, without being reflected in energy use statistics. Changes such as these will operate in various directions in the energy balance and will probably not be revealed by statistics. Defined measurement and analysis is often necessary.

In the present-day situation, we have to use the services of individual consultants who, on the basis of their competence and availability of equipment, provide an assessment of current operational status. A specification of which and how various parameters are to measured and analysed would be of considerable value.

Computerisation of operational monitoring could initiate a change to more rational operation. Existing routines need to be listed, and a performance specification drawn up on the basis of specific needs. The National Association of Local Authorities has developed an aid for this, in the form of a checklist of over 50 points. Tariffs and presentation of costs are sometimes regarded as important points: no amount of computerisation can help if good data is not available.

Control and supervision

Control and supervision can be performed both manually and by advanced technology, with the emphasis in recent years being on the technical side. The ideal is a combination of good technical equipment and direct contact with the installation. The purely physical contact with the system, the building and the user can easily be undervalued if the actual technology is advanced and heavily marketed. It is also common to fail to allow for the dynamics of the building itself in the control process. Building services systems may be substantially oversized and prevent temperature variations from occurring, which is of decisive importance in reducing both heating and cooling requirements.

It is difficult to decide whether computerisation generally tends to reduce the use of energy and whether it is profitable. When savings do occur, it is often unclear how much can be credited to computerisation and how much to generally improved supervision of the system. Although supervision may often be manual, it does generally require extra work by personnel.

International standardisation work in progress

The lack of communication between different control and supervisory systems has become an increasingly serious problem. Most communication protocols are at present proprietary, i.e. different makes of equipment cannot communicate with each other. However, international standardisation work is in progress. Open System Interconnection (OSI) is a model for standardisation[9]. However, practical results from standardisation are likely to be a few years away. Some manufacturers already employ OSI protocols, which could be developed into de facto standards. Familjebostäder and the Gothenburg Energy Authority have developed their communication system under the name of Hermes.

Development must result in more open systems, with more functions being integrated with the purely

technical functions. Property documentation and administrative functions, for example, could be included in the system. Any change made to any part of the system could result in appropriate immediate updating of operational records, drawings and procedural descriptions. Another development relates to the building services systems and cable-running, with the electricity distribution system itself being used for the transfer of signals. This facilitates and reduces the price of building services systems, not least in existing buildings.

Nevertheless, by far the most important measure for the future is to increase understanding of the interaction between the building, its service systems and its occupants.

This chapter is based on material by Karin Engvall, Stockholm City Council Office of Research and Statistics, Per Wickman, Stockholm City Council Department of Operational Analysis and Sven-Olof Eriksson, Division of Building Technology, the Royal Institute of Technology, Stockholm.

REFERENCES

1 *Informations- och utbildningsbehov rörande el- och energihushållning* (Information and training requirements for electricity and energy conservation). National Energy Administration, 1990.

2 *Framtidens kunskaper* (Future knowledge requirements). The Swedish Building Maintenance Workers' Union, ABL-konsult, 1990.

3 *Utbildning för el- och energieffektivitet i den byggda miljön - ett 90-talsproblem* (Training for electricity and energy efficiency in the built environment - a problem of the 1990s). The Swedish Association of Heating and Air-conditioning Engineers.

4 See Swedish Federation of Rental Property Owners, 1993.

5 Annual costs, 1994 - Offices. REPAB Program AB.

6 1994 Building Regulations, National Board of Housing, Building and Planning, 1994.

7 Wånggren B, *Idrifttagning av installationssystem i Stockholmsprojektet* (Commissioning of building services systems in the Stockholm project). Swedish Council for Building Research, R42:1990.

8 Engvall, K and Norrby, *Upplevt inomhusklimat i Stockholms bostadsbestånd* (Subjective indoor climate in Stockholm housing stock). USK 1992:4.

9 *Datorsystem för fastighetssektorn* (Computer systems for the property sector). Swedish Federation of Rental Property Owners, 1993.

ATTITUDES AND LIFESTYLE AFFECT ENERGY USE

SUMMARY

The factors behind human behaviour relate to individual motivation and to the receipt of thorough and comprehensible knowledge that arouses feelings. This knowledge and these feelings should be the motivators of action. However, the difference between word and deed is affected by the obstacles to, and potentials for, change that exist in the social surroundings of each and every individual. Such obstacles may very well be anchored in the individual's life form.

Life form is defined as categories of persons sharing the same living conditions. Within each residential area or in each workplace, there are the right conditions or obstacles for responses to environmental actions that accord to a greater or lesser extent with the individual's motivation. An important basic condition for achieving changes in individual and household habits seems to be identification of the individual or household with the area. Interest in, and

willingness to perform, environmental actions have a greater chance of leading to results that can be collectively measured in areas where individuals or households feel relaxed and at home. The worst conditions for attempting to change behaviour to the benefit of the environment are to be found in large residential areas with very heterogeneous populations and a high rate of turnover.

In many areas, difficulties have been noted both in changing human attitudes and actions and in retaining those changes that have been made. At a general level, it appears as if knowledge and a constant stream of information result in a saturation level, at which every additional change requires excessive effort. Behind this general observation, it is often possible to discern several underlying processes, with very different obstacles and opportunities for development and change, requiring different types of information strategies.

Spreading information with the objective of influencing persons so that it results in lasting changes is associated with many problems which, in general terms, can be described under a number of points. The factors that lie behind human behaviour are concerned with:

■ *The individual's motivation for, and interest in, changing attitudes and actions.* It is not sufficient merely to possess the appropriate knowledge and, through it, to understand that it is necessary to modify a pattern of actions. Each attitude must be anchored in the fundamental values of the individual and of society. These values give rise to many attitudes and actions, all pulling in the same direction and towards the same objective, e.g. within the environmental field.

Persons in a society are often exposed to conflicting pressures. Information on the importance of conserving energy is opposed by the marketing of new products, services and experiences that result in greater use of energy. Those exposed to such conflicting pressures have a tendency to retain their 'old' behaviour: information and new knowledge are not absorbed. Where new information is absorbed and results in conservation, there is an increased probability of the released resources being used to achieve a higher standard through the consumption of new products or services. Savings resulting from energy conservation can thus quickly be offset by new consumption to the 'old' level again.

■ *Knowledge of a phenomenon needs not only to be correct*

and relevant, but must also be so thorough and comprehensible that it encourages further thought and analysis. It needs a link to concrete experiences in the daily life of the individual. Each individual or household must be able to translate the message into experience and measures that are relative and feasible to their own daily life.

■ *Knowledge needs to arouse feelings in the individual.* By awaking feelings, knowledge can motivate changing a bad habit or enhancing an existing good habit. However, it can also awake feelings that result in the reverse, i.e. reinforcement of undesirable behaviour. In general, information alone results in only slow changes. There is much inertia in individuals and obstacles in the world around them which are overcome only slowly. Other guide measures can act as catalysts in order to accelerate the process of change, such as financial guide measures (pricing, rebates, taxation, fees) or normative changes (legislation, inspection systems, sanctions). The same guide measures seldom have the same effects on everyone. General guide measures act as catalysts to different extents on different groups of individuals/households.

■ *Knowledge and feelings motivate action,* whether in the form of the individual modifying a pattern of action or further developing an existing pattern of action. In many contexts, persons say that they intend to modify their actions, without subsequently actually doing so. There can be a considerable difference between what is said and what is done. The probability of changing a pattern of actions is greatest if the effect/profitability of changing is noticeable by the individual in the short term. It must alays be possible to translate information into concrete actions and situations in the individual's own daily life. At the same time, it should be possible to experience the consequences of the actions at as close hand and as directly as possible.

■ *The difference between word and actual deed is affected by the obstacles and opportunities for change that exist in the individual's social surroundings.* Such barriers may be firmly anchored in the individual's life form, i.e. the context in which he/she lives his/her daily life. Important contexts of this type are the environments in which the individual passes his/her daily life, e.g. workplaces and residential areas. In these contexts, many persons share the same living conditions, the same life form. Within each residential area and/or workplace, there are conditions for, or obstacles against, the performance of environmental actions that accord to a greater or lesser extent with the individuals' motivations.

Life form involves sharing the same living conditions

Life form is defined as categories of persons who share the same living conditions. The content of the concept of life form is related partly to the housing structure in the urban environment, and partly to demographic and social characteristics of those living there.

At the level of Swedish society, the physical characteristics of a shared life form can be described in a number of ways, including living conditions in terms of type of housing, disposition and ownership category of their residences. The social and demographic characteristics of a shared life form are the type of household, age and socio-financial circumstances. Using this analysis, the urban life forms in Swedish society can be described by three main groups, based primarily on the physical structure, namely rented from a commercial owner, rented from a cooperative owner and privately-owned residences.

A general description of the demographic and socio-financial variables for these forms of living reveals differences between them. However, a more thorough analysis of the different forms of living identifies several sub-groups in each main category. The degree of population stability and population heterogeneity seems to be particularly important in determining this classification. Residential areas with a low population turnover but with both heterogeneous and homogenous populations can serve as cohesive life forms. On the other hand, high population turnover in combination with high population heterogeneity and a large number of households are criteria that indicate that such residential areas do not operate very well as cohesive life forms.

In areas of privately owned detached houses, most of the owners are prepared to modify their living habits to suit the environments of their own households, but it is more difficult to persuade them to act together in the interests of the entire area. Photographer: Beppe Arvidsson, Bildhuset

Well-being and environmental actions belong together

An investigation of behaviour in the various life forms analysed persons' identification with their dwelling and their environmental actions as manifested by sorting of refuse, water and energy conservation measures in the various life forms. In order to achieve changes in individual and household actions, an important basic prerequisite seems to be that there should be identification between the residential area and the home area. Interest in, and willingness to implement, environmental actions have a greater chance of leading to results that can be measured collectively in areas where persons live and feel at home, and not just in the

individual apartment but in the residential area as a whole. In these respects, the urban life forms differ. On this basis, the best prospects for environmentally considerate actions are to be found in tenant ownership association areas and in older and smaller commercial ownership areas with a low turnover rate. In privately-owned detached house areas, there is a high willingness to perform environmentally considerate actions on a household basis, but it is more difficult to achieve corresponding actions on an area basis. The worst prospects for changing patterns of actions for the better are to be found in large residential areas with high population heterogeneity and a high turnover rate.

The results indicate that not only is it important to

aim at both individuals and households when attempting to establish willingness to act and to change living patterns in respect of such environmentally considerate measures as sorting of refuse or energy conservation and water conservation measures, but it is equally important to identify the conditional factors for environmentally considerate measures associated with different life forms and to modify the approach strategy to suit the conditions applicable to each life form.

Freedom of choice in preference to forced savings

There is a close relationship between public planning and individuals' choice of living forms and environmental responses. One investigation, for example, found that improved infrastructure in the form of easier and faster journeys to and from work results in both a saving of time and a saving of money for the individual. These savings are then evaluated by the individual in such a way as to increase the freedom of choice between an improved living standard or a higher quality of free time. Within quite a short time, the savings in journey time and cost have been replaced either by moving to a new home with a longer journey distance, but with the same journey time, to work, or by an increased use of energy in free time. At present, this seems to be a general feature of many different types of consumption. As long as freedom of choice is available, individuals and households choose freedom of choice and enhancement of welfare before both individual and public savings[1].

This chapter is based on material by university lecturer Anna-Lisa Lindén, Department of Sociology, Lund University.

REFERENCES

1   This essay is based mainly on the following literature:

Lindberg, G. and Lindén, A-L, 1989. *Social segmentation på den svenska bostadsmarknaden* (Social segmentation on the Swedish residential market). The Living and Built Environment Research Group, Department of Sociology, University of Lund.

Lindén, A-L, 1989a. *Vem bor i bostadsområdet? Bostadsutbud - befolkningsstruktur - förändringsmönster* (Who lives in the residential area? Availability of housing - population structure - patterns of change). The Living and Built Environment Research Group, Department of Sociology, University of Lund.

Lindén, A-L, 1989b. *Bostadsmarknadens ägarstruktur och hushållens boendemönster. Förändring och utveckling 1975-1985* (Ownership structure and household living patterns of the residential market Change and development, 1975-1985). The Living and Built Environment Research Group, Department of Sociology, University of Lund.

Lindén, A-L, 1994. *Människa och miljö. Om attityder värderingar, livsstil och livsform* (Man and the environment. On attitudes, valuations, life style and ways of life). Carlssons förlag, Stockholm.

Lindén, A-L, 1994. *Livsstil och konsumtionsmönster - drivkrafter och motkrafter i energianvändning. I-världen som trendsättare* (Life style and consumption patterns - driving forces and counter-forces in energy use. The industrialised world as a trend-setter). In SOU 1994:138. Report from the Climate Delegation.

Lindén, A-L, 1995. *Urbanismens livsformer och samhällets avfallsproblem* (Urbanism's life forms and society's waste problems). Nordisk arkitekturforskning, Vol. 8.1 (in publication).

OTHER LITERATURE

Energi är livet. Energikonsumtionen och sparande. Livsstilar och energikaraktärer. Marknadssegmentering och kommunikation (Energy is life. Energy use and conservation. Lifestyles and energy characters. Market segmentation and communication). Ericsson, T. and Hamrin, U. Swedish Association of Electrical Utilities, 1991.

SOCIETY AND ENERGY

Money, rules and information - policy measures that affect energy use
Time to think of energy and environmental costs at local community level
The importance of correct siting
The built environment affects transport requirements and vice versa
Deregulation changes the electricity market
Let market forces assist the introduction of new technology

Photographer: Bruno Ehrs, Bildhuset

MONEY, RULES AND INFORMATION – POLICY MEASURES THAT AFFECT ENERGY USE

SUMMARY

In recent years, energy policy has become increasingly associated with an awareness of the importance of environmental aspects. It has also become more market-orientated, which has changed the requirements in respect of the State's policy measures. The planned phase-out of nuclear power production in 2010, for example, means that policy measures to assist the introduction of alternative energy sources must have high priority. The importance of price as a policy measure has increased, but there is some doubt as to whether market forces alone are capable of leading development in the desired direction.

Research is needed to illuminate the extent to which standards and rule structures are needed, and to make more refined investigations of the factors that determine domestic energy use. Behavioural science investigations, linked to individuals' energy decisions, are also needed. More in-depth investigations of price structures in the energy market are required, as are investigations of various means of financing different types of overall heating systems. The decision-making process at different levels needs to be studied, and it is important to look at the relationship and interaction between different policy measures. Ancillary effects of policy measures, such as health and environmental effects, competition and productivity aspects, also need to be investigated. Information as a policy measure is another important research area.

Historically, public authorities have long attempted to influence energy use patterns in the built environment for a number of reasons and in varying ways - through legislation and administrative standards, through financial policy measures, through information and training and by direct support for research, development and demonstration activities intended to develop and demonstrate new technical designs and systems.

However, it was not until the more cohesive energy policy of the 1970s that energy use in the built environment came up onto the political agenda in its own right, with application of more active policy measures. It was also not until then that any real debate - whether political or scientific - came about concerning the costs, effects and efficacy of various policy measures and incentive systems.

The stick, the carrot and the sermon

The term 'policy measures' is by no means self-explanatory. Vedung[1] points out that the concept is defined in respect of the relationship between those issuing the policy measures and those whom they are intended to influence. A policy measure consists of a 'substance' component (its issuer's/the authority's wishes or requirements concerning what is to be achieved) and an 'effect' component, e.g. what the addressee is expected to do and what the results of this may be.

There are various ways of classifying policy measures. Vedung[2] distinguished between regulatory policy measures ('the stick'), financial incentive policy measures ('the carrot') and information ('the sermon'). This classification is by no means closed to discussion: on the contrary, there is an extensive debate concerning the advantages and drawbacks of various classification bases and on how various policy measures can be characterised. There is often substantial confusion. The term 'administrative policy measures', for example, is often used to refer to various types of prescriptive regulations. But administrative policy measures can also refer to conditions associated with the availability of financial incentive policy measures, e.g. the conditions to be fulfilled in order to receive a State building loan.

Various types of policy measures are often used in conjunction with each other. Information, for example, is in many cases a prerequisite for achieving the effect intended by application of financial support or regulatory standards.

Over the years, many different types of policy measures have been employed to influence energy use in the built environment, and many appraisals of the results have been performed[3]. Examples include loans and grants for energy conservation investments, standards for new building and refurbishment, information, loans and grants for demonstration and experimental building projects and support for local authority inspection and advisory services.

Different types of policy measures are used in different environments and for varying purposes. It therefore seems to be equally important to investigate the interaction between different policy measures as the effects of the individual policy measures.

Three different time frames

An important aspect in this context is the time frame, i.e. matters relating to the time taken for policy measures to work and the length of time for which they are applied or are available. When discussing the choice between different policy measures, there is therefore reason to distinguish between at least three different time frames:

- An **acute shortage situation**, when energy use needs to be reduced very quickly or directed in another direction, necessitating the use of some particular technology and utilizing existing capital equipment.
- In the **medium term**, where the objective is to give energy use a different direction within, say, a 5-10 year period. This focuses interest on technology changes and the effects on production and use structures.
- In a **long time perspective**, when considering the likelihood of energy shortages in the longer term, policy measures can also aim to affect the main features of developments in the structure of society through changes in business or commerce, siting of the built environment or the structure of transport systems.

A comparison of policy measures

It is of some interest in this context to consider whether Swedish energy policy differs from energy policy in other countries in respect of the types of policy measures. The National Board for Industrial and Technical Development (NUTEK) has performed an investigation[4] in which it described the policy measures used in other IEA countries, as well as making a comparison between Sweden and other countries in respect of their choices of policy measures.

According to the NUTEK report, many different types of policy measures have been employed in the various countries. The commonest instruments were information and advisory services, building regulations, grants and loans and support for the introduction of new energy technology. Other policy measures included tax reductions, training and work carried out by energy utilities.

A comparison between Sweden and other countries drew the conclusion that Swedish work in the energy conservation sector is no longer dependent on grants. However, substantial elements of support programmes are still employed in other countries. At the same time, there has been a shift in responsibility for energy conservation from the State to regions, local authorities and energy utilities. The report states that it is more difficult to draw conclusions concerning support for the introduction of new technology, partly due to difficulties in obtaining comparable details.

In 1993, on behalf of the Government, NUTEK prepared a presentation of the results of earlier evaluations of Government energy policy measures that had been applied[5]. In the case, for example, of energy conservation support for homes, the conclusion is drawn that the energy conservation measures that were applied have produced an effect that was in line with the initial objectives, but that the savings achieved were only partly the result of the availability of public grants.

A similar conclusion is drawn in respect of building regulations, on the basis of the reviewed material. This indicates that the regulations and standards may have had a certain energy conservation effect, but that their direct effects were probably limited.

As far as other policy measures are concerned - e.g. local authority energy planning, advisory and inspection services and various types of information campaigns - it is difficult to draw any definite conclusions concerning the effects of the policy measures on the basis of the information in the available evaluation reports.

Objective of policy measures is at the centre

When evaluating the effects of policy measures, it is the fundamental objectives to be achieved that are central. It can be pointed out that even if, in certain respects, energy is given special treatment in the political process, the overall objective of energy policy can still be said to be aimed at bringing about good utilisation of resources. Energy policy should be based on what nature and the environment can withstand.

By its nature, research is a long-term process. Nevertheless, society's priorities are naturally concerned most closely with today's problems. As the world around us changes, so also are research and energy policy values correspondingly changed.

The latest five-year period has been characterised by many substantial changes, all of which have left their mark on the political objectives to greater or lesser extents. One of these important changes is the increased awareness of environmental aspects, which are progressively affecting an increasing number of areas. An effect of this has been that energy policy, which was originally concerned first and foremost with achieving security of supply of energy, has nowadays become effectively a part of environmental policy, or at least an important instrument of it.

Re-evaluation of economic policy

Another important change is that of the method of working of the world economy and of economic development. Since the latter half of the 1980s, there has been a substantial re-evaluation of economic policies throughout most of the world. The breakdown of the centrally planned economies has given a boost to the concepts of market economies. At the same time, a deep, persistent recession in the market economies has resulted in growing public borrowing and permanent budget deficits in many countries, contributing to a review of the role of the public sector. Following in the wake of this have been deregulation and changes in competition rules relating to businesses and activities that have previously been regarded as clearly the

providence of the State. In Sweden, the recently decided deregulation of the electricity market[6] is an example of the sea change that was started at the end of the 1980s. Energy policy as a whole has also been given a more market-orientated direction[7], from previously having had largely quantitative objectives in respect of the use of various forms of energy.

New building work in Sweden has more or less stopped, with general levels of investment - and thus the rate of renewal of capital investments - being considerably lower than they have been for much of the post-war years. The rates of expansion, too, of district heating and electricity in particular are at present low or non-existent, and it is not clear whether the natural gas distribution system will eventually continue to be expanded. All told, this means that repair and maintenance (both in the built environment and in energy supply systems) can be expected to become increasingly important.

The effects of internationalisation

A third important change is that of internationalisation. Several important international agreements have been reached in recent years, including the Rio Agreement and conclusion of the Uruguay Round within the framework of the GATT Agreement. Membership of the European Community has brought the Swedish economy closer to the European economy. As a result, Sweden has to take increasing account of the world around it when determining its political programmes and the measures needed to realise them. Special case requirements can be seen as obstacles to trade, conflicting with the GATT Agreement. New taxes and levies can conflict with EU rules in an integrated Europe and procurement rules can prevent us from employing the type of technology procurement programmes that have been common in Sweden.

However, there are also important conditions that, in some respects, have not changed. One of these is the Swedish Parliament's decision to phase out nuclear power generation. Although this is debated at regular intervals, Parliament's decision is still in force, concentrating interest on new production capacity, electricity conservation and electricity substitution. It seems clear that nuclear power in the Swedish energy system will continue to play an important part in connection with energy-related research, with the result

Price is an important guide measure, and much energy can be saved simply through 'correct' market pricing of electrical energy. Photographer: *Bruno Ehrs, Bildhuset*

that policy measures for electricity conservation and the introduction of alternative energy sources are still very relevant fields of research.

Price is the most important policy measure

As far as deciding on the choice of most appropriate policy measures for direction of energy policy is concerned, there is a growing tendency to use price as the most important policy measure. Sweden's 1991 Energy Policy Bill[8] stated that price was an important policy measure as a signal to the parties in the market, and that it ought to be possible to bring about part of the expected improvement in the efficiency of energy use without any other policy measures than the market price of electrical energy.

By 1994, the tone had sharpened in the Directive to the Energy Commission. This simply states that "Price is the most important policy measure as a signal to the parties in the market". The Directive discusses two types of system-related measures that have been tested primarily in the USA: 'Integrated resource management' and 'The balance principle'. The Directive did not want to prescribe the use of these principles, but felt that the desired balance could be achieved with the help of market prices in an operating market.

The environmental sector, too, has been strongly affected by the new winds of change. Previously, the means of achieving environmental policy objectives consisted mainly of granting of concession and surveillance under the Environmental Protection Act. The restructuring of taxation and fees that was started at the beginning of the 1990s has meant that economic policy measures have become increasingly important in reducing the environmental impact of the energy system.

Effects of policy measures

Today, we possess relatively good statistics concerning the effects of energy conservation measures that have been applied in various building categories and by different user categories. However, to what extent these measures can be said to represent direct or indirect effects of policy measures is a different, and considerably more difficult, question. As far as the effects of policy measures on energy use in the built environment are concerned, two aspects stand out as key ones:

- To what extent would the applied measures have been taken without policy measures?
- What are the effects on the overall system of the measures taken on the user side?

Many measures would in fact very probably have been undertaken even without policy measures, and so the question is what net effect has the 'additional policy measure pressure' had?

How are consumers affected?

If the mechanisms behind investment behaviour in the building sector seem difficult to interpret, this is even more the case in respect of how policy measures affect consumers' day-to-day behaviour.

- How do different decision-makers react to effects such as altered prices, taxes and fees?
- What is the importance of various types of information campaigns?

This, too, is an area in which the surrounding world and current mood ('crisis awareness') play an important part; probably, for example, information campaigns have greater effect in a situation when acute rationing (e.g. of oil) is imminent, rather than in a situation when energy supply appears to be cheap and assured.

Rules and standards

Both new building and refurbishment are still largely controlled by rules and standards, and it is difficult to imagine that this situation would be significantly changed in the short term, at least in respect of fundamental building performance requirements relating to life, health and safety. Naturally, this does not prevent us from wondering whether the standards should be investigated to see if they are effective, whether they reflect market requirements or whether there might be justification for restricting the number of standards and applying some other alternative.

Property-owners, for example, claim that the present energy standards result in excessive building costs and that, as a result of changes in the energy markets and elsewhere, they may be neither in the interests of society nor of the running costs of buildings. In addition, it has been claimed that local circumstances - including the availability of district heating and waste heat - should determine the energy characteristics and equipment of new building developments to a greater extent than they do today. Health aspects and international aspects have also sometimes been quoted as reasons for reviewing present energy standards. The National Board of Housing, Building and Planning constantly reviews this aspect[9].

New standards are also attracting attention, e.g. the above report also discusses standards for governing maximum electricity use in domestic appliances etc. As new dwellings have become increasingly well insulated and airtight, the characteristics of electric equipment etc. have an increasingly important effect on the total energy requirement of buildings[10]. Summarising, it can be said that a review of current administrative policy measures is on its way, but that this does not necessarily mean that the number of standards will be reduced.

Greater need for more knowledge

In general, it seems to be of interest to continue to compare the application of policy measures in Sweden and other countries, and to perform the comparison in more depth, not least through Sweden's membership of the European Union. A concrete example of this can be found in the work for which NUTEK and the National Board for Consumer Policies have been carrying out investigations, namely to introduce mandatory standards concerning domestic and electric appliances[11]. One of the points made in the Directive is that the framework of trading rules must be considered when carrying out the work.

As the energy markets become more and more similar to other goods and services markets, economic analyses become increasingly important. This includes aspects such as analyses of the effects on the public economy of different choices and application of policy measures, including the costs of applying different policy measures. A given area for research would seem to be to determine to what extent standards and regulations are required, and to what extent more market-conformal solutions could result in similar or better fulfilment of objectives.

The price sensitivity of different user groups is central to application of price-related policy measures such as taxation and fees. Many investigations have been carried out, for example, into the determining factors behind households' energy demands[12]. A recently published report[13] on the price of electricity states that households are not insensitive to the price, and that only a smaller part of individual households' demand for electricity can be explained by variables that relate directly to electricity use. Other factors, such as more general behaviour variables etc., therefore seem to be important to investigate. An interesting attempt in that direction is that presented by American research[14]. Certain researchers claim that individuals' lifestyles are just as important in determining overall energy use as are energy standards, well-insulated houses, efficiency of various appliances etc.[15] We need, in other words, more refined investigations of the factors that determine domestic energy use, as well as more genuine behavioural-related research linked to energy habits and individual energy decisions.

Pricing needs to be investigated

We also need to consider what prices consumers have to pay and to what extent these prices reflect true costs. More in-depth investigations of pricing in the energy markets appears important, not least in connection with deregulation of the electricity market. This also includes matters relating to tariffs for electricity, district heating and natural gas. It is sometimes claimed that some energy utilities lock subscribers into their systems through low initial connection fees that do not reflect the total system costs for providing the supply.

A most important area of investigation is that relating to the decision-making process at different levels. Key questions to which answers are needed include who is expected to be affected by the policy measures, who actually makes the decisions and on what basis the decisions are made. Closely related to this is the question of institutional frameworks in the form of legislation and regulations, industry agreements etc.

A particular aspect of this relates to the State's (assumed) control of local authorities. For several years, for example, the State has expressed a wish that local authority energy utilities should operate as energy service companies. To what extent these pious hopes have actually led to results is largely unknown. The same can be said about the 1977 legislation that requires local authorities to prepare energy plans[16].

System relationships - both in terms of the balance

between supply and use of energy as a whole, and those within the built environment - have previously been investigated, by such means as economic/mathematical models[17]. Although such analyses may easily lead thoughts towards centrally planned systems, it is clear that even in a more market-orientated system it is important to design policy measures and control systems that are intended to bring about systems with good overall efficiency.

The question of how links and interaction between different policy measures can be brought about is particularly important. A programme publication from the Swedish Council for Building Research (BFR) in 1987[18] claims, for example, that a common feature of the use of policy measures up to that time had been a unilateral concentration on consumer investments, without sufficient consideration of system relationships such as local availability of waste heat. Regardless of whether this situation has changed since that report was written, it is still the case that efficient policy measures must be designed in such a way as to allow for such factors as local variations in the price and availability of various forms of energy.

The effects of various financing arrangements

As a result of weakened State finances, in combination with a more market-orientated view of the method of working of the finance markets, the question of the effects of various forms of financing is a key one. Closely related to this are questions relating to the overall costs of various heating systems, such as solid fuel firing, solar heating, heat pump systems etc. Questions concerning such matters as methods of calculating capital costs under different conditions seem to be particularly relevant in this context.

As pointed out above, the great reduction in new building activity has placed increased emphasis on operation and maintenance. Bearing in mind such factors as local authorities' poor finances, questions relating to optimum maintenance and the factors that determine maintenance frequency and type must be seen as important[19].

Information as a policy measure has been used primarily during crisis situations. However, there are examples of information measures intended to increase consumer awareness of their levels of energy use. Helsingborg Energi AB, for example, has worked together with NUTEK and EllipsData to conduct trials intended to make energy bills better and easier to understand[20]. The report points out, for example, the importance of noting the effect of background variables. This is another example of the conclusion that investigation of the factors that determine domestic decisions is of considerable importance in deciding the effects of policy measures.

Research is also being conducted at present at Uppsala University into more general aspects of information programmes for energy conservation[21].

Market transformation

The concept of market transformation is an area into which a considerable amount of research is at present being conducted. It relates to measures aimed at stimulating a market for which the demand is only diffuse. Measures that are being considered include bringing forward the introduction of new technology, acceleration of market penetration and increasing market share[22]. Technology procurement is an example of a method belonging to this area. This has been employed by NUTEK and others, and can be applied not only to hardware, such as domestic appliances, lighting and windows, but also to software such as training, demonstration activities etc.

Investigation of the side-effects of policy measures, whether positive or negative, seems to be a somewhat neglected area. This includes matters such as health and environmental effects of various measures, as well as those that relate to competition and productivity in the markets affected by various types of policy measures. Support or standards that have been drafted in excessively specific terms, for example, can result in increased market concentration, thereby stifling market dynamics and technical development. In addition, certain policy measures (e.g. loans and grants) often have significant (although in many cases overlooked) effects on income distribution between different groups.

The problems of policy measures are largely general ones, and research into other areas of society having political links, such as the transport sector, has substantial relevance in many cases. However, there are certain special features of the built environment that need to be noted, not least the long life of buildings in comparison with other capital items and the fact that the rate of new building work is at present, and is expected to remain, low, with the result that more attention is focused on aspects such as operation and maintenance and on the rules and other policy measures that affect installation and modification of heat supply systems.

Naturally, this imposes special requirements on the policy measures aimed at the built environment sector.

This chapter is based on material by Bo Diczfalusy, MBA.

REFERENCES

1 Vedung, E.: *Statliga regleringsprocesser och sektoriella nätverk - Byggnadsstadgan och energinormerna 1972-1992* (Government control processes and sectorial networks - Building legislation and the energy standards, 1972-1992. Unpublished report.

2 See Vedung.

3 For a review of such evaluations, see for example *Utvärderingar av svensk energipolitik - en kommenterad biografi* (Evaluations of Swedish Energy Policy - a Commented Biography). NUTEK R.1993:34.

4 *Styrmedel för effektivare energianvändning och förnybara energikällor i IEA-länderna* (Policy measures for more effective use of energy and renewable energy sources in the IEA countries). NUTEK R.1993:33.

5 *Utvärdering av svensk energipolitik 1975-1993* (Evaluation of Swedish energy policy, 1975-1993). NUTEK R.1993:12.

6 Bill 1993/94:162, bet. NU 1993/94:NU22, rskr. 1993/94:358.

7 Directive 1994:67.

8 Bill 1990/91:88, Page 11.

9 See, for example, *Utredning av kravet på värmeåtervinning i byggnader* (Investigation of the Requirement for Heat Recovery in Buildings). National Board of Housing, Building and Planning, 1991.

10 See, for example, Swisher, J.: *Dynamics of Electric Energy Efficiency in Swedish Residential Buildings*, NUTEK, Stockholm, 1993.

11 Standards for maximum electricity use of domestic appliances etc. NUTEK R1992:24.

12 See, for example, Nilsson, C.: *De svenska hushållens energianvändning 1950-1987* (Swedish Domestic Electricity Use,

1950-1987). Memorandum 125, Department of Economics at the University of Gothenburg.

13 Andersson, B.: *Electricity Demand - a Study of the Swedish Residential Sector.* EFI Research Paper No. 6511, the Stockholm School of Economics.

14 Schipper, L. and Meyers, S. et al.: *Energy Efficiency and Human Activity: Recent Trends, Future Prospects.* Cambridge University Press, USA 1992.

15 Schipper, L., Johnson, F. et al.: *Energy Use in Sweden: An International Perspective.* Lawrence Berkeley Laboratory, Spring 1993.

16 The National Audit Office has, for example, claimed in an audit report that the Act Concerning Local Authority Energy Planning has had little or no effect and should therefore be repealed.

17 See, for example, *Energy Systems Technology. Annual Report 1993.* ISRN CTH-EST-R-94/1-SE.

18 *Energi i byggd miljö - 90-talets möjligheter* (Energy in the Built Environment - Potential for the 1990s). BFR G 16:1987.

19 Professor Göran Bergendahl et al. are conducting, for example, an investigation for Gothenburg Energy on optimum maintenance of electricity, gas and district heating distribution systems.

20 *Utvärdering av energispareffekter* (Evaluation of Energy Conservation Effects). NUTEK R.1994:38.

21 Vedung, E.: *Staten som predikant: Svenska energisparkampanjer* (The State as Preacher: Swedish Energy Conservation Campaigns). Stencil, Uppsala University 1994.

22 See, for example, Nilsson, H.: *Market Transformation by Technical Procurement and Demonstration.* NUTEK, Stockholm, 1992.

OTHER LITERATURE

Energi och miljö i Norden - användning av skatter och avgifter som miljöpolitiska styrmedel inom energisektorn (Energy and environment in the Nordic countries - taxes and levies as environmental policy guide measures in the energy sector) Nordic Council of Ministers NORD 1991:23.

Energirapport 1994 (Energy Report 1994). NUTEK B1994:9.

Hur kan elförbrukning i svenska hushåll och lokaler påverkas? En

dynamisk analys till år 2010 (How can we influence electricity use in Swedish households and commercial premises? A dynamic analysis to 2010). Swisher, J. N. and Christiansson, L. NUTEK R1994:54.

Utvärdering av svensk energipolitik. En kommenterad bibliografi (Evaluation of Swedish energy policy. A commented bibliography). Vedung, E. NUTEK R1993:34.

TIME TO THINK OF ENERGY AND ENVIRONMENTAL COSTS AT LOCAL COMMUNITY LEVEL

SUMMARY

Local communities are obliged to plan for energy conservation and take steps to ensure an adequate and reliable supply of energy. In 1991, the Swedish Parliament decided that these energy plans should be complemented with environmental impact appraisals. However, even though the local authority energy plans have been politically decided by the local council, they are not binding on authorities or individuals.

Major improvements have been effected in reducing the pollution and environmental impact of stationary energy installations, while the transport system is still being allowed to grow without consideration of the environmental impact of such growth. In future, much greater attention needs to be paid to the environmental effects of energy use in the transport system, both in terms of research and of planning. Opportunity can be taken, in connection with local authorities structure plans and detailed plans, to take account of energy considerations in the built environment with the aim of reducing energy demand, although in practice this is seldom done.

Membership of the European Union requires environmental impact appraisals to be produced for plants having a major effect on the environment. In accordance with agreements reached at the Rio de Janeiro Conference, all of Swedens local authorities have been instructed to develop local level Agenda 21 action programmes before the end of the century.

The most important needs at present, in terms of research and knowledge, are to investigate the effects of a more deregulated energy market on safety, the environment, willingness to invest and energy planning at local level. We also need to develop environmental impact appraisals of energy systems within the remit of improving the efficiency of energy use, and to develop methods for costing environmental measures in order to provide a basis for a selection of measures. Sweden also needs to perform system investigations, concentrating on the use of renewable energy sources, more efficient use of energy, the use of waste heat and industrial backpressure generation, CHP production and the use of refuse for energy production.

Since 1977, local authorities have been required to draw up energy plans for their areas, aimed at encouraging energy conservation and to take such steps as necessary to ensure a reliable and efficient supply of energy[1].

Since 1977, the Swedish Parliament has changed the text of the Act three times, transferring its ambitions in respect of local energy planning to local authorities. Originally, energy conservation was the primary objective. From July 1982, each local authority was to provide a plan showing how it intended to reduce the use of oil within its area. In 1984, planning was extended to be comprehensive, covering the entire administrative area of each local authority.

At the end of the 1970s, energy conservation plans for the existing built environment were drawn up by the majority of local authorities: energy advisers, paid for by the State, were employed at local authority level. During the 1980s, local authorities oil reduction plans resulted in substantial reductions in the use of oil, while comprehensive energy plans were drawn up for the majority of local authority areas during the second half of the 1980s[2].

The most recent change in the legislation concerning local authority energy planning occurred in June 1991, when the Swedish Parliament decided that the energy plans must be complemented by environmental impact appraisals[3].

The most important point in the Act is this: Each municipality shall have an uptodate plan for the supply, distribution and use of energy in the municipality. This plan shall include an environmental impact appraisal to permit an overall assessment of the effect that the activities described in the plan have on the environment, health and conservation of natural resources. The plan shall be approved by the municipality council.

Non-binding plans

Although the municipality energy plans are approved and issued at a political level by the municipality council, they are not binding on authorities or individuals. This became clear when the Act was first passed. It was then realised that a system of municipal energy plans which, after State scrutiny, would bind subsequent detail plans, concession decision etc., would involve significant drawbacks, e.g. by acting against the need for freedom of action of planning. The conclusion was therefore that this planning should be prescribed in law, but not have formal legal implications.

The requirement for municipal energy planning provides no guarantee of implementing State energy policy at local level. The municipalities and energy companies have very free hands in their planning for new energy systems, although they often follow the general guidelines set out by the State for restructuring of the energy system, e.g. the policy during the 1980s to reduce dependence on oil.

The question of assigning a special role in the energy sector to the regional county councils was taken up on a number of occasions, including during the 80s in connection with energy policy Bills concerning expansion of municipal energy planning. At that time, it was not felt suitable to construct a regional level within the energy field. One reason for this was that changing conditions relating to various energy forms in different regions made it difficult to find consistent solutions for application throughout the country.

The starting point for the expanded municipal energy planning and its implementation is that all responsibility shall lie with the municipalities. There is no continuous collection of statistics for the State authorities, and the county councils have no formal role in the energy sector. However, the position of the county councils in the hierarchy close to the municipal councils puts them in a special position for acting as a link between the municipalities and the central level of energy planning.

The regional environmental strategies developed by the county councils can have importance in determining their actions in the energy sector, even at local level and

in respect of concrete projects. Establishing a relationship between regional environmental objectives and local energy supply planning is one of the most important aspects needed in order to achieve improved links between energy and the environment.

Energy planning must be concrete and up to date

An evaluation of municipal energy planning that was carried out in 1991 shows that the requirement for comprehensive municipal energy planning has been regarded as far too ambitious and burdensome. The 1984 change in the law placed a considerable emphasis on the municipal plans covering all forms of energy, and on planning covering the entire area of the municipality. However, it has been difficult to digest all this at once, and several municipalities have refrained from planning.

Working with the municipality councils, the National Board for Industrial and Technical Development (NUTEK) has developed a new and simpler way of planning for the municipalities. The result of this work is described in the information publication 'Environmentally sensitive local energy planning' which was sent out to all local authorities in the country in 1991[4].

The objective is to make municipal energy planning simpler, more concrete and up to date. The requirement to draw up major, allembracing plans has been toned down: instead, planning can be concentrated on what is actually happening, or what the municipal council wants to happen, in the municipality. The publication has been written primarily for those in municipality staffs and energy companies who have to prepare the necessary data for a decision on restructuring the energy system.

A wider decisionmaking basis

The objective of environmental impact assessments is to create a wider basis on which decisions can be made. They help the energy planner to select appropriate energy systems, as analysis of the environmental impact can provide useful information, including how to achieve the least possible environmental impact per unit of energy produced[5].

Sweden is well to the fore in the use of district heating systems. During the 1970s, local authorities position in the energy sector was substantially strengthened, and many district heating systems were constructed. In many cases, it was the local authority

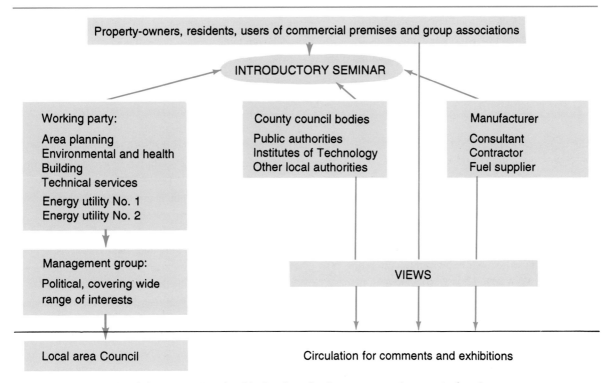

Figure 1. An example of the parties involved in local authority energy environment planning.

energy plant that was responsible for supplies of both heat and electricity. With the coming into force of the Municipal Energy Planning Act and changes in legislation concerning electricity, local authorities were also formally given increased responsibility.

In 1975, district heat production amounted to about 22TWh. Now, in 1995, production capacity is about 43TWh/year. Oil prices provided strong incentives to get away from the use of oil and to use solid fuels instead. Local authorities played an active part in the introduction of indigenous fuels such as wood chips, processed pellets and peat, and also involved themselves in development and demonstration of new energy technologies.

Energy policy uncertainty

Local authority investments around 1980 in solid fuel boilers for burning indigenous fuels were based on an expectation of continued high oil prices and were in line with the Governments intentions to reduce dependence on oil. However, the subsequent fall in the price of oil during the 1980s created problems for these investments. Sweden did not, as did certain other

countries, increase taxation on oil to a level that would maintain its price and make alternatives competitive. The resulting uncertainty relating to the country's energy policy, coupled with experience of the substantial investments in energy systems intended to use indigenous fuels, has made local authorities more wary of new longterm commitments. However, the relatively high prices of oil and coal today have favoured the use of indigenous fuels, on which there are no energy or environmental taxes.

Partly as a result of legislation concerning the design of combustion plant for solid fuels, Sweden has maintained a tradition of production from highly flexible firing systems that can quickly be modified to suit different fuels. This is a valuable strength both in terms of readiness for crisis situations and of environmental consideration.

A major problem in longterm energy planning has been that Government decisions on taxation, charges and public grants for the construction of energy systems have often been changed, with the result that the relationships between energy prices have changed. Major investments in energy systems intended to accommodate new taxation or charges structures have become unprofitable as a result of closelyfollowing decisions concerning new taxes or charges. Many energy utilities in Sweden, for example, converted plant to burn coal, whereupon new charges shortly after made it unprofitable to use coal.

A freer energy market affects local energy decisions

Deregulation of the electricity market has started and there is a tendency in all aspects of politics to encourage a greater element of freer market forces in the energy sector. In future, the energy utilities will probably employ shorter writedown times as they restructure themselves to deal with unrestricted competition and improved efficiency. This will apply both to those that solely distribute electricity (i.e. not having their own generation plant) and to energy utilities having both production and distribution either of electricity alone or also of other energy carriers. Increased competition can increase efficiency in the energy sector and shorten decisionmaking paths.

Unfortunately, this development could also result in a deterioration in the environment, reduced conservation of resources and greater vulnerability. Planning that attempts to arrive at proposals for good overall solution may be ignored. Private companies start by looking at the financial conditions needed to ensure a good return on investment. Private investments often require shorter payback times than public investments. There is a risk that, in future, there will be less interest in building robust energy systems such as combined heat and power plants.

Many local authority energy utilities which at present supply electricity and heat to public systems may find themselves in a competitive situation where they are forced to build whatever is the cheapest energy system at the time and which, although financially sound if regarded in total isolation, is not a good energy system in a larger perspective. Purely financial considerations can arrive at what are, taken in isolation, the most profitable refuse disposal systems, the most profitable electricity production systems, the most profitable electricity distribution systems and most profitable heat production and distribution systems. However, with several different independent parties in the same geographical area, each of whom decides its own cheapest solutions, a cheap and lowpollution overall

solution, such as construction of a refusefired CHP plant, may be ignored.

Major adverse environmental effects of traffic and transport

Traffic and transport use considerable quantities of energy and severely affect the environment. Since the 1970s, energy use in this sector has grown more rapidly than in any other sector. Traffic and transport are the major sources of atmospheric emissions of NOx.

Systems for stationary energy installations (electricity, heat, processes etc.) and systems for transport are essentially very different. This is also reflected in planning methods. There is justification for saying that it is essentially the stationary energy installations that have been restructured and which have taken steps to reduce pollution. For many years, the transport sector has been allowed to grow without any environmental restrictions, although the introduction of catalytic exhaust cleaning for private cars will make an important contribution to reduction of NOx emissions.

There are limits to what can be effected by tightening up environmental requirements relating to the production of electricity, heat and industrial output without simultaneously considering corresponding measures in the transport sector. Research and investigations are needed to develop methods of tackling the problem of transport rather than those of stationary energy installations.

Energy systems to match the built environment

The siting of energy production plant is often discussed in connection with local authority energy planning, e.g. the siting of refuse incineration plants or district heating systems and, in recent years, also smallscale CHP production. However, the situation could be reversed by discussing how to plan the built environment in order to reduce its energy requirements. This could cover passive measures such as orientation of buildings and appropriate siting, which have been shown capable of reducing heat requirements by 10 - 30%. It is at the structure planning and detailed planning stages of work by local authorities that measures such as these can be considered. However, this is unfortunately seldom done: tradition says that it is the energy system that should be made to match to the built environment. A more

Traffic and transport are the main sources of emissions of oxides of nitrogen to the atmosphere. Photographer: Thomas Wester, Bildhuset

unconditional planning process with several inputs (Figure 2) would be preferable.

Matters of physical planning have hitherto been regarded by the European Union as national concerns. There are no indications that existing planning legislation in the Nordic countries needs to be changed in response to EU membership. Denmark, for example, did not alter its planning legislation as a result of its membership.

EU membership will probably not affect specific energy planning as practised in the various countries. Denmark, for example, has retained its restrictive statecontrolled energy planning system, constructed to suit its own national needs and wishes. Nor will there be any effect on other local authority plans or arrangements that indirectly affect energy, e.g. traffic planning, planning for crisis preparedness, refuse disposal or reservation of areas for energy production plant and distribution facilities for energy production.

The European Commission has taken initiatives in a few points that affect planning. Environmental impact appraisals are required in connection with more important siting decisions for plants having substantial

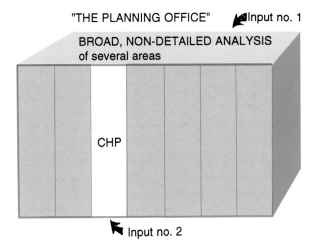

Figure 2.The local authority energy planning process, with two postulated inputs. Input 1 is used when the objective is to perform a strategic overview of the energy and environment situation, while Input 2 is used to arrive at a more detailed decisionmaking basis for a given matter or a particular project. In the diagram, this has been illustrated by CHP.

environmental impact. These appraisals assist local authorities and regions. The Commission is also considering adopting maximum permissible emission limits or air pollution quantifiers although again it is the local or regional authorities that have the main responsibility for environmental decisions[6].

Greater importance of environmental costs

Through their publication 'New Approaches to the Economy, Energy and Environment at Local Level'[7], NUTEK and the Environmental Protection Agency emphasise the increasingly important environmental link between the local and global energy perspective. The economy and the environment are linked by starting from commercial budgeting procedures, which are then complemented by environmentallyrelated costs.

The publication is aimed at those involved in local environmentallyaccountable energy systems, such as local authorities, energy utilities, property owners and energy advisors. It has also been written so that it can be used for training. It provides examples of concrete applications, describing in each case the environmental and energy benefits that can be achieved. Projects of the type described can be included in a municipal energy plan: examples provide the ideas for active environmental impact appraisals.

Full speed ahead on Agenda 21

At the UN Environmental Conference in Rio de Janeiro in 1992, one of the most important conclusions was that environmental protection work needs to be developed at the local level. In accordance with the Conference decision, all of Sweden´s local authorities have been urged to develop local Agenda 21 action programmes by the end of the century. Work on preparing these documents has already started extensively, and it is expected that by 1996 all local authorities in the country will be fully engaged in preparation of their local Agenda 21 programmes.

Actions and input of the type described in 'New Approaches to the Economy, Energy and Environment at Local Level' can be included in the energy section of Agenda 21 at local level. Local authorities can also decide to regard a municipal energy plan as part of their Agenda 21 work. During 1994, the Environmental

Protection Commission has published its 'Local Agenda 21 - A Guide document'[8].

Poor links between energy and the environment

A problem in the environmental context is that environmental work and energy work are performed largely isolated from each other. The environmental authorities operate mainly as inspection and approval authorities by setting limits for permissible pollution. They monitor environmental impact and set rules for the permissible environmental load of energy production processes. It could be said that their work is concentrated primarily on reducing existing or planned pollution. There is no indepth dialogue between the environmental authorities on the one hand and energy utilities and authorities on the other a dialogue that would, for example, discuss new lowpollution energy systems from which pollution can be partly or wholly eliminated.

Flue gas cleaning, effluent treatment, the use of betterquality fuels or improved combustion processes in a given energy system can be characterised as damagelimitation applications. However, other types of measures could have greater positive effects on the environment: examples include improvements in the efficiency of energy use, resulting in elimination of the need to use certain quantities of energy at all, selection of efficient energy systems that can result in more efficient energy production and thus eliminate pollution to some extent (e.g. CHP instead of separate production of heat and electricity), or selection of energy systems that use lowpollution fuels, thus partly or wholly eliminating a certain amount of pollution. Unfortunately, improvements of these kinds are not included in the remit of the environmental authorities.

Investments in energyefficient production systems evaluate their profitability in terms of investment requirements against energy savings. Reduced costs for the purchase of energy must pay for the investment: the environmental benefits resulting from reduced energy use are essentially not considered, apart from the fact that energy prices include environmental levies, although these are too low in relation to the damage caused by energy production processes. However, when investments are made in pollutionreducing processes such as flue gas cleaning, there is hardly any consideration of profitability, as this is seen as an environmental measure.

There are no new economic approaches that can simultaneously consider both energy economics and environmental economics. The environmental levies that have now been introduced are a first step on the way towards including consideration of environmental profits in an investment.

Central questions in future energy planning

Many local authorities and energy utilities are faced with continued change of their energy systems. Examples of central questions that need to be considered are:

- Should we concentrate on renewable energy sources at local level?
- How can we improve the efficiency of energy use?
- Can refuse become an important energy resource?
- Can smallscale CHP plants, for the provision of local electricity supply, be built?
- How can local/regional air pollution be reduced?
- Should new residential areas have electric heating or district heating?
- What part will district heating play in future energy systems?
- Which environmental measures are most profitable?
- Can industrial waste heat be used?
- How can air pollution from transport systems be reduced?
- How can we counter the effects of the deregulated energy market on the environmental impact of energy systems?

Future research and knowledge requirements

The most important research and knowledge require-ments can be summarised by the following points.

Consequences of a deregulated energy market:

- What will be the effects of a more deregulated market on safety, environment, willingness to invest etc.?
- What will be the effects of a more deregulated market on energy planning at local level, including municipal energy planning?

Natural gas versus other energy carriers:

- Improved information for evaluating markets, guide measures and interfaces with other energy sources and systems for extension of the natural gas distribution system.
- Collection and presentation of experience of natural gas systems from other countries, including effect analyses.

Energy systems and recycling:

- Development of environmentally accountable energy strategies, including overall resource consideration.
- System studies, with the emphasis on the use of renewable energy sources, more efficient production of energy, more efficient use of energy, the use of waste heat and industrial backpressure generation, combined heat and power production and the use of refuse for energy production.
- Development of energy cycle models for use on PCs.

Environmental impact appraisals:

- Development of methods for environmental impact appraisal of energy systems, including the effects of improvements in the efficiency of energy use.

Costeffectiveness of environmental measures:

- Development of methods for economic evaluation of environmental measures as a basis for choice of measures.

This chapter is based on material by Nils Moe, MSc. Eng., NUTEK, Stockholm.

REFERENCES

1 The Act Concerning Local Authority Energy Planning, 1977:439, 1991:738.

2 *Kommunernas energiplanering* (Local Authorities Energy Planning). National Energy Administration, 1986:12.

3 The Act Concerning Local Authority Energy Planning, 1991:738.

4 *Miljöanpassad lokal energiplanering,* MILEN (Environmentally sensitive local energy planning). NUTEK and the Swedish Environmental Protection Agency, 1991.

5 *Metodik för miljökonsekvensbeskrivning* (A Method Description of Producing an Environmental Impact Appraisal). The Swedish District Heating Association, 1993.

6 *Energipolitik i plan och verklighet* (Energy Policy Planning and Reality). Niels Moe, Nordic Council of Ministers, 1994.

7 *Nya grepp om ekonomi, energi och miljö* (New Approaches to the Economy, Energy and Environment). NUTEK and the Swedish Environmental Protection Agency, 1994.

8 *Lokal Agenda 21- en vägledning* (Local Agenda 21 - A Guide). The Environmental Protection Commission, 1994.

OTHER LITERATURE

Ekonomi - miljö - metod - i lokal energiplanering (Economy environment methods in local energy planning). Moe, N. and Mensson, T. NORDPLAN Report 1992:1.

Energi och miljö. Möjligheter och hinder vid samordningen av den kommunala miljö- och energipolitiken (Energy and the environment. Opportunities and obstacles for coordination of local authority environmental and energy policy). Fransson, B. Swedish Association of Local Authorities, 1991.

Kommuner och småföretag i samspel för ett framtida energisamhälle. Slutrapport från ett försök med energirådgivning (Local authorities and small companies working together for a future energy society. Final report from energy advisory trials). Eden, M. Chalmers University of Technology, Department of Industrial Planning. IACTH 1991:1.

THE IMPORTANCE OF CORRECT SITING

SUMMARY

The three main components that affect energy demand are climate, the energy supply system and transport. The problem is to find the correct strategy for siting building developments that provide the most favourable combination of these components.

A prerequisite for finding the most favourable structure in terms of climate, energy, transport, environment and cost is the use of computerised planning programmes integrated with geographical information systems. A particular problem is that arising from the changes in climate that are caused when a built environment replaces a greenfield site. In

this context, it is important to investigate the role of green areas. Making the various planning programmes dynamic in respect of the spread of urban climate should therefore be the next stage of research.

Insufficient investigations have been carried out into how traffic reduction measures and other restrictions affect the siting of built environments and thus the extent of transport required. The most important research requirements at present are:

■ to attempt to develop models explaining the relationships between physical variables in the urban

environment, overall transport requirements and the choice of transport system,

■ to develop basic theories governing the relationship between energy turnover, energy qualities, transport and the structure of society,

■ to develop coherent models for assuring the energy aspects in urban development,

■ to quantify permissible emission quantities area by area on large-scale municipality maps in order to provide a basis for structure planning, and

■ to analyse the effects of different types of systems of energy supply.

There are several links between the physical organisation of the physical aspects of a community and its energy requirements. One component of these relationships is influenced by the fact that climate varies from one part of a community or region to another. This affects the demand for energy for thermal comfort, depending on where the development is sited. As a result, differences in energy requirements for an average built environment can vary between some areas by 0-50 %.

Conditions can also vary from one part of a larger area to another in respect of energy supply. In one part, for example, the use of district heating based on woodchips might be the most favourable energy source. In another, there might be an accessible aquifer at an elevated temperature, constituting an attractive energy source. Elsewhere again electricity, biogas or oil might be the preferred alternatives. If the development is sited with potential energy sources for thermal comfort in mind, this provides a further main component in the relationship between energy and physical structure. In this context, physical structure refers to the built environment of homes, businesses, service installations and infrastructure.

The third component in the relationship is transport. This includes not only transport of persons and materials, but also that of media such as water and waste water. In terms of transport, a municipality or region is never homogeneous. Some areas may be suitable for rail transport, while others require buses for public transport. Other areas again might have to resort to the car as the main alternative. Some structures can also include pedestrian, cycle and moped routes. Home working using electronic links further complicates the picture. Supplies of water and drainage can also alter the picture in different parts of a community.

The problem is therefore to find a strategy for siting urban elements that provides the most favourable combination of the three main components that affect its energy turnover, i.e. climate, energy system and transport.

Using energy for thermal comfort and powering machines involves energy conversion, which releases residual or waste products such as sulphur dioxide, oxides of nitrogen, carbon dioxide, particulates and heavy metals. The above problem is therefore further complicated by the need to find a structure that results in the least environmental pollution associated with the energy conversion process. The fact that these processes also have an economic aspect of the greatest importance is also a very relevant component. Taken together, the overall problem picture is so complex that only powerful computerised planning programmes, working in combination with geographical information systems, are likely to be able to provide the necessary help for public planning.

The size of the problem is indicated by the UN assessment of the world's future urban mass. The present world population of 5500 million is expected to stabilise at about 8000-14 000 million within a century. Most of these persons are assumed to be living in urban areas. If they are all to be provided with reasonable living conditions in terms of homes, work and services, we are facing the most extensive urban development programme in history. As the energy needed to run urban systems accounts for between 50 % and 75 % of total energy demand, we can obtain a rough idea of the scale of the problem in connection with development of a sustainable long-term urban structure.

A review of research development is given in the dissertation 'Physical planning with respect to energy'[1]. The literature is now so extensive that it would require regular work by a university department to keep up with it[2].

The present review of the Planning and Building Act has given notice that local authority structure planning will be given increased importance as a means of bringing all factors together in public planning. Structure plans must be updated and adopted by municipality councils every second year. As an increasing proportion of the material on which the work is based exists in computerised form, updating will require computer assistance.

A prerequisite for finding the most favourable structure in terms of climate, energy, transport, environment and cost is the use of computerised planning programmes integrated with geographical information systems. Basic systems exist today at research levels in universities, but further technical development and demonstration activities are needed before this basic knowledge can be used at the municipality planning level.

Methods and programs are available today within the climate sector that can be employed for community planning purposes. They require special knowledge to make proper use of them, and it is therefore important that they should be compatible with current geographical information systems. A particular problem is that arising from the changes in climate that are caused when a built environment replaces a greenfield site. In this context, it is important to investigate the role of green areas. Making the various planning programmes dynamic in respect of the spread of urban climate should therefore be the next stage of research.

Greater emphasis on structure planning

The Planning and Building Act (PBL)[3] states: *"Built environments, and installations that require a supply of energy for operation, shall be sited in such a way that is compatible with conditions governing energy supply and energy conservation."*

New developments in the transport sector

The transport sector has a long tradition of research. As a result, models therefore exist for most given patterns of built environment and traffic networks, with the help of which it is possible to forecast traffic flows in various parts of the network with good accuracy. Recently, several of these models have been complemented with energy and emission calculation modules which make it possible to calculate which combinations of types of transport would have the greatest positive effect on the environment. There are also extensive empirical investigations of travel habits, choice of type of transport etc.

The problem with these earlier investigations is that not much work has been done on investigating the structuring effect of new transport networks, different types of traffic reduction measures and other restrictions on vehicular traffic on the siting of developments and thus on the extent of transport work required. Current research demonstrates that the construction of new, larger roads around urban areas, intended to reduce through traffic, often results in peripheral establishment e.g. of out-of-town shopping centres, which substantially increase the amount of transport and thus energy demand and emissions. Another example is that the introduction of artificial slaloms or sleeping policemen to force vehicles to slow down often results in subsequent acceleration with resulting increase in energy demand and pollution.

Energy plans should be updated every second year

If energy supply considerations are to be included as an element in structural planning, it is necessary for the local authority energy plans to be all-embracing. However, the starting point for these energy plans is the structure plan for future development of the area. As this is supposed to be updated every second year, the energy plan should also be updated on the same basis. Development work in this area therefore seems to be important: again, with an eye to integration with the relevant geographical information systems.

The problem of current research within the transport sector can be expressed as a search for explanatory models rather than one for forecasting models. What are the physical variables in urban development that play a part in determining total transport requirements and the choice of methods of transport? Can these variables be affected by local planning decisions? What part does the traffic environment play in determining usage patterns of vehicle-owners? It is important to locate problems at levels that are accessible for decision.

Quantify permissible emission quantities

From the community planner's perspective, it is important to quantify permissible emissions on an area-by-area basis within those parts of the environment sector that are linked to energy use. Comprehensive community maps, with permissible limits marked on them, are needed as a basis for describing the built environment and its energy and transport systems. This is a necessity if the structure plan is to be able to include consideration of emission quantities. Here, too, certain fundamental investigations have been made, although the results and knowledge have not been developed to a stage where they are applicable at community level. It might be possible to formulate such an integrated environmental index, although economic models can be used instead, to the extent that they consider emissions as criteria for siting larger urban development areas.

In Sweden, physical planning is formalised mainly at the local authority level. However, environmental problems are no respecters of local authorities and have a totally different, cross-border nature. In addition, the cost parameters in current planning models are static. However, the trend towards EU integration is likely to result in greater emphasis on the regional and international aspects, as indicated in Europe 2000 (published by the European Union) and elsewhere. Concentration on the regional level of this problem area is therefore important.

The European Union has developed its 'Towards sustainability' programme. This gives priority to five sectors, one of which is '... improved land-use/economic development planning at local, regional, national and transnational levels.' The 1992 Rio Conference also discussed these problems. The conclusion is that the urbanisation process and its links to energy supply must be considered in any and every strategy for ecologically sustainable development.

Cooperation shortcomings

This broad subject area has been investigated widely over the last 20 years. We can therefore wonder why there are still significant shortcomings in cooperation between the two planning disciplines of energy and land-use planning. A reasonable answer might be that it is due to the fact that most of the extensive investigations that have been performed have been field

Climate differs from one part of a region to another, with the result that the demand for energy for thermal comfort also differs, depending on where buildings are located. Photographer: Kjell Johansson, Bildhuset

studies. There are only a few investigations at the method plane level, while fundamental theories of the relationship between energy turnover, energy qualities, transport and the structure of society are essentially lacking.

Today, at the stage where planning results are to be converted into design, construction and occupation, there are few overall models for considering the energy aspects of urban development. The implementation consequences at the detail level of various energy supply systems are also largely untouched research areas.

This chapter is based on material by Dr. Johan O. Lamm, Department of Urban Design and Planning, School of Architecture, Chalmers University of Technology.

REFERENCES

1 Lamm, J., *Fysisk planering med hänsyn till energi* (Physical planning with reference to energy). Dissertation, Department of Heat and Power Engineering, Lund University of Technology, 1990.

2 One way would be to update this knowledge review at regular intervals, e.g. every second year, which would require about two months' work based on searches of the Diss.Ab.Internat and Compendex (Urbline) international databases concerned.

3 The Planning and Building Act, SFS 1987:246, Page 2.

OTHER LITERATURE

Bebyggelse och infrastruktur. Planering av bostäder, energi och service med hänsyn till transporter och miljö (The built environment and its infrastructure. Planning of housing, energy and service with relation to transport and environment). Lamm, J. O. and Görling, A. Chalmers University of Technology, Department of Urban Planning, 1994.

Environment, energy and housing. A location model. Lamm, J. O. and Görling, A. BFR D1:1992.

Projektmetod för modern energiteknik i små utbyggnadsetapper (A project method for modern energy technology in small building expansion developments). Planning and implementation. Modin, B. O. BFR R19:1990.

THE BUILT ENVIRONMENT AFFECTS TRANSPORT REQUIREMENTS AND VICE VERSA

SUMMARY

The relationship between the built environment and transport can be described as a two-way relationship, in which the structure of the built environment affects transport requirements and the structure of the traffic systems, while the traffic systems in their turn affect the structure of the built environment.

Passenger transport requirements in Sweden can be roughly divided into 25 % to and from work, 25 % working/business journeys and 50 % recreational, pleasure and social journeys. The energy used by the transport sector is substantial, with 57 % of it being used by private cars. Most of this energy is supplied from fossil fuels. Future trends towards homeworking - IT commuting - will allow individuals to choose their place of work and residence more independently of distance, which will result in reduced energy demand by the transport sector.

Important areas of research are to:

- illuminate the relationship between the built environment and transport over time and at different spatial levels,

- investigate how a built environment might be structured in order to reduce travel requirements,

- investigate how goods distribution can be coordinated,

- develop methods for consequence analyses in which various aspects can be processed,

- develop user-friendly planning and decision-making models,

- develop methods for cooperation across sector and administrative boundaries.

The relationship between the built environment and transport is multi-faceted. Greatly simplified, it can be described as a two-way relationship:

- *The structure of the built environment affects transport requirements and the structure of traffic systems.*
- *Traffic systems affect the structure of the built environment.*

Conditions are similar for both goods transport and passenger transport. The following pages are concerned mainly with the relationship between the built environment and passenger transport.

Passenger transport requirements in Sweden can be roughly divided into 25 % to and from work, 25 % working/business journeys and 50 % recreational, pleasure and social journeys. The journeys that can most clearly be identified and coordinated are commuting journeys to and from work. This enables public transport solutions to be provided for them to a certain extent[1].

Homeworking - what will it mean?

The 1980s saw the start of an increasing tendency towards distance working or homeworking. In 1986/87, over 800 000 persons in Sweden worked at least two hours a week at home. About three-quarters of them usually worked for up to ten hours per week at home[2]. The development tendencies showed that about 180 000 of those who already performed some work at home could increase their time spent doing so, while about 400 000 of those who did not work from home found that they could start doing so, with an estimated working time of 2-10 hours per week.

Later investigations[3] show that commuting to and from work can be reduced by up to a quarter as a result of greater use of IT commuting. These investigations indicate several effects on travel to and from work:

- the proportion of public transport traffic will fall,

Future ways of working - known as telecommuting - will allow homes and workplaces to be chosen without regard to distance, and may result in reduced energy use for transport. Photographer: Kjell Johansson, Bildhuset

- travel times, both by car and public transport, will increase,
- total traffic mileage will decrease, while traffic mileage by private car will increase.

IT commuting allows home and workplace to be chosen with less consideration of distance. Reduced total traffic mileage results in reduced energy use by the transport sector.

Other investigations, on the other hand, indicate that this IT commuting is unlikely to become extensive in future. In its work on Vision 2009, the National Board of Housing, Building and Planning[4] has looked at the effects of such an increase in IT commuting on building development patterns and communications, and feels that it is likely to affect mainly only trips to and from work, which make up only about 25 % of total travel. If 10 % of all persons in work are full-time commuters, while 10 % exhibit some reduction in their amount of work commuting, the total physical travel mileage of this group will be reduced only marginally.

The structure of the built environment has a very high inertia, and will not be changed to any greater extent by changes in working habits resulting from a shift towards the IT community. However, smaller communities in peripheral sites may develop as a result of this new technology. Through their unique environmental values and good living conditions, small towns and rural areas may become attractive for telecommuters. An important area of research is to investigate how new networks of communities, both large and small, can cooperate with each other in respect of work, homes and public resources such as public transport and energy supply.

Shift away from hypermarkets?

A large number of hypermarkets has been established in recent years, with the result that total transport work for shopping has increased by 3-13 times in comparison with the era before these hypermarkets.

There is, however, a growing tendency by consumers to question the value of spending time and money, and creating pollution, on travelling to these hypermarkets and shopping malls. In the UK, large grocery chains are starting to re-establish themselves in town centres[5]. There are also many other factors that indicate increasing interest in local services in town centres. IT allows more people to work at home, with the result that there will be more persons around. Increasing environmental and energy costs may result in reduced use of the car.

Growing awareness of the importance of recycling, and new requirements in respect of the contents and quality of what we buy, are other factors that change the conditions for local and small-scale solutions. The provision of services can change, so that a tobacconist, for example, might start providing services such as faxes or e-mail. The need to coordinate deliveries of goods, both in the existing built environment and in a spread and diversified service structure, can become an important area of research. Another important R&D

area is that relating to how a built environment should be structured in order to reduce travel requirements.

Much energy used by the transport sector

Energy use within the transport sector is substantial. 57 % of transport energy is used by private cars: less than 1.1 % of passenger transport is based on electricity as the energy source.

Table 1. Energy use within the transport sector in 1989[6].

Type of transport		Energy use (Twh/year)
Private car, petrol		44.3
	diesel	1.9
Bus,	petrol	0.05
	diesel	2.6
Passenger train, tram, underground railway, electric		0.87
Passenger train, diesel		0.14
Aircraft		3.6
Ferries, inland		0.1
Truck,	<3.5 tonne, petrol	5.1
	>3.5 tonne, petrol	0.15
	<3.5 tonne, diesel	1.0
	>3.5 tonne, diesel	12.5
Goods train, electric		1.5
	diesel	0.20
Cargo vessel		6.7
Total		**80.71**

As can be seen from Table 1, almost all energy used in transport is supplied by fossil fuel. Energy use in the transport sector therefore accounts for a large proportion of Swedish local, regional and global environmental problems. If the efficiency of energy use was improved, and if best present-known technology was used for exhaust emission cleaning, emissions of oxides of sulphur and NO_x could be reduced by 70-90 % by 2015 relative to 1989[7].

Coordination and cooperation

The Swedish Environmental Protection Agency's work on the Low-pollution Transport System project[8] shows that work will be required by a large number of different interests at local, regional and national level in order to achieve good solutions. One important aspect of the work is to affect the spatial organisation - ground use. This needs to be done in cooperation by many parties - the National Board of Housing, Building and Planning, the County Councils, local authorities, the National Roads Administration etc. The Environmental Protection Agency is proposing to collect and present research results etc. that illustrate the importance of the structure of society in achieving various environmental objectives. Examples will illustrate the parts played by urban planning and structure to minimise transport requirements and energy supply, while facilitating means

of disposing of waste and processing effluent. Other points to be investigated include: What can improved coordination between area planning and infrastructure planning produce in the way of local, regional and national results? How can improved coordination between sector planning and physical planning be achieved, and how can these instruments be best made to work with common resource conservation and environmental objectives?

One area in which investigation of cooperation between parties has started is coordination of road planning and other area planning[9].

Engström and Landahl[10] have presented another example of how cooperation can be realised and energy aspects linked to physical planning. They indicate where in the physical planning process it can be appropriate to deal with various energy problems (Table 2). Their

Table 2. The three stages of planning.

Stage 1	Stage 2	Stage 3
CLIMATE CONSIDERATIONS Outline climate analysis	Planning and built environment investigations	Guidelines for shaping the development
HEAT SUPPLY Investigation of possible ways	Alternative strategies	Guidelines for energy supply

Table 3. Physical planning and energy planning.

Physical planning	Energy aspects affect:
Municipality level	Siting of the development area. Built environment structure. Land use and development factor.
Area level	Boundaries of the area. Siting of built environments. Traffic and open areas. Planning standards. Access and use of open areas. Local climate and ground conditions. Vegetation and landscape. Development in stages.
Detail planning	Layout plan, building height and separation. Vegetation.

method considers both the siting and the design of built developments and the space requirements of the energy supply installations.

Their proposal for a working method was based on a number of factors, including research that had been carried out up to the middle of the 1980s and which had provided the following knowledge concerning the effect of energy aspects on various parts of the content of physical planning[11] (Table 3).

No general conclusions on layout planning

Despite this, there are no conclusions of general validity concerning the design of the built environment structure in order to reduce the amount of transport work required and to facilitate good energy conservation. This is an area of which few theoretical models have been constructed, although some work has been done, e.g. in connection with the Major Urban Areas Traffic Investigation[12] and the Gothenburg Environment Project[13]. The importance of municipal and regional planning is emphasised. One important research area is investigation of the relationship between the built environment and transport over time, at different spatial levels, and the link to other infrastructure systems such as the energy system, all of which affect or are affected by the built environment and the traffic system. There may be a need to develop models, such as IMREL (Integrated Model of Residential and Employment Location), developed at the Royal Institute of Technology and used today for analysis of built environment and transport systems. Coupled with geographical information systems (GIS), the two could create powerful analysis tools.

Local authority planning responsibility has hitherto involved working with structure plans for the local authority area, more in-depth urban area plans and small detail plans. There has been some coordination and cooperation across local authority boundaries, mainly in respect of corridors for railways and gas pipelines.

The role of the county council is to review the plans on the basis of a number of criteria relating to health and safety, inter-area aspects and national interests and, if necessary, to return the plan to the local authority for further work. The role of the county councils in pressing for coordination and cooperation needs to be developed.

The Planning and Building Act states that the Regional Planning Institute is a form of cooperation body for matters involving a number of local authorities. There are similar linking organisations within the water area, such as the water management associations and the water protection associations. As far as public transport is concerned, there is a coordinator, the Public Transportation Authority, at regional/county level. However, methods for cross-boundary cooperation in the building and transport sectors need to be developed. User-friendly planning and decision-making models are also required.

Physical planning is important

The structure of the built environment offers several potential opportunities for traffic and energy supply. Energy plants and distribution systems, for example, together with traffic systems, provide a structural skeleton basis in physical planning. A certain density of building is needed for collective services such as public transport, district heating etc., and physical planning play an important part in the development of this structure. Although there may be only small additions each year, it is important that they are made in the right place and with a long-term plan policy behind them in order to grow into viable solutions.

Following the thoughts and intentions behind Agenda 21, and moving forward into the recycling community, many flows of materials should be in recycling loops, of varying geographic extent. Many of these loops return at local level, which results in a greater need of land for cultivation and return of nutrients, This, in turn, can result in greater differences between built-up areas and perhaps also between individual units, which in turn can result in less favourable conditions for public transport and a greater demand for transport energy.

It is important to conduct research into how these various claims on closeness and distance manifest themselves and can be reconciled, and into the effects that they have on the structure of the built environment and transport systems.

Four main elements in planning

Planning work involves four main elements:
1. Determination and description of the planning conditions.

2. Description of the objectives that the plans are to achieve.
3. Proposals for ways in which these objectives might be achieved.
4. Analysis of the effects of the proposed measures.

There are often no consequence analyses that investigate advantages and drawbacks of various alternatives, and thus provide a basis for selection between them. During the last year, local authorities have developed their own routines for performing their environmental impact assessments in various types of plans and projects. Draft proposals for manuals on performing environmental impact assessments are, or have been, out for comment from the Swedish National Rail Administration, the National Board of Housing, Building and Planning and the Swedish National Road Administration.

In work on the new 'Advice and instructions for planning urban traffic networks'[14 15 16], views have been put forward concerning the need to produce traffic impact assessments. Social impact assessments have also been discussed in other contexts. Development of methods for consequence analyses, in which various aspects can be handled, is an important area of research.

Hagson & Reneland[17] have investigated how local authorities have complied with the legislation calling for local authority energy planning. Their work shows that there is a need for strategic local authority energy planning. They present a method of planning, centered around strategy and policy formulations, and from which subsequent action programmes are developed and the roles of the politicians clarified. In addition, R&D is needed into the parts played by politicians and local authority employees, as well as of decision-making processes.

This chapter is based on material by Glenn Lundborg, Department of Environmental Planning and Design, Luleå Institute of Technology.

REFERENCES

1 Bjuhr, H.; Engström, C.-J.; (1993): *Framtidsstaden* (The City of the Future). BFR T12:1993.

2 Engström, Mats-G.; Eriksson, Gunnar; Johansson, Rikard; (1990): *Att flexa i tid och rum. Distansarbetets struktur och tendenser* (Flexible Working in Time and Space. Structure and Tendencies in Homeworking). BFR T8:1990.

3 Scheele, Siv & Säfvestad, Kjell (1995): *Bebyggelsemönster och resande i ett informationssamhälle* (Built Environment Patterns and Travel in an Information Society). Article in Plan No. 1, 1995, pp 12-16.

4 Husberger, Lars (1995): *Telematik, kommunikationer och bebyggelsemönster* (Telematics, Communications and Built Environment Patterns). Article in Plan, No. 1, 1995, pp 35-39.

5 Hedberg, Lotta & Baurne, Ellinor (1994): *Dagligvaruhandel - tur och retur. En uppsats i bebyggelsens mångfald* (Comeback for the Grocery Trade. An essay on the many forms of the built environment). Editor: Louise Nyström. National Board of Housing, Building and Planning, Karlskrona.

6 Johansson, B., 1993: *Kan transporterna klara miljömålen?* (Can Transport Meet its Environmental Objectives?) Swedish Transport Research Board Report 1993:11.

7 See Johansson (1993).

8 Environmental Protection Agency (1994): *Miljöanpassning av transportsystemet - Förslag till program för att åstadkomma ett miljöanpassat transportsystem* (A low-pollution transport system - Proposals for a programme to bring about a low-pollution transport system). Report No. 4341.

9 National Board of Housing, Building and Planning, National Roads Administration (1994): *Samverkan för bra vägar. Erfarenheter och rekommendationer med utgångspunkt från tio exempel* (Cooperation for Good Roads. Experience and recommendations on the basis of ten examples). National Board of Housing, Building and Planning Report 1994:5. Karlskrona.

10 Engström, C.-J., Landahl, Gustaf (1987): *Energifrågor du vinner på att ställa tidigt i planeringen* (Energy questions that should be put at an early stage of planning). BFR T15:1987.

11 Engström, C.-J. (1985): *Forskning om kommunal energiplanering - Vad har vi lärt oss? Uppsats i kommunal energiplanering* (Research into public energy planning - what have we learnt? An essay on public energy planning). Five essays. National Energy Administration, 1988:R5. Allmänna Förlaget, Stockholm.

12 *Storstadstrafik 4. Ytterligare bakgrundsmaterial* (Major Urban Areas Traffic 4. Further background material). Allmänna Förlaget. SOU 1989:79.

13 Hagson, Anders & Reneland, Mats (1989): *Kommunala energistrategier - analys och värdering av planprocess och resultat* (Local authority energy strategies - Analysis and evaluation of the planning process and results). SACTH 1989:1 (R). Urban Planning - Architecture - Chalmers University of Technology, Gothenburg.

14 *Allmänna råd för planering av trafiknät samordnat med bebyggelse i städer och tätorter* (General guidelines for planning urban traffic networks) TRÅD-92. Consultative document. National Board of Housing, Building and Planning.

15 *Goda exempel, nr. 8. Bebyggelse på landet i den kommunala översiktsplaneringen* (Good examples: No. 8. Buildings in the rural areas in local authority structure planning). National Board of Housing, Building and Planning, 1994, Karlskrona.

16 *Goda exempel, nr. 9. Tätortsbebyggelse i den kommunala översiktsplaneringen* (Good examples: No. 9. Urban area built environments in local authority structure planning). National Board of Housing, Building and Planning, 1994, Karlskrona.

17 See Hagson & Reneland (1989).

OTHER LITERATURE

Bärkraftig infrastruktur. Nordisk essäsamling om stadens framtida försörjnings- och kommunikationssystem (Sustainable infrastructure. A collection of Nordic essays on future urban supply and communication systems). BFR T14:1994.

DEREGULATION CHANGES THE ELECTRICITY MARKET

SUMMARY

With the new Electricity Act, which deregulates the electricity market, the Swedish electricity market will become an integrated national market, open to competition between both producers and suppliers. The State's control over pricing will be restricted to monitoring transmission and distribution tariffs.

The demand for electricity can be expected to increase relatively rapidly. Competition between the power utilities may result in them keeping down production in order to increase their profits through higher prices, which could result in price rises of 35-40 %. If, on the other hand, they go in for aggressive price competition, prices could fall by 15-20 %. The most likely scenario is lower electricity prices and greater competitiveness of electricity in the energy markets that are of importance for the built environment.

As far as energy and environmental policy are concerned, the State was previously able to use Vattenfall as an instrument of its energy and environmental policy. With Vattenfall's transition to an independent commercial organisation, the State now disposes only over general and competitively neutral policy measures such as ensuring that emission charges are the same for all, or standards applying to all sectors of the industry. The State's policy measures must have long-term credibility and be designed so that the various energy and environmental policy measures are commercially viable.

There will be less need for technical/-economic knowledge to be supplied to companies, but a greater need for across-the-board consumer information on the companies and their production methods.

The supply of heat, lighting and ventilation services to the built environment provides a market for a large quantity of energy in the form of electricity, fuels and district heating. In comparison with the requirements of industry and the transport system, low-temperature heat constitutes a substantial proportion of the energy used in the built environment. This means that the built environment is a significant real or potential customer for 'new' fuels such as different types of bio fuels or solar energy. It also constitutes an important potential customer for locally produced electricity from wind power plants.

Energy use in the built environment is affected relatively significantly by various types of energy and environmental policy measures[1]. The most important of these are the Local Authority Energy Planning Act and taxation rules relating to various types of fuels. Other factors of significance include the Building Regulations, the regional allocation funds for subsidising electricity distribution costs and the group billing of electricity and heating charges in many apartment buildings. Finally, ownership conditions and taxation of national and local authority energy utilities affects electricity and district heating prices.

Against this background, it is clear that changes in the internal markets for various fuels and forms of energy carriers will be of importance for energy supply to the built environment. However, the close interchangeability of electricity and other forms of energy carriers in the built environment means that developments in the electricity market will have a greater effect on this sector than is indicated by the simple numerical proportion of its energy use accounted for by electricity. Higher or lower electricity prices can have an immediate effect on the competitive situation of other forms of energy carriers and thus on the conditions relating to energy supply. A concrete example of this was given at the end of the 1980s, when falling real prices of electricity were regarded by many as a key obstacle in preventing the successful introduction of new forms of energy carriers and the implementation of energy conservation measures.

Sweden's new Electricity Act has been interpreted at times by the electricity market as deregulation and at other times as re-regulation. Regardless of the terminology, the Act makes sweeping changes to the rules of play in the Swedish electricity market. The Swedish power and electricity distribution utilities will probably be subjected to considerable 'conversion' pressure during the next few years, which can be expected to affect prices and terms for electrical energy and thus also the use of energy in the built environment as a whole.

Local and regional market areas were the norm

The 'old' electricity market was regulated by the 1902 Electricity Act. An important element of this was the system of network and area concessions. A holder of one of these concessions was obliged to meet all 'normal' requests for supply of electrical energy within a given area. However, the concession also brought with it sole right to all supplies of electricity within the regional (a network concession) or within the local distribution area (an area concession). The Swedish electricity market therefore in reality broke down into a number of regional and local markets, where neither larger electricity users such as industries or distribution companies or small users such as individual households could freely choose their electricity supplier. At the same time, the power producers developed close links between themselves, covering not only day-to-day operation of the existing system but also planning of new capacity construction.

Apart from this 'structural' regulation that was provided by the old Electricity Act, formal regulation of the Swedish electricity market has been limited. However, through the State's ownership and direct control of Vattenfall, and through the latter's dominant position within the power industry, the State has effectively had very extensive influence over developments on the electricity market. Electricity prices at the high-voltage level have been largely determined by Vattenfall's tariff principles and the requirement for return on State capital invested in the company. However, at the low-voltage distribution level, it is the principle of full cost coverage by local authority utilities that, together with distribution utility costs and the price of high-voltage electricity that they have purchased, has controlled prices.

The new situation - unrestricted pricing

With the new Electricity Act, the situation on the electricity market will be completely different in several respects. The high-voltage transmission network will be strictly separated from production and sale of electricity, with all parties in the electricity market being given access to the high-voltage transmission system, regional transmission systems and local networks on the same terms. With this open network situation, the Swedish electricity market will become a single integrated national market, opening the way to competition both between high-voltage producers and low-voltage distributors. The State's control over pricing will be limited to monitoring and possible regulation of network tariffs. There will, in other words, be essentially free pricing of electricity. At the same time, the new Anti-trust Act will mean that old forms of cooperation or cartels within the power industry will be declared illegal or at least regarded with strong disfavour.

Short-term and long-term effects[2]

The intention of the 'open network' rules is to encourage greater competition and thus lower electricity prices. However, when discussing the effects of electricity market reform on electricity prices, it is important to distinguish between short-term and long-term effects.

In the short term, when national production capacity and import arrangements are essentially given, there are two main conditions that determine electricity price development. The first of these is demand development at given prices, i.e. the shift in demand that reflects mainly production and income developments within the country, while the second is the intensity of price competition on the electricity market.

Increased demand

After some years of declining production, the Swedish economy is now in a strong export-led upturn - not least in the energy-intensive industrial sectors. This indicates that the demand for electricity can be expected to increase relatively rapidly over the next few years. This will mean that the surplus capacity that has existed in the Swedish power sector since the middle of the 1980s will be mopped up, increasing the power utilities' marginal production costs. The fact that the summer of 1994 was very dry will only reinforce this trend.

As prices on a competitive market are dictated by marginal costs, any increase in marginal cost will have an immediate impact on market prices. However, the high-voltage tariffs on the 'old' electricity market were also based on the power utilities' marginal costs. This became apparent not least during the latter half of the 1980s, when falling marginal costs immediately resulted in lower electricity prices for all customer categories. As a result, the new Electricity Act is hardly likely to have any effect on the rapidity or magnitude of any electricity price increases powered by marginal costs, and which seem likely to occur during the second half of the 1990s.

Increased price competition is, however, a direct result of the new Electricity Act. When attempting to assess how increased competition in the electricity market affects price developments, it is necessary to consider the high concentration on the high-voltage market seller side. At present there is a large number of power utilities, although the market is dominated by only a few of them. Vattenfall's market share, for example, is about 50 %, with Sydkraft's share following at about 25 %. Judged by accepted criteria for quantification of seller concentration on a market (Herfindahl's index), these figures indicate a very high degree of concentration. The high-voltage market, in other words, is one with a high degree of imperfect competition. In such a market, prices are determined largely by the companies' choice of competition strategy.

Bertrand or Cournot competition?

There are a number of more or less plausible models of imperfect competition, known as oligopoly models, with different implications for pricing. Starting from various oligopoly models, we can simulate pricing on the Swedish market after a change to open networks and free pricing[3]. We then find that if the power utilities concentrate primarily on aggressive pricing competition in order to win market shares, electricity price levels are likely to fall by 15-20 %. Literature on the subject refers to this type of fall as Bertrand competition. If, however, the power utilities attempt to hold production down (but without cooperating with each other) with the aim of increasing their profits through higher prices, the price level could rise by 35-40 %. In its pure form, this is known in the literature as Cournot competition.

When the Norwegian electricity market was deregulated in 1991, intensive price competition broke out and high-voltage prices fell dramatically, with newly-establish electricity trading companies - i.e., companies with no production capacity of their own - playing an important part. It was also significant that there was a good trading market for electricity (a 'power exchange'). However, the fall in price seems primarily to have been due to a growing surplus capacity on the electricity market: a number of rainy summers had resulted in large quantities of power being available, while the recession and a mild winter reduced demand.

When the recession bottomed out, and a dry summer was followed by a cold winter, prices rose. During the coldest part of the winter, Norwegian electricity prices reached very high levels. It is also clear that the power utilities have learnt to work under these new conditions, and that the initial Bertrand competition was gradually replaced by something approaching Cournot competition.

Increased price competition

Bearing in mind what has previously been said above concerning the basic supply and demand conditions on the Swedish electricity market during the next few years, it is unlikely that there will be any significant surplus capacity on the new deregulated market, which means that any fall in price motivated by a need to find a market for a larger quantity of power is therefore unlikely. Instead, it more likely that prices would rise as a result of a Cournot-type response on the part of the largest utilities. However, this can occur only if these utilities are prepared to reduce their production - and thereby perhaps lose some of their market shares - in order to achieve a higher price level. However, there is much that indicates that the larger Swedish power utilities are far more interested in winning market shares rather than losing them. This supports the belief that increased price competition can be expected, thus exerting a downward pressure on high-voltage prices.

Substantial potential for rationalisation

However, the parameter that is important for energy use in the built environment is electricity price at the low-voltage level. It is commonly felt that there is significant potential for rationalisation in electricity distribution, and the incentive to take up this potential can be reinforced both by the price monitoring that will be carried out by a special unit within the National Board for Industrial and Technical Development (NUTEK) and by mergers and take-overs of distribution utilities. However, in the short term it is unlikely that there will be any dramatic changes in distribution costs.

In the longer term, increased competition will affect electricity prices primarily by a greater incentive to cost efficiency and technical developments, i.e. effectively increased productivity. Experience of the last couple of decades' deregulation of air travel, telecommunications etc. and other sectors in the USA indicate that increased competition results in lower consumer prices, and that this is due primarily to significant productivity gains, i.e. to lower costs rather than lower utility profits. The pressure on companies' profit margins resulting from increased competition has thus been compensated by cost-reducing rationalisation measures.

It is in the nature of things that it is not so easy to say exactly which cost-reducing rationalisations will result from increased competition. However, we can draw some conclusions from the Norwegian experience, where reduced investment resulted in higher capital productivity, and from the UK where substantial reductions in employee numbers resulted in higher labour productivity. These factors indicate that, in the long term, increased competition is likely to force down the producers' and distributors' costs, thus contributing to lower electricity prices than would otherwise have been the case.

Probably lower electricity prices

Taken together, all this means that the increased competition on the electricity market will probably result in relatively lower prices of electricity, and thus greater competitiveness for electricity on the energy markets that are of importance for the built environment.

However, it must be remembered that electricity prices are increasingly sensitive to various types of energy and environmental policy requirements and policy measures[4]. The question then becomes a matter of considering if, and if so by how much, the new Electricity Act and the utilities' response to it can be expected to affect the conditions and directions of energy and environmental policy. In this context, the energy and environmental policy guidance under consideration is that intended to facilitate the introduction of 'new' forms of energy carriers and application of energy conservation measures, as well as to restrict emissions of sulphur, NOx and carbon dioxide from the power industry.

The new Electricity Act and energy and environment policy

In a market in which companies are protected from both foreign and home competition, and where there is a large or dominant element of public ownership, the State appears to have a considerable potential for using regulation and other policy measures to affect the companies' choice of technology, production policies etc. Much of the extra cost that arises can be passed on to the consumers, and public ownership constitutes a protection against the returns required by the capital market. This means that, in other words, the costs of environmental policy are less visible in a sector in which competition and exposure to the capital market are limited. However, the costs as such are no lower. In actual fact, a sector exposed to competition may be more used to reacting cost-effectively to rapid changes in the conditions around it, and thus be better able to do so.

Following this reasoning, we can say that the State was able partly to use Vattenfall as an instrument of energy and environmental policy on the 'old' electricity market, and that the costs for doing so were only partly apparent. A concrete example of this is Uppdrag 2000, a major Vattenfall project involving ambitious concentration on both energy conservation and utilisation of new forms of energy carriers, and for which the commercial return was apparently low, both as indicated by the initial budget and by the final evaluation. It is also likely that the lack of international competition, coupled with the power utilities' monopoly-like positions in their regional markets, assists the introduction of relatively extensive environmental requirements in respect of electricity production plant, including CHP plants.

With less restricted and more extensive competition in the electricity market, it is hardly possible to employ individual companies as instruments of energy or environmental policy. In future, therefore, energy and environmental policy control of the power industry will need to be based on general and competition-neutral policy measures. Specifically, this involves the use of policy measures such as uniform emission charges, industry-wide standards or general support for research and development. A common feature of all of them is that they make the costs for the energy and environmental policy requirements visible in the utilities' accounts or in the State's budget.

Investment vs. returns

The privatisation of Vattenfall and the partial divestment of Stockholm Energi have contributed to creating a situation in which an increasing proportion of power industry investment in future will have to meet the rates of return requirements of the strongly international capital market. This development will probably continue and will reduce the utilities' interest in energy or environmental policy measures having a low or uncertain commercial value. Companies exposed to competition both in the capital market and in their sales markets will not be able to undertake any unpaid energy or environmental policy work. This will mean that, as far as environmental policy is concerned, the power industry will become very similar to other heavy industrial sectors, particularly if the international trade in electricity increases and the power industry becomes a sector involved in significant international competition.

The conclusion of this discussion is that deregulation of the Swedish electricity market will have clear consequences for the choice of energy and environmental policy measures. Opportunities for an informal, direct 'command-and-control' regulation will be reduced. However, this does not necessarily mean that energy and environmental policy objectives must be revised. What is needed is a change to general, indirect (incentive-affecting) policy measures such as uniform emission charges, transferable emission quotas etc. What is important is that the policy measures should be formulated so that the necessary concrete actions that contribute to fulfilment of the agreed energy and environmental policy objectives (and which should preferably also be viable in terms of the public budget) should be profitable when judged against the rate of returns required from the energy utilities.

An example to indicate that high environmental

policy ambitions can be achieved, even in an industry exposed to competition and which is itself responsible for the environmental pollution that is to be reduced or eliminated, is shown by the progress of eliminating chlorine emissions by the pulp and paper industry. Despite the fact that this is a sector exposed to strong competition, and which is financed largely by the regular capital market, it has been possible greatly to reduce the amount of chlorine emission per tonne of pulp in a quite short time. In this particular case, the environmental policy measure has been in the form of technical development for part of the time, complemented by strong incentives to maintain or exceed these requirements through adverse consumer response to the use of chlorine-bleached paper.

Expensive targets reduce guide measures' plausibility

However, there are also clear limitations in respect of the ability to realise ambitious energy and environmental policy objectives using general, indirectly acting guide measures. If the objectives are regarded by many parties as too expensive in relation to the achievable energy or environmental objectives, they will lose their credibility. Energy utilities and consumers, expecting energy and environmental policies to be reviewed in the near future, together with their associated emission charges, grant rules etc., will not modify their behaviour in line with these guide measures.

Swedish nuclear power policy is a clear example of this problem. The views of the parties involved on the costs for complete early phase-out of nuclear power production have resulted in them doubting that the declared policy will be fulfilled. As a result, they have not felt justified in taking the appropriate steps that would be needed to facilitate the phase-out. Comprehensive political declarations and agreements have not changed this situation. In itself, this credibility problem has little to do with the new Electricity Act. However, to the extent that the Act can result in a choice of policy measures that make the costs of energy and environmental policy objectives all the more visible, associated credibility problems can become more pressing.

The conclusion of this reasoning is that deregulation (or re-regulation) of the Swedish electricity market is not in itself an obstacle to retaining and realising ambitious energy and environmental objectives. Nevertheless, the new institutional framework and increased competition will gradually convert the power industry into just another sector of industry, with only limited possibilities to pass on energy or environmental policy costs to customers and owners. This circumstance will have serious effects on energy and environmental policy: policy measures will need to be long-term in their application and be drafted so that energy or environmental policy measures are commercially viable.

Profitability before environment

The changes in the electricity market that have been discussed above can also be expressed as saying that the electricity market and a number of closely associated fuel markets will become more commercialised. Competition and the need to be profitable will become more obvious features of the energy markets. The question then is how such a development, in the light of given forms of

Deregulation of the electricity market will place greater emphasis on competition and profitability requirements. Profitability will probably come before environmental considerations.
Photographer: Anna Gerdén, Bildhuset

taxation, subsidies and other energy and environmental policy measures, can be expected to affect the utilities' and households' interests in energy conservation and new forms of energy. Will the power utilities concentrate on increasing electricity's market share at the cost of new forms of energy carriers and energy conservation? Or will profitable conservation measures be realised to a greater extent than has previously been the case?

It is unfortunately so that the only way to obtain a definitive answer to these questions is to wait and see. At present, we can only indulge in informed speculation. We will then be able quickly to identify factors that favour energy conservation and the introduction of new forms of energy carriers, as well as factors that oppose such developments. As far as opposition is concerned, it is clear that no effort will be put into concentrating on energy conservation or new forms of energy carriers that do not exhibit a sufficiently high and long-lasting potential profitability. Any loyalty towards most of the declared energy and environmental policy objectives that the energy utilities have hitherto demonstrated will probably be eroded in the struggle for market shares and profitability.

A commercialised electricity market can stimulate new approaches

It seems to be a widespread belief that commercialisation of the energy markets could retard energy conservation and the introduction of new forms of energy carriers. But what factors might encourage a development in the opposite direction? First and foremost is the simple fact that companies that wish to survive on the capital market's terms must, in the long term, have an unsentimental attitude towards their history and their products. In the long term, a power utility cannot capture market shares with a price policy that bears no relation to its costs situation and therefore results in losses or insufficient return on capital. Nor can it continue to employ traditional technology and traditional fuels if new technology and new fuels could give higher profits. The fact that a utility may always have produced and supplied electricity must not indefinitely prevent a gradual product development towards becoming involved in customers' energy conservation work. In other words, commercialisation of the Swedish energy market could encourage a new

approach and openness towards new alternatives and strategies for energy utilities.

Pressure from an environmentally sophisticated public

Another, closely related, effect of commercialisation of the energy market is that the various utilities will achieve clearer profiles. When consumers can choose their electricity supplier, there will be more incentive to become aware of the various suppliers' strengths and weaknesses. Such a trend will reinforce the companies' incentive to get to know their customers and to develop products that suit their requirements or preferences. In the energy sector, such involvement might very well take the form of active assistance for effective utilisation of the energy supplied, or of particular care to limit the environmental impact of the energy production process. In other words, 'green' consumers or employees create (or necessitate) commercial reasons for energy and environmental conservation measures on the part of the energy utilities.

The phenomenon of 'green consumers' has attracted a considerable amount of attention in recent years, including, for example, the above-mentioned reaction towards chlorine emissions by the pulp and paper industry. In a number of often quoted cases, it is clear that concern for a company's or its products' image, in combination with an increasingly environmentally aware public, has forced individual companies to go further in their environmental protection work than was required by current statutory requirements or regulations. However, there does not appear to be any quantitative determination of this phenomenon or of any well-founded assessment of its relevance to energy-producing companies.

Greater need for consumer information

Finally, we can reflect over to what extent the emergence of the new electricity market affects the need for knowledge of those responsible for energy and environmental policy, and how and to whom this knowledge should be supplied. Energy and environmental policy control of the old electricity market was based to a very large extent on technical/financial knowledge, i.e. knowledge of the technical aspects of energy production and conservation processes and of their costs. This knowledge circulated among energy utilities, sector and interest organisations and, to some extent, individual households. It had the characteristic of public availability: in principle, all relevant technical/financial information was made available to all parties on the energy market. The underlying objective of this R&D and information work was to facilitate companies' and households' adjustments towards the objectives set out in energy and environmental policy. In all main respects, the need for knowledge of this type should be the same in a more commercialised energy market. However, as far as the public character of the information and the target groups for information activities are concerned, the situation is likely to be different in at least two respects. Companies working in a competitive market can strengthen their position by developing new technologies and new products, but this means that they will try to prevent their competitors from benefitting from such knowledge and R&D work. This will also mean that the public knowledge developed and obtained by authorities and other public bodies, will be of less value to the utilities, as it is primarily exclusive knowledge that can strengthen their market positions.

The second difference is that deregulation will result in consumers becoming the most important target group for the receipt of information: the lower the costs of obtaining and processing information by consumers, the more effectively a market works. This means, for example, that consumer information on the utilities' 'green' profiles can mean much in terms of pressure on the companies to choose low-pollution technologies and fuels. In relative terms, this means that there will be less need for the utilities to acquire technical/financial knowledge, but a greater need for across-the-board consumer information on the companies and their production methods.

This chapter is based on material by Professor Lars Bergman, Stockholm School of Economics.

REFERENCES

1 As energy policy is often dictated by various environmental considerations, we could equally well talk about 'environmental policy'. However, in the rest of this section, I shall use the term 'energy and environmental policy' to refer to the entire system of objectives and actions/measures intended to avoid or limit various types of environmental problems by means of changes in energy production or energy use.

2 This section, up to the heading 'The new Electricity Act and energy and environmental policy' is based partly on Bergman, L. et al , *'Den nya elmarknaden'* ('The new electricity market'), Stockholm, SNS Förlag, 1993. See it for a more detailed discussion of pricing in markets in which there are few competitors and on the effect of increased competition on productivity.

3 *Den nya elmarknaden* (The new electricity market) *op. cit.* gives a more detailed description of the factors behind these calculations.

4 Here, we disregard the effects of the planned phase-out of nuclear power production. The reason for this is that it is not possible comprehensively to consider how the new Electricity Act will affect conditions for implementing the nuclear power production phase-out in this short chapter.

OTHER LITERATURE

Elmarknad i förändring. Från monopol till konkurrens (The changing electricity market: from monopoly to competition). NUTEK B1991:6.

Fri elmarknad. Produktion, hushållning och EG (The free electricity market: Production, conservation and the EC). Söderström, M., Karlsson, B. G. and Björk, C. Linköping Institute of Technology, IKP-R-728, 1993.

Konkurrenslagstiftningen och elmarknaden (Legislation for competition and the electricity market). Danielsson, I-M., Diczfalusy, B., Eriksson, C., Henricson, L. and Szatek, K. Monopolies Commission, 1993.

LET MARKET FORCES ASSIST THE INTRODUCTION OF NEW TECHNOLOGY

SUMMARY

Many common ways of thinking, attitudes and arguments stand in the way of large-scale restructuring of Sweden's energy system.

The improvement in efficiency that can be effected depends on the potential of each measure and the acceptance that it can win. Potential and acceptance are affected in turn by several other factors, such as the time factor associated with the rate at which society's infrastructural capital is renewed, improvements in technology, increases in use or production volume that result in cost reductions, the parts played by parties on the market, the structure of goods distribution systems and the characteristics of the products themselves.

Market force potentials to get products out into the markets must be utilised and enhanced, while many customers need improved instruments for becoming aware of, understanding and trusting new technology. This can be done by such means as demonstrations, training and marking.

More knowledge is also needed of practical marketing of the concept of efficiency improvement. This applies, too, to knowledge of how energy-efficient technology can improve industrial productivity and of how such improvement programmes can make better use of market mechanisms for synergic effects. Finally, it is important to improve general knowledge of system relationships that can result in improved conservation at lower cost.

Ever since the oil crises of the 1970s, Swedish energy policy has comprised a mix of major programmes on the one hand and various forms of support intended to motivate consumers in general on the other hand. The hope has been that, by concentrating on the large users of energy and making the best use of research and analysis, new production technology would evolve that, 'in one bound', would solve almost the entire problem. It was further hoped that improved information would turn one and all into energy-conscious kilowatthour-savers and, with minor improvements, arrive at modest market improvements. Information and activities have been strongly sectorised, so that applied information could be directed to each particular target group. The following pages describe some of the commonest ways of thinking, attitudes and arguments that stand in the way of change.

Ingrained habits are a strongly contributory reason for energy efficiency in companies often being low. A worn-out part is replaced by another of the same type. Everyone does what they normally do, and can rely on the equipment working. This is an understandable attitude, as the most important objective of those responsible for production is that it should be kept going without interruptions. Why take any risks? However, the result is that particularly ancillary systems in companies, such as motors, lighting, ventilation, climate control plant etc., are oversized and operated without any thought of energy efficiency. Such items may be many times larger and run more often or for longer periods, than are really needed for the purpose.

For many years, too, we have also employed a "What's in it for us?" approach before doing anything. Instead of asking whether some particular action is worthwhile, we ask instead whether there is any financial support for carrying it out.

Large companies are usually more hidebound than small companies, despite their greater overall competence. Small companies can make decisions more quickly: large companies have procedures to be gone through, although they be more persistent once they have reached a decision. This means that it may be preferable to introduce new technology to the market through groups of small companies, as this also results in more rapid introduction to the consultant and installation contractor sectors.

'Biggest first'

A common starting point when deciding what to deal with is 'Biggest first'. This approach is based on applying optimum measures or achieving maximum effect. According to this, it is industrial processes that should first be tackled, thus quickly solving major problems. However, it is generally the case that decisions that need to be taken in order to improve the efficiency of major sectors of industry are concerned with matters completely different from energy efficiency improvement. Energy tends to be treated as considerably less important than future markets, the availability of raw materials, cooperation with other companies, competition etc. Decisions in matters such as these take a long time to be made, and are made at a high level within companies.

Major improvements in the energy context certainly exist, but they can be realised only in connection with some other ongoing natural investment process in a company. They are never realised solely for their own benefit, but only if the resulting improvement in the efficiency of energy use can be combined with other significant benefits in the form of environment, production etc.

It may instead be the case that minor potentials for efficiency improvements, which can quickly be realised and of which the effects can be seen in everyday applications, can result in a better spread and awareness of energy and environmental factors. However, important everyday applications mean the most.

'It costs more to use energy more efficiently'

Quality is assumed to be more expensive, and energy-efficient products often have a higher quality, although this is not always reflected in the price. Many low-energy domestic appliances are cheaper to buy and cheaper to run, or are at any rate cheaper when both buying and running costs are added up. The reason for some items being more expensive may be due to something entirely other than low energy demand: technical design, visual design, service organisation, even the brand, etc.

A closely related problem is that most persons, whether ordinary consumers or professional purchasers, do not make their choices on the basis of total life cycle cost. Purchase price and running costs are not added up: instead, it is the lowest purchase price that decides. The subsequent higher running costs will either be borne by someone else, or simply postponed as tomorrow's problem.

'Improving energy efficiency becomes more expensive the further it is pursued'

"Obviously we intend to improve our efficiency of energy use," say some, "but only as long as it pays." There are several examples of pursuing energy efficiency improvements so that they pass the break-even point in the cost curve. If this is to be achieved the entire system in which the efficiency improvement is made must be affected. A good example is given by the use of high-performance windows (with U-values lower than 1.0) which means that radiators can be reduced in size, moved or - in extreme cases - dispensed with altogether. The resulting savings in installation costs exceed the higher costs of the windows. The same effect can be observed between ventilation/climate control/electrical systems on one hand and office equipment on the other.

An American experiment by Art Rosenfeld and Amory Lovins shows that radical system changes can be employed on an extensive scale. Similar experience has been gained in respect of greater utilisation of daylight in office premises, which has also resulted in parallel increases in working productivity.

'If energy prices rise, we shall save more'

The above claim is correct, but does not tell the whole story. Many improvements in energy efficiency have been made, despite the fact that they are not financially viable. This is the result of inadequate controls within the companies and of insufficient decision-making capacity. Many companies have delegation rules that mean that improvements are made only if the pay-off time is shorter than 2-3 years: everything else is rejected. In addition, priority is given to investments that increase production rather than those that reduce costs. To this must be added the factor that the results of efficiency improvements are regarded as uncertain, as there is no experience of similar measures.

There is, in other words, a systematic difference that results in lack of investment in improving energy efficiency. As investments in new production capacity are more carefully evaluated, using more correct criteria, considerable resources will always be invested in new energy production. If, instead, the same sums were to be invested in improving energy efficiency, better use would be made of dwindling resources.

The traditional response to these problems has been to improve information. Information has been too careful and too general. It has been issued in the form of glossy brochures, describing general principles, rather than as reports relating to real cases. It has also been aimed at triggering guilty consciences in respect of waste instead of pride concerning good deeds.

It is not primarily everyday habits of energy use that we aim to affect, but purchasing behaviour, i.e. the product that we choose when we buy. Maintenance routines need to be improved. Information naturally needs to be matched to this, and to have more of the character of marketing for the improved products and applications. Information needs to be available where and when the purchases are to be made, which may be made only at intervals of decades.

'We need more energy, not less'

More efficient use of energy is the cheapest, largest and most underestimated conservation resource for Sweden and Swedish industry as they face the future. There are many reasons for this underestimation, and some of them are well documented. However, most users feel that the energy that they waste is insignificant, or that its cost is modest. Nevertheless, in many common domestic, office, commercial and industrial applications, energy use can be halved without loss of amenity or benefit. In fact, efficiency improvements generally result in higher productivity, improved working conditions, more light, more comfortable indoor climate and more easily-run building services systems. A number of examples are described below.

Improved office equipment can reduce problems of surplus heat and the risks of magnetic fields. Computers, VDUs, printers, faxes and copiers are all available that shut themselves down when not used.
Photographer: Anne Mette Welling, Mira

■ Better lighting of workplaces in offices, industry, hospitals and schools can reduce discomfort and absence due to sickness as well as increasing productivity. Such lighting can be provided by new high-frequency lamps, improved light sources, better control of lighting to make maximum use of daylight and occupation and with improved luminaires. Energy savings are in the range 30-80 %, and profitability lies in both reduced energy use and increased productivity.

■ Better ventilation can reduce problems of allergies and increase comfort and performance. This can be effected through more accurate sizing of air ducts, correct choice of types of fan impellers, types of motors and drives and by closer control of air flow rates. These changes can be introduced during building refurbishments, which are carried out in most buildings at regular intervals. Energy savings are often of the order of 50 %, and profitability is realised by choosing the right opportunity for the right measure.

■ Improved office equipment can reduce problems of excessive heat and the risk of electromagnetic fields in office premises. Computers, VDUs, printers, faxes and copiers that turn themselves off when not in use are all available. Energy efficiency of such machines is usually between 40 % and 80 % better than those of their energy-hungry equivalents. Savings come in the form of lower energy bills, reduced costs for cabling and cooling installations and higher productivity.

The combination of efficiency improvement and improved productivity or better comfort is typical of successful schemes.

How much can we gain by improving efficiency?

The best investigation that has been performed in Sweden was Vattenfall's Uppdrag 2000. This was an extensive investigation, carried out using consistent methodology. It included experimental work, performed at a range of sites. The results indicated that there was a financially viable potential for savings amounting to about 17 % by the end of the century. Factors that could further increase the potential for savings included the

possibility of systematic replacement of equipment/appliances by better equipment/appliances whenever replacements were made.

However, a potential for savings or improvement indicates only that such savings or improvement could be made. If the potential is to be realised, it must also be accepted by its potential users:

$$\textit{Improvement in efficiency}$$
$$=$$
$$\textit{Potential } \textbf{x} \textit{ Acceptance}$$

We cannot, in other words, hope that the entire potential will be realised: this would require an acceptance of 100 %. However, despite the assessments in Uppdrag 2000 and the matter of acceptance, it can definitely be claimed that the total potentials for conservation exceed 17 %. From the results of the Uppdrag 2000 report, the following observations can be made.

■ *The time factor.* Uppdrag 2000 based its figures on the turn of the century, while the need to restructure the energy system looks further ahead, to 2010. However, the decisive time factor is that resulting from the turnover of 'capital' in society, in the form of buildings, machinery, equipment, building services systems etc. Several important parts of this have lives, or times between refurbishment, that exceed ten years: windows, for example, tend to be replaced about every 30 years.

■ *The importance of technology.* Uppdrag 2000 prepared its results on the basis of the best known technology. However, technology procurement involves attempting to accelerate the rate of introduction of new technology, or improving the technology itself. In the domestic white goods sector, for example, the average performance of equipment available on the market is 75 % less than that of the best available products. At the same time, it has been found possible significantly to improve the performance of the best products.

■ *The volume factor.* By increasing the market volumes for the best and improved technologies, costs can be radically reduced. This is the foundation stone of the Technology Procurement Programme, aimed at increasing volumes to attract manufacturers to improve their products at reasonable (lower) prices. This is sometimes referred to as the 'learning curve': in its most recent report, 'The Power Surge'[1], the Worldwatch Institute has noted these factors as decisive for success in the sector. A doubling of volume can reduce costs by 20-30 %: if this doubling can be effected more quickly, market penetration will be achieved more rapidly.

- *The importance of the parties.* Wider roles for the market's parties, through the creation of energy service utilities or utilities that concentrate more on the benefit of the energy than on purely numerical kilowatt-hours, can mean much for customers' faith in energy efficiency. This could create a better balance between the willingness to apply and the willingness to save energy.

- *The importance of goods distribution.* Better means of achieving extensive spread of good technology are needed if such technology is to come to widespread use. This involves aids such as sector practices, purchasing rules etc. It also involves product identification, e.g. with marking systems that facilitate proper choices. It requires aids for consultants and installation contractors, so that unusual system combinations can more easily be tested and selected, e.g. in CAD systems. It also requires back-up from promotional campaigns to improve the image of the companies that make the correct choices. An example of this is the Swedish ELOFF Strömsnål (Current Miser) campaign on low-energy-requirement domestic white goods.

- *The importance of product characteristics* This is perhaps the most important element of all. Energy efficiency is only part of a product's characteristics. Others are generally much more important: does the product perform the right task: is it easy to install and look after: does its function affect other factors? Products that have positive answers in these respects will achieve more widespread use, whether they are energy-efficient or not. Correspondingly, products that cannot be justified solely because of their good energy performances may be selected on other grounds.

Collating all these factors results in the following table:

	Potential	Acceptance
Time	+	
Technology	+	
Volume	+	+
Parties concerned		+
Distribution		+
Characteristics	+	+

It can be seen, therefore, that there are many factors that increase both potential and acceptance relative to the previous reference level.

Most of the discussion concerning improvement in efficiency relates to specific improvement, i.e. the number of kilowatt-hours used per square metre or per litre of volume in a refrigerator etc. In this latter context in particular, it is often pointed out how the performance of refrigerators and freezers constantly improves from one generation to the next. This is true, and it is therefore important to note that these specific improvements can be further accelerated, as was done by the technology procurement programmes. The energy policy that was established by the Energy Conservation Delegation[2] and which resulted in establishing the Technology Procurement for More Efficient Use of Energy programme, is better suited to commercial reality than were previous energy policy measures. For the first time, a serious attempt has been made to utilise market forces, rather than just hoping that they would arrive at the correct results by themselves.

Three coordinating factors

There are three coordinating factors in society that affect our use of energy: specific intensity (kWh/benefit), activity (total benefit) and structure (the make-up of the benefit). The activity is generally on a rising trend, and cannot be affected by energy policy measures. The structure can be affected to some extent, but over a longer period of time. Certain changes in these parameters are autonomous, i.e. they will occur without additional external pressure. All these factors serve only to confuse the current energy debate still further. What do the figures really mean? The following table illustrates some practical examples of movement in various directions.

	Increasing	Decreasing
Intensity	More sophisticated equipment (e.g. colour copiers).	Developed equipment (e.g. refrigerators).
Activity	Increased population.	More resource-conscious consumption.
Structure	Lifestyles that require more goods. Increased industrialisation.	Mutation of an industrial society into a service society. Changed infrastructure for transport (e.g. vehicles instead of petrol-powered electric vehicles)

As these factors constantly affect total energy use, it is also difficult clearly to indicate the magnitude of the efficiency improvement that can be effected and what will really bring about the changes. The latest energy report[3] of the National Board for Industrial and Technical Development (NUTEK), for example, states that the aggregated effect of efficiency improvements and structural changes is expected to amount to 16 TWh/year (11 %) in terms of electricity by 2005. Industry accounts for about 9 TWh/year of these savings, with about 2/3 of this being structural effect. This indicates that the maximum figure for efficiency improvement, including autonomous change is about 10 TWh/year (7 %).

The report from the Energy Use Council[4] has investigated certain segments of energy use, equivalent to over half of the country's total energy use, and assesses the autonomous improvement in efficiency by 2010 as amounting to 8 %. The same report assesses the possible total improvement in efficiency use by the investigated sectors as amounting to 22 % by 2010. The figures, in other words, are a jungle, although there do seem to be good prospects of forcing the rate of efficiency improvement over and above that which would result from normal technical development and normal structural change.

Shaking up the markets

If all this is to be achieved, there will have to be changes in the markets, making better use of their inherent powers. We need better products than the very best ones that are available today. Marketing and sales of the best products must be increased, in order to take every opportunity to improve efficiency. The poorest products must be eliminated from the market.

All this must be done simultaneously. In a pattern such as this, there is no question of different measures excluding each other: instead, if anything, they must be welded together into a single policy.

Product improvements nowadays are often made in an international environment. Most products are manufactured in one country and sold in several others. Any lasting change therefore often requires international participation. This can be done most effectively in defined projects between interested countries and companies, but can be given valuable support by international cooperation between countries under the auspices of IEA's various agreements and by the two EU development programmes for spreading more efficient products, SAVE (a programme for more efficient use of energy) and THERMIE (a programme for energy-efficient technology within the areas of energy use, renewable energy sources, solid fuels and hydrocarbons).

Technology procurement

Better use needs to be made of market forces in spreading products, while assisting the parties involved in the market to come into contact with each other in their work of developing even better products. On the other side, the organised market needs strong customers who are in a position to express their requirements clearly[5]. Technology procurement is a very powerful instrument in this context.

The many customers need improved instruments for obtaining information on, understanding and trusting new technology. They need to be exposed to a cross-fire of activities to enable them better to make their choices, and so that it is the positive beneficial aspects of efficiency improvements that attract them to making decisions, rather than purely the improvement in efficiency itself[6]. These instruments include demonstration, training and marking systems.

For the purchaser, low-performance equipment that was perhaps sold cheaply in a sale, or of which the price was simply low because of poor quality, can become an unexpected future financial burden. For society, its existence and requirement for disproportionally excessive energy quantities represents an obstacle in the way of good environmental and energy intentions. Unfortunately, such equipment can always find purchasers who do not base their choices on rational considerations[7]. These products should be removed from the market by application of standards.

International projects under development

Within the framework of IEA's innovative technologies programme, a sub-programme under the name of Market Pull Activities has been in progress since 1993, establishing itself in a number of areas:

- Wet Appliances, which is concerned with washing machines, dishwashers and dryers.
- Copiers.
- Lighting equipment.

Two new areas are at an early planning stage:

- Vending Appliances, for hot and cold drinks.
- Home Electronics, for automatic power-down of equipment.

More needs to be done

There is, in other words, much to be done, both as concrete measures and as determination of suitable improvement measures. As far as technology is concerned, it is primarily further development of systems and knowledge of system relationships that need to be developed, enabling us to save more at lower costs. We also need to know more about how energy-efficient technology can complement increased industrial productivity. As far as ways of organising the spread of energy-efficient technology are concerned, we need to learn more about cooperative measures so that the various energy efficiency improvement programmes can make better use of market forces.

This chapter is based on material by Hans Nilsson, Manager of the Department of Energy Efficiency, National Board for Industrial and Technical Development (NUTEK), Stockholm.

REFERENCES

1   Flavin, C., Lenssen, N. 'The Power Surge'. Worldwatch Institute 1994.

2   SOU 1987:68 and SOU 1987:69.

3   Energy report 1994. NUTEK B1994:9.

4   Energy Use Council. NUTEK B1994:8.

5   Lundvall, B. Å. Innovation, the organised market and productivity slowdown.

6   Robinson, John B. The Proof of the Pudding. Making Energy Efficiency Work. Energy Policy, September 1991.

7   Sanstad, A., Howarth, R. Consumer Rationality and Energy Efficiency. ACEEE Summer Study, 1994.

5

THE ENERGY SYSTEM

Effective energy supply is a question of balance
Energy conservation is better than new electricity

Photographer: Bengt Olof Olsson, Bildhuset

EFFECTIVE ENERGY SUPPLY IS A QUESTION OF BALANCE

SUMMARY

It is necessary to consider both energy conservation and ways of changing heating systems when minimising the cost of energy supply to a property.

The potentials for energy conservation are admittedly substantial, but conservation measures should be differentiated depending on the types of built environment and the type of heating system. In areas with district heating, the financially viable room for manoeuvre in terms of conservation is relatively restricted, while substantial investments can often be justified in properties in most other areas. The possibility of changing heating systems also affects the optimum level of conservation.

The cost of replacing heating systems is high in properties having direct-acting electric heating, which results in the financially optimum conservation level being higher in such types of properties than in those having other heating systems.

Model studies forecast further extension of district heating systems, which is often justified by the potential for expansion of CHP, or may be due to availability of an appropriate supply of waste heat. The Building Regulations and other guidelines for building need to distinguish between properties having heating systems that can provide a potential heat sink for CHP (whether now or in future) and other properties.

About 50 % of the energy conservation potential that was estimated in 1979 has now been implemented. Taxation of fuels should be independent of what the fuels are used for: if not, such taxes can result in increased emissions.

A wise property-owner conserves energy and modernises or replaces heating equipment simultaneously. This enables energy conservation to be balanced against corresponding measures on the supply side, keeping down heating costs.

All too often, energy conservation assessments and determination of suitable types of heating systems are made independently. This method of thinking also applies to most of the calculation aids that are available, resulting in sub-optimisations and unnecessary costs. A balanced assessment enables the property-owner to avoid the most expensive conservation measures while making limited investments in the supply side.

The balance problem, i.e. finding a balance between supply and conservation, varies depending on the demand-dependent variables such as the type of property, its age etc. and on the energy-system-dependent variables such as possible forms of heating, distance from a district heating supply etc. It is therefore necessary to consider both groups of variables when calculating the financially optimum conservation level[1].

Much research has been done in this sector. As long ago as at the end of the 1970s, the first results were being produced at the Department of Energy Systems Technology at Chalmers University of Technology. An investigation from Jönköping in 1980 is discussed below as an example[2 3]. This has been followed up by investigations in about a dozen other local authority areas between 1985 and 1994. Analysis of the Jönköping case showed that energy conservation to a level of at least 25 % of the net energy demand was justifiable. How much further savings should lie above this level depends on the type of heating systems and type of built environment, i.e. on both energy-system-dependent and demand-dependent variables.

Optimum energy conservation

The Jönköping investigation indicated that, in those areas where district heating was feasible, the optimum energy saving level was about 5-6 percentage points less than the optimum saving level in areas with no feasibility of district heating supply. In addition, the optimum energy saving level was a few percentage points lower in the centre of the town, where distribution costs and culvert costs were lower than in the outer areas of the town.

When the Jönköping investigation was performed, the town's district heating system had not been extended to any significant extent. The dependence of the optimum saving level on different types of heating systems becomes more marked when we look at areas having established district heating systems and with relatively low marginal production costs. Figure 1 shows the results from four local authority areas having established district heating systems.

The width of the band in Figure 1 depends on differences from one local authority area and another and between the studied scenarios.

There is little room for further conservation measures in apartment buildings and commercial premises that are already connected to district heating systems. However, in areas outside those supplied by district heating, the potential savings are about 10 % higher than within the district heating area. It is interesting to note that the latter also applies to properties that are next on the list for district heating supply. When properties on the periphery of the town centre area are connected to a district heating supply, it becomes economically viable to keep down investments in distribution capacity[4].

An important result from the investigations is that energy conservation measures should be differentiated depending on the type of built environment and the type of heating. The optimum savings level in properties already connected to district heating is relatively low (when considering an average assessment for all district-heated properties), while continued substantial investment is often justified in most other types of properties (again on the basis of average figures)[5,6].

This conclusion concerning a differentiated input level remains throughout the scenarios studied in the various projects. It is therefore safe to say that this is a robust conclusion.

Replacing heating systems affects conservation

The possibility of replacing, or having to replace, the heating system also affects the optimum savings level. The example described below is from the Värnamo investigation[7], in which an important assumption was that the price of electricity is expected to rise around the end of the century.

Figure 2 illustrates the greater incentive for conservation in detached houses with direct electric heating as compared with other detached houses. In the case of the directly electrically heated houses, the potential conservation level (including recovery of heat in ventilation exhaust air) is about 40 %, but lower in other houses. In the latter, it is easier to replace the heating system when the price of electricity rises, and it will be more cost-effective to do so than to implement the most expensive conservation measures.

Percentage relative to 1978

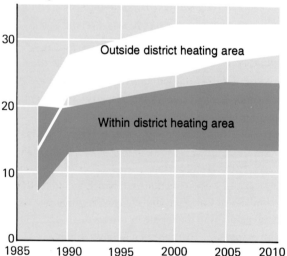

Figure 1. Financially optimum conservation level for apartment buildings and commercial premises outside and within district heating areas, relative to 1978 costs. The district heating system is assumed to be supplied by CHP. The results shown in the diagram are taken from investigations performed in Värnamo, Uppsala, Gothenburg and Karlstad.

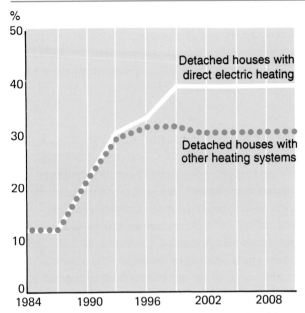

Figure 2. Financially optimum conservation level in detached houses having direct electric heating and those having other heating systems.

As the need or pressure for a new energy carrier often results from changes in external circumstances, e.g. in fuel prices, taxation or environmental charges, changes of energy carrier are often seen in a large-scale perspective, both in terms of inputs to models and in reality. This could be referred to as conversion waves, and the tendency was noted as long ago as in the Jönköping investigation from 1980-81[9] [10].

As far as appropriate measures for detached houses in the Jönköping investigation were concerned, two conversion waves were foreseen:

■ In the first wave, which was expected to occur during the 1980s, there would be a change from oil-fired boilers to electric heating, primarily using electric boilers, although individual heat pumps would be installed in some houses.

■ The second wave of conversion is expected to occur in response to the substantial increases in electricity prices that are expected to occur when the phase-out of nuclear power production starts. Various dates have been put for this, as well as various effects for detached houses depending on whether they are within or outside district heating zones.

A maximum optimum conservation level exists

In other words, it can be seen that greater flexibility in the choice of supply system reduces the financially optimum conservation level, regardless of whether it is a waterborne heating system in a single house or a public district heating system that results in this flexibility. Work on deriving key indicator quantifiers found that, in practice, there is a maximum optimum conservation level for each type of property[8]. Above this level, conservation does not pay, as it then becomes more profitable to change the type of heating in order to minimise heating costs. The key indicator investigation was based on extensive sensitivity analysis, including assumed energy price shock rises.

Changing the heating method becomes particularly interesting when an existing heating system has worn out. In this case, even the alternative of retaining the original heating system or heating method requires new investment, which thus naturally increases the competitiveness of a new heating method, which always requires new investment.

The first forecast was right

The first conversion wave forecast by the Jönköping investigation has largely occurred in practice: conversion of electric heating in detached houses and connection of apartment buildings and commercial premises to district heating. Whether the second conversion wave will actually occur in reality remains to be seen. As we know, the substantial rise in the price of electricity that was forecast as a result of the phase-out of nuclear power production, and which would be the reason for this second wave of conversion, has not yet occurred.

In comparison with most other energy carriers, district heating and electricity are special cases in the context of changing the mix of supply by energy carriers. By using these two energy carriers, we are able to adapt centrally in order to suit changing circumstances. This can often be done more cost-effectively than if the changes were made on a property by-property basis. Flexibility increases and heat supply is less sensitive to external changes.

District heating expands

The local authority energy system investigations that the Department of Energy Systems at Chalmers University of Technology and Profu AB carried out at the end of the 1980s and at the beginning of the 1990s identified a conversion wave to further district heating connections. It is primarily to apartment buildings and commercial premises that connection is viable, although certain suitably sited detached house areas could also be converted to district heating.

These later investigations show that it is only partly a need for oil substitution that is the driving force behind district heating expansion. In most of the investigations (Uppsala[11], Värnamo[12], Gothenburg[13] and Karlstad[14]) it is instead primarily the potential for increasing CHP production that lies behind the expansion of district heating. In turn, the reason for the improvement in CHP competitiveness is that, in all cases, electricity prices are forecast to rise substantially. Further conversion to district heating increases the size of the heat sink, thus also allowing more electricity to be produced.

There are, however, exceptions to the rule accounting for the expansion of district heating, as can be exemplified by the Piteå investigation[15]. There, too, the result indicated further expansion of district heating, but in this case because of the excellent availability of good quality industrial waste heat. The amount of waste heat available was such that it could provide cheap district heating to a considerably larger number of properties than those that already were connected to the district heating supply.

These examples show that it is external factors such as a high electricity price (partly caused by the assumed phase-out of nuclear power production) or the availability of industrial waste heat that indirectly affect the choice of energy carrier for heating various types of built environments by making the production costs of district heating more competitive in relative terms.

A recently completed investigation[16] compares the conservation potentials as estimated during the 1970s with subsequent actual development of energy demand, to show that about 50 % of the estimated conservation potential for space heating and domestic hot water production has been achieved.

At present, we have a situation in which electricity production is, in principle, unconnected with heat production. The electricity used in Sweden is produced almost entirely by hydro power or nuclear power. Hydro power involves no heat production, while the waste heat from the condensers in nuclear power stations is not used for heating.

CHP's time is coming ...

We can foresee a need for new electricity production capacity in the future. This need may arise earlier if the phase-out of nuclear power production is brought forward, but many factors indicate that it will arise in any case as a result of increased demand for electricity and possible future exports of electricity. Under such conditions, it will almost certainly become viable to build new CHP production plant, which will increase the link between electricity and heat production.

More expensive electricity production plant will result in an increase in the difference in production costs between electricity and heat (not direct electric heating). This will be particularly apparent in those areas where heat supply is based on district heating where most of the district heat is produced by CHP. It may be so that heat production will be regarded purely as a by-product of electricity production, despite the fact that the presence of the heat sink for which the heat is produced is essential for this resource-economical production of electricity. It justifies properties of this type being given special consideration when deciding on measures intended to reduce heating requirements.

Setting heat conservation targets too high in properties that form part of the heat sink for CHP production is often an overall waste of resources for the country's energy system as a whole. It would result in reducing electricity production from the CHP plants, necessitating other, less-efficient electricity production instead. The situation becomes particularly serious if the high conservation ambitions require an input of electricity for powering heat recovery systems, as we then both lose the heat sink for CHP production and increase the demand for electricity. When drafting building standards and general guidelines for building, a distinction should therefore be made between properties that provide a heat sink for CHP production (whether now or potentially in the future) and other properties. This is not the same as deliberately wasting heat in district-heated properties, but the financially optimum energy conservation level is definitely lower in such properties than in similar properties that are not in district heating areas.

Technical potentials provide a different picture

The following presentation[17] is based on the Masterfile database, which is a comprehensive register of the built environment and energy use in various areas, properties and buildings throughout the country.

Heat demand is expressed as the net heat demand of the buildings. There are two figures: the present demand and a calculated post-conservation demand. This post-conservation demand is based on a generalised calculation of the technical conservation potential. This involves insulating each building up to the Building Regulations standard for new buildings, upgrading windows to triple-glazed units and installing heat recovery if the building has mechanical ventilation. At the same time, all incidental heat input is reduced by changing all electrical appliances up to the level of the most electrically-efficient appliances available on the market today, which would in turn increase the amount

of energy needed from radiators. These calculations have been performed individually for each building, with allowance for the type of building, its age, its equipment standard and whether conservation or improvement measures have already been applied.

Expressed as total net heat use for the entire country's built environment, the result is as shown in Figure 3. Areas where properties have their own boilers have been divided up into 'dense' and 'sparse'. 'Dense' represents a thermal heat load of 30 GWh/km², year or more, and includes group heating plants. The remainder is categorised as 'sparse', and is dominated by detached houses.

The total net heat demand as shown in Figure 3 amounts to about 98 TWh/year, with the theoretical technically feasible conservation potential amounting to about 19 TWh/year. The conservation potentials shown in Figure 3 can be summarised for the various types of built environment as follows:

Buildings with district heating: There still remains a considerable technically feasible potential, amounting to about 6.6 TWh/year. The conservation potential

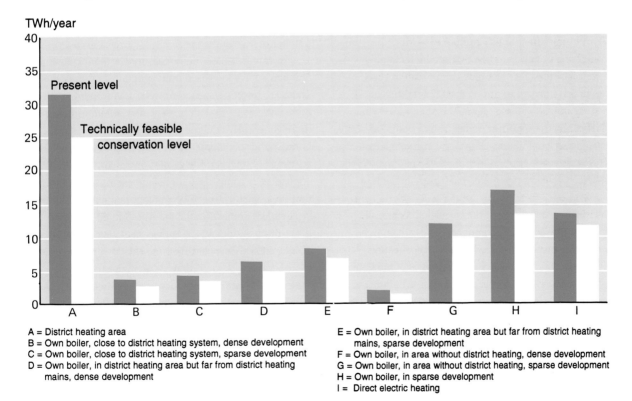

A = District heating area
B = Own boiler, close to district heating system, dense development
C = Own boiler, close to district heating system, sparse development
D = Own boiler, in district heating area but far from district heating mains, dense development

E = Own boiler, in district heating area but far from district heating mains, sparse development
F = Own boiler, in area without district heating, dense development
G = Own boiler, in area without district heating, sparse development
H = Own boiler, in sparse development
I = Direct electric heating

Figure 3. Total net heat use for the Swedish building stock. The left-hand column shows present use, while the right-hand column shows use after application of technically feasible conservation measures.

expressed in kWh/m², year is high, while the proportion actually dealt with is relatively small, i.e. conservation to date appears to have been relatively little.

Other properties in district heating areas:
Densely-built areas in the vicinity of district heating systems present a quite high technically feasible conservation potential in kWh/m², year terms, despite the fact that many of these properties have already been improved. The conservation potential in kWh/m², year in sparsely-built areas close to district heating systems is less. In the case of houses with their own boilers in urban areas, it is therefore important to ascertain whether they can be connected to a district heating supply or not, so that the appropriate level of conservation can be applied, rather than what is purely physically feasible. Expressed in TWh/year, most of the conservation potential (amounting to about 4.6 TWh/year) is found in sparsely-built areas well away from district heating systems in district heating areas. The conservation potential in the corresponding densely built areas amounts only to about 2.5 TWh/year, as indicated by these calculations. These latter areas include those having group heating plants.

Own boilers in sparsely built areas: Much has already been done in these areas, although the remaining technically feasible potential is high, both in specific terms (kWh/m², year) and in total (3.6 TWh/year).

Direct electric heating: Conservation potential in this category is less in both relative and absolute terms (1.8 TWh/year) than in other areas, despite the fact that relatively few improvements have been applied.

As much as over 50 % of the calculated technically feasible conservation potential exists in areas already having district heating or close to district heating systems. This is equivalent to over 40 % of the floor area of the country's residential buildings and commercial premises (excluding industry). Against the background of the analysis results described above, this is to be expected. There are good reasons to assume that conservation measures already applied have been taken after cost analysis that has led to the conclusion that the economically optimum savings level is lower in areas with district heating than in areas outside district heating networks. This means that there is still a considerable technically feasible, but not financially viable, potential

for energy conservation in district heating areas.

This emphasises the value of looking at the balance against heat supply when assessing how much of the technically feasible potential can be achieved.

Energy use is reduced by improving the efficiency of its use. This may seem obvious , but the examples below show that this not necessarily the case, at least not in respect of the use of electricity.

Greater use of electricity

The Gothenburg project[18] investigated various points, including the potentials for limiting the use of electricity by means of improvements in efficiency. The investigation found that the use of domestic electricity in Gothenburg had increased by 3 % per year since 1973. During this period, the number of inhabitants of the city had decreased somewhat, although the number of electricity subscribers remained approximately constant. This meant that per-capita domestic electricity use had increased from 750 kWh/person in 1973 to 1200 kWh/person in 1987, equivalent to an annual rate of increase of 3.4 %. In other words, the increase in the use of domestic electricity is the result of increased use, not of an increase in the number of inhabitants or the number of dwellings.

We can speculate on the reasons for the increase. Standards have increased both generally and in homes. There are fewer persons per dwelling unit today than there were in 1973, with present-day dwellings being more generously equipped with refrigerators, freezers, home laundry equipment etc. than they were about 20 years ago. However, the greater ownership of domestic appliances is compensated to some extent by the fact that the appliances have become more energy-efficient.

In 1988, domestic appliances accounted for three-fifths of domestic electricity use. General technical development has meant that present-day appliances are more resource-efficient than those in use in 1973. Despite this, we use 60 % more domestic electricity per person.

One interpretation of this analysis is that electricity use would be 20-30 % higher still if the appliances had not become more energy-efficient. Another interpretation is that, through the improvements in the efficiency of domestic appliances, consumers have money over for other consumption, which has increased electricity use. If the appliances had not become better, electricity use would not have increased so much.

Present-day domestic appliances such as refrigerators, freezers, fans etc. use less energy than those of the 1970s. Despite this, we still use 60 % more domestic electricity per person than we did in the 1970s. Photographer: Bengt Olof Olsson, Bildhuset

The example shows both that improving the efficiency of energy use is nothing new, but something that has gone on steadily, and that improvements in the efficiency of electricity use do not necessarily result in a reduction in energy use.

More stringent environmental requirements raise the optimum conservation level

Several investigations have included the environmental effects of energy conservation. The Värnamo and Gothenburg investigations[19][20] looked at the part played by the conservation programme in the reduction of emissions of sulphur, NO_x and carbon dioxide. Emissions would increase by 3-23 % if the cost-effective conservation measures in dwellings and commercial premises were not implemented. These figures include the emission effects on national electricity production.

The Värnamo investigation looked at how the part played by the conservation programme would be affected if environmental requirements were tightened up relative to those of the present day. The results from the analysis naturally show the obvious effect that enhanced environmental requirements would increase the optimum savings level. However, at the same time, such requirements would also mean that it would become more profitable to improve supply-side technology to reduce emissions per MWh produced. Nevertheless, a further result is that the improved environmental conditions resulting from each MWh reduction in demand would also be diminished.

The Värnamo and Gothenburg analyses weighted the result of these two effects of the enhanced environmental requirements (i.e. that the conservation level would increase but that the emission reduction per saved MWh would be reduced). The conclusion was that conservation's proportion of the measures to meet the reduction in emissions would be unchanged.

As far as emissions of various pollutants are concerned, it is important to ensure that total levels are minimised. It is not sufficient simply to consider the use of energy in buildings. If, for a given energy requirement, we change from combustion of a fuel to electricity, it is important to be aware of how the electricity has been produced. Admittedly, emissions at the point of use stop, but electricity demand is increased and if marginal increases are produced by fuel-fired power stations the change can, in the worst case, increase total emissions.

Actual environmental effect must be measured at national level, while decisions on types of heating systems are taken at local level. At these levels, the decision-makers do not have access to, and are probably not concerned with, the facts at national level when making their decision, which can result in environmental sub-optimisations. The analyses that have been performed give reason to believe that both district heating and electric heating are gaining market shares which, in the worst case, can result in unintended increased environmental impact.

Differentiated taxes can increase environmental impact

Present-day energy taxes have a strong limiting effect on carbon dioxide emissions from the country's energy system. If we calculate the effects of a scenario in which these taxes were totally removed, total carbon dioxide emissions from the country's energy system in 2005 would be about 40 % higher than if the present level of taxation is retained[21].

The current differentiated taxes mean that:

- fuel use for electricity production is exempt from energy and carbon dioxide tax,
- electricity and fuel use in manufacturing industry is exempt from energy tax, and pays only 25 % of the normal level of carbon dioxide tax.

If, however, we look at environmental effects other than carbon dioxide emission, the picture becomes less consistent. Several investigations have compared scenarios with present-day tax levels with other scenarios without tax. These comparisons show that the present-day taxes:

- favour the use of electricity,
- act against CHP,
- favour biofuels, wind power and, to some extent, natural gas, and
- discourage the use of coal and oil.

The two last points accord with national energy objectives, while the two first points are less desirable. One example of the effects of exempting electricity production from tax is that CHP is put at a disadvantage. If the turbine exhaust heat in a power station is sold for heating (CHP), tax becomes payable on that portion of the fuel used for heat production. If this heat is not used (as in a cold condensing power station), however, the entire fuel quantity is exempt from tax. This encourages a waste of resources, as tax is levied if the exhaust heat is used, but not if it is not used.

However, not even with regard to carbon dioxide emissions do present-day taxes have a reducing effect under all conditions. One project looked at the effects on carbon dioxide emissions resulting from different levels of carbon dioxide tax. It was expected that increasing levels of tax would reduce emissions through changes to other fuels, greater conservation etc. However, one scenario came to the paradoxical conclusion that a higher carbon dioxide tax increased carbon dioxide emissions from the energy system. The explanation for this was that competition between electricity and fuels had been changed to the benefit of electricity, as fuels utilised for electricity production are exempt from tax, while fuels used for heating are heavily taxed. This results, to some extent, in electricity replacing the use of fuels for heating. At the marginal levels, direct heat production at 70 % efficiency is replaced by electricity production at 40 % efficiency: in other words, more fuel is needed for the same heating requirement, resulting in increased emission.

Guide measures should therefore be designed to effect uniform taxation, with the use of fuels being taxed in the same way regardless of what they are used for. However, we must understand that there are many reasons why future taxes are unlikely to be entirely logical in their energy and environmental effects. Taxes remain one of the largest elements of uncertainty in the energy sector, if not the largest.

Databases and calculation tools

Much of the work of the above-described analyses has been carried out using the MARKAL energy system model[22]. This model optimises energy supply, conservation measures and emissions. The Department of Energy Systems at Chalmers University of Technology has also developed a method of integrated analysis of energy system development and measures intended to reduce environmental risks[23]. The HOVA[24] energy conservation model was used as an ancillary programme to prepare the energy conservation input needed for the MARKAL model.

Experience from the MARKAL model has been used to produce a simple model for small and medium-sized communities (KRAM)[25]. This new model cannot perform total optimisations, but does instead have a modular structure that allows the user to make trial and error attempts to arrive at the best solution. This model is now in use in all 17 local authority areas in Skaraborg county.

This chapter is based on material by Professor Clas Otto Wene, Department of Energy Systems, Chalmers University of Technology, Håkan Sköldberg and Bo Rydén, PROFU AB, and Anders Göransson, Energidata Göteborg AB.

REFERENCES

1 Rydén, B.: *Integrerad miljö/energistudie i Värnamo kommun 1987-1988* (An integrated environment/energy investigation in Värnamo, 1987-1988). Gothenburg, Profu AB, 1988.

2 Wene, C-O. & Andersson, O.: *Långsiktig kommunal energiplanering: Stockholm, 1983* (Long-term local authority energy planning: Stockholm, 1983). Efn/AES, 1983:4.

3 Wene, C-O. & Andersson, O.: *The optimum mix of supply and conservation of energy in average size cities.* In Proc. IEA Conf. on New Energy Conservation Technologies and their Commercialisation, 6-10 April 1981, Berlin. J. P. Millhone & E. H. Willis (editors). Berlin, Springer Verlag, 1981.

4 Rydén, B., Johnsson, J. & Wene, C-O.: *Combined heat and power production in integrated energy systems.* Energy Policy, February 1993, pp 175-190.

5 See Rydén et al. (1993).

6 *Göteborgs energisystem - ett forskningsprojekt: slutrapport* (Gothenburg's energy systems - a research project: Final report). Gothenburg Energi AB, Chalmers University of Technology and Profu AB, Gothenburg, 1990.

7 See Rydén (1988).

8 Rydén, B., Johnsson, J. & Larsson, T.: *Underlag för energiprognoser, nyckeltalsutredningen. Studie av variationer i nyckeltalen för energisparande i bostäder och lokaler m.m. MARKAL-modellen - praktikfall Jönköping* (A basis for energy forecast, a key indicator quantifier investigation. Investigation of variations in key indicators for energy conservation in dwellings and commercial premises using the MARKAL model - the Jönköping case). August 1986. National Energy Administration.

9 See Wene & Andersson (1983).

10 Wene, C-O. & Andersson, O.: *District heating in the long-range planning for the city's total energy system.* Proceedings of the Fifth International District Heating Conference, September 1981, Kiev, USSR. Section III, Part II, p. 90.

11 Johnsson, J., Björkqvist, O. and Wene, C-O.: *Integrated energy - emission control planning in the community of Uppsala.* International Journal of Energy Research, Vol. 16 (1992), p. 173.

12 See Rydén (1988).

13 See Profu (1990).

14 Sköldberg, H.: *Strategisk energi/miljöstudie med MARKAL-modellen som underlag till energiplaneringen för Karlstads kommun* (Strategic energy/environmental investigation using the MARKAL model as a basis for energy planning for Karlstad). Gothenburg, Profu AB, 1990.

15 Sköldberg, H.: *Integrerad energi- och miljöstudie för Piteå* (An integrated energy and environment investigation for Piteå). Gothenburg, Profu AB, 1991.

16 Niklassson, I., *From Conservation Supply Curves to Energy Demand.* YSSP 1994, ECS, IIASA.

17 Calculations made by Anders Göransson, Energidata Göteborg AB.

18 See Profu (1990).

19 See Rydén (1988).

20 See Profu (1990).

21 MARKAL calculations for NUTEK, Winter 1994/95. Profu AB, Gothenburg.

22 Abilock, H. et al.: *MARKAL - A multiperiod linear programming model for energy systems analysis.* Proceedings of the International Conference on Energy Systems Analysis, 9-11 October 1979, Dublin, Ireland, p. 482. Reidel, Dordrecht, 1980.

23 Wene, C-O.: *The optimum mix of conservation and substitution.* Int. Journal of Energy Research, Vol. 4 (1980), pp 271-282.

24 Wene, C-O. & Andersson, D.: *HOVA: Nettoenergibehov och energisparpotential i befintlig bebyggelse* (HOVA: Net energy requirements and energy conservation potential of the existing built environment). January 1983. Chalmers University of Technology Department of Energy Systems, Internal Report 183-05.

25 Josefsson, A., Johnsson, J. and Wene C-O.: *Community-based Regional Energy/Environmental Planning.* NOTA DI LAVORO 78.94, Fondazione Eni Enrico Mattei, Milan, 1994.

ENERGY CONSERVATION IS BETTER THAN NEW ELECTRICITY

SUMMARY

Per-capita electricity use today in Sweden is twice as high as in West Germany and three times as high as the average for the European Union. However, in the long run, a deregulated electricity market will make conditions in Sweden the same as in the rest of Europe, i.e. the price of electricity will be substantially increased.

Simulation models have been used to investigate a number of possible changes to the Swedish electricity system such as environmental charges, improvements in the efficiency of use, conversion to other fuels and demand side management. The results show that electrical energy can be a major new export product, that electricity conservation is cheaper than building new power stations either in Sweden or on the continent, and that carbon dioxide levies (which are at present not charged on electricity production) would be cost-effective on such production. Other reports indicate the same results - electricity conservation measures are much cheaper than building new electricity production capacity, and electricity conservation measures in industry are the cheapest and most cost-effective.

Energy-efficient buildings are an extremely cost-effective way of conserving resources, and this will be even more the case in the future.

Simulation models for optimisation/-simulation of local authority electricity and district heating systems have reached commercial maturity, although we would like to see the description of buildings in such models being much more extensive.

The Swedish energy system has changed substantially during the 1970s and 1980s. The use of oil has been greatly reduced, while the proportion of electricity supplied by nuclear power has increased substantially. Today, electricity use in the built environment is about ten times as high as it was in 1960, while fuel use is approximately the same as it was then. Since 1970, the use of oil in industry has ceased almost entirely, while electricity use is twice as high. This pattern of development is something in which Sweden is almost alone.

Throughout the 1980s the decision to phase out nuclear power production, and particularly the decision on early phase-out of two reactors, has restricted the discussion almost entirely to supply side aspects. The present situation, with considerable excess production capacity during most of the year, and the prospect of future deregulation, has resulted in dumped prices. This, together with low-price imports of electricity from Norway, can also result in low electricity prices in the longer term, which means that improvements in efficiency will not be cost-effective. All this is occurring at the same time as world market prices for oil have fallen to 1960s levels. In addition, the trend in Europe is towards allowing market forces to control events. Under all these circumstances, is there any justification for performing research into more energy-efficient buildings?

If we analyse the demand side, with the nuclear phase-out as a condition, we find that electricity conservation measures are much cheaper to implement than is the building of new electricity production capacity. This has been described in a number of reports, including 'A free electricity market, production, conservation and the EU'[1], from a project financed by the National Board for Industrial and Technical Development (NUTEK). Similar conclusions are reached if we study the changes that the Swedish electricity market is expected to undergo during the next few years, i.e. contradicting the claims in the first paragraph above.

In an international electricity market, it would be reasonable for Swedish electricity prices to rise to the level encountered in the rest of Europe. In the longer term, our per-capita electricity use must become about the same as within the rest of the EU. Today, the per-capita use of electricity in Sweden is over three times that of the average within the EU. Photographer: Morten Løberg, Samfoto A/S Oslo 1, Mira

The Swedish electricity system is at present undergoing massive changes from having been a monopoly to a free market, from an isolated national market to an open international market, from a supply-orientated system to a user/customer-orientated system. A number of possible changes in the Swedish electricity system have been investigated through simulation of such parameters as environmental charges, potentials for efficiency improvement, conversion to other fuels and demand side management[2]. The results show that electrical energy can become a new major Swedish export product, that electricity conservation is cheaper than building new power stations, whether in Sweden or in other countries, and that carbon dioxide levies on electricity production as well as on the burning of fuels for other purposes would be cost-effective.

Swedish electricity use is very high

In an international electricity market, it is reasonable to expect that Swedish electricity prices will rise to levels encountered on the continent. Per-capita electricity use today is almost twice as high in Sweden as in West Germany, and three times as high as the average for the European Union. With growing cross-border transmission capacity to the continent, Sweden will export electrical energy and import continental electricity prices. This will result in greater profitability of conservation measures on the part of Swedish electricity customers.

Other reports indicate similar results, although the analyses have been performed at different levels. One of these, at industrial level[3], is the MINTOP project, while 'Demand side management of electricity use' is concerned with end-user level in local authority electricity and district heating systems[4]. A third report[5] is concerned with the energy distributor level. In all cases, electricity conservation measures are much cheaper than building new production capacity, with conservation in industry being the cheapest and most cost-effective. This result was also reached by Sydkraft's TOPPKAP project. The same conclusions have also been reached on the international plane.

Constant development

New developments constantly take place: for example, new agreements have been reached concerning the supply of electrical energy from Norway. Planning has

also started for new undersea cables for the interchange of electricity with the continent. The first of this new group of links, with a capacity of 600 MW, was the Baltic Cable between Sweden and Germany, commissioned in November 1994. Norway intends to construct a link to Germany and another to Holland. An open electricity market can result in an entirely new situation for both distributors and producers. The producers will have to compete with each other to sell to distributors and end users. In addition, completely new operators may emerge, e.g. power brokers acting as intermediaries on the power exchange.

The reasons for electricity and district heating users, electricity distributors and power producers to implement energy and electricity conservation measures are many and important. This will become even more significant on a deregulated electricity market, with incentives being enhanced in step with the introduction of new tariffs, contracts and supply forms. Greater ease of transporting electrical energy between the continent and Sweden will also have a very marked effect on price levels. An additional aspect is concerned with the environment and costs for environmental impact. If a price is put on environmental impact, there will be an incentive to take steps to limit the effects.

Today, there is insufficient financial incentive for applying cost-effective measures to the extent that is possible and financially viable for a local authority energy system[6][7]. If conservation measures are applied only on the user side, with present-day electricity tariffs as the determinants, the users reduce their energy system costs while the distributor, the local authority energy utility, instead sees its energy system costs increased. The two interests are thus mutually opposed.

An energy system analysis has been performed for a Swedish town with a population of about 90 000[8], investigating various combinations of cooperation between customers and distributor. The results show that if the largest industries in the town applied conservation measures, their total energy system costs would be reduced by SEK 12 million over a ten-year period, while the local authority electricity utility would see its energy system costs increased by SEK 6 million. This means that the loss of revenue from industry exceeds the reduction in the cost of electricity that the utility buys from the producer. As a result, the total system savings for the local authority are SEK 6 million over ten years. The industrial conservation measures that were investigated were proposals for real measures that were identified after visits to the companies and after metering and analysis of their electricity use.

Greater profits from a single system

If, instead, we regard the local authority electricity company and industries as a single common system, instead of as two systems as is the case today, we can identify cost-effective energy system measures that would result in a major reduction in total energy system costs, i.e. in a significant reduction of resource consumption. Regarding the two parties as a single system means that conservation measures can be identified by investigating the true cost of electrical energy within the local authority energy system, instead of (as now) using the existing electricity tariffs as the references. On this basis, calculations for the same town indicate a total energy system cost saving of SEK 330 million over ten years, if distributor and customers could be regarded as a single system.

The postulated system solution would involve conservation measures on the local authority supply side in the form of a biomass-fuelled CHP plant with an output of 40 MW of electricity, complemented by conservation measures on the industrial user side in the form of demand management, efficiency improvements and conversion to other fuels. This overall single-system concept is now beginning to find acceptance, with efforts to introduce it being made in a number of local authority areas. Similar results can also be demonstrated for the building sector, and this approach will become essential when the Swedish electricity market is integrated with the continental market.

When we today analyse buildings from a system perspective, far too little allowance is made for the fact that buildings are in fact systems of different components, and that they form part of a larger supply system with characteristics that vary throughout the day and the year. If we start with the building as such, it has a heat source or a heat input point for such purposes as maintaining a suitable indoor temperature and providing the occupants with hot water. In order to prevent excessive demand for heat, the building is insulated, the ventilation system incorporates heat recovery and so on. The amount of insulation used is determined today largely by standards, such as the Building Regulations. As a result, analysis of a building

as an energy system is not normally performed: instead, it is the regulatory framework that is simply followed.

All electricity eventually becomes heat

Electricity is used in buildings also to meet requirements for lighting etc. It is sometimes also used as a direct heat source, but at least during the heating season all electricity used in the building will eventually benefit the building in the form of heat, even if this had not been its primary purpose from the beginning. If, for example, low-energy lamps are installed, this will reduce electricity demand but will simultaneously result in higher energy demand from the heating system, which perhaps also obtains its original energy from electricity. The low-energy lamp may therefore contribute to energy saving only outside the heating season, although at this time of year there is also likely to be little demand for lighting. Any financial saving will therefore occur only if the energy from the heating boiler is cheaper than the energy used for lighting.

An investigation[9] has shown that many office buildings could be heated almost entirely by the waste heat from lighting, computers and other office equipment. Office buildings require additional heat input only at times when they are unoccupied. Today, public buildings are insulated in the same way as are dwellings. Buildings are insulated as if it was heating that is the problem, while at the same time attempting to minimise cooling requirements by specifying performance requirements in respect of more energy-efficient office equipment.

How are electricity and heat produced?

If we widen our horizons somewhat, we need to consider how the electricity and heat used in a building are produced. The district heating may have been produced by electric boilers on an interruptible supply tariff. If we consider the case of the low-energy lamps as above, electricity as such may be saved in the building and the user may receive a lower electricity bill, but the heat that is needed to replace the free heat that would otherwise have been provided by the old lamps may in its turn also have been produced by electricity. As a result, there is no real saving of resources for the country as a whole. Instead, there has been a cost for the more energy-efficient lamp, which is at least ten times as high as that of the old lamp. However, low-energy lamps have a clear place in the Swedish energy system: the fact that the above argument has been concentrated on their downside has been done only because this provided a simple example.

It may be necessary to resort to the use of oil-fired cold condensing power production (or some other form of expensive power production) during the winter, while nuclear power and hydro power production are sufficient during the rest of the year. An oil-fired cold condensing power station has an efficiency of only about 30 %, so each kilowatt-hour of electricity that is saved reduces oil consumption by 3 kWh. Electricity saved during the summer, on the other hand, has a value of only 0-10 öre/kWh. From a cost viewpoint, therefore, it is important that the conservation measures employed are directed primarily to reducing use of the most expensive forms of power, i.e. oil-fired cold condensing power.

Additional insulation and ventilation heat exchangers have the greatest effect when conditions are coldest, i.e. when oil-fired cold condensing power production is likely to be used. They have no significant effect during the summer, but this is less important as only cheaper forms of power production are then in use. The performance of an outdoor air heat pump, on the other hand, improves as the temperature of its air heat source rises. The resulting saving is therefore greatest during the summer. The same applies, for example, to solar collectors without seasonal heat stores.

Conservation measures as described above can save a considerable quantity of energy in a building. However, for the nation as a whole, it is important that these savings should not be evaluated in the same way as if they resulted solely in a reduction in (for example) oil-fired cold condensing power production. In fact, it is the case that the more solar heat that is used, the greater becomes the proportion of low-efficiency oil-fired cold condensing power production, as the utilisation time of electric heating is reduced.

Energy conservation where it is most needed

From the above, it can be seen that it is important that energy conservation measures should be applied where they are most needed and where they are most profitable. However, in some cases, the national

perspective may demand that heat needs to be saved only during the summer, while electricity should be saved mainly during the winter. In a district heating system supplied from a CHP production source, the built environment acts as a heat sink, which means that the heat is effectively a form of energy that must be removed[10]. A combined heat and power plant produces electricity, while the heat that would be removed in a cold condensing power station is here supplied to the district heating system. During the summer, a certain minimum flow is required in the country's rivers, which in turn means that hydro electricity from these rivers is virtually free.

The system under investigation therefore needs to include both the buildings and the energy-producing installations. However, the problem with this approach is that there are today no sufficiently refined models of reality, taking account of the complex relationship between primary energy input to the system and its progress right through to the final customer. There are, for example, at least two different tariff structures for electricity that must be incorporated. In Europe, daytime power demand is determined by the needs of industry. There is little use of electric heating, and so there is less difference in demand between electricity use in the summer and winter, although demand varies between night and day in parallel with industrial demand. In Sweden, the maximum power demand on the year's coldest day is determined effectively by the demand for electric heating.

The same factors as in the rest of Europe

With a deregulated electricity market, conditions in Sweden will become, in the long run, the same as in the rest of Europe, i.e. substantially different from now, with much higher electricity prices.

The previously-mentioned report, 'A free electricity market, production, conservation and the EU'[11], states that the total system cost of Sweden's existing electrical energy system, as calculated by the present value method, is about SEK 130 000 million. This has assumed that no measures to improve the efficiency of the system have been taken. If nuclear power is phased out and replaced by 'traditional' power generation, i.e. if it is replaced by fossil-fuelled cold condensing power generation, the cost would increase by about SEK 125 000 million. If, on the other hand, appropriate conservation measures were employed, the additional cost would be reduced to about SEK 70 000 million, i.e. a saving of SEK 55 000 million. A necessary condition for this would be that all parties involved in the market - producers, distributors and end users - act financially rationally, i.e. that they implement all the viable conservation measures. This is not the case today, as various incentives are missing for the different parties involved.

Electricity prices will increase

The system savings resulting from a conservation measure applied by an end user do not benefit the end user: instead, some of the savings are retained by the producer, who no longer needs to install additional production capacity. This has been described in more detail in a degree thesis[12], which discussed the matter of incentives in detail. As mentioned above, electricity may be sold to Germany and other countries when the Baltic Cable is commissioned. In a totally unrestricted electricity market, Swedish electricity producers would naturally try to sell electricity to the continent. As marginal electricity production in central Europe is coal-based, power producers there would want to purchase electricity from Sweden or Norway as long as the Swedish or Norwegian electricity prices were below the price of electricity produced from coal. At the same time, the Swedish producers would see no incentive to sell electricity within Sweden at a lower price than they could get by exporting it. This will mean that, effectively, we will export electricity but import central European prices. Price levels in Sweden will therefore rise.

Financially rational behaviour on the part of the end users would therefore mean that a number of conservation measures that had previously not been regarded as viable would be implemented - provided that the resulting savings could be retained by those paying for the measures. Some local authorities also operate energy utilities that both produce and sell electricity and/or energy. Most of these have their own district heating distribution systems, allowing them to sell the heat produced by CHP production. Several investigations have looked at energy systems of these types, in which the supply of more fuel has to compete with conservation measures on the demand side[13 14.]

High electricity use by Swedish consumers

As European conditions begin to bite, we will need to make maximum use of low electricity tariffs during the night, in order to reduce the effect of higher daytime prices as far as possible. Conditions in Sweden and the rest of Europe will become more or less similar, and in the long term our per capita use will become much the same as throughout the rest of the European Union. Today, Swedish per capita use of electricity is approximately three times as high as the European average, which is fairly similar throughout the EU states. Electricity for less sophisticated purposes will simply become out of reach in Sweden.

In a future non-nuclear situation, or when conditions have harmonised with those in the rest of the European Union, buildings may be heated using the same power stations and distribution capacity as industry. This condition will apply as long as we prefer to work during the day and sleep at night. All this means that, from the supply point of view, the system is of classical structure.

With appropriately designed building services systems, a building can use much of its electricity during the night, when industrial demand is low. This reduces the need to install additional production and distribution capacity, while enabling consumers to use cheap night-time tariff electricity without having to sacrifice comfort.

Measurements in experimental buildings show that it is possible almost entirely to eliminate daytime power demand for heating and domestic hot water production between 06.00 and 22.00 during the winter without any significant sacrifice of comfort. This of course requires the design, construction and quality of components and systems (e.g. walls and windows) to be correct, as well as appropriate designs of heating and ventilation systems.

The thermal inertia of buildings must not be overlooked

It is important to point out that this philosophy cannot be employed in its entirety with a mechanical exhaust air ventilation system with a heat pump. In such a system, it is obviously difficult to turn off the heat when the supply air temperature is, say, -20 °C. It is against this background that many feel that it is difficult to turn off direct electric heating for any longer period of time in detached houses. A house with mechanical exhaust ventilation could be cold while a similar house with balanced ventilation and heat exchangers is still warm. This makes it possible to utilise the building itself for demand management, depending on the price of electricity on the spot market. However, this requires the house's heat exchanger to use the heat to warm the house, rather than heating the domestic hot water tank, which is unfortunately often done.

Simulation models and their applications

New and existing detached houses and apartment buildings can be modelled in a number of programs as is already dome to some extent. The results obtained were used, for example, in the previous sections of this chapter. In such cases, the system boundary was usually around the buildings, with tariffs and other conditions, such as refurbishment costs, being regarded as defining parameters. This means that production conditions were assumed to be of lesser importance. Other models have been used for processing the energy demand of the country as a whole, although they have treated the built environment and other end users in a more summary manner. By combining results and experience from various models, it should be possible to produce a very much more refined picture of the country's energy use in the built environment.

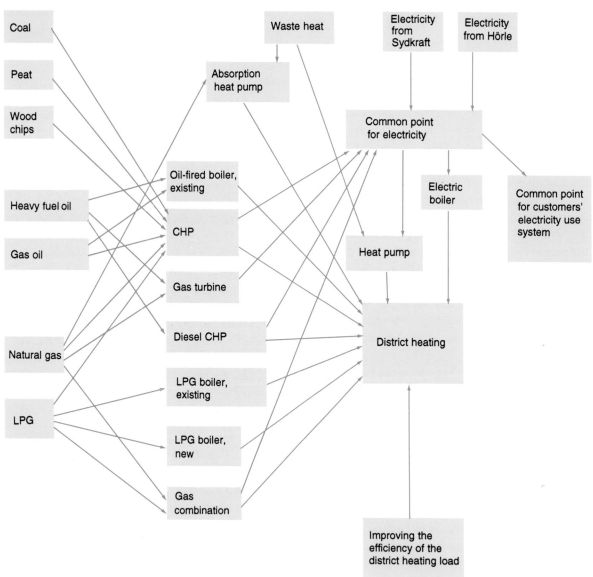

Figure 1. The Värnamo energy system.

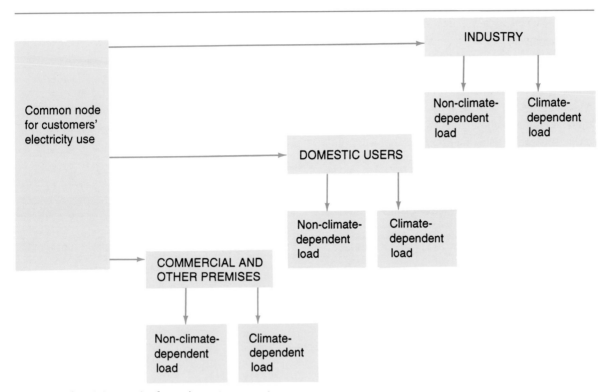

Figure 2. Electricity use in the main customer sectors.

It is possible to calculate conservation measures that really would be of value in terms of making best use of the country's resources. This does not mean only resources in the form of money, but also in the form of the environment. In addition, the method employed would mean that the system would be optimised, i.e. it would not be possible for some other combination of the measures processed by the model to produce a better result.

In an investigation of Värnamo and other towns[15], the energy system has been described mathematically. Figure 1 shows how fuel input is illustrated on the left. It is then burnt in a number of boilers to produce heat and electricity which, in turn, are used directly or to power various items of apparatus. It can be seen that the production side is relatively well described, while the district heating and electrical loads are represented by aggregated nodes. These nodes are, in turn, intended to represent industrial loads, domestic loads and a commercial premises load, as shown in Figure 2. It can be seen that the entire building stock in the model has been summarised under the heading of 'Commercial and other premises'.

What we would like to see is a very much more extensive description of the buildings in the energy system. A first attempt to do this has been made, dividing the sector up into climate-dependent and climate-independent loads. There is also a node for efficiency improvements, but this has nowhere near the degree of detail required in order to show what is cost-effective in buildings: for example, it is not possible to illustrate the effects of additional thermal insulation. Nor have more complicated solutions, such as bivalent heating systems that have been shown by other model studies to be competitive, been represented mathematically.

Today, the methodology of optimising/simulating local authority electricity and district heating systems has reached commercial maturity, and about 20 local authority areas have been analysed[16]. The financial savings have been so substantial that it has been relatively simple to justify implementation. What has been described here is how user conservation measures that could provide even greater financial savings could be identified. Energy-efficient buildings are an extremely cost-effective way of conserving resources, and this will be even more important in the future. Sweden could export both electricity and Swedish houses(!) to the continent, and introduce electric heating, provided that the houses have sufficient thermal inertia to allow them to be heated during the night, (instead of using night set-back which, from a resource conservation point of view, is directly wrong).

This chapter is based on material by Professor Björn Karlsson, Department of Energy Technology, Linköping University.

REFERENCES

1 Söderström, M., Karlsson, B.G., Björk, C. *Fri elmarknad. Produktion, hushållning och EG* (A free electricity market. Production, conservation and the EU). Report IKP-R-728, Linköping Institute of Technology, 1993.

2 See Söderström et al. (1993).

3 Larsson, L., et al. *Projekt MINTOP* (The MINTOP Project). Sydkraft AB, Malmö, 1988.

4 Ottosson, H., Söderström, M. *Teknikstyrning av elanvändning, rapport 1 och 2* (Demand side management of electricity use, Reports 1 and 2). Sydkraft AB, 1990.

5 Andersson, M. *Cost-effective Incentives for Local Electric Utilities and Industries in Cooperation, Modelling of Technical Measures.* Degree thesis no. 370, LiU-TEK-LIC-1993:12, ISBN 91-7871-103-7, ISSN 0280-7971, Linköping Institute of Technology, 1993.

6 Gustafsson Stig-Inge, Karlsson Björn, G. *Är det lönsamt att spara fjärrvärme?* (Does it pay to save district heating energy?). Energimagasinet No. 7, pp 33-37, 1992.

7 Gustafsson Stig-Inge, Karlsson Björn, G. *Lönsamma energisparåtgäder i 60-talets flerbostadshus. Fallet Grevegårdsvägen* (Profitable energy conservation measures in 1960s apartment buildings. A case study: Grevegårdsvägen). Report LiTH-IKP-R727, Linköping Institute of Technology, 1992.

8 See Andersson (1993).

9 Gustafsson Stig-Inge, Karlsson Björn, G. *Is Space Heating in Offices Really Necessary?* Applied Energy, Vol. 38 (1991), pp 283-291.

10 See Gustafsson, Energimagasinet 1992.

11 See Söderström et al., 1993.

12 See Andersson (1993).

13 See Ottosson et al., (1990).

14 Henning, D., *Energisystemanalys Kalmar Energi* (An Energy System Analysis for Kalmar Energi). Report IKP-R-720, Linköping Institute of Technology, 1993.

15 See Ottosson et al., (1990).

16 Henning, D. *Energy Systems Optimisation Applied to Local Swedish Utilities.* Linköping Institute of Technology, 1994.

OTHER LITERATURE

The balance principle. NUTEK R1993:14.

Om elsparandets samhällsekonomiska intäkter och kostnader (On the public revenues and costs of electricity conservation). Johansson, P-O. National Energy Administration, 1990:R7.

ENERGY CONVERSION IN THE BUILT ENVIRONMENT

Solar heating – energy conservation and energy production
Energy storage is a prerequisite for a change of technology
High energy prices favour the heat pump
Heat distribution – development of simpler and cheaper technology
Solar electricity – great interest in other countries
Natural gas – a future potential
Bio-energy – improved combustion technology is required
Wind power is best in open country
Small-scale combined heat and power production must be user-friendly

Photographer: Kjell Johansson, Bildhuset

SOLAR HEATING
– ENERGY CONSERVATION AND
ENERGY PRODUCTION

SUMMARY

Swedish technology for large-scale group solar heating systems is renowned world-wide and is one of the most economical solar heating system technologies. Solar heating applications can be regarded in the dual categories of energy conservation and energy production. However, in recent years, the Swedish lead has been reduced as a result of a cutback in grants and lack of funding for full-scale experiments. Although Swedish solar heating research is of a high quality, its competence rests in practice on individual workers, who are unfortunately spread over the entire country.

At present, solar heating technology is in a consolidation phase and looking for commercial niches. In the case of larger solar heating systems, the natural niche is oil-fired group heating plants and smaller district heating systems. With the backing of an organised advisory service, small-scale solar heating for individual house applications could also expand its commercial niche.

The performance of solar collectors can be enhanced by the addition of horizontal mirrors in front of the collectors, improvement of absorber coatings, anti-reflection treatment of the cover glass and through the provision of more efficient transparent insulation within the collectors.

The most important areas for research are to develop system designs that combine solar heating with other environmentally-friendly additional heating systems, to improve the efficiency of present designs of solar collectors, to develop cheaper collectors through new methods of manufacture and the use of lighter materials and to develop heat storage technology. It is also important to produce design manuals and other design aids, to provide additional training for research workers and engineers and to include solar heating technology in the engineering courses run by the institutes of technology.

Solar heating applications can be seen from two different angles. One regards a solar heating installation as part of the building, thus making it comparable with other measures adopted to reduce the need for purchased energy, i.e. an energy conservation measure. Domestic hot water systems with roof-integrated solar collectors, solar walls and solar roofs are examples of technologies that meet this description. Such systems make no pretensions to meet a high proportion of energy requirements, but can continue to work as long as the building works, in just the same way as other heating, ventilation and sanitation services. There is considerable scope in this application quickly to spread well-proven and prefabricated dual-function designs such as solar walls etc. In addition, the spread of the technology in connection with both new building and refurbishment can also be influenced through appropriate formulation of the Building Regulations. Examples of larger systems of this type, installed in connection with refurbishment, are the roof-integrated water-cooled solar collectors in Hammarkullen and the air-cooled solar collectors in the Järnbrott development, both in Gothenburg. The EKSTA housing company in Kungsbacka has built several new residential developments incorporating roof-integrated solar collectors, while the Konsolen block in Stockholm incorporates solar walls and the Kejsaren block incorporates air-cooled solar collectors. Most of the solar heating systems intended for use in private houses also fall into this category.

The second way of regarding a solar heating system is to see it as an energy production system. Systems of this type are incorporated generally in group heating systems with larger central arrays of collectors or with roof-mounted collectors. Their output is connected to a common distribution system, which may also be linked to a heat store. Systems of this type have been demonstrated in Sweden during the 1980s, but have not yet achieved financial viability. However, later system designs have become simpler and less expensive.

Group heating systems with daily heat stores can supply about 10 % of the total annual heat requirement. Typical specific performance parameters for systems of this type are 0.5 m^2 of solar collector surface area per annual MWh of total heat demand, with a water heat store with a volume of about 0.1 m^3 per m^2 of collector surface area. New systems with ground-mounted solar collectors have been built in a number of places, including Malung (1988), Falkenberg (1989), Nykvarn (1991) and Säter (1992).

Other applications in the energy production category are systems for heating outdoor swimming pools. Such systems should already be competitive due to high yield and simple installation technology, which is reflected in a relatively stable market amounting to about 2000-3000 m^2 per year. Vessigebro in Falkenberg can be taken as representative of an optimally designed system, and produces an annual heat yield of over 500 kWh/m^2 of collector area. This is probably a Swedish record for energy yield from flat plate solar collectors.

Special systems for hospitals, with a high domestic hot water proportion, have also been designed and a number have been built, e.g. in Ljungby and Jakobsberg. The market for both the system designs was felt to be so interesting that design guidance was prepared through the Swedish Council for Building Research (BFR).

Only a few parties involved in group solar heating systems

The Swedish solar collector market for group heating systems is characterised by being made up of only a few parties. This had the advantage of allowing the developers consciously to complete the design and development of what was regarded as a specifically Swedish design of solar collectors for larger systems; namely, relatively large-scale modules that could be installed either at ground level or on roofs. In principle, the collectors still look the same as they did at the beginning of the 1980s.

Technically, the design is based on Teknoterm's Sunstrip absorber. Ground-mounted solar collectors are assembled in modules of about 12 m^2 or larger. The absorber is contained in an insulated aluminium case. In the normal design, the anti-convection baffle on the front of the collector consists of an outer cover glass and a thin Teflon film between the absorber and the cover glass. This design has also been produced for integration in roofs, with the outer cover in this case consisting of an acrylic sheet. Today, solar collectors for group heating systems are available from three suppliers, all using similar design principles. Differences lie in the details and in what is prefabricated and what is assembled at site.

It is interesting to note that, after 11 years' use, the performance of a solar collector of the type used in Lyckebo was measured at the Älvkarleby Laboratory and found to be essentially unchanged. This should increase the security for the long amortisation times that need to be employed when costing solar heating systems.

Excellent performance of full-scale experiments

Ground-mounted solar collector arrays have been further developed in several projects incorporating short-term heat stores, e.g. in Nykvarn, Malung, Säter and Falkenberg (see Figure 1). In general, it can be said that these systems are operating well and are substantially more efficient than those that were built at the beginning of the 1980s, although there are some individual problems. One such is that the means of securing the Teflon™ film between the glass and the absorber is not without problems. On the other hand, it has been found that even those solar collectors in which the Teflon™ film is close up to the absorber or to the glass are operating well, with no greater difference between actual performance and expected performance. The performance of the Falkenberg system is somewhat lower than had been expected, but on the other hand the system was cheaper per square metre than, for example, Nykvarn 1b, which was built in 1991. The main reason for this is thinner insulation on the back of the absorbers, which at the time was regarded as experimental. Further cost savings were achieved in Säter (1992), and capital costs have been halved since

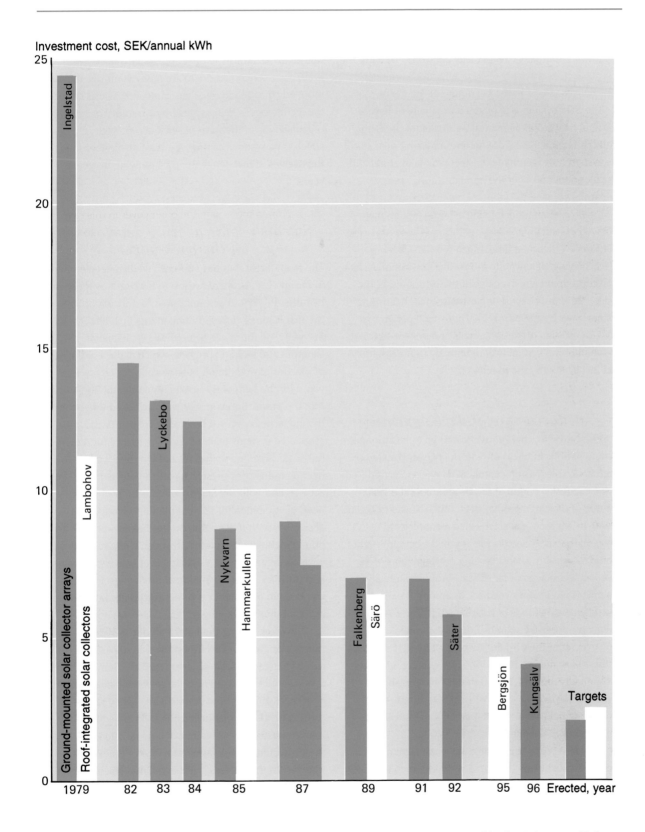

Figure 1. Costs of larger solar energy schemes in Sweden, expressed as SEK per annual kWh. Prices as of July 1994 (indexed by E84 Contractors' Index). Schemes shown for 1995 and 1996 are planned.

the beginning of the 1980s.

Systems with roof-integrated solar collectors have become substantially cheaper (see Figure 1). In Särö, the solar collectors cost only 60 % of what roof-integrated solar collectors cost at the beginning of the 1980s.

The Särö system was planned originally to have a seasonal heat store. However, as a result of problems with the original heat store design (a rock pit heat store) the system now has a smaller steel tank heat store, and provides about 50 % of the annual heating energy demand.

Price developments for single-house system have followed essentially the same pattern as those for larger systems. At the same time, much work has been put into achieving significantly more efficient system designs than those that were available at the beginning of the 1980s. Present prices of single-house solar heating systems vary between SEK 7:00 and 15:00 per annual kWh, depending on design details and system size and on whether the system is bought ready or for assembly and installation by the purchaser.

Reduced rate of development

During the 1990s, Sweden will continue to be among the leading nations in terms of performance and quality of large-scale solar heating systems. However, as opposed to the expansive period at the beginning of the 1980s, the rate of development has been much slower in recent years. In addition, the established technology of large-scale solar collectors has reached a certain level of maturity, possibly almost verging on stagnation. The Swedish technology of large-scale group solar heating systems is world-renowned and is among the most cost-effective methods of solar heating. The costs of energy produced by solar heat have continued to fall. However, after the drop in the price of oil in the middle of the 1980s, market interest in solar heating has been substantially reduced, although it is now possible to discern some degree of upswing in response to other environmental problems - the greenhouse effect and depletion of the ozone layer.

In recent years, from being the leading country in terms of solar heating technology development, Sweden has now become only one (albeit important) country among several others. As far as group solar heating systems are concerned, Germany has demonstrated a number of major initiatives in recent years, with several projects that have either been started or are planned,

both with and without seasonal heat stores. Sweden has initiated a fruitful bilateral cooperation with Germany in this area. As far as solar heating systems for individual houses are concerned, there are many countries that are more advanced than Sweden. However, as this sector of the technology is being spread by a number of organisations in the form of self-build projects, small-scale systems of this type have also established themselves in Sweden, with sales growing in recent years.

Swedish solar heating development on the back burner

The main factor that has affected Swedish development in recent years is the reduction in R&D grants for solar heating. In 1994, these amounted to only about 30 % of the real value of corresponding grants in 1984. Secondly, no funds are being made available for experimental building projects, which is the usual motor of practical development of solar collector technology. It was with the help of these experimental building loans that the production volumes were achieved that enables the industry to develop both solar collectors and associated systems technology. The lack of funding for full-scale experiments has resulted in the Swedish solar heating industry at present having a very low level of activity, and with the largest manufacturer of solar heating equipment at present manufacturing only absorbers, with most of the output being exported. In purely manufacturing terms, Sweden's remaining solar collector manufacturing industry is effectively operating as a not very impressive manual production industry: increases in production volumes would allow significant rationalisation to be carried out.

However, during the latter half of the 1980s, a number of project feasibility studies were performed that could change the solar collector market. Some of them investigated the feasibility of large district solar heating systems in Kungälv and Nynäshamn. They showed that the solar collector manufacturing industry could rejuvenate itself by a number of bold decisions. A larger project would provide a basis for one of the companies to invest in the necessary industrial manufacturing process, thus substantially reducing manufacturing costs. The most likely candidate seems to be Nynäshamn, where a now unused complex of underground oil storage caverns could be used as a seasonal heat store. A solar collector array of about 120 000 m² would be large enough to create the right conditions for halving the cost of the collectors, thus making solar heat profitable. What is primarily needed now is a form of financing that will take the sting from the high initial costs.

Solar heating technology looking for commercial niches

Summarising, it can be said that solar heating technology is at present in a consolidation phase, and that the market can no longer be seen as remote. Today, the technology is looking for commercial niches.

Results from a number of investigations[1][2] show that solar heating system costs can be reduced for present-day technology and for further developments thereof as a function of array size for both 24-hour and

seasonal heat stores. In addition, it can be assumed that the costs of small systems will also be affected by the fact that there is a steady market and that industry has invested in efficient production technology. Costs of heat storage, too, are expected to respond to a larger market, as it provides experience and arrives at methods of lowering costs relative to those of single systems.

Figure 2 shows the results of these cost calculations as a function of system size and investment costs per annual kWh, expressed in 1993 cost levels. Costs for both present-day technology and expected further technical development of solar collectors and 24-hour/seasonal heat stores are shown. The figure also shows present-day permissible maximum costs for oil-firing, based on an annuity of 10 %.

Table 1 shows the potentials for group heating plants

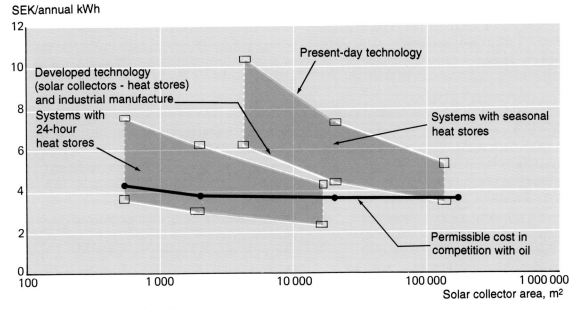

Figure 2. Costs as a function of system size.

Table 1.   *Number of typical systems of different sizes*

Size	District heating		Group heating		DH + GH
	Heat load, TWh/year	No.	Heat load, TWh/year	No.	Of which oil, TWh/year
7-10 GWh/yr	0	0	2	>500	2
10-32 GWh/yr	0.7	50	2.7	200	2.7
>32 GWh/yr	3.0	50	1.1	20	1.4

(GH) and smaller district heating networks (D H)[3].

There is, in other words, a potential for converting at least part of the oil used in about 800 boiler plants, group heating plants and smaller district heating systems to solar heating. If all these were converted to systems with short-term heat stores, there would be a market for about 1.5-2.0 million m[2] of solar collectors. If, in addition, about 20 % of these systems were converted to systems with seasonal heat stores, the total collector market would increase to about 3-4 million m[2]. These figures indicate that there is sufficient potential to realise our assumptions, i.e. of technology and market development resulting in lower costs. It also means that a conscious programme of market stimulation could achieve the desired effect of kick-starting a market that could then subsequently develop under its own power.

A rich flora
of small systems

As far as the small systems (intended primarily for single-family houses) are concerned, there is a wider range of products available on the market. However, most of these suppliers have only small market shares. The largest market share is held by the LESOL system for DIY installation, using solar collectors based on the Sunstrip absorber. The marketing method, involving evening courses in DIY construction/installation or cooperative associations, is very popular in other countries (i.e. in Austria) and has expanded substantially in recent years in Sweden. In 1994, about 7000 m[2] of solar collectors were sold for DIY installation of single-family house systems in Sweden. However, it must be pointed out that there are also other attractive solar collectors for small systems on the market, of which some are also particularly suitable for mass production and have high energy yields.

P-marking
for quality control

At the beginning of the 1990s, the Swedish National Testing and Research Institute developed its P-marking approval scheme for monitoring quality control of the range of solar collectors available. Working with the solar industry sector, SP developed a test procedure that consists of both performance testing and materials testing. If solar collectors are to qualify for State grants, they must have passed at least the initial acceptance

testing. By 1994, there were a score of collector designs that had passed this test, and about a dozen that had also passed the entire P-marking testing process. One of the results of this general development trend is that the energy yield from present-day small solar collectors is almost twice what it was at the beginning of the 1980s, so that a good solar collector in a domestic hot water system should be able to produce about 400 kWh/m[2] or more.

Solar heating systems
are only part of the answer

In Sweden, as throughout central Europe, solar heating systems provide only part of the answer for heat supply. Although a considerably oversized seasonal heat storage system could produce 100 % heating energy coverage, cost considerations show that it is best to complement solar heating systems with some form of ancillary heating system with a low capital cost. For this reason, oil-fired boilers or electric boilers are good complements to solar heating.

As far as summer heating systems with short-term heat stores are concerned, it is preferable that oil-fired boilers (which would have low efficiencies during the summer) should be taken out of service. This requires careful system optimisation. The same operating benefits can be achieved using biofuels as the additional heat source. However, the incorporation of a solar heating system can hardly affect the power demand, as this depends mainly on winter conditions. In principle, all types of additional heating are permissible, as there is little competition between summer solar heating and winter heating systems. In addition, the heat store can very well be used for storage of heat from cheap night-time electricity. However, there is little point in using heat pumps for domestic hot water production in combination with solar collector systems, as the reduced operating times of the heat pumps also reduce the time available during which they can pay for themselves.

70 % of annual heat demand can be
supplied by solar heat

A seasonal heat storage system can be designed so that the solar heating system supplies about 70 % of the annual heating energy demand, together with a given base load level during parts of the year. The top-up heating system can be oil-fired or biofuel-fired, although

A solar heating installation can be regarded as an energy conservation measure or as an energy production system. Photographer: Tomas Åhlén

cheap night-time electricity is also suitable through availability of the heat store. A typical power rating of the top-up heating system is about half of the maximum power demand. Here, too, the addition of a heat pump system is unlikely to be viable. An investigation for the Kungälv solar district heating system showed that it would be profitable to combine a seasonal heat storage system with biofuel-fired CHP: both systems benefit from the presence of the heat store.

The points previously made for summer heating systems are also valid for the owners of detached house systems. A somewhat oversized summer heating system consisting of 10 m^2 of solar collector area and a heat store with a volume of about 1 m^3 has recently been developed in conjunction with a number of institutes of technology and manufacturers. It is highly suitable for combining with a log-fired boiler that supplies the house's entire heating requirements throughout the

winter, with heat requirements during the spring, summer and autumn being met by the solar heating system.

A conflict can arise when attempting to determine how a given amount of money, earmarked for energy conservation measures, should best be employed. An interesting assessment criterion[4] has been introduced in Germany, involving the principle of the least primary supply of fossil fuel. The investigation shows that summer solar heating systems come in third place after additional wall insulation up to a certain thickness and after upgrading windows to triple glazing. This ranking order might be somewhat different in Sweden as a result of a different electricity production system, although it does show that, despite everything, solar heating systems can compare well with many other energy conservation alternatives in terms of profitability.

Swedish solar heating research at a high level

Swedish solar heating research has always been regarded as being of a very high standard. Relative to the number of scientist engaged in the solar heating sector, Sweden also has a strong position in the European research world. However, this competence and expertise is vested in only a small number of researchers and scientists, who are unfortunately, in addition, scattered throughout the country. On the other hand, it can be claimed that cooperation between institutions and between institutions and industry is better than is the case in many other research areas.

Solar heating-related fundamental research, concentrating on the solar-optical aspects, is conducted at Uppsala University. The university supports a group of research scientists in the classic meaning, who also perform important industrial technical development of individual components such as absorbers and reflectors. Other groups of scientists concentrating on solar heating are to be found at Vattenfall's Älvkarleby Laboratory, which plays an important part in the general further development of solar heating technology. In Borås, the Swedish National Testing and Research Institute has a high competence in quality assurance of solar heating systems. Another group of scientists is to be found at the Falun/Borlänge Institute of Technology (SERC), which is consolidating its expertise in conjunction with other research groups, e.g. from Uppsala and Chalmers University of Technology.

Elsewhere, there are scientists who play an important national and international part in solar heating research at many institutes of technology, e.g. at Chalmers University of Technology, the Royal Institute of Technology, Lund Institute of Technology, Luleå Institute of Technology and at the Swedish University of Agricultural Sciences in Lund. At all these universities there are renowned scientist who are boosting Sweden's competence with important work on international projects from organisations such as the IEA and EU. Sweden also has a long tradition of performance measurement technology and system design technology, which are areas in which it has contributed much to international expertise in respect of the operation and design of large-scale technology. Several of these scientists are working for their PhDs and will constitute a future highly valuable asset in research centres at institutes of technology and within industry.

A leading role in international cooperation

Sweden has played, and continues to play, a leading role in international cooperation. In particular, the country is well represented in many IEA Annexes for solar heating, in some of which it has had, or has, the management function as Operating Agent. At present, Sweden is involved in most of the active joint IEA projects. Within the Solar Retrofit area (installation of solar heating in connection with refurbishing of roofs), Sweden is both the initiative-taker and Operating Agent. In addition, the country contributes actively to international testing and standardisation work in this field. However, it is primarily the exchange of scientists and of results with other institutions or countries that encourages and advances research.

In the solar heating field, Germany occupies a special position. There is cooperation between the two countries at several different levels: at public authority level through jointly arranged seminars, study trips and information exchange programmes, and at informal level through direct links between German and Swedish consultants and research groups which have resulted, for example, in a number of joint project proposals within the EU. Denmark, too, is an important joint working partner in the solar heating field. The three countries also have good cooperation in respect of technical development of seasonal heat stores.

Short-term objectives dominate

The short-term objectives of present and future R&D work are aimed primarily at reducing the price and increasing the performance of solar heating systems. Certain R&D projects also support the transfer of knowledge from the research level to users. In the longer term, development of new and improved solar collector designs has high priority, although lack of resources means that the short-term objectives take precedence over long-term technical development.

Highest priority is given to development and production of system technologies that can contribute to improved system efficiency and more reliable operation of solar heating systems. An important area of work is to integrate solar heating technology with conventional technology, so that best use can be made of the characteristics of solar heating systems. Examples of such working areas are the design and rating of heat exchangers and consumer service units[5] for low return temperatures, and the combination of solar heating systems with low-temperature heating systems. In addition, there is a need for system designs that combine solar heating with other environmentally-friendly top-up heating systems such as woodchip boilers or small CHP units burning biomass fuels.

Solar collectors can become more efficient

Development aimed specifically at methods of improving the efficiency of solar collectors is being carried out by Vattenfall's Älvkarleby Laboratory. Starting from present-day designs, four areas have been identified in which collector efficiency can be improved:

- The positioning of mirrors on horizontal surfaces in front of the collectors.
- Improvement of absorber coatings.
- Anti-reflection coatings on cover sheets.
- More efficient transparent insulation within the collector.

Much of current and future R&D should be concentrated on these points[6].

We can now increase the incident radiation on solar collectors by incorporating reflector surfaces between the lines of collectors. In the simplest case, these reflectors consist of corrugated and protectively painted aluminium sheet. The first trials installations were built in 1994 in Östhammar, Örebro and Denmark. Theoretically, this should result in an increase in yield of at least 150 kWh/m^2 of installed solar collector area.. As aluminium sheet is relatively cheap, the result should reduce the cost of heat by about 10 %.

In addition, Uppsala University is conducting intensive R&D aimed at improving the characteristics of absorbers. Reduced thermal emission could increase thermal yield by about 30 kWh/m^2. At the same time, it should be possible to improve optical efficiency somewhat. The Älvkarleby Laboratory has proposed a process for anti-reflection treatment of the cover glass. Together, these two processes could improve the loss-free efficiency, 0, to about 0.8, thus improving the total yield by about 60 kWh/m^2. However,

anti-reflection treatment requires close cooperation between the solar collector manufacturers and the glass industry. At present, the cost effectiveness of these improvements is uncertain.

Reducing the heat losses of solar collectors through the use of advanced transparent anti-convection baffles is being investigated both in Sweden and other countries. Today, most designs are far too expensive to be considered, but this is an area that should be seen in a longer development perspective.

Storage technology is a weak link

The economics of solar heating systems are naturally also dependent on the availability of reliable and cost-effective methods of storing heat, whether in short-term (24 hour) or seasonal heat stores. Throughout the 1980s, it was storage technology that was found to be a weak link, both technically and in cost terms. 24-hour stores in larger systems, such as Falkenberg and Nykvarn, are based on traditional steel tank heat stores, as used to even out the heat load on back-pressure district heating power production. Despite this, there are still problems with expansion systems: solar heating systems are subject to wider temperature swings, and lower operating temperatures, than conventional district heating systems, which means that designs involving steam cushions do not work well.

As far as seasonal heat stores are concerned, it is the capital cost that is the major problem. By the end of the 1980s, two new methods of construction had been evaluated in two smaller trials installations. These were in Särö (using an insulated tank of spiral-wound galvanised sheet steel) and in Malung (using an insulated excavated pit heat store with a stainless steel liner). Both concepts seem to be promising designs for systems requiring storage capacities of about 10 000 m^3 of water. The tank design is also suitable for smaller sizes, while the excavated pit heat store is suitable for larger sizes up to about 50 000 m^3. However, if the costs of systems with seasonal heat stores are to be reasonable, the costs of the stores themselves must be halved. In addition to water heat stores, ground heat stores in clay or rock could be interesting alternatives. In the case of even larger systems, uninsulated rock caverns are still the best alternative.

The borehole heat store in Luleå. Borehole heat stores and aquifer heat stores seem to offer promising lines of development. Already, most of the commercially constructed heat storage systems use one of these two principles. Photographer: Roland Lindfors Mediateknik, Luleå Institute of Technology

ENERGY STORAGE IS A PREREQUISITE FOR A CHANGE OF TECHNOLOGY

SUMMARY

The recently developed storage concepts for energy storage can be divided into the main groups of excavated pit heat stores, rock cavern heat stores, borehole heat stores, earth hose heat stores aquifer heat stores and ice heat stores. Steel tanks, closed borehole heat stores, surface aquifer heat stores (low temperature) and ice tanks are all commercially available and technically proven. Open borehole heat stores, deep aquifer heat stores (high temperature) and earth hose heat stores

are almost viable and technically fully developed. Excavated pit heat stores and existing rock cavern stores are financially promising and fully technically developed, while ice heat stores below ground are technically promising but financially doubtful.

All the investigations that have been carried out indicate that all storage concepts are competitive with steel tanks for long-term heat storage. Energy storage technology has very little

destructive effect on the environment.

What is particularly needed now is to disseminate more information on the results and performance of steel tank heat stores, closed borehole heat stores, surface aquifer heat stores and ice tanks, to train operators, designers and builders, to make risk capital available for commercialisation of certain types of stores and to ensure that research and development of the types of stores that are felt to be most promising in cost terms continue.

Research in the field of energy storage is concerned primarily with thermal storage, i.e. storage of thermal energy at elevated temperatures ('heat') or at below-ambient temperatures ('cooling'). Storage technology and its applications are concerned with 'moving' energy in time, through either hours, days or months. Storage is used for purposes such as replacing expensive peak load energy with cheap base load energy or to lop power peaks. Energy stores can also be used as reserve energy sources in the event of power failures etc. In new energy systems, energy stores work in conjunction with other energy systems, generally solar energy or heat pumps.

For several years, the building industry in Sweden was overheated, resulting in overproduction. The market is now having difficulty in digesting this overcapacity of building volume, and no substantial new building work is likely in the near future. The fact is that, even if new building should increase to something approaching a 'normal' level, the additional resulting construction would be small in comparison with the existing building stock. There is therefore no reasonable prospect of introducing thermal storage techniques to the market in conjunction with the construction of new buildings.

Those market segments in which thermal energy stores therefore have their prime potential are to be found in the Refurbishment/Conversion/Extension

projects. Much of the country's existing building stock is in this sector. The building companies are today reviewing their organisations and will probably emerge leaner and fitter from the present building crisis. One effect of these internal re-organisations and of the increasing competition - not least in an international perspective - will probably be that building costs are forced down. If development goes in this direction, it would make thermal energy stores more cost-effectively competitive, as much of the cost of thermal storage is associated with the initial investment, of which the building and civil engineering costs make up a significant proportion.

Short-term storage involves charging and

discharging the store several times a year; storage periods can often be as short as parts of a day. Common heat storage methods employ steel tanks, as used in district heating systems, group heating systems, apartment buildings and individual detached houses. Rock caverns can also be used for both short-term and long-term storage.

With increasing primary energy prices and the development of alternative energy forms, a number of new storage concepts have developed both nationally and internationally. In Sweden, the emphasis has been on development of technologies involving the use of sub-surface strata and groundwater as the storage medium. Contact with the store is either by means of water as the energy carrier or, if there is a risk of freezing, by a glycol/water mixture. Calcium chloride ($CaCl_2$) is sometimes used instead of glycol.

Heat exchangers and heat pumps often form an interface between the store and the user. A control and supervisory system, with a greater or lesser degree of sophistication, will also be required to control the flow of energy to and from the store. Storage is usually controlled by temperature sensors which, in turn, control valves and pumps.

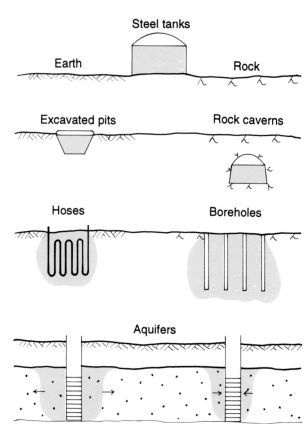

Figure 1. Some types of heat stores.

Many different types of stores

The recently developed storage concepts can be divided up into the following main groups:

- Excavated pit heat stores
- Rock cavern heat stores
- Borehole heat stores (boreholes in rock)
- Earth hose heat stores (hoses in the earth)
- Aquifer heat stores
- Ice heat stores

These various technologies have been the subject of experimental development for a number of years, and so sufficient data is now available to permit a general assessment of performance and applicability. In general terms, it can be said that:

- Long-term storage (seasonal storage) at low temperatures normally requires a heat pump in the system. Systems in which heating/cooling is provided directly to a process or central ventilation system through heat exchangers are excepted from this rule.

- Short-term storage at high temperatures normally does not require a heat pump.

Whether or not to incorporate a heat pump in the system is a matter of technical design and cost considerations.

40 sub-surface stores built between 1979 and 1994

Almost 40 sub-surface heat stores were built in Sweden between 1979 and 1994. Of these, three from the end of the period are described below.

The aquifer heat store at SAS Frösundavik outside Stockholm was built in 1987[1] [2]. It is connected to an office complex with a floor area of 64 000 m². The energy system incorporates five boreholes which are used both for injection and recovery of water. Three 25 m deep boreholes are situated at the centre of the store, and are used for storing cold water, at temperatures down to +2 °C. Two 10 m deep holes are used for storage of warm water. One of these holes is situated 250 m north of the middle of the store, while the other is 100 m south. The temperature in the warm boreholes is 14-17 °C, and 6-8 °C in the cold boreholes. The store has operated well, with only minor problems of water chemistry in the circulating water. (One borehole has been cleaned twice since 1988.)

The borehole heat store at the GLG Centre north of Stockholm was built in 1989[3]. It supplies a modern office complex with a floor area of 110 000 m². It consists of 64 vertical boreholes at a distance of 4 m apart and with a diameter of 115 mm. The depth of the boreholes is 110 m, and they contain U-shaped hoses for heat exchange. During the summer, heat from the air-conditioning refrigeration condensers is stored, for use during the winter via a heat pump. No serious operating problems have been encountered.

The aquifer heat store in Lomma was built in 1990[4][5][6]. Much of the district heating system's heat is supplied through a heat pump system that abstracts heat from the Höje River in the vicinity, either directly or via the aquifer heat store. During the summer, surplus heat is loaded into the aquifer at a temperature of about +14 °C. During the winter, this heat is recovered via the heat pump. Of the low-temperature heat input to the heat pump, about two-thirds comes from the aquifer and one-third directly from the river. Some problems with biological contamination of the heat exchangers have been encountered: apart from this, the system is working well.

Regardless of market conditions in general, there are considerable requirements on the technology of thermal heat stores in connection with any market introduction. In addition to budgets that clearly demonstrate profitability, such systems need to be simple, reliable and robust. The calculated saving must not require the use of advanced control technologies or substantial input from operating personnel etc. Systems must be simple, operating modes few and technical aspects well-proven.

Heat stores for apartment buildings

Of the country's four million dwelling units, 2.2 million are in apartment buildings. The overall age profile agrees quite well with the age profile of apartments owned by, for example, HSB (a major Swedish property developer). On the basis of information supplied by HSB, estimates indicate that about 3000 oil-fired boiler plants and about 500 electric boiler plants could be complemented by 24-hour heat stores, e.g. in connection with refurbishment.

Data on group heating plants is available from a report by the National Energy Administration, which stated that, in 1985, there were 1825 group heating plants operated by housing companies. The criterion for classifying a boiler plant as a group heating plant was whether it used more than 100 m³ of oil per year or not.

Shopping centres, sports centres and offices are the most interesting

Appendix 1 indicates that about three-quarters of the heating energy used in commercial premises is supplied by district heating or oil. The types of developments regarded as most interesting for energy storage are shopping centres, sports centres and offices. Although many of these were built during the 1980s, we can hardly expect any further new production during the next few years. Developments of these types have large quantities of surplus heat to dispose of at times. Energy storage then becomes particularly appropriate in order to capture this surplus heat and allow it to be used later. Prospects are therefore probably better for cost-effective energy storage in developments of this type than in, say, apartment buildings. Utilisation of existing tunnels, rock caverns etc. are also applications with good expected cost effectiveness.

Energy storage in larger systems

We have so far discussed the conditions relating to, and prospects for, energy storage for individual apartment buildings, smaller groups of apartment buildings or commercial premises. In a longer time perspective, we should also examine what scope there is for energy storage in larger systems, e.g. for use in large district heating systems. Steel tanks are already used today for peak-lopping purposes in many larger district heating systems. A report[7] from the Swedish Council for Building Research (BFR) states that seasonal storage of heat for use in district heating systems could be interesting from a thermal performance point of view at about 40 sites throughout Sweden. However, unfavourable geological conditions would probably mean that about 20 % of these sites could not be developed.

Another BFR report[8] from 1989 discusses the conditions for using solar heating with seasonal heat stores in large heat supply systems (district heating and group heating plants larger than 2 MW). According to this report, there is a maximum solar heating potential of about 6 TWh/year in district heating systems, and about 0.5 TWh/year in group heating plants.

Cost consideration

When investigating the cost considerations associated with thermal energy stores in a heating system, it is important to distinguish between:

■ Heating/cooling systems in which the store is a component that improves system efficiency, but where the system can still operate without the store. An example of a heating system of this type is one using an outdoor air heat pump with a ground heat store that can be charged with heat from the outdoor air.

■ Heating/cooling systems where the store is an essential component if the system is to operate as intended. A typical example of this type of store is that of a solar heating system with a seasonal heat store.

When discussing thermal energy stores in systems of the first type, a financial model should be employed that allows for the marginal benefit of the store. In the same way that other marginal improvements to any system are analysed against the requirement that each additional part of the system must pay for itself, the same approach should be used when analysing the cost performance contribution of a thermal energy store to a heating system. If an investment is to be viable on strictly economic grounds, the marginal cost of the store must be less than the marginal cost of alternatives.

If, instead, systems of the second type are being considered, it is essential to use a financial model that considers the total cost of the entire system. In this case, the store is an essential element of the system, and so there is no point in attempting to put a value on its marginal benefit.

Depending on the type of heating/cooling system into which the thermal energy store is to be integrated, the type of alternative system against which it is to be compared will vary from case to case. However, for each type of system, it is reasonable to use the type of heating/cooling system that is most commonly employed for this application as the comparison system. If, for example, we are investigating a load that needs only heating, and has no cooling requirement, and which is also in the vicinity of a district heating system, it is appropriate to use district heating as the alternative heating system, with the district heating tariff as the highest permissible cost.

Storage requirements

A need for short-term thermal storage is encountered primarily in the following cases:

■ peak-lopping in district heating systems and group heating plants (night/day, weekend/weekday, shorter periods of extreme cold),

■ cost saving through differentiated tariffs, e.g. in systems with waterborne electric heating (night/day, weekend/weekday),

■ utilisation of industrial waste heat (day/night, weekday/weekend),

■ utilisation of solar energy (day/night, week),

■ peak-lopping in cooling systems (night/day).

The need for seasonal storage is considerably greater and encompasses potentially all types of energy production systems. However, in more concrete terms, storage requirements are associated primarily with:

■ utilisation of solar energy for heating purposes (summer/winter)

■ utilisation of thermal energy in the outdoor air (natural heat) for space heating purposes and with the use of heat pumps (summer/winter),

■ utilisation of outdoor air cooling for process and comfort cooling (winter/summer),

■ utilisation of cheap energy production capacity during the summer in district heating systems and group heating plants, possibly complemented by

heat pumps (summer/winter),
- utilisation of surplus production of waste heat (summer/winter),
- more efficient utilisation of the heat from CHP plant (spring and autumn/winter).

In the rest of this section, we shall refer to the concepts of heat storage at 'high' and 'low' temperatures. High-temperature storage operates at temperature levels that require no further temperature elevation of the heat carrier (usually water) between the store and the user, while low-temperature storage involves raising the temperature of the heat carrier between the store and the user (usually by means of a heat pump).

Viability lies in savings

Regardless of the technology employed, a heat store should generate sufficient savings to meet its own capital and running costs. Preferably, the store should actually produce a financial surplus if it is to be regarded as profitable.

There can, however, be storage requirements without expressed profitability requirements. Such needs may be dictated by environmental or operational reliability factors, long-term energy planning needs or perhaps a purely development project. However, if we start from the more short-term commercial viewpoint, there are still potential requirements for both short-term and long-term heat stores in which the potential viability lies in the value of the various savings that the store can effect. Savings potentials in the form of reduced use of primary energy (electricity, fossil fuels), reduced environmental charges, operational optimisation etc. can justify investment in a heat store.

It can be seen that there are several different technical alternatives, each having particular characteristics and application areas. Another important factor in the choice of technology is the ground conditions at the site. This makes it extremely difficult to make any general comparison of one alternative with another, whether in respect of costs or of savings. However, on the basis of experience from about 30 experimental installations that were constructed under the auspices of BFR's heat storage programme, together with the results from several theoretical investigations, it is possible to provide cost indications for most types of store design.

Lowest capital cost for borehole and aquifer heat stores

All the investigations that have been carried out with the aim of comparing the specific investment costs of different storage technologies indicate that all alternative storage concepts are competitive with steel tanks for long-term storage. However, there are substantial differences in costs between different alternative concepts. Apart from the scale effect, the tendency here is that the less work that needs to be done in the ground, the lower the cost: a relationship that should be fairly obvious.

The specific costs of steel tanks are SEK 7-8/kWh, and of excavated pit stores are SEK 4-5/kWh. The costs of large heat stores vary with size, with larger volume resulting in somewhat reduced costs. In the case of water-filled rock cavern heat stores, the cost is between SEK 3 and 4:50/kWh. Boulder-filled rock caverns can be somewhat cheaper. Borehole heat stores lie in the range SEK 0.50 to 2.00/kWh. Although comparison cost analyses have still not been performed in genuinely comparable manners, most factors indicate that earth hose heat stores should cost much the same, or possibly a little more, than borehole heat stores, while aquifer heat stores have the lowest specific cost. This assessment is also supported by the fact that the largest number of commercially built storage system are of the aquifer or borehole type.

Some years before savings start

Today, we have only fragmentary information on the financial operating performance of different types of stores and thus of payback of investment. However, in general, it can be said that the design savings have seldom been achieved during the first few years of operation. There are several reasons for this, such as:

- significant problems during commissioning as a result of unfamiliarity with the systems,
- problems with control systems arising from difficulties in integrating the storage function with existing conventional energy systems,
- unforeseen technical shortcomings, due to technical complexity or unfamiliarity with new system components, and
- unexpected problems with lime/precipitation and/or corrosion in systems using surface water or

groundwater as the energy carrier, resulting from insufficient consideration of water chemistry.

Another reason for certain experimental installations not returning positive operating cost surpluses within the short time during which they are usually monitored (usually for two years after commissioning), can be the attitude of the recipient of the financing loan. This person or organisation might prefer to see the experimental building loan written off, rather than have the system perform so well that repayments on the loan become due. However, after a few years' work and adjustments, most experimental installations do seem to achieve the savings performance on which the design had been based. Where this is not the case, they have simply been taken out of use.

A difference between heat and heat

The heat that is supplied to seasonal heat stores is normally either surplus heat or easily-available solar energy. From an environmental point of view, there is a difference in principle between heat that is a by-product of other activities and which cannot be used in any other way, and heat that has been 'produced' specifically to be supplied to the heat store. In the first case, the heat storage system cannot be regarded as contributing to the environmental impact resulting from the original energy conversion process. Instead, there is an environmental gain through the elimination of new heat production (e.g. using oil). However, in the case of short-term storage aimed at peak lopping, no energy is normally saved. Any environmental differences are then associated with the plants as such, with differences in efficiency and with any local effects associated with maximum load.

The use of materials in ground heat stores is usually in the form of piping, sealing membranes and insulation, which is usually plastic, while storage tanks are manufactured from stainless steel. Plastics have varying degrees of environmental impact during production and recycling/destruction. Previously, foamed insulations were produced using CFCs, but these have now been replaced by less harmful foaming gases. Polyethene, used for piping and in sealing membranes, is relatively innocuous from a destruction/recycling viewpoint. The use of copper

can result in elevated copper concentrations in mobile ground water.

Possible coordination problems

Ground use means that natural resources will be used throughout the life of the store, and might involve conflict with other ground use. Rock cavern heat stores and aquifer heat stores make little demands in terms of ground surface area, although aquifer heat stores present a clear risk of conflict with other users of ground water resources. Borehole heat stores in rock and vertical hose systems in earth involve occupying a smaller area of ground above the store for piping and valves etc. However, the ground above the store is not rendered unusable, but can be used for other purposes. Stores in the form of horizontal hose systems in lake bed sediments or peat bogs can cover areas up to about $50\,000\ \text{m}^2/\text{GWh}$. Excavated pit heat stores and large tanks require a ground area of $1000\text{-}9000\ \text{m}^2/\text{GWh}$, which normally cannot be used for any other purpose at the same time.

Particular problems can arise when using the spaces in abandoned oil storage chambers or mines as heat stores. In the latter case, dissolved metal concentrations in the store water can be so high that the store needs to be carefully isolated from the heat distribution system, while the water cannot be discharged untreated to a recipient. Old oil storage caverns can be cleaned relatively easily, although the oil will partly dissolve in the storage water.

Minimum environmental impact

As a final assessment, it can be said that heat storage technology must be regarded as having very little adverse effect on the environment, although some environmental impact cannot be avoided. However, the adverse effects that can arise are local and limited in time. No extensive subsequent environmental monitoring is needed, provided that appropriate water treatment methods are employed. Problems during the constructional period can be caused in urban areas. From a system operating perspective, heat storage technology offers the prospect of substantial environmental gains when in operation in those cases where storage results in a reduction in the required supply of primary energy from fossil fuels.

Enhanced cooperation with IEA

In the field of energy storage, Sweden has participated in joint international work under the auspices of IEA since the end of the 1970s. This work has been concerned mainly with thermal storage in aquifers. However, towards the end of the 1980s, it expanded to include latent heat stores, i.e. short-term heat stores where phase changes in solid materials are employed, making use of the latent heat associated with changing from the solid phase to the liquid phase and vice versa.

Requests for further cooperation have been put forward during 1995. This work with IEA now includes various forms of electricity storage, such as hydro power reservoirs, flywheels, batteries, compressed air energy storage (CAES), thermochemical storage, latent stores and system aspects. IEA also wants to move closer to concrete applications. In 1995, Sweden was made the Operating Agent for dealing with these aspects within IEA's Executive Committee. Increased links with other IEA activities are planned.

Maturity of storage techniques

Some types of heat stores are in commercial use today; others can be regarded as promising while others again are unlikely to be developed to the stage where commercial market introduction becomes possible. Both technical and economic aspects must be considered when making these decisions. Any attempt to bring together all these aspects to produce some form of maturity ranking is naturally difficult and involves a large subjective element.

In attempting to make this assessment, it has been assumed that we consider both system design and market conditions, so that any heat store system best matches the conditions at site. Technical maturity and economic potential have been separately assessed. Both depend naturally on the type of energy system in which the various types of stores are installed, i.e. between what temperature levels they are to work, but we have nevertheless attempted to give a simplified picture of the various methods in the tables below. However, they must be seen only as a rough guide in an attempt to present a comparison of the level of maturity of various storage techniques in terms of technical maturity and economic potential.

This rough comparison presupposes the most favourable application for each type of store, i.e. favourable conditions in respect of system integration (storage capacity, power transfer capacity and operating conditions) and geology.

Significant factors that affect energy losses and energy quality are the temperature level (low or high), the length of the storage cycle (short or long), storage capacity/energy quantity (large or small), power transmission performance (low or high) and thermal stratification (little or marked).

Expected and desirable development

We can distinguish a number of trends in future development, either desirable and/or expected.

■ Technical development to improve performance and reduce costs should continue.

■ We should concentrate on technologies of which we have the most local experience.

■ Systems need to be simpler in respect of input from several disciplines and areas of technology.

■ Information needs to be more effective, particularly when aimed at groups with no previous contact with storage technology.

■ The number of aquifer heat stores will probably increase first.

■ When the market breakthrough approaches, we shall probably also see an increase in the number of borehole heat stores.

■ In the longer perspective, we should be able to develop stores for solar heat that can compete with steel tanks. As yet, the optimum design has not been developed.

■ Development of phase change heat stores will probably be led by industrial applications, which means that such stores may not necessarily automatically be suited for installation in buildings.

■ The framework of public rules and regulations has a considerable effect on development. A deliberate concentration on a sustainable energy system would favour the development of energy stores.

An important question relates to the work that needs to be done for the various methods. In the case of the commercial, technically developed systems, it would seem to be important to disseminate information on results and performance. It may also be necessary to

Long-term heat stores - high temperature (>50 °C)

Type of store	Storage capacity (MWh)			Technical maturity
	-1000	1000-5000	5000-	
Aquifer store, shallow		**	***	●●●
Rock cavern, existing		**	**	●●
Rock cavern, new		*	**	●●
Borehole store, open	*	**	***	●●
Borehole store, closed	*	**	***	●
Excavated pit	*	*	*	●
Steel tank	***	*		●●●

Long-term heat stores - low temperature (<30 °C)

Type of store	Storage capacity (MWh)			Technical maturity
	-1000	1000-5000	5000-	
Aquifer store, shallow	*	***	***	●●●
Aquifer store, deep		**	***	●●
Rock cavern, existing		**	***	●●
Borehole store, open	*	**	***	●●
Borehole store, closed	*	**	***	●●
Earth hose	*	*	*	●

Profitability:

*** = Commercial ** = Close to commercial * = Promising

Technical maturity:

●●● = Some development remains ●●= Development remains ●= Capable of development

provide some training support for operators, designers and builders. Continued technical development should be monitored.

In the case of systems that are close to commercial introduction, it will probably be necessary to provide risk capital in order to see them built. It is not until this occurs that it is likely that development will continue towards improved performance and lower cost. Suitable agencies are the Swedish Council for Building Research, the Thermal Engineering Research Institute and the National Board for Industrial and Technical Development (NUTEK).

In the case of the financially promising systems, it will probably be necessary for their performance to be substantially improved or for their cost to be substantially reduced in order to bring them to the commercial development level. This requires an unconditional discussion of the possibility of making heat stores of these types commercially viable. It will be appropriate to apply R&D for storage systems that are felt likely to reach the stage of financial viability and/or which is needed if a particular type of heating system is to continue to be developed.

A major programme of research for the utilisation of

solar heating has been performed, and is still being performed, in Sweden. In the long term, this is both right and essential. However, in the medium-long term perspective, it is difficult to see solar heating being introduced without substantial financial support.

Widespread introduction of solar heating requires thermal energy storage. If solar heating applications without heat pumps are to be brought about, quite special requirements are imposed on the heat store, in the form of seasonal storage at high temperature, with the ability to accept high input storage powers. Heat stores providing these characteristics and already having good technical maturity are steel tanks, excavated pit heat stores and rock cavern heat stores. Borehole heat stores and deep aquifer heat stores can also be seen as capable of promising development. However, today, neither of these types of systems is viable under the given conditions.

Further development of solar heating technology, which needs to be supported by positive political will, requires continued research and development of these systems.

This chapter is based on material by Professor Gunnar Gustafsson, Department of Geology, Chalmers University of Technology, Gothenburg.

REFERENCES

1   Johansson, S. SAS Frösundavik - *An Office Heated and Cooled by Groundwater*. Swedish Council for Building Research, D5:1992. Stockholm.

2   Åbyhammar, Eriksson, Johnasson, S. *Akviferbaserat energisystem - Projektering, byggande och idrifttagning* (An aquifer-based energy system - Design, construction and commissioning). Swedish Council for Building Research, R13:1991.

3   Nordell, B. *GLG Heating/Cooling Storage System*. Proc. of IEA Workshop on Generic Configurations of Seasonal Cold Storage Applications. Utrecht, The Netherlands, Sept 18-19, 1991.

4   Andersson, O., Sellberg, B., 1992. *Swedish ATES Applications - Experience after Ten Years of Development*.

5   Nilsson, L., Andersson, O., Probert, T., 1994. *Akvifervärmelagring i Lomma - Utvärdering* (Aquifer Thermal Energy Storage at Lomma - Evaluation). BFR R35:1994.

6   Svensson, C., 1994. *Experiments on the Clogging and Rehabilitation of a Laboratory Well in the Lomma ATES Plant*. Lund Institute of Technology.

7   Hydén, H., Töcksberg, B. *Potential för säsongslagring av värme i svenska fjärrvärmesystem* (Potential for seasonal storage of heat in Swedish district heating systems). BFR R112:1985.

8   Lundborg, H. *Möjligheter för solvärme med säsongsvärmelager i stora värmeförsörjningssystem* (Potentials for solar heating with seasonal heat stores in large heat supply systems). BFR R81:1989.

OTHER LITERATURE

Borehole heat store design optimisation. Nordell, B. Luleå Institute of Technology, Department of Water Engineering. Doctoral thesis 1994:137D.

Markvärmeteknik. Handledning för planering och projektering (Ground heating technology: a planning and design guide). Magnusson, C. and Sundberg, J. BFR T6:1990.

HIGH ENERGY PRICES FAVOUR THE HEAT PUMP

SUMMARY

The market for very large heat pumps is saturated, and it is smaller units that have dominated the supply of new heat pumps in recent years. However, there is some recovery for larger domestic heat pumps.

Maintenance costs of a good heat pump installation are lower than for a corresponding oil-fired boiler, and compressor efficiencies have increased from 50 % at the beginning of the 1980s to 60 %. The fact that the coefficient of performance today is still not more than 2-3 is due to several different types of losses in the systems. Technical development will gradually reduce these losses.

It is important to retain and encourage research and training facilities in order to assure Sweden's competence in the field of heat pumps. This also means that there is a need of training at several levels, ranging from development engineers and designers to system installation contractors.

Sweden needs to develop new refrigerants that can replace the present HCFC media and to develop components and systems suitable for them. Further development is needed of low-energy pumps and fans, and we need to optimise operating modes, e.g. through speed control. We also need to improve the efficiency of simple and reliable heat pump systems, capable of providing a high proportion of annual energy requirements, in conjunction with commercial product development.

Heat pumps provide a means of improving the efficiency of heating processes[1] as they make use of low-grade heat from the surroundings ('natural heat'), or other heat sources that are freely available. However, in order to do this, it is necessary to provide a certain amount of drive energy input. This drive energy can be either in the form of electrical energy, of fuel for a combustion engine that drives the heat pump or of thermal energy to power an absorption heat pump.

The ratio between the output thermal energy from the heat pump system and the drive energy input is referred to as the Coefficient of Performance (COP), and is always in excess of unity.

With electrical energy as the drive energy (electrically-driven compressor heat pumps), the coefficient of performance of present-day systems is around 2.5-3 (relative to the net electrical energy input), or somewhat more. This means that, relative to direct electric heating, energy savings can amount to between 60 % and about 70 %. Thermally powered heat pumps always have lower COPs than electrically driven heat pumps, often about 1.3 to 1.6 or 1.7, with the result that savings are correspondingly less (25 % - 40 % as compared with using the drive energy to provide heating directly).

The principle of operation of a heat pump is essentially the same as that of a cooling system; the difference lies in the method of use. If, in a given building or its vicinity, there are *simultaneous* needs of both cooling and heating, conditions may be suitable for appropriate systems that can provide unbeatable energy and cost efficiency, as it is possible to make use of both the hot and cold sides of the heat pump. Even if the needs of cooling and heating do not occur at the same time, it is still possible to use the same equipment to meet both needs. This involves the use of 'reversible' heat pumps which are used for heating during the winter and for comfort cooling during the summer. This is a very large market in countries such as the USA and Japan. There is

Heat pump technology can be seen as a means of recovering the thermal energy that 'leaks' from buildings. This heat pump, recovering heat from sewage effluent, is installed at the Rya heating plant in Gothenburg, and is the largest in the world. Photo: Du Pont de Nemours

no great benefit with this in terms of energy conservation, but there are financial savings, as it is easier to accommodate the capital cost of the heat pump if the installation can also improve comfort.

Greater use of cooling technology and heat pumps in the built environment seems to be intimately associated with development trends in society and with rising living standards. An investigation carried out by Ångpanneföreningen in December 1994 estimated that about 11.6 TWh/year of electrical energy is at present used in Sweden for driving cooling and heating pump systems. This is equivalent to about 8 % of the country's total annual electricity use. The corresponding figure in the USA is even higher.

It goes almost without saying that any heat pump system must be exceedingly interesting from an environmental point of view. The technology can be seen as a way of recovering the thermal energy that escapes from our buildings. However, whether it is also financially interesting for the user depends on equipment costs, interest rates etc. This is an aspect that is widely discussed, and the discussion is not new. We can refer, for example, to an article in Teknisk Tidskrift by Matts Bäckström in 1940 entitled 'Wood firing, electric boilers or electrically-driven heat pumps?', which gives a cost comparison. Although the question is the same today as it was over 50 years ago, much has happened to the technology itself.

High energy prices favour heat pumps

Success in selling heat pumps is due to several factors. An important quantifiable aspect is the potential for saving money by the user. Savings potentials are closely linked to energy prices for the necessary drive energy and for competitive forms of heating, i.e. to electricity and fossil fuel prices (oil and coal) or, in special cases, biofuels. Where installation is being considered in urban areas, the two energy carriers concerned are almost always electricity and/or oil.

Analysis of technology and price relationships indicates that there is only a relatively narrow band in which fuel-powered heat pumps (absorption heat pumps) are superior in cost terms. Conditions need to be quite special before this type of heat pump comes into its own. This is reflected in general in market behaviour (including international markets), where absorption heat pumps account for only a very small proportion. In Sweden, there are a few very large absorption heat pumps that have been integrated in industrial processes. As far as is known, there are no absorption heat pumps in use in applications associated with the built environment.

A general conclusion is that high energy prices favour the use of heat pumps. This is hardly surprising, as the savings resulting from the use of heat pumps increase as the price of energy increases.

Hard times at the end of the 1980s

Heat pump applications expanded very rapidly during the second half of the 1970s and first half of the 1980s. This market expansion covered several different size ranges and varied applications - everything from exhaust air heat pumps for single-family houses, with an output of only a little over 1 kW, up to very large heat pumps for supplying district heating systems with outputs of up to 30 MW. Table 1 illustrates various applications and shows the range of heat sources that are commonly used for different types of heat pumps.

A few larger companies involved themselves seriously in development. A large number of other companies - over 100 - later surfed on the wave and involved themselves in the heat pump market. Unfortunately, expertise in many of these companies was low: some of them promised much and delivered little. Many of them installed over-complicated systems that caused various types of problems. Much of the market collapsed when the price of oil fell in 1985/86 and the Government withdrew public subsidies. The end of the

Table 1

Thermal power output, kW	1	10	100	1000	10×10^3
Application:	Domestic hot water Space heating	Detached houses Domestic hot water in apartment buildings	Apartment buildings Industries	Industries Group heating	District heating
Heat sources:	Exhaust air (outdoor air)	Outdoor air Surface earth Rock Groundwater Lake water Exhaust air	Exhaust air Rock Groundwater Lake water	Outdoor air Lake water Industrial waste heat Sewage effluent	Lake water Waste heat Sewage effluent

1980s was a hard time for most heat pump manufacturers.

100 large, 250 000 small

The market for very large heat pumps must be regarded as saturated: today, hardly more than one such installation is being built each year. However, there are about 100 large heat pumps in operation, with an average output power of about 13 MW for each of them.

In 1994, the total number of installed heat pumps amounted to about 250 000. Of the heat pumps sold, a large proportion were Swedish-manufactured up to the middle of the 1980s. At that time, about 100 000 heat pumps were installed and in operation, of which over half were of the liquid/liquid type, abstracting heat from the ground, rock, lake water or groundwater. Most of them had been developed and manufactured in Sweden. The remainder used outdoor air or ventilation exhaust air

as their heat source: again, there was a certain proportion of Swedish-manufactured heat pumps in this group.

In recent years, the number of heat pump installations has been dominated by considerably smaller units: ventilation exhaust air heat pumps for detached houses and 'room heat pumps' using outdoor air as their heat source for heating indoor air. Swedish manufacturers produce a good range of exhaust air heat pumps, which are also successfully sold on the export market. Most of the small air/air heat pumps are imported: Figure 1 illustrates the proportions.

Some changes have occurred over the last year, and there is an encouraging trend by which the proportion of Swedish-manufactured heat pumps is rising.

Swedish heat pump manufacturers include ElektroStandard, Eufor, IVT and Thermia. Manufacturers of large heat pumps include ABB Refrigeration, while the very largest of all (for district heating systems) are manufactured by ABB Stal.

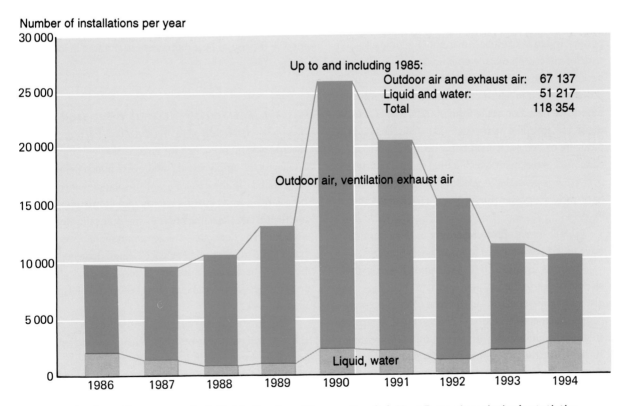

Figure 1. Number of heat pumps installed in Sweden. (Source: Swedish Heat Pump Association's statistics, 1981 - 1994).

Table 2.   *Heat yield of different types of heating processes*

Type of heating system	Heat yield / Fuel thermal content
Boiler	0.80
Electric boiler:	
Electricity from cold condensing power	0.45
Electricity from back-pressure power	$(0.35 + 0.45) =$ 0.80
Electrically-driven heat pumps:	
Electricity from cold condensing power	$0.45 \times 3 =$ 1.35
Electricity from back-pressure power	$(0.35 \times 3 + 0.45) =$ 1.50
Absorption heat pumps	$0.80 \times 1.5 =$ 1.20
Combustion-engine-driven heat pumps	$(0.25 \times 3 + 0.5) =$ 1.25

Drive energy for heat pumps

A common reservation against the use of heat pumps is that they require a drive energy input in order to work. The Swedish electricity system is based at present, as known, almost entirely on hydro power and nuclear power. In terms of global environmental impact - particularly carbon dioxide emissions - this is highly desirable. However, after the phase-out of nuclear power production, electricity generation will probably have to be based on some form of fossil fuel. Of these, the least harmful is natural gas. New condensing power production capacity will probably be in the form of combined cycles, with which a total thermal efficiency of over 50 % is possible. A greater proportion of back-pressure power production (CHP) can also be expected.

Table 2 shows approximate efficiencies of primary drive energy for different forms of heat supply.

The table assumes 10 % distribution losses in the electricity distribution system and 10 % heat losses in district heating systems. In the case of back-pressure power, electricity output has been assumed to represent 40 % of the fuel input, with heat output representing 50 % (before the above-mentioned distribution losses). The annual efficiency of local firing has been assumed to be 80 %. Annual COPs for heat pumps are 3.0 for electrically-driven heat pumps and 1.5 for heat-driven absorption heat pumps. In the case of

combustion-engine-driven heat pumps, the engine thermal efficiency, as measured at the output shaft, has been assumed to be 25 %, with 50 % of the heat energy in the fuel being recovered from the cooling water and exhaust gases.

It can be seen from the table that all systems that involve the use of heat pumps are favourable in energy terms.

Electrically-heated detached houses are not efficient

Electricity is highly suited for energy distribution, with an electricity supply to each and every house being taken for granted. In the case of a well-insulated detached house, the annual heating energy requirement is of approximately the same order as the domestic electricity and domestic hot water energy requirement. Sweden has a large number of electrically heated detached houses. This is clearly not an efficient use of electricity: heat pumps would make the best use of the electrical energy.

Ensuring adequate heat supply on the coldest day of the year is a particular problem. Heat pumps abstracting heat from surface earth layers, rock or water (groundwater or lake water) are obviously preferable in this case. Using outdoor air as the heat source, it is difficult to design a heat pump so that it is capable of supplying sufficient heat on the coldest day, as it would be grossly oversized during the rest of the year. Speed control might be one way of starting to tackle this problem. Nevertheless, some source of supplementary heating would still be required: in the interests of avoiding overloading the electricity distribution system, supplementary heating should preferably not be direct electric heating. From the point of view of limiting electrical demand, it is definitely preferable to use an oil-fired or log-fired boiler as the soursupplementary heating. Systems of this type, which can use two types of drive energy inputs, are referred to as bivalent systems, which provide the additional advantage of making a standby source of heat supply available. From the point of view of the power utilities, there is reason to encourage such arrangements - at least if the electricity distribution system suffers from load peaks during the winter.

The refrigerant question

Much of the public funding invested in research and development of heat pumps has been spent on developing heat sources with seasonal storage characteristics, such as surface earth heating, rock or water. It is in the nature of things that systems of this type are often more expensive to build than simpler designs in which outdoor air is the main heat source. As a result of the depressed market situation, these more sophisticated systems have been difficult to sell since the middle of the 1980s.

Discussion of refrigerants has been high on the agenda over the last ten years. The discovery that CFCs were depleting the ozone layer has resulted in restrictions and prohibitions on their use. The debate on the environmental effects of leaking CFCs has harmed heat pump technology and perhaps also been partly misdirected, as the use of heat pumps actually reduces the environmental impact of heating systems. Much of the research carried out in the last five years has been concentrated on development and obtaining experience of new, less environmentally hazardous, refrigerants. Not all the problems have been solved, but much development is being carried out[2][3].

Heat pumps manufactured in Sweden today do not contain CFCs. Much work is in progress on replacement of the HCFC media that are used instead. This is a more difficult area than replacement of CFCs, although HCFCs are less harmful to the environment than CFCs. Possible replacements include mixtures of HFC media, 'natural' media such as hydrocarbons[4], ammonia or carbon dioxide.

Compressor efficiencies have improved

The development of small compressors has been very interesting. If used in a well-designed system today, they are highly reliable. Efficiencies have also been improved: a typical hermetic compressor (including the electric motor) from the beginning of the 1980s had a total isentropic efficiency of 50-55 %. The corresponding figure for a 1994 compressor is over 60 %, and a further few percentage points' improvement can be expected.

New working principles have been developed, of which the most successful for smaller compressors is the use of the scroll compressor. This provides benefits in the form of good efficiency, almost vibrationless operation and a more compact design than reciprocating compressors.

Sweden leads the market in compact heat exchangers

Heat exchangers with interesting performance have also been developed. This includes development of various types of compact heat exchangers, particularly flat plate heat exchangers for heat exchange between the primary heat transfer medium and the refrigerant. In this area, Swedish industry leads the world. For liquid/liquid heat pumps, this means that the unit can be made more compact, using less refrigerant and with a higher COP as a result of low temperature differences.

Further examples of technical development can be found in control equipment. Systems with integral microprocessors have reached everyday applications. Systems of this type also allowed advanced logic control sequences for optimum operation to be cheaply and reliably implemented. In addition, the systems allow operating conditions to be recorded, which can facilitate, for example, service and maintenance.

From the point of view of making maximum use of energy, another interesting possibility is that of speed control of compressors, fans and pumps. This can be effected by using inverters for supplying the drive motors. It provides a means of capacity control, enabling the output of the heat pump to be better matched to the load than was previously possible.

Reliability
- number of faults declines with increasing age

Heat pumps have sometimes been represented as very demanding in terms of service. This was probably true at any early stage of their introduction (not least when considering the large number of parties on the market, as mentioned above). However, statistics for properly built units, and particularly for those that were supplied ready to use with complete control equipment from the factory, indicate good availability. If anything, maintenance costs of heat pumps are less than for burner service of a conventional oil-fired boiler, and

which also involves expense for chimney-sweeping. Service requirements of heat pumps have been investigated in a number of ways, including questionnaire investigations[5] (see Figure 2).

In order to investigate how heat pumps operate in practice after some years' use, about 100 heat pump owners in Danderyd, north of Stockholm, were interviewed on four repeated occasions between 1985/86 and 1990/91. The response frequency was good throughout the period. Service requirements were revealed through details in the replies concerning the number of faults that had occurred during the last year. Among the results, it could be noted that heat pumps

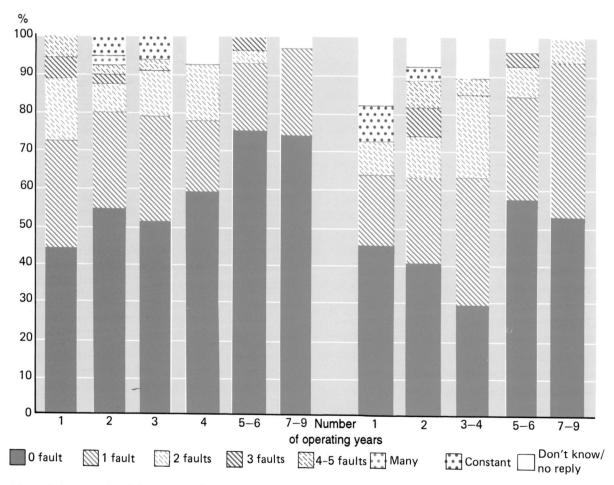

Figure 2. An example of the results of a questionnaire survey of experience of heat pumps.

that used outdoor air as their heat source had somewhat more faults per year than those using rock or surface earth as their heat sources. According to the latest set of replies, 65 % of the systems had suffered no faults at all, and none had had more than two faults. A clear effect, applicable to all the systems, is that the 'number of faults in the last year' had declined with increasing age of the systems. One reason for this may be that, after a few years' operation, any teething troubles have been cured.

COP
- a measure of
energy conservation

As mentioned at the beginning of this chapter, the coefficient of performance is a measure of the energy saving produced by a heat pump. It varies with operating conditions, and is quite strongly dependent on the temperature rise produced by the heat pump. This temperature rise is, in turn, affected by the temperature of the heat source, the required temperature for supply of the heat and temperature differences in the heat pump evaporator and condenser.

It is interesting to work out what would happen if we could build a totally loss-free heat pump. Using outdoor air as its heat source, it would need to work between the ambient air temperature and the required indoor temperature. With a room temperature of +20 °C and an ambient temperature as encountered during a statistically average climatic year in central Sweden, the thermodynamic limit would be a coefficient of performance of about 15! This means that the energy requirement for a well-insulated detached house, having a total heating demand of 15 000 kWh, could be met for an electrical energy input of 1000 kWh. This is approximately what the radiator pump in a detached house uses if it runs for a whole year.

The reason that we today, in reality, only achieve a COP of 2.5-3.0 is to found in the various types of losses. The temperature differences have a very strong effect, as described above. Losses in the cycle itself, in the electric motor and in the compressor further reduce the coefficient of performance. As a rule of thumb, we can say that the actual heat pump process itself achieves about half of the theoretically possible coefficient of performance for the particular temperatures of the heat source and the hot side of the heat pump. In addition, the energy demand of ancillary equipment needs to be considered, and is often underestimated[6 7.]

What energy requirements are included?

In order to be able to compare different systems, we need to have defined which ancillary items of equipment have been included in the total energy demand. This is self-apparent, but when defining the efficiency of an oil-fired boiler, allowance is seldom made for the energy demand of the radiator pumps, despite the fact that their energy costs are not negligible.

In order to characterise the annual energy requirement of a heat pump system, we employ the concept of an annual heating factor. In order to calculate this, it is necessary to add together the heat requirements at various outdoor temperatures, with allowance for the number of hours per year that the temperature has lain within a particular interval. It is important to be aware of which energy requirements are included when comparing energy demand for a house. Is the supplementary heating that is needed to complement the heat pump during the coldest days included? Has allowance been made for heating domestic hot water? How is domestic electricity accounted for? The results can easily be misinterpreted, and the heat pump installation is often unjustifiably blamed for not producing the expected savings.

Example:

A good heat pump can produce an annual heating factor (coefficient of performance) of 3.0, which means that it saves 2/3 of the energy requirement for heating. What it does not do, of course, is affect the demand for domestic electricity, and (depending on the type of heat pump) it may not either contribute to heating domestic hot water. A well-insulated detached house can have a heat demand of, say, 12 000 kWh/year, with perhaps 6000 kWh/year for lighting, cooking, refrigeration, washing etc. and a further 6000 kWh/year for domestic hot water production. In this case, the heat pump saves 2/3 of 12 000 kWh, i.e. 8000 kWh, and requires an electrical energy drive input of 4000 kWh. Total electrical energy demand (after installation of the heat pump) is thus 4000 + 6000 + 6000 = 16 000 kWh. This must be compared with the energy demand prior to installation of the heat pump which, if the house was electrically heated, was 24 000 kWh. The heat pump has thus saved only 8000/24 000 of total electricity demand, i.e. one-third. However, this does not mean that the heat pump is a failure: it saved 2/3 of the house's heating requirements.

Very high coefficients of performance are often put forward as being very important. A high COP has a psychological value, but it is easy to exaggerate the cost savings resulting from this improvement. This is an area of diminishing returns: with a COP of 2.5, the heat pump will supply 60 % of the house's total heat requirement from the free heat source; a COP of 3 will increase the heat pump contribution to 67 %, while a COP of 4 will increase it to 75 %.

Must not cost more than it is worth

The additional saving must not cost more than it is worth. The additional investment for a heat pump with a COP of 4.0 (which saves 75 % of the heating energy) relative to that having a COP of 2.5 (which saves 60 % of the energy) must not exceed the resulting saving if it is to give the same return on the capital invested (i.e. 75/60, or one quarter more).

Figure 3 illustrates the effect of the annual COP on annual savings for a number of cases in relation to the investment for various energy price combinations. The figures assume the same price for each kilowatt-hour of heat, regardless of the annual COP. It can be seen that the cost of input drive energy is extremely important in determining the savings potentials. The payback time has also been plotted on the y-axis. The diagram assumes an annual operating time of 4000 hours, with a marginal capital cost of SEK 4000/kW as the marginal investment cost of the heat pump.

Essential to tackle all losses

All losses must be tackled if the COP is to be improved. We need to improve the efficiencies of the electric motor and compressor, radically reduce the temperature

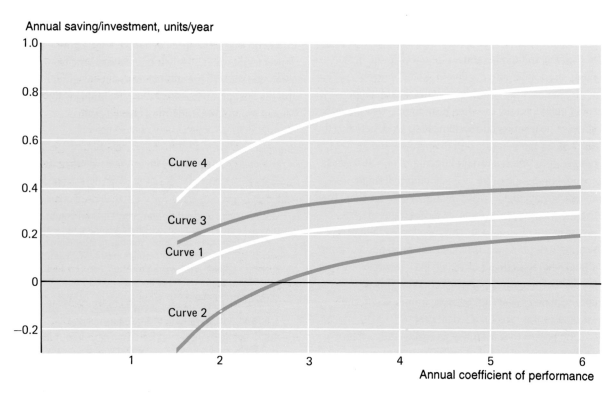

Figure 3. The effect of annual COP on annual savings. The annual COP is plotted on the x-axis, while the y-axis shows 'A' = the ratio of annual savings and capital investment (1/'A' is the payoff time for the investment). The heat pump is assumed to require a marginal additional investment cost of SEK 4000/kW, and the operating time is 4000 h/year. The diagram shows a comparison between an electrically-driven heat pump and:

Curve 1: an oil-fired boiler (80 % efficiency), oil price SEK 3000/m³, electricity price SEK 0.50/kWh for heat pump operation.

Curve 2: an oil-fired boiler (80 % efficiency), oil price SEK 3000/m³, electricity price SEK 1.00/kWh for heat pump operation.

Curve 3: electric heating, electricity price SEK 0.50/kWh (the same for electric heating and the heat pump).

Curve 4: electric heating, electricity price SEK 1.00/kWh (the same for electric heating and the heat pump).

differences in the heat distribution system, the evaporator and the condenser (using gliding temperatures on the refrigerant side if possible), and develop extremely low-energy fans. In addition, the control system needs to be optimised and output power made to match the demand, e.g. through speed control. In the same way, heat losses from the warm to cold side need to be minimised.

One of the heat pump development programmes in Japan has given itself the praiseworthy objective of demonstrating that it is possible to increase the COP to twice present value. This is an ambitious challenge: to meet it, all the measures indicated above will have to be considered.

High energy coverage and high savings

'The market' is looking for cheap, simple systems that are reliable and easy to operate. This is very praiseworthy, but can easily result in sub-optimisation. Research and development support is needed in order to encourage the design and production of systems capable of providing a high proportion of the annual energy demand and high savings, without sacrificing reliability or simplicity. Integrated systems with bivalent features are likely to be very interesting to electricity utilities in the future, as they provide a means of highly desirable demand management.

When developing systems towards the target of reduced losses and higher energy savings, it is necessary constantly to remember that the final system must not be significantly more expensive - the price must not increase by more than the value of the increased savings. Development to be supported by public funding needs to be concerned partly with fundamental aspects, but must also be carried out with close links between commercial organisations and the institutes of technology. The power utilities, too, are important parties in encouraging development along the correct path.

Research into refrigerants is needed

It is highly probable that there will be a need for fundamental research into the use of new refrigerants throughout the remainder of the 1990s. The National Board for Industrial and Technical Development (NUTEK) is supporting a three-year group research programme that was started in 1994, with industry and the institutes of technology working together on clearly targeted and application-specific projects. A prerequisite for this is that there is the necessary competence in the institutes of technology: fortunately, as a result of earlier work initiated by the Swedish Council for Building Research (BFR), this competence is in place. However, it is important that fundamental and more long-term research can be retained in the future as well. The NUTEK project indicates that the research that has been carried out has been successful and that it represents the correct priorities. Continued fundamental research is required in respect of such areas as thermal characteristics and the heat transfer characteristics of pure media and of mixtures. Low-temperature heat transfer media for use in indirect systems also need to be further developed.

Systems and components - an enormous working area

Component development and system design to suit new working media is an enormous working area. The institutes of technology can contribute to this with basic knowledge, partly in the form of results from fundamental investigations of heat transfer characteristics, with data for optimisation, through the provision of specialised measurement equipment and independent testing activities, e.g. of compressors and heat exchangers. Another area in which much has already been done, but where more can certainly be done, is the field of control, as influencing the function and performance of the heat pump. Important components on which development is required include expansion valves.

Priority should be given to greater emphasis on measures for energy saving in heat pump systems. This is an area in which research should be carried out in conjunction with companies skilled in product development. It is also important to encourage measures intended systematically to integrate heating and cooling technology: possible energy savings through the use of such systems are extremely interesting.

An important objective of research by the institutes of technology is to retain and enhance research and training environments to ensure retention of competence within the country. It is in this way that we can also follow - and influence - international development and provide industry and society with skilled engineers. Training activities are also important for this objective. Training is needed at several levels, from development engineers and designers to installation contractors.

This chapter is based on material by Professor Eric Granryd, Chair of Applied Thermodynamics and Refrigeration, the Royal Institute of Technology, Stockholm.

REFERENCES

1 Granryd, Eric: *Heat Pumps. Cycles, Applications and Economy.* Lecture at the UN Workshop on Advanced Technology Assessment Systems, Issue VI. Moscow, 1988/New York, 1991.

2 Rohlin, Peter: *Köldmedelsblandningar som arbetsmedier i kyl- och värmepumpanläggningar* (Refrigerant mixtures as working media in refrigeration and heat pump plants). Report from the Department of Energy Technology, Royal Institute of Technology, 1994.

3 Granryd, Eric and Melinder, Åke: *Secondary refrigerants for indirect refrigeration and heat pump systems. A comparison of thermodynamic properties of aqueous solutions and non-aqueous liquids.* SCANREF International, No. 4, 1994.

4 Tengblad, Niklas: *Resultat från prov med liten luft-luftvärmepump med propan/gasol som köldmedium* (Results from tests of a small air/air heat pump using propane/LPG as its refrigerant). Trita REFR Report 93/12.

5 Melinder, Åke: *Enkätundersökning av villavärmepumpar i Danderyds kommun* (Questionnaire investigation of domestic heat pumps in Danderyd). BFR Report, ISRN KTH/REF/R-92/5-SE, Stockholm, 1992.

6 Tengblad, Niklas: *Resultat från prov med liten luft-luftvärmepump med propan/gasol some köldmedium* (Results from tests of a small air/air heat pump with propane/LPG as its refrigerant). Report to BFR, ISRN KTH/REF/R-93/12-SE, Stockholm, 1993.

7 Granryd, Eric, Tengblad, Niklas and Nowacki, J-E.: *Propane as refrigerant in a small heat pump. Safety considerations and performance comparisons.* Paper for IIF/IIR-Conference, Hanover, 1994.

OTHER LITERATURE

Industriell värmepumpteknik. State of the art. (Industrial heat pump technology: state of the art). Berntsson, T. Thermal Engineering Research Institute Report 461, 1992.

Konkurrenssituationen mellan kraftvärme och värmepumpar. Miljöavgifters inverkan på konkurrenssituationen i fjärrvärmenät (The competitive situation between CHP and heat pumps. The effect of environmental levies on competition in district heating networks). Isaksson, H. and Westerlund, R. National Energy Administration 1989:R18.

Uteluftvärmepumpar i gruppcentraler (Outdoor air heat pumps in group heating plants). Glas, L-O. BFR R16:1991.

Värmepumpar för direktelvärmda villor (Heat pumps for detached houses with direct electric heating). Glas, L-O. and Figueroa-Karlström, E. BFR R28:1992.

Värmepumpar för bebyggelse (Heat pumps for the built environment). BFR G2:1992.

HEAT DISTRIBUTION
– DEVELOPMENT OF SIMPLER AND CHEAPER TECHNOLOGY

SUMMARY

Between 1970 and 1990, the number of public district heating systems in Sweden increased from 24 to more than 150. If we include the local distribution networks of group heating plants, about 60 % of the country's space heating and domestic hot water supplies are distributed through hot water mains. During the 1980s, the amount of oil used for supplying district heating decreased from 85 % of the fuel input to 10 %.

Distribution technology has become simpler and cheaper, and district cooling is now gaining ground. Sweden has a strong position in research and development of distribution technology. Research into materials technology and consumer service units technology is of high international class. Advanced methods of system monitoring, leak tracing and renovation are being developed. However, only surprisingly small amounts of research funding are made available for R&D of district heating distribution.

Important R&D areas include:
- the development of methods for inspecting and repairing networks that do not require excavation,
- the development of additives that increase energy distribution capacity in existing mains,
- the development and introduction of intelligent control technology and different types of heat exchangers,
- the development of new metering technology,
- the development of data banks to facilitate preventive maintenance,
- the development of thermodynamically efficient designs for consumer service units,
- improving the efficiency of existing production plant, distribution networks and consumer service units.

In Sweden, hot water is distributed both in larger district heating systems, which are often owned by local authority utilities, and in smaller local hot water distribution systems, referred to as group heating systems. These latter are often owned by property companies, county councils or industry.

Between 1970 and 1990, the number of public district heating systems in Sweden increased from 24 to more than 150. During this period, about SEK 50 000 million have been invested in various heat distribution systems, and it is estimated that the same amount has been invested in the 2000 or so group heating distribution systems in the country. Some of the reasons for this relatively substantial expansion have been Sweden's previous heavy dependence on oil, pollution in urban areas and cost comparisons with other forms of heating. Sweden, Germany and Denmark are the countries in which district heating is most widely used. If we include the local distribution networks of group heating plants, about 60 % of the country's space heating and domestic hot water supplies are distributed through hot water mains.

In recent years, however, expansion of district heating systems has stopped, despite the fact that about a third of Sweden's local authority areas still have no district heating services. District heating has found it increasingly difficult to compete in present-day energy markets. Even the construction of new group heating plants has declined substantially in recent years, although this is mainly due to the fact that new building work in general has practically stopped. For both types of distribution system, competition problems are most marked in areas with less dense building densities (and therefore with less dense heat loads), such as smaller communities and the outer areas of towns. The lengths of mains required become too great relative to the amount of energy supplied or per subscriber.

Another problem is that many distribution systems

are reaching the age when they need to be replaced and/or renovated. In several areas, maintenance costs have risen steadily, at the cost of general network expansion, the construction of boiler plants or establishment of new systems.

A third factor is that the heat load supplied by the existing network has fallen progressively from year to year. In 1970, specific mains load in Sweden was about 10 MWh/km of mains, while in 1985 this had fallen to about 6 MWh/km. To this must be added also the effects of shorter utilisation times, i.e. the relationship between the quantity of energy supplied (MWh) per year and the power (MW) that is needed in order to make this supply. Two conclusions can be drawn:

- District heating and group heating plants have left the expansion stage and, in most places, have entered the operational administration stage.
- New building developments that are less wasteful of energy, together with energy conservation measures in existing building stock, have reduced the profitability of existing distribution systems.

A trend towards lower temperatures in district heating systems

All existing mains systems for district heating are designed for a supply temperature that can reach 120 °C, with a design pressure rating of 1.6 MPa. The media pipes are generally of steel in order to ensure the necessary strength. Conventional distribution technology is used throughout in areas of relatively high thermal load density, down to moderately densely built-up areas of linked/terrace houses or closely sited detached houses.

Present-day development, however, is moving towards simpler and more efficient distribution technology. Most networks have succeeded in dropping the maximum distribution temperature to about 100 °C, or sometimes lower. Secondly, various methods of laying have been developed, intended to simplify branch connections and to reduce the need for compensation for thermal expansion. Thirdly, work is in progress on adjusting or replacing consumer service units with the aim of reducing their return temperature (i.e. the temperature of the water returned by them to the mains). In parallel with this, advanced methods of network monitoring and leak-tracing are being developed, while it is expected that, in the longer term,

new methods of repairing mains that do not require excavation will be developed. All this will reduce the costs of heat distribution, thus allowing areas of lower thermal low density to be connected.

District cooling can contribute to more even loading

District cooling constitutes a new market, employing a technology that has the same connections with building services systems as does district heating. As the need for district cooling is greatest during the summer, when district heating requirements are low, it can contribute to more even loading of the production facilities, and also of the networks if absorption coolers, powered by district heat, are used in the central service units. Another interesting possibility has been demonstrated in Västerås, where heat pumps that abstract heat from sewage effluent are used during the summer to produce both heating and cooling at the same time. The availability of cheap district cooling can be of considerable importance in determining the future design of indoor climate comfort systems for residential buildings, offices and industrial premises.

GRUDIS - plastic mains for group heating systems

At the beginning of the 1980s, the Swedish Council for Building Research (BFR) initiated research and development of simpler distribution systems for use in group heating systems. The objective of the work was to develop a cheap, simple technology, intended for use in areas where conventional distribution technology was not competitive. In conjunction with what was then Studsvik Energiteknik AB and the manufacturers, a new distribution technique using plastic pipes was developed, having the working name of GRUDIS and being described in a manual issued by the Council[1].

GRUDIS is a system for distribution of domestic hot water and hot water for space heating employing flexible (bendable/coilable) insulated prefabricated plastic mains intended for burial in the ground. It comprises a complete system structure for linking production units, distribution networks and consumer service units. The design differs from conventional technology, and allows for the characteristics of plastic piping such as limited strength and limited resistance to diffusion.

GRUDIS - plastic pipe technology for the supply of district heating and domestic hot water.

The pipes are flexible and can be installed in complete lengths. As no jointing or welding work is needed in the pipe trenches, the trenches can be very narrow. The method also allows considerably higher rates of laying than can be achieved using conventional methods. All this means that groundworks and installation costs are substantially less than for steel pipe mains.

The main drawbacks hitherto have been the limitations of plastic materials in respect of pressure and temperature performance, and the fact that the material is not totally diffusion-resistant to oxygen. However, life tests indicate that plastic media pipes have progressively improved, and we can today expect lives of 50 years if the maximum temperature is limited to 90 °C. The corresponding pressure limit is 0.6 MPa (1.0 MPa for smaller pipe sizes), which should be sufficient for smaller distribution systems or secondary systems.

Plastic pipe distribution systems have considerable potential for connecting areas of lower heat load density, such as edge-of-town areas, detached house areas or less densely built urban areas with power demands of up to 1-2 MW. The method is also suitable for conversion to water borne heating systems in areas at present heated by direct electric heating.

Plastic pipe systems have been evaluated in a number of demonstration projects, after which more general application started. However, there is still a need to make the method known to planning and design consultants.

Consumer service units are the link

In mains-borne heat distribution systems (district heating etc.), it is the consumer service units that form the link between the external heat distribution system and the internal systems in the building (radiator system, domestic hot water system, air heating system etc.). Consumer service units generally contain heat exchangers that provide hydraulic separation between the two systems, at the price of a certain temperature drop. Other important components included in the units are shut-off valves, control systems, pumps, pressure-holding vessels and heat meters.

The heat exchangers are generally either spiral-wound tube heat exchangers or flat plate heat exchangers. Development has resulted in the production of increasingly compact heat exchangers, with ever more efficient heat transfer. Increasingly, fully-brazed flat plate heat exchangers have replaced the classic design of flat plate heat exchangers with gaskets.

The control valves may be electronically controlled or mechanically self-powered. The self-powered valves are commonest in small consumer service units, e.g. in detached houses.

Domestic hot water may be heated either with or without storage. In the latter case (with on-demand heating), it is the thermal capacity of the heat distribution system that is utilised, coupled with diversity effects between the many consumer service units as a whole. On-demand heating saves space, but results in greater load variations, particularly when used in detached house areas.

Heat meters consist almost always of two temperature sensors, a flow meter and an integrator. The flow meters were previously mechanical, but several types of electronic flow meters now compete for the market. The two most commonly used types are magnetic/inductive meters and ultrasonic meters. As heat metering is the basis on which supplies are charged, type-testing and subsequent checking of heat meters has been introduced. It is difficult to measure both small temperature differences and low flow rates with sufficient accuracy.

New methods and new regulations

During the last five years, discussions have started concerning new technical regulations intended to complement the present regulations. This would involve the introduction of a new standard, with rated supply temperatures up to 90 °C and a design pressure of 0.6 MPa[2]. These levels would allow materials other than steel mains to be used. There are several supporting factors:

- As an increasing number of CHP plants, heat pumps and condensing boilers come on line, interest in low system temperatures is increasing. The underlying reason is naturally that of cost, as plant and equipment of these types become increasingly efficient at lower system temperatures. Reducing system temperatures will also reduce network heat losses.

- In newly built areas, houses are often designed for considerably lower secondary heating temperatures than was previously the case. This means that the primary temperatures have also been able to be progressively reduced.

This opens up new prospects for alternative system connection arrangements, e.g. with the direct connection of subscribers. Direct connection on the space heating side is common in Germany and Denmark, and can reduce installation costs in areas such as smaller detached house developments.

If ordinary direct connection is to be avoided, one alternative can be to utilise the pressure exchanger that has recently been developed at Chalmers University of Technology, and which enables two distribution systems, operating at different pressure levels, to be connected to each other, without any thermal losses arising as is the case with heat exchangers.

Direct connection is also possible for the domestic hot water circuits, using the method as employed by the GRUDIS system. As the supply main temperature is lower for new building areas, the domestic hot water temperature is also sufficiently high throughout most of the year for heat exchange to the space heating system. This would allow the secondary distribution system (i.e. within the building) to have only two pipes instead of four pipes as now, which would also help to reduce the

costs of the heat distribution systems within the buildings.

Individual heating versus district heating

Central heat distribution, and district heating in particular, demonstrated its superiority to individual or local heating systems during the 1980s, when major efforts were made to reduce the country's dependence on oil. Figure 1 shows the change in energy production mix of Swedish district heating systems between 1980 and 1990, with the proportion of oil used as the primary fuel falling from about 85 % to about 10 %.

Changing the production system to district heating took surprisingly little time, thus making it possible to supply subscribers with heat that was both cheaper and which created less pollution. There is not the same flexibility with group heating plants, where about 50 % of the energy is still supplied by oil[3]. The reason for this is probably that small-scale investments are often more expensive (in specific terms) than large-scale investments. However, it must also be accepted that there are many maintenance measures competing for the funds available to property-owners.

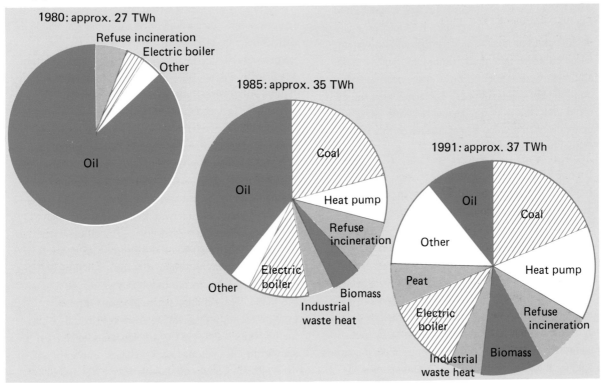

Figure 1. Energy supply sources to Swedish district heating systems, 1980 - 1990.

Which form of heating is the most cost-effective?

It is difficult to draw any general conclusions concerning which form of heating is most cost-effective. The boundary between smaller district heating systems and group heating systems becomes ever more diffuse, while the price of district heating varies substantially from area to area, ranging from about 20 öre/kWh to over 50 öre/kWh. Further, as property administrators often include their energy costs in their operating budgets, it is also difficult to determine the actual market prices of heat distributed from group heating plants to individual households.

If new areas are to be connected, the initial connection charges must not be too high. In newly-built detached house areas, these costs can be of the same order as that for a modern boiler, i.e. about SEK 20 000-30 000:-. This provides a simple, modern consumer service unit and about 10 m of supply main. However, the average length of supply main in a detached house area is usually considerably longer, at about 20-30 m. We therefore need extremely simple system designs in order to meet the total overall cost. However, in mixed development areas, i.e. with detached houses, apartment buildings, schools, child day-care centres, local shops etc., it should generally not be difficult to produce a modern distribution system based on low-temperature technology, flexible mains and mainly direct connection of space heating and domestic hot water supplies. The actual heat source could then be a central dual-fuel boiler or - which is generally even better - a heat substation in a larger district heating system.

The competence is there

The traditional research-related distribution technology knowledge exists at the established sector research institutions. These include Chalmers University of Technology, Lund Institute of Technology and the Umeå Institute of Technology. Projects, commissioned work and programmes are generally performed by the institutes on their own, but sometimes in conjunction with local energy utilities, industrial companies or consultant organisations, such as the Swedish National Testing and Research Institute (SP) or the District Heating Development Company (FVU AB). Specialised knowledge exists at Lund Institute of Technology, which has a special laboratory for work on consumer service units, and at Chalmers University of Technology in the same field. Other important areas include metering technology at Lund and control dynamics and insulation materials at Chalmers.

For some years, the district heating industry has carried out performance tests of heat exchangers etc. for use in consumer service units at Studsvik Energiteknik AB (now FVU AB). Studsvik Material AB's Plastics Laboratory was a leading organisation, with high international profile, which became known for its pioneering work on polymer distribution pipes for hot water.

Further R&D resources also exist at the country's larger energy utilities. A number of housing associations, too, have invested funds for development work in the field of heat distribution. All told, the country's distribution technology competence is extremely high on an international level.

Modest research funding

Unfortunately, the amount of funding made available for district heating distribution R&D is at present surprisingly small: a total of about SEK 10 million from the State and about SEK 20 million from sources within the industry over a three-year period. However, about the same is invested in R&D by the energy utilities and property companies directly. This must be compared with an invested capital of about SEK 50 000 million, and with an annual revenue of about SEK 4000 million for heat distribution services (4-5 öre/kWh).

As far as the industry itself is concerned, the picture is split. Today, only a few smaller piping and mains manufacturers remain in Sweden. The others have moved their activities to other countries for a variety of reasons, the main one being that the stagnating building market in Sweden meant that business was no longer profitable. The situation is less gloomy for heat exchangers and valves etc., as there are several manufacturers active in these fields, assisted also by significant international market shares. A number of examples are Cetetherm, Landis & Gyr, TA and ELGE. These companies also have a strong responsibility for R&D.

International cooperation

Sweden has a strong position in research and development of distribution technology. Sweden and Denmark are traditionally regarded as being pioneers in the work of reducing distribution temperatures and simplifying distribution systems and installations. Sweden also participates in several joint projects within IEA, and is at present Operating Agent for work concerned with status monitoring of district heating systems. The country also makes a substantial contribution to Nordic work on district heating, and plays an important part in the development of new environmentally friendly foamed insulations in a joint project with Germany and Denmark. Sweden also participates actively in international development work in the field of testing and standardisation. There is also a considerable amount of bilateral activities with Sweden exporting its specialised knowledge to the Baltic countries, USA and Canada.

Important areas of R&D

In a futures study, the district heating research development group of the National Board for Industrial and Technical Development (NUTEK) has presented its views on the needs for research and development[4]. The report names the following areas in which R&D is required, which can also be taken largely to apply for group heating systems.

■ **Consumer service units**

Consumer service units constitute a key component in efficient operation of the entire system. Thermodynamically efficient consumer service unit designs, cheap, compact and robust designs and domestic hot water systems that are resistant to lime build-up need to be further developed. An important area is the prevention of microbial growth of pathogenic bacteria, such as those involved in Legionnaires' Disease etc.

■ **System integration**

These areas include new, computerised operational monitoring and billing systems, as well as advanced metering systems with higher accuracy. In addition, methods and techniques for adaptive control of consumer service units need to be developed.

■ **Network maintenance**

Costs can be minimised by developing methods for status inspection and repair that do not require excavation. Interesting methods include the use of tracer gases and other means of detecting leaks, measurement of wall thicknesses and thermography. Methods of eliminating excavations such as internal lining and sealing of pipes are also needed, as are life length forecasts for the materials concerned.

■ **New mains systems**

Application of new materials and new methods of laying mains, depending on system size and purpose. The introduction of new standards and regulations allowing systems to operate at lower temperatures and pressures, such as plastic pipes or flexible metal systems suitable for burial by ploughing or slit trenching. Development of new CFC-free insulation is also particularly important.

■ **Improving the efficiency of distribution**

Develop additives that increase the energy distribution capacity of existing mains ('slippery' or 'high-energy-density' water). This area also includes improving the efficiency of consumer service units through the introduction of intelligent control technology and different types of heat exchangers. New meter technology is also felt to be an important working area.

■ **System aspects**

It is expected that many district heating distribution problems can be solved by improved logistics. This includes development of system models for quality assurance, operational optimisation, improvement of operational efficiency and the development of data banks and databases to assist preventive maintenance. In this respect, the district heating branch can probably learn much from other, more advanced, energy technologies.

■ **Market development requirements**

Despite everything, the situation constitutes a challenge to the sector. Simplified technology and new system designs open the way not only to improved operation of existing systems but also to new areas. Development is needed in three areas in order to increase efficiency and profitability while retaining the heat load and subscribers:

* Optimisation and improving the efficiency of existing production plant, networks and consumer service units, as far as is possible using 1990s' technology.

* Complementation of existing systems, components and regulations with technology, rules, design requirements and monitoring of simpler systems, e.g. for operation at lower pressures and temperatures that allow cost to be reduced but which also meet requirements in respect of security of supply and minimum pollution.

* Revision of tariffs in a way that encourages consumers' efforts to conserve energy. The old view that tariffs should spread the costs are now regarded as unacceptable and would sabotage the belief in 'efficient district heating' in a deregulated market.

This chapter is based on material by Dr. Heimo Zinko and Håkan Walletun, MSc., of ZW Energiteknik, Nyköping, and by Dr. Svend Fredriksen, Department of Heating and Power Technology, Lund Institute of Technology.

REFERENCES

1 Eriksson, L and Zinko, H., *Plaströrskulvert för värme och varmvatten* (Plastic mains for heat and domestic hot water). Report T24:1993, Swedish Council for Building Research, Stockholm, 1993.

2 *Alternativ fjärrvärmeteknik* (Alternative District Heating Technology). The Swedish District Heating Association, Stockholm, 1994.

3 *Energistatistik för småhus, flerbostadshus och lokaler - Sammanställning avseende åren 1990-1991* (Energy statistics for detached houses, apartment buildings and commercial premises - Summary for 1990/1991). E 16 SM 9303, Statistics Sweden, Stockholm.

4 Mattsson, C., *Fjärrvärmebranschens behov av forskning och utveckling - En framtidsstudie* (Research and development needed in the district heating sector - A futures study). CGM Rationell Planering AB, 1993.

OTHER LITERATURE

Fjärrvärme. Teori, teknik och funktion (District heating. Theory, technology and operation). Frederiksen, S. and Werner, S. Studentlitteratur, Lund, 1993.

Fjärrvärmemarknaden. Struktur och marknadsförhållanden (The district heating market. Structure and market conditions). SPK R:1991.

SOLAR ELECTRICITY – GREAT INTEREST IN OTHER COUNTRIES

SUMMARY

There are today two types of photovoltaic solar cell systems (PV systems): stand-alone systems for 12 V applications and grid-connected systems for connecting to the public electricity supply.

The solar cell modules available today are standard modules, assembled from monocrystalline or polycrystalline silicon cells or thin-film modules having an active film of amorphous silicon. The latter type has a low efficiency. However, other thin-film materials are expected to become available over the nest few years: those which are most promising are cadmium telluride (CdTe) and CIS (copper-indium-selenium).

Solar cells can be fitted to the roofs of buildings in a number of different ways. They can also be mounted on facades. The practical potential for electricity from PV systems in Sweden is estimated to be about 5 TWh/year. Today, such energy costs about ten times as much as energy from the normal electricity supply system. Scope for reducing the price depends on new manufacturing technology and mass production.

On an international level, Sweden is very passive in the solar electricity sector. The country provides no investment support, no objectives have been established for its introduction and the price paid for any electricity supplied to the public system is much lower than in other countries.

Continued architectonic and building research and development are needed for the integration of solar cell panels into building structures, and further development of thin-film modules is needed. However, above all, we need a change of attitude on the parts of decision-makers, power utilities and users.

References in Sweden to solar energy for buildings are usually concerned with solar heat - solar collectors, using water or air as their heat transfer medium, and supplying space heating and domestic hot water. Passive solar heating, too - the reduction of a building's heat requirements by appropriate construction methods and orientating it to make best use of insolation - is a known and practised method. In international terms, Sweden is well to the fore in solar heating, with cost conditions being so favourable that the 25-35 % grants available from the National Board of Housing, Building and Planning have motivated many private persons to install solar heating systems on their houses.

A different form of solar energy utilisation is the production of electricity using PV systems. This is another aspect of solar energy that is rapidly gaining ground in Sweden. Solar cells that directly convert solar energy to DC have been available on the Swedish market since the middle of the 1970s, although their use has been restricted to smaller systems such as power supply of remote telecommunications repeaters and navigation beacons. Instead of 'solar cells', they are often referred to as 'photvoltaic cells' (PV).

In recent years, PV systems have found increasing application in the recreational sector, with modules fitted to summer cottages, caravans and boats today being a common sight. Common to all these applications is that the ordinary electricity supply system is not available or that the distance from the nearest point of supply is so great that the cost of connection would be prohibitive.

By installing PV systems to charge batteries, energy is available without having to transport batteries to somewhere where they can be charged from the mains. Today, between 15 000 and 20 000 summer cottages meet their energy requirements through the use of small PV systems. These systems are available in the form of complete DIY packages consisting of a solar cell module, a battery, charging regulator, wiring, lamps and a frame for mounting the modules on a wall or roof. The entire cost is less than SEK 10 000, which can be compared with the cost for connection to the public mains, which could be anything from SEK 10 000 and up, depending on the distance to the nearest supply point. A particular advantage of the solar cell system is naturally that the subsequent energy is free, and that there are no fixed charges after the system has been installed. It is important to emphasise that, if actual energy use in a summer cottage connected to the mains is low, the annual fixed charges will substantially inflate the cost of energy.

Today, there is a growing conviction that decentralised PV systems, as opposed to large centralised power stations, will be one of the first photovoltaic applications that achieves widespread commercialisation. Among such decentralised applications it is photovoltaic systems for buildings, whether connected to the mains or as stand-alone systems, that are expected to be the most important.

Where a public electricity supply is not available, a photovoltaic supply can be a cost-effective alternative to the use of diesel generators, with such systems comprising an enormous potential market.

Integration of solar cell modules into buildings

Building-integrated photovoltaic systems represent a special form of PV systems used for power supply to buildings. Interest in such systems, with the solar cell modules forming an integral part of the building, is increasing throughout the world. The modules often form part of the building's outer cladding, and thus become architectonically and in energy terms a part of it.

An important aspect of such systems is the fact that the modules have a dual purpose. Besides producing electrical energy, they may also act as part of the roof or the external cladding. In addition, they can be used as sunshading, or can even be made partly transparent to permit lighting of stairwells or similar areas. Systems of this type are usually, but not always, connected to the mains, and are suitable for use both in dwellings and commercial buildings.

'Photovoltaics in Architecture'[1] is recommended as a good source of information for a more comprehensive view of the architectonic possibilities.

Building-integrated PV systems have many

advantages over large centralised systems or non-integrated systems:

- Their use results in an architectonically uncluttered design that is considerably more attractive than non-integrated arrangements (with solar modules mounted on supporting frameworks or in ground-level arrays). The aesthetic value can be an important factor in penetrating a potentially large market.
- Building-integrated photovoltaic systems replace conventional building materials and their installation costs, reducing the cost of the photovoltaic system. In addition, integration of such systems in a building means that their foundation and framework mounting costs are already paid.
- An important advantage of decentralised grid-connected systems is that the electrical energy is produced where it is used. This eliminates both transmission and conversion losses, which can amount to as much as 25-30 %.
- Finally, these systems have a number of other advantages that are shared with all PV systems. PV systems have no moving parts that can wear out, no fuel costs and the energy produced by them is sustainable, with no environmental pollution.

Low-power use of domestic electricity

Domestic electricity is generally used at 230 V AC and at relatively low powers. If we disregard houses with electric heating, the normal rating of the main supply fuse is 16 A, equivalent to a power of 3.5 kW per phase. (Swedish houses are normally connected to a three-phase supply.) Maximum power demand is likely to be from the cooker and any immersion heater.

Typical annual energy use for purely domestic electricity (i.e. excluding heating) is somewhat over 3000 kWh per detached house or apartment (see Appendix 1). A PVsystem installation, with a peak power rating of 3 kW, can produce an annual output of about 3000 kWh in Sweden.

The Association of Swedish Electric Utilities' 1991 report[2] shows that about 40 % of Swedish domestic electricity use occurs during the period from April to September (inclusive), and that the mean power demand during the day is about 0.5 kW (somewhat lower during the summer and somewhat higher during the winter). A

PV system installation on the latitude of Stockholm would produce about 80 % of its annual energy output during the same period.

Large power stations or small individual systems

As far as more large-scale use of PV systems is concerned, such that the energy produced would have a noticeable effect on a country's total energy supply, there are two lines of international development. One is to build large centralised PV power stations, with the direct current being converted to alternating current in an inverter, after which it would be supplied to the distribution system. The second alternative is to employ a decentralised arrangement, with a large number of smaller grid-connected systems installed on the roofs or walls of buildings. Most of the energy would be used where it was produced, with any surplus being fed into the grid.

At the international level, both the above alternatives are being tried, although development during the last few years has been increasingly concentrated on the smaller individual systems. Development started in Europe, with Switzerland, Germany, Holland and Austria as leading countries. The USA and Japan subsequently joined in the trend, and large demonstration and technology development projects have been built, and are being operated, in those countries.

Switzerland and Germany first

Switzerland today has about 500 grid-connected individual house systems, with an average power rating of 3 kW. The country has a large number of small power utilities, many of which have shown themselves very willing to receive surplus energy from the PV systems. One way of doing this is to allow the house's electricity meter to run backwards when the house is producing surplus electricity.

Germany is operating a project under the name of the '1000 Roofs Project'. The original 1000 systems increased in number as a result of the fall of the Wall, so that there are now about 2250 PV system installations, with the Federal Government bearing about 50 % of the cost and the Länder Governments bearing a further 20 %. This total 70 % subsidy relates to small grid-connected systems, with power outputs in the range 1-5 kW, for single and two-family houses and with an upper total cost limit of DEM 27 000 per kW. In Germany, as in Switzerland, there are power utilities which, in certain cases, even pay considerably more for electricity from PV systems than they charge householders for the electricity that the latter buy from the utilities.

In its New Sunshine Project, Japan has started an important programme with its Ministry of International Trade and Industry (MITI) paying two-thirds of the installation cost of single-house systems with a maximum output of 3 kW. 1000 systems were planned for 1994, the first year of the programme. Over a period of seven years, it is intended to install 62 000 systems, with a total power rating of 185 MW. The two-thirds cost subsidy will apply for the first three years, and thereafter be progressively phased out over seven years.

Sweden is active in the field of building-integrated photovoltaic systems (BIPV) through its participation in the IEA Solar Heating and Cooling Programme, Task 16, PV in Buildings project. The objective of Task 16 is to increase awareness of BIPV, both in respect of its architectonic aspects and of purely technical aspects.

Stand-alone PV systems - DC used for battery charging

Stand-alone systems are those in which the direct current from the solar cells charges batteries for use at 12 V. Systems of this type are common today for summer cottage installations. The cost of a complete system, capable of providing power needed during the summer for lighting and radio/television, is about SEK 7000:- for a PV module power output rating of about 50 W. There are also a few larger installations of this type in Sweden: the largest is on the island of Huvudskär in the Stockholm archipelago, where 16 modules, with a total output power of 1 kW, are mounted on the roof of the old Customs House.

Grid-connected PV systems - DC converted to AC

The second main category of PV system is that in which the DC output of the cells is converted to AC in an inverter, connected to the public electricity supply. Installations of this type range in size from 1 kW and upwards. In principle, there is no technical difference between a smaller installation on the roof of a house and a ground array power station. Sweden has five such installations in operation today, of which the largest (10 kW) is installed on the Ringen Shopping Centre on Södermalm in Stockholm. This was commissioned in 1993, is owned by Stockholm Energi and is Sweden's contribution to IEA Task 16. Each country involved in Task 16 undertakes to build and evaluate the performance of at least one single-house system of this type.

Standard modules and thin-film modules

The solar cell modules that are used today are usually standard modules of the type that has been available on the market for the last 10-15 years. Their lives can be expected to be of the order of 20-30 years.

The standard module consists of monocrystalline or polycrystalline silicon cells, connected in series as required to produce a suitable output voltage - usually about 15 V - for charging of batteries. The conversion efficiency of these cells is about 15 %, which means that the efficiency of the entire module (i.e. of the whole surface area, including the frame) is about 12 %. In Sweden, a module of this type can produce about 100 kWh/m^2, year. Production of larger modules has started in recent years: previously, an output of 50 W per module was the maximum output power, but it is now common for module outputs to be over 100 W. It is also possible to purchase modules without frames, in the form of laminated sheets, which makes it easier to integrate them in roofs or facades. In Switzerland and some other countries, a number of smaller companies have started manufacturing modules intended specifically for buildings.

Solar cell modules are also manufactured in Sweden. The company is called Gällivare Photovoltaics (GPV), and started production in 1992. The range comprises solar cell modules with 55 W or 110 W outputs, available with or without frames. GPV also supplies special modules to suit specific requirements.

Another type of module available on the market is the thin-film module, having an active layer of amorphous silicon. The advantage of this type of cell is its extremely low use of materials and suitability for high-volume production methods. Together, these two factors result in a lower cost per unit of area than for the crystalline silicon cells. However, the major drawback is

that this type of cell has a low efficiency (about 5 %). The Finnish company, Neste, manufactures amorphous thin-film modules in France. Other thin-film materials are expected to become available on the market over the next few years, with efficiencies exceeding 10 %. Materials that seem most promising in this context are cadmium telluride (CdTe) and copper-indium-selenium (CIS). Working with the Royal Institute of Technology, IMC in Kista has achieved efficiencies of over 16 % on small surface areas. An architectonic advantage of thin-film modules is the ability to produce a visually more regular surface than can be done with silicon cell modules.

Four ways of mounting solar cells on roofs

Mounting solar cell modules on south-facing roofs is the best way of making the most use of sunlight. This provides both an optimum slope and reduces the risk of shading from trees or other buildings.

There are four different ways of mounting solar cell modules on roofs: directly, integrated, stand-off and on a frame.

- **Direct mounting** means that the modules are fitted in direct contact with the existing roof. This method is relatively simple and saves the cost of extra support structures. The drawback is the high cell temperature that can be reached, and which reduces output power from the modules by about 0.4 % per degree C. Vattenfall Utveckling in Älvkarleby has tested a method in which laminated cells are adhesively bonded to corrugated sheet.

- **Integrated mounting** means that the modules replace the outer layer of the roof. Integrated mounting is intended primarily for new building work, and can produce a more aesthetically pleasing result. An additional advantage is the saving resulting from replacement of other roof covering materials. The drawback is that careful design is required in order to avoid problems with leakage. Special 'tile modules' have been developed in order to facilitate this type of installation.

- **Stand-off mounting** means that the modules are fitted to a structure that provides an airgap between the roof and the module. This provides good cooling of the modules by convection, while its simplicity means that it is the method most commonly used

204

Solar cells can be mounted in a number of ways, on roofs or walls. At present, electricity generated by them costs about ten times as much as mains electricity. Potential for price reduction lies in new technology and mass production.

today. The drawback is primarily the appearance of the whole, and the fact that there are no savings in conventional roofing materials.

- **Frame mounting** is a method that is used primarily on flat roofs, so that the modules can be mounted at a suitable angle. As such installations are not visible from ground level, appearance is of no particular importance.

Facade mounting of solar cells is architectonically interesting

Although the incident radiation angle is less suitable on a vertical surface than on a sloping surface, mounting of cells on facades may become a widely used method. In addition to producing energy, the modules can provide an architectonically interesting facade. This is particularly the case when the building has glass cladding so that parts of the cladding can be replaced by solar cell modules. The appearance of the modules then becomes important: colour and size should preferably match the other cladding elements. Alternatively, the modules can be used to provide some form of patterning of the facade.

There are also other ways in which solar cells can be mounted:

- Through fitting standard modules on an existing facade, in such a way as to provide a decorative function. An example of this, dating from 1994, can be seen on the newly built County Museum in Härnösand.
- As laminates, bonded directly to the metal wall of a factory to provide a low-cost method of mounting.
- Specially manufactured transparent thin-film modules as wall elements in stairwells, glazed verandas or other areas where light admission is required.

Grid-connected PV systems for buildings

A grid-connected PV system is intended to be able to supply electricity both to the building on which it is mounted and to the public electricity supply. Its main elements are the solar cell modules, an inverter and two meters, one recording the electricity supplied to the public network and one for electricity purchased from it (see Figure 1).

A common size of a grid-connected PV system of this type, suitable for a single-family house, is 3 kW. With the modules commonly used today, this means that it requires an area of about 25 m^2 which, in most cases, leaves sufficient space for installation of a solar heating system as well.

Two types of inverter

The second important component in a system of this type is the inverter that converts DC from the solar cells to AC, either at 230 V single-phase or at 400 V three-phase. There are two types of converter; self-commutating and mains-commutating. The self-commutating inverters generate the correct frequency from their internal circuitry, and can thus continue to operate independently even if the mains supply is not connected. This means that, if the system also incorporates batteries, a supply of AC can be maintained to the building during shorter power failures. The duration of such a supply depends naturally on the storage capacity of the batteries.

Mains-commutated inverters, on the other hand, require the mains supply to be connected in order to operate. If the supply is interrupted, inversion will stop. However, this can be an advantage, as it is important that the system should not unintentionally supply energy to a system that has been disconnected for service work.

An important function of all inverters is the Maximum Power Point Tracker (MPPT) which ensures that the solar cells are operating at their maximum power point. A solar cell produces maximum power at a voltage that depends on the level of incident solar radiation and the cell temperature at the time. As both insolation and temperature are constantly changing, the output voltage needs to be correspondingly varied in order to ensure maximum output, which is the purpose of the MPPT feature.

5 TWh of seasonal storage in hydro power reservoirs

In the case of decentralised PV systems, building roofs and walls provide suitable mounting positions. An investigation performed by VBB[3] estimates that, at the end of the century, there will be about 160 million m^2 of roof surface area in Sweden suitable for fitting solar cells.

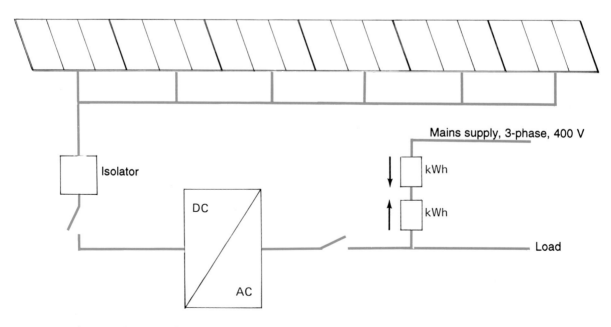

Figure 1. Schematic diagram of a photovoltaic solar cell system operating in parallel with the mains.

Insolation on these surfaces amounts to about 1000 kWh/ m², year. Assuming continued improvement in the efficiency of solar cells, a system efficiency of 20 % would represent a potential of about 32 TWh/year of PV system electricity output. However, the practical potential would be considerably less, as much of this energy would have to be stored for use during the winter. According to VBB, about 5 TWh/year could be stored in the country's hydro power reservoirs, thus making up the practical potential.

A major advantage of mounting PV cell systems on buildings is that the electricity is produced where it is to be used and at the right voltage level, reducing transmission and conversion losses. However, the amount of energy that can be used directly depends on how well production and use track each other during the day. Domestic electricity use naturally varies, as does insolation, and it is not particularly likely that the two would track each other. However, it is relatively simple to introduce load control devices that would start certain domestic appliances when electricity is available. For example, much energy could be used for water heating if no other load needed to be supplied at the time. On the other hand, if the local electricity utility is prepared to purchase surplus power for a good price, such load control would be less important.

PV systems are ten times too expensive

By far and away the greatest obstacle in the way of wider use of PV systems today is their high cost. SEK 80/W is a good approximation of the cost of a grid-connected PV system today. In Sweden, each installed watt can produce about 1 kWh/year, and its life is expected to be of the order of 20-30 years. The resulting energy cost will vary, depending on the method of costing employed and on the interest rates used. However, it is impossible to avoid the conclusion that electricity from PV systems today is about ten times as expensive as electricity purchased from the grid.

However, there are undoubtedly potentials for major cost reductions, based both on new technology and the benefits of large-scale production. Thin-film CdTe and CIS modules will almost certainly be available on the market within the next 5-10 years. Their production technology is suitable for large-scale manufacture, while the amount of materials used in them is very low, so that the resulting price is likely to be considerably less than present-day prices. One condition, of course, is that the size of the market should increase, although increasing environmental pressure is likely to assist this. In addition, many buyers today are already prepared to pay a higher price for 'green' products, ranging from fruit and vegetables to clothes produced from biocide-free fabrics. There are no doubt also many persons who are prepared to pay a higher price for their energy for the same reason.

At times, these installations will produce more energy than is being used in the house. This will therefore require two separate energy meters; one registering energy purchased from the supplier and one registering energy supplied back to the mains. The Association of Swedish Electrical Utilities has published recommendations for connections of such systems to the mains, and there are also recommendations concerning the payment aspects. At present, a private person who supplies energy back to the mains receives only about 50 % of what he/she would pay for the energy. This means that savings are greatest when as much as possible of the solar electricity is used within the house.

Sweden among the most passive

Within the IEA Photovoltaic Power Systems programme, a summary[4] describes the national situations in this sector. From this, it can be seen that Sweden is unfortunately one of the most passive countries.

- Only Sweden, Finland and Portugal have no Government programmes to support the use of PV systems.
- Eight countries (of which Sweden is not one) have established objectives for the use of PV systems: 50 MW in Switzerland, Japan and USA by 2000, 30 MW in Canada by 2000, 25 MW in Italy by 1995 and so on.
- Only Sweden and Turkey have no investment grants for PV systems. Grants of up to 80-90 % of the system cost are available in France and Italy for stand-alone systems in cases where such systems are cheaper than conventional mains connection. The corresponding grant in Germany is up to 70 %, while Japan provides 50-67 %, Switzerland 30-50 % and Canada 33-72 %.
- Buy-back rates are higher in most other countries than in Sweden. Sweden sets the rate on the basis of

avoided costs, equivalent to about 25-30 öre/kWh. This can be compared with 60 öre/kWh in Denmark and Finland, 70 öre/kWh in Germany and at least 80 öre/kWh in Switzerland.

Attitudes must change

The greatest obstacles in the way of wider use of PV systems in the built environment are the high initial cost and the attitude of decision-makers, power utilities and the general public. The cost of electrical energy produced by PV systems is high in comparison with the cost of conventional electricity. Our low electricity prices, in conjunction with the low buy-back price for solar electricity, also constitute part of the problem. A further problem is to be found in Sweden's energy policy and its effects in this context. The general public needs to receive the right signals in order to be motivated to go in for new energy technology.

Today, the most important development area is solar cell modules and their costs. The answer is probably to be found in the use of thin-film modules, and particularly of CIS modules. Sweden is one of the leading countries in this area, and the prospects for Swedish manufacture look favourable.

Inverters are another important area. Several good designs are available on the European market, and prices will undoubtedly fall as manufacturing volumes increase.

This chapter is based on material by Mats Andersson, MSc., Catella Generics AB, Kista.

REFERENCES

1 *Photovoltaics in Architecture*; O. Humm, P. Toggweiler; Birkhäuser Verlag, Basel, Switzerland, 1993.

2 Association of Swedish Electric Utilities, Annual Report, 1991.

3 *Solceller i bebyggelsen* (Solar Cells in the Built Environment). Efn/LET 1984:18. Details in a report to Efn project no. 5260241, Construction Potential, VBB.

4 IEA Photovoltaic Power Systems, Task 1, Exchange and Dissemination of Information on Photovoltaic Power Systems. Status report, for publication at the beginning of 1995.

OTHER LITERATURE

Byggnadsintegrerade solcellssystem (Building-integrated solar cell systems). IEA Project PV in buildings. Annual Report 1994. Perers, B., Spante, L., Thunell, G., Andersson, M. and Holmström, S. Elforsk report 94:15.

Solceller. Forskning, teknik och ekonomi (Solar cells. Research, technology and costs). NUTEK 1993.

NATURAL GAS
– A FUTURE POTENTIAL

SUMMARY

Internationally, the market for natural gas has grown substantially in recent years. In Europe, natural gas' market share is now about 20 %, or 300 000 million m³/year. Of this, Sweden uses about 800 million m³/year. Market development in Sweden is along two lines: acquisition of new customers for established technology and the introduction of new technology.

The most important research requirements are:

■ a systematic review of unconventional applications for gas as used in other countries,

■ the development of systems suited to Swedish conditions,

■ the production and verification of computer programs for designing and placing infra-red heaters,

■ demonstration installations of infra-red heaters,

■ theoretical and experimental investigations of new types of boilers employing catalytic burners, pulsed combustion and sand bed combustion.

In addition, further knowledge is needed in respect of condensing technology and the interaction between condensing boilers, the rest of the heating system and the building. As far as the use of gas for cooling and micro-CHP production are concerned, we should monitor international development.

In Sweden, current energy gases - i.e. gases of which the energy content is used for heating, electricity production, powering of vehicles, industrial processes etc. - are natural gas, LPG, town gas, biogas, producer gas, blast furnace gas and hydrogen.

As far as the use of gas in buildings is concerned, it is in practice only town gas and natural gas that are used. Biogas produced in sewage treatment plants and waste tips is not transported over any longer distances but is used either in premises on the site or in boilers supplying district heating systems. Most of the LPG supplied is used in industry and in heating plants, with a small amount being used in holiday cottages, caravans and boats.

Coking gas and blast furnace gas are produced in few steel works and are used on site. The hydrogen that is produced in Sweden, mostly within the petroleum industry, is used mainly in the production plants concerned.

In 1992, Sweden used 0.5 TWh of town gas and 8.0 TWh of natural gas[1]. Town gas customers, amounting to about 150 000 in total, are in Stockholm and Gothenburg, and most of the gas is used for cooking, with a lesser part being used for heating.

The natural gas trunk main extends from Malmö to Gothenburg, with connections to 26 communities along, or close to, the line. In these areas, natural gas supplies 20 - 25 % of total energy needs.

Natural gas supplies are made up as follows:

	Percentage	*TWh*
Power and heat plant	*47*	*3.8*
Industry	*38*	*3.0*
Residential, service etc.	*15*	*1.2*
Total	*100*	*8.0*

The rest of this chapter concentrates on natural gas, although many matters concerned with technical development etc. are also relevant for other energy gases, e.g. LPG.

The main reason for the introduction of natural gas to Sweden in 1985 was an energy policy decision to 'diversify' the Swedish energy system and thus help to reduce the relatively high dependence on oil. Some parties also saw the introduction of natural gas as a first step towards the phase-out of nuclear power production. However, natural gas does have advantages of its own, which mean that in many cases it is superior to alternative fuels. Gas is easy to distribute and has a high energy density. It produces very little pollution, and the environmental problems that can arise depend on the combustion process as such, rather than on the actual fuel.

The fact that natural gas is a gaseous fuel also makes it suitable for applications for which oil or solid fuels are not realistic alternatives. Examples of such applications, of which some are applicable to the use of gas in buildings, are:

■ infra-red radiation heaters
■ fibre burners
■ catalytic burners
■ regenerative burners
■ fuel cells
■ directly-heated drying cylinders
■ combustion heat exchangers ('sand box' type)
■ domestic applications such as cooking stoves, tumble dryers and air conditioning.

Substantial increase in the natural gas market

Internationally, the natural gas market has grown substantially in recent years. In Europe, the market share of natural gas is now about 20 % which, in real figures, means about 300 000 million m³/year[2].

Since natural gas was introduced in Sweden in 1985, its use has increased steadily, to its present value of about 800 million m³/year. The backbone of the distribution system stretches from Malmö in the south northwards to Gothenburg, with branches to 26 towns along, or in the vicinity of, it. In these towns, natural gas supplies 20-25 % of the total energy supply[3].

At present, no further extension of the trunk main is planned, nor are any larger expansions of the regional distribution networks along the trunk main route. There are plans to extend the Hyltebruk main to Värnamo and to run a connection from Trelleborg to Ystad, although no decisions have yet been made.

A project that is at the discussion stage is a pipe from the Norwegian Haltenbank field to Finland via Sweden. If this project comes to fruition, it can be assumed that a number of central Swedish towns and companies would be connected to the pipe.

During the next few years, market development must be restricted to established natural gas areas through an increase in the number of their customers. This can be done along two parallel lines:

1. Acquisition of new customers for established methods of use of gas.
2. The introduction of new technology particularly suitable for natural gas.

'New technology', in this context, refers both to technology that is already established in other countries but which has not yet been employed in Sweden, and to technology which is under development, either at the national or at the international level.

It is estimated that application of both the above market paths would find a relatively large potential for further use of natural gas, and that the use of gas in buildings could be increased from the present 1.2 TWh/year to 2.4 TWh/year by 2010.

Applications for gas[4]

- **Space heating using conventional boilers.** Gas can be used in everything from large CHP power stations to small decentralised individual room heaters or IR panels installed directly in the area to be heated. The boundary for 'gas in buildings' has been drawn at boilers installed in the building to be heated, i.e. district heating and group heating are not considered here.

  In addition to low costs, an objective of the gas alternative is to simplify system designs (including that of flue gas systems) to reduce environmental impact and to improve efficiency. These are also the objectives of research and development.

  Of the gas that is at present used for space heating, most is supplied to boilers in apartment buildings, most of which, in turn, have replaced older oil-fired boilers. However, in some cases, the existing oil-fired boiler has been retained and the burner replaced by a gas burner.

  Conversions of this type that have been carried out to date are of essentially mundane nature, and have not needed to be supported by any special research or development programmes. Even in those cases where an oil-fired boiler has been replaced by a condensing gas boiler, only known technology has been involved.

  As far as gas heating of detached houses is concerned, most has been provided by new gas boilers installed in new houses. Known and commercial technology results in good designs in terms of high efficiency and low NO_x emissions. However, there is potential for improvement, e.g. in improved interaction between the building and heating system, improvement of condensation methods and continued development of pulsed combustion.

- **Space heating using IR radiant heaters.** IR radiant heaters are used in this context primarily for heating commercial premises, such as stores, although they can also be used in 'small-scale' applications, e.g. for domestic verandas and terraces. Several makes of gas-fired radiant heaters are available on the market, and some consultants also have suitable computer programmes for determining ratings and positions. The market for gas-fired radiant heaters is very small in Sweden.

- **Space heating using heat pumps.** Heat pumps that use gas as their energy supply may be of compressor type or absorption type. In the first type, the compressor is driven by a gas engine, which can be a conventional Otto cycle engine or, for example, a Stirling engine. An absorption heat pump is almost silent, but has a lower coefficient of performance than a compressor heat pump.

  In Sweden, all small-scale heat pumps are powered by electricity. The price relationship between electricity and gas is such that, at present, gas-powered heat pumps are not competitive.

- **Other space heating.** Other applications for which gas is suitable include open fires, tiled stoves, conventional stoves and gas convector heaters.

  A gas-fired mock fire, consisting of atmospheric gas burners with ceramic or lava coals or logs, can be installed in an existing open fireplace. At present, only one type-approved fireplace insert is available in Sweden for use with natural gas. In the traditional Swedish tiled stove, the flue gases are led through passages in the firebrick in the interior of the stove, so that heat is stored in the bricks and released to the room over a period of several hours. Newer designs incorporate an integral heat exchanger, to provide a more immediate flow of warmed air. Air from the room enters at the bottom of the stove, is heated by the flue gases in the heat exchanger and discharged at the top. Tiled stoves intended for firing by gas are normally totally enclosed, as no fuel needs to be inserted by hand as is the case with coal or log firing. At present, there are no gas-fired tiled stoves available in Sweden.

  A traditional wood stove is free-standing, made of cast iron and with an enclosed firebox with doors at the front. New designs have a glass door so that the flame can be seen from the outside. A wide selection of stoves of this type is available for use with natural gas on the market in other countries: at present, very few are available in Sweden.

  Gas convector heaters are similar to small fan

heaters, and are often installed on the inside of an exterior wall. Combustion air enters from the outside and the flue gases are discharged through a pipe through the wall or via a chimney. A heat exchanger heats the air in the room. There are no type-approved gas convector heaters available in Sweden, and the few units that are in use in the country have individual approvals.

■ **Domestic hot water heating.** Fuel-fired boilers usually incorporate domestic hot water storage as an integral part of the boiler. Alternatively, there may be either a separate storage tank or a through-flow heat exchanger. The latter type requires a high heating power, as the water flowing through it must be heated immediately to the required final temperature. Gas heating can be suitable in such cases, as a normal gas installation permits a very high power supply.

■ **Comfort cooling using gas.** Comfort cooling - air conditioning - is employed primarily in hotels, restaurants and offices. In other countries, particularly in the USA and Japan, there is also a substantial market for domestic air conditioning units.

Cooling normally employs the heat pump principle and, as previously mentioned, the heat pumps may be of compressor or absorption type. If the air to be cooled is first dried, less cooling power is needed. This drying process can also be gas-based.

■ **Shop cooling.** Other non-industrial cooling apart from comfort cooling is employed primarily for cooling foodstuffs in grocery stores. This cooling application extends down to about -20 °C, as needed for the shop's well-cases. Normally, electrically-driven compressors, installed in each well-case or other item to be cooled, are used for cooling. An alternative is to employ a central gas-powered cooling unit that supplies cooling to all the loads at the correct temperature.

As yet, no gas-based shop cooling systems are installed in Sweden, again due to the price superiority of electricity.

■ **Decentralised small-scale electricity and heat production.** Large-scale CHP production, i.e. with power ratings of some tens of MW and upwards, has long been profitable in Sweden. However, the economics become poorer with reducing size, and 'micro-CHP' units intended for detached houses are today not viable. (See the chapter entitled 'Small-scale CHP must be user-friendly'.) However, small-scale CHP has many advantages and the tendency in other countries, e.g. in neighbouring Denmark, is towards smaller and smaller units, which are usually powered by gas engines.

A few smaller gas engines with combined heat and power production are installed in Sweden, although they are to be regarded almost as experimental and demonstration installations. Complete packaged units are available in other countries: in Germany, for example, a unit is available with 23 kW heat output and 3 kW electricity output comprising a condensing boiler, a Stirling engine and a hot water storage tank.

■ **Food preparation equipment.** Cooking by gas does not have the same tradition in Sweden as in many other countries. Gas cooking stoves have previously been found only in towns with town gas supplies, and new gas stoves in Sweden are sold almost exclusively as replacements for older stoves. A few domestic users purchase gas stoves instead of electric stoves, but the market is very limited.

■ **Heating of swimming pools.** The conventional means of heating a swimming pool employs a boiler and heat exchanger. A few gas-heated pools exist in Sweden. Other methods are also used in other countries, e.g. heat pumps or immersion heaters.

■ **Sauna units.** The heating principle is usually the same as in an electrically-heated sauna unit, i.e. partly by warm air that flows out into the room and partly by hot stones for steam production. A Finnish natural gas sauna is installed as a demonstration unit in Sydgas' premises in Åstorp.

A natural-gas-fired sauna has been developed in Japan, with the heat radiated from black infra-red radiant heaters mounted on the wall. This allows the air temperature to be reduced, but no steam can be produced. This Japanese design has still not yet reached Sweden.

■ **Tumble dryers.** Several commercial laundries have

gas-powered tumble dryers, but as far as domestic users are concerned, this is quite a new line. The advantages over electrically-powered tumble dryers are shorter drying times and lower energy costs.

- **Installation materials.** The installation of gas-powered equipment at several points in a building requires gas pipes to be run to the various loads and suitable connectors fitted. This is quite expensive, and is probably one of the reasons for gas applications other than a main boiler being fairly uncommon in, say, domestic applications. Several gas suppliers, particularly in other countries, are working on simplifying and reducing the cost of internal piping, and a few designs of compact connectors, e.g. for outdoor grills, have been developed.

Coordination through the Swedish Gas Center AB

At the beginning and around the middle of the 1980s, i.e. in connection with the introduction of natural gas in Sweden, there was a large number of individual research and development organisations working in the natural gas field, e.g. Vattenfall, SwedeGas, Sydkraft, Sydgas, Västgas and some of the larger local authority energy utilities, such as Stockholm, Gothenburg and Malmö Energi. In addition, there was a central programme of gas technology research, operated by the National Energy Administration, the National Board for Technical Development and the Swedish Council for Building Research, together with another programme that was operated by the Thermal Technology Research Foundation.

In 1990, the gas industry decided to coordinate its work through a special development company, the Swedish Gas Center AB (SGC). SGC was also appointed to finance industry's contribution to the gas element of the Thermal Engineering Research Institute's research programmes.

As a result of the stagnation in the natural gas market at the beginning of the 1990s, the gas companies decided to concentrate their work through SGC, leading to conclusion of the Thermal Engineering Research Institute's work on gas in the summer of 1993. State participation in the gas sector has been cut back, and that part of the financing provided by the National Board

for Industrial and Technical Development (NUTEK) that is not concerned with fundamental gas technology research is now channelled through SGC via a non-specific gas research programme.

Continued need of research and development

On the hardware side, gas in buildings is concerned primarily with apparatus (equipment, components, units etc.) and systems. As the market for gas apparatus in Sweden is very small, most of the equipment is manufactured in other countries. Research and development of apparatus is therefore conducted almost exclusively by manufacturers in other countries, often with financial support from the national gas utilities, e.g. British Gas, Ruhrgas and Gaz de France. However, for certain types of components and apparatus, there may be justification for carrying out research and development in Sweden. Regardless of where some item of apparatus may have been developed, it can be important to build demonstration installations in order to accelerate general acceptance of the particular technology.

Greater effort is justified on the system side, as system designs are often different in Sweden from those in other countries. This applies also to the 'software' side, i.e. environmental aspects, performance, operation and maintenance.

Some of the technical areas are described below, with suggestions for new or continued research, development and demonstration activities.

Gas burners

Regardless of the intended application, the objective of development of new gas burners is to achieve high combustion efficiency, low NOx and other emissions and, where appropriate, good controllability.

As mentioned above, most burner development is carried out by the burner manufacturers in other countries. However, Swedish work on certain types of special burners, e.g. catalytic burners, can be justified. Two different designs have been developed by the work of the Thermal Engineering Research Institute, which has also investigated the feasibility of combining catalytic combustion and heat exchanger in a single compact unit[5].

Development within the field of radiant heaters should be concentrated on system aspects. SGC is preparing instructions for installation of such heaters. Further work is needed, e.g. in producing and verifying computer programmes for optimum rating and positioning of radiant heaters, together with the installation of one or more demonstration installations.

Condensing boilers

Much of the research into gas-based building heating has been, and is being, carried out by the Department of Heat and Power Engineering at the Lund Institute of Technology, with financing from a number of sources, including NUTEK, the Swedish Council for Building Research (BFR) and the Thermal Engineering Research Institute. The work at Lund has included condensing boilers and, in connection therewith, reheating of the flue gases in order to avoid condensation in the chimney[6].

There is a need for improved knowledge of condensation technology and also of the interaction between the boiler, the rest of the heating system and the building. Continued research, that can be expected to result in practical technology, is therefore desirable.

Boilers with pulsed combustion

Research into the formulation of theories and models involved in the process of pulsed combustion is also in progress at the Lund Institute of Technology. On the practical side, a Swedish manufacturer has developed a domestic boiler, intended primarily for oil but suitable also for use with gas, and having excellent performance in terms of efficiency, compactness and low environmental impact.

Continued work in the field of pulsed combustion should be aimed at completing research and producing design principles for larger boilers employing pulsed combustion, for use in apartment buildings and industrial applications. This work should be carried out in conjunction with boiler manufacturers or other manufacturing industry.

Other boilers and heatgenerating apparatus

There is a potential for a larger market for gas convector heaters, particularly for use in industrial premises. This is a technology that is well-developed, so that any development work needed can be restricted to specific points, e.g. optimisation of power and positioning, together with performance monitoring.

A new, interesting concept of heat generation using gas is combustion in a sand bed. The principle can be likened to that of fluidised bed combustion, but with the difference that the bed here is not fluidised and the fuel is a gas/air mixture that moves upwards through the bed. The bed contains cooling tubes that extract the heat produced. The method is a further development of an earlier design for cleaning ventilation air that contains hydrocarbons ('Adtec's sandbox filter')[7]. The method should be further investigated, both with regard to its theory and in experimental applications and then, when successful results have been obtained, should be tested on a larger scale. Companies that could be interested in taking over possible continued commercial development should also participate in the development work.

An investigation carried out by SGC shows that on-demand (through-flow) heaters for domestic hot water can save up to 1800 kWh/year in a detached house, as compared with the use of a gas-fired or oil-fired storage heater[8]. This, together with other benefits, makes the concept of on-demand heating attractive. A properly operating system requires a sophisticated control system, capable of operating over a wide control range, and various other features. Initially, suitable work would involve testing of a number of manufacturers' products, intended to show where further development work might be needed.

A review of system designs

The fact that natural gas is a clean, gaseous fuel means that in some cases it is possible to select system designs that would be impossible or impractical using other types of fuels.

There is a need for a systematic review of unconventional gas-based systems available in other countries. This should be followed by appointing a suitable Swedish body to attempt to arrive at new designs. The results of this work would then constitute a basis for a decision on further work. Certain system designs might require detailed calculations or experimental investigations, while others could perhaps be incorporated directly in demonstration or commercial installations.

Substantial development potential for cooling using gas

A medium can be cooled by a large number of different principles. As far as gas is concerned, only compressor cooling and cooling using absorption heat pumps have found practical application. However, it would be desirable to conduct a careful review of the suitability of other methods of cooling for using gas as their drive energy.

Purely generally, there is a major development potential for gas-based cooling technology, as witnessed not least by the previously described conditions in the USA. International development of 'established' gas cooling technology should be monitored, possibly complemented by installation and operation of one or more systems using absorption cooling pumps. This would provide practical experience of gas-based cooling. It could also result in a realisation of the potentials for simplification and cost reductions, intended to improve the competitiveness of the technology with respect to electrical systems.

International development in the field of micro-CHP needs to be carefully monitored. As there is already a market for small-scale CHP in other countries, it can be assumed that extensive technical development is being carried out by the manufacturers of traditional gas engines and by other parties.

Two concepts with Swedish links need to be investigated in more detail. One applies to the use of Stirling engines as power units for electricity generation. This concept has been developed by a number of bodies, including TEM in Malmö, and is on the way to achieving commercial establishment in other countries. The second concept involves the use of gas turbines as prime movers, with directly-connected high-speed electricity generators. System investigations and experimental applications need to be performed around both these concepts.

The gas meter - an important component

The gas meter is an important component in gas installations. The most widely used type is the bellows meter, which is characterised by simplicity, good accuracy, long life and low price.

Developments in the field of electronics have given gas meters a range of additional features over and above measuring the total volume of gas flowing through them. 'Intelligent' meters can incorporate, for example:

- instantaneous measuring of volume flow rate,
- temperature measurement,
- temperature compensation of the volume flow rate,
- maximum flow restriction,
- sensors for extremely low gas flow rate.

Development of gas meters with no moving parts is also in progress. An example of this type of meter is the ultrasonic meter that measures the speed of sound in the gas with and against the direction of flow, from which it calculates the flow velocity. Research is being carried out into ultrasonic meters and methods of calibrating them at the Department of Heat and Power Engineering at Lund Institute of Technology. This research should continue, although it should now be linked to companies or organisations interested in further commercial development. The feasibility of the Department acting as a test site for calibration of extremely highly accurate gas meters should be further investigated.

As gas customers are billed on the basis of the amount of gas energy that they have used, measured volume flows need to be converted to corresponding energy flows. However, technology for directly measuring the energy flow rate is being developed in several parts of the world, as well as at the Department of Heat and Power Engineering at Lund Institute of Technology, where work is in progress using an ultrasonic method. If this should produce promising results, work should be concentrated on developing a prototype meter.

This chapter is based on material by Jörgen Thunell, MSc., the Swedish Gas Center AB, Malmö.

REFERENCES

1 1993 Annual Report of the Swedish Gas Association.

2 AB Svensk Energiförsörjning, Energy Facts (Natural Gas).

3 Sydgas AB. Annual Report, 1993.

4 Kastensson, P., Ivarsson, S.; *Utvecklad teknik för gasinstallationer i småhus* (Developed technology for gas installations in detached houses). The Swedish Gas Center AB Report 049, February 1994, 27 pages.

5 Ahlström-Silversand, F., Hargitai, T.; *Katalytiska värmeväxlare för industriella tillämpningar* (Catalytic heat exchangers for industrial applications. Thermal Engineering Research Institute Report No. 496, January 1994, 132 pages.

6 Näslund, M.; *Experimentell undersökning av kondenserande panna med avgasåtervärmning* (Experimental investigation of a condensing boiler with flue gas reheating. Thermal Engineering Research Institute Report No. 487, November 1993, 31 pages.

7 Swedish Gas Technology Centre AB. Information Sheet No. 13, April 1994, 2 pages.

8 Forsman, J.; *Gaseldade genomströmningsberedare för tappvarmvatten* (Gas-fired on-demand heating of domestic hot water). The Swedish Gas Center AB Report 036, June 1993, 26 pages.

OTHER LITERATURE

Konkurrensbetingelser i Sverige för elenergi och naturgas (Competition conditions in Sweden for electrical energy and natural gas). A consultation document. NUTEK R1992:8.

Naturgas i Sverige. Ett bidrag till diskussionen om statens roll i samhället (Natural gas in Sweden. A contribution to the discussion on the State's role in society). Moberg, E. Industriförbundet, 1991.

Naturgasteknik i småhus. Utvärderinhg av uppvärmningssystem (Natural gas technology in single-family houses. Assessment of heating systems. Berggren, B. BFR T15:1989.

BIO-ENERGY
– IMPROVED COMBUSTION
TECHNOLOGY IS REQUIRED

SUMMARY

About 20 % of Sweden's total heating requirements for detached houses are met by bio-energy. Most of this is in the form of logs, with the proportion of woodchips, pellets and briquettes being very small. Present-day boilers are largely designed for oil firing.

The Swedish Environmental Protection Agency's performance requirements for log-fired boilers were introduced at the beginning of the 1980s. For the best products, they have resulted in a reduction in emission of tar of 20-30 times for boilers and 5-10 times for stoves and tiled stoves. With present-day methods, a requirement for incorporation of a hot water tank would further improve the situation. However, unfortunately, boilers are still being installed today that exceed the permissible emission limits because building permission is not consistently applied by local authorities.

In principle, bio-energy has substantial advantages from an environmental viewpoint, and it would be desirable if it could be developed into a substantial sustainable resource in the future. However, if this is to be the case, the environmental downside effects that are associated with its use must be eliminated.

The most important training and research requirements are to provide information and training for manufacturers, installation contractors and individual users, to develop combustion equipment that produces significantly lower emissions of volatile organic substances than do present-day designs, to develop control equipment that better responds to the transient processes in log combustion and to develop combustion equipment for pellets, including their use in wood stoves.

It is also important to optimise the thermal inertia of boilers - mainly by reducing the need for heavy firebricks around the combustion chamber - and to optimise heating systems that include hot water storage tanks. Development of control equipment capable of controlling the power output of local heat sources would eliminate the need for an expensive hot water tank. Finally, there is a need to develop cost-effective heat distribution systems for local heat sources.

The use of bio-energy for the provision of heating supplies has a long tradition in Sweden. Up until the 1950s, bio-energy played a central part in heating homes and commercial premises. As oil, and later electricity, began to take over the market, the importance of bio-energy diminished. However, interest is again increasing in the wake of the oil crises of the 1970s, now starting from partly new positions. Security of supply was a central theme of the debate, as did the assumed reduced environmental impact of bio-energy.

The use of this old 'new' energy source was discussed along two lines: as a provider of energy for individual buildings, and as fuel in larger district heating and CHP plants. In this latter area, development has been relatively rapid in the last 15 years: today, several district heating plants use biofuels in one form or another. To date, it has mainly been woodchips and/or forest waste that have been used, although processed fuels such as pellets and briquettes have started to be used in recent years. The progress of bio-energy in these larger-scale contexts has largely followed changes in energy policy and taxation. For example, the present taxation of carbon dioxide emissions from fossil fuels has made the use of biofuels very attractive, and several plants have been modified to allow them to burn them.

However, this presentation will concentrate on the integrated use of biofuels in the built environment. Today, this means almost exclusively individual heating of homes and industrial premises.

Problems with too little or too much air

Logs and other wood fuels are more difficult to burn than, say, oil. They make great demands on both the equipment and the firer's knowledge. Combustion air must be supplied so that the fuel is uniformly gasified and so that the air is effectively mixed with the combustion gases. The flame itself must also be insulated from cooling surfaces in order to maintain a high combustion temperature.

Insufficient air results in incomplete combustion, with the temperature of the flame being reduced. Combustion becomes pyrolysis. Excess air, on the other hand, can also cause problems: air which is not really needed for combustion cools the combustion chamber and increases flue gas velocities, thus affecting the flame temperature and reducing the amount of heat absorbed by the convection zone of the boiler.

Combustion air can be divided up into primary and secondary air. The primary air dries the fuel and produces a hot combustible gas. The secondary air needs to be supplied where the gas stream is at its hottest and most dense. We can therefore regard the primary air as gasification air and the secondary air as the true combustion air which completes combustion of the volatile gases that comprise 85-90 % of the total energy content of the fuel.

Combustion principles and boiler types

Among boilers that have been designed purely to burn logs, there are many different combustion systems, each of which has its particular advantages. The one to be chosen depends on the application.

The first classification is into refractory and non-refractory boilers. The second is into natural-draught and mechanical draught (fan-controlled) boilers. The list below summarises the main combustion principles and boiler types.

Natural draught boilers:	The traditional boiler. The chimney provides a negative pressure which draws combustion air into the burning zone and evacuates the flue gases.
Fan-assisted boilers:	Combustion air is supplied by a fan. This provides more stable combustion, but also introduces problems in connection with starting and stopping the fan.
Non-refractory:	The flame is cooled by cold water-cooled surfaces.
Refractory boilers:	A secondary combustion chamber prevents the flames from being cooled.
Top burning:	Through burning. The primary air enters from below, passing up through the fuel. The flue leaves from the top of the combustion chamber. The whole log charge burns together. This type of boiler has a high power.
Bottom burning:	The combustion air passes up through a grate, with the exit to the flue from the lower edge of the firebox. The wood burns from the bottom. This is the traditional way of burning wood and, with a ceramic secondary combustion chamber, results in good performance.
Reverse combustion:	The primary air flows from the top downwards, with combustion from the bottom. This arrangement results in good combustion.
Thermally lightweight fireboxes:	These stoves or open fires are of sheet metal or cast iron. They provide radiant heat and/or convection heating. They quickly reach working temperature, but store very little heat.
Massive fireboxes:	Tiled stoves or steatite stoves. Can be fired harder than a thermally lightweight stove without risk of overheating. Good combustion and extended heat release, but slow to start.

It should perhaps be pointed out here that there has not hitherto been any environmentally approved log stove that does not incorporate refractories. This means that refractory boilers are always preferable if fuel is to be put on in batches. However, automatic firing of woodchips, or continuous firing with, say, pellet burners, can be done without excessive pollution even in non-refractory boilers, because combustion is completed before the flame comes into contact with cooling surfaces.

Burning sawdust, woodchips or processed wood fuels such as briquettes or pellets often requires additional equipment in the form of a pre-combustion chamber, stoker or burner. This equipment is connected to the existing boiler, and can be a good choice when the objective is to reduce heating costs. It is also possible to obtain boilers and stoves that have been specially designed and built for use with a particular type of fuel.

Hot water storagetanks are essential

With present-day technology, it is almost impossible to control the power of a boiler to suit the varying demands of a domestic application. A hot water storage tank is therefore essential for use with all combustion of biofuels in water-cooled stoves or boilers.

We distinguish between two different types of heat storage; heat storage from one point in time to another and evening-out of both power demand and power input (i.e. in the form of hot water from the boiler). Heat storage improves both cost and convenience. Consumption is evened out and the boiler can be fired at what has been established as an average rate.

20 % of energy supplies from biofuels

In 1993, Sweden used a total of 50 TWh of energy for space heating and domestic hot water supplies in detached houses. About 11 TWh was supplied by bioenergy, equivalent to almost 20 % of total energy use for space heating in detached houses. The proportion of this supplied by logs has varied over the years, but has been increasing steadily since 1980 (see Figure 1).

By far the greatest part of bio-energy use is as combustion of logs. The proportion of wood chips, pellets or briquettes today is very small.

Most logs are fired in boilers that supply the house's central heating system. Most boilers today are intended primarily for oil firing. This also applies for the majority of dual-fuel boilers, which admittedly can burn logs in purely practical terms, but in which the actual combustion chamber design is not intended primarily for log firing.

A small proportion of logs are also burnt in stoves, tiles stoves etc. The main idea of these is that they should provide a visually attractive fire and also some additional heat. However, in a few cases, stoves/tiled stoves can provide a significant proportion of a house's heating requirements.

Wood chips are burnt to a limited extent, mainly in rural areas, but their use has declined after a surge in interest in the 1970s as a result of problems with handling and storage of the fuel. The use of pellets and briquettes today is marginal, mainly in areas around the plants where such fuels are produced.

The overriding consideration in connection with wood firing during the last decade is the environmental impact. As a result of problems that came to light at the beginning of the 1980s with emission of unburned hydrocarbons, environmental performance requirements have been introduced for wood-fired boilers and stoves/tiles stoves. These requirements are expressed in the form of maximum permissible emissions of tar per unit of input energy. In the case of boilers, the limit is a

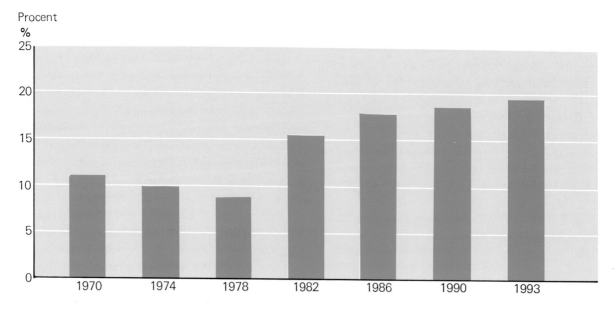

Figure 1. Proportion of wood fuel as an energy source in relation to total energy use for space heating and domestic hot water production in detached houses from 1970 to 1993.

maximum of 30 mg of tar per MJ. These requirements have resulted in greatly improved methods of combustion, relative to earlier designs.

Emissions have been reduced

However, it should also be noted that a simultaneous improvement in efficiency has contributed to a drastic reduction in emissions per unit of energy produced. Today, about 50 designs of log-fired boilers are approved, together with almost 200 designs of wood stoves/tiled stoves. Tar emissions from boilers have been reduced by 20-50 times, and that of stoves/tiled stoves by 5-10 times, both relative to the performances of earlier designs.

However, as a result of the relatively long life of boilers, about 20-30 years, it will be some years before the new products begin to make up a significant proportion of the total units in use. Administrative factors, too, have hitherto restricted introduction of the new technology. Replacement of boilers, for example, does not require building permission if the same type of fuel is used. This means that conventional, non-environmentally-approved boilers are still being installed. The National Board for Industrial and Technical Development (NUTEK) and the Swedish Environmental Protection Agency have therefore proposed changes in the legislation in 1994 that would result in more rapid introduction of the new stoves and boilers. It has also been suggested that local authorities should be empowered to restrict the use of log firing in the most densely built areas. However, the proposal has aroused criticism, and it is uncertain what will happen.

Pellets and briquettes can best meet future requirements

Future increased use of sustainable building-integrated bio-energy implies a number of requirements, both technical and economic. Schematically, the use of bio-energy can be divided up into the following elements:

- fuel supply,
- combustion technology,
- heat distribution, and
- emission aspects.

Further development is required within each of these areas.

A biofuel intended to facilitate substantially greater use of bio-energy than is the case today must fulfil a number of requirements if its use is to be increased. The most important of these requirements are:

- an established market,
- a working distribution system,
- ease of handling for the user,
- high energy density relative to that of logs, and
- environmentally positive characteristics.

The fuels that can be foreseen as best fulfilling these requirements are primarily pellets and briquettes. These are processed fuels, manufactured from various residual products from the forest industry and woodworking industry, e.g. wood chips, sawdust and bark. The material, possibly with a suitable binder, is forced under high pressure through a die to produce compact pellets/briquettes. Typical diameters are 8-12 mm for pellets and 75 mm for briquettes. Fuels of this type have a moisture content of about 10 %, a relatively uniform shape and are easy to handle. Calorific value is about 4.8 kWh/kg, and density about 650-700 kg/m^3. This gives an energy density of over 3 MWh/m^3, which can be compared with about 1.6-1.8 MWh/m^3 for logs. The energy density is therefore considerably higher for the processed fuels.

As pellets in particular can be transported by screw conveyors, firing can be automated. This applies both to transport from the storage bunker to the boiler and supply to the burner, making the fuel relatively easy to handle by the user.

Environmentally, both pellets and briquettes have good characteristics. Emission of tar is very low in comparison with that from combustion of logs. This is a result both of the characteristics of the fuel itself and of the automated firing. Emissions of volatile organic substances are probably relatively low. Overall, the processed fuels must be regarded as clearly preferable from an emissions viewpoint. Unless taxation conditions are adversely changed, a smoothly operating market should be a fact within the near future. Pellets and briquettes are the bio-energy form that are best suited for future developments.

New combustion technology must be developed

Extrapolation of available measurements indicates that log firing accounts for about 20-25 % of total emissions of volatile organic compounds in Sweden. Bearing in mind the environmental and health effects of substances such as ethene, benzene and butadiene, all of which are VOCs, this situation cannot be allowed to continue indefinitely. We therefore need to develop a second generation of combustion equipment that will result in substantially lower VOC emissions than present-day designs. However, our knowledge of the factors that influence emissions of unburned substances is today limited, and further research is required. A positive factor, however, is that the necessary technical development is a logical continuation of the successful work to date.

A critical factor in connection with the use of logs as fuel is load control and thus combustion intensity control. It has been found to be extremely difficult to comply with current environmental requirements when operating at part load with existing control methods. Today, all type approvals for boilers require the use of hot water storage tanks, i.e. of full-load combustion. In the longer term, it would be desirable to arrive at designs that do not require the heat storage tank, as it takes up space and makes the system more expensive. However, this will require significant development of control methods and firebox design. As the nominal output rating of the boilers is often considerably greater than the design power demand, development of smaller boilers would be desirable.

A more immediate control problem arises in connection with the transient process of log combustion. There is every reason to concentrate work on methods that measure the flue gas characteristics (excess air, temperature) as control signals for boiler control. With the present rapid rates of development of sensors and microprocessors, it should be possible to make major advances in this respect. However, development in this direction has hitherto been surprisingly slow.

Optimisation of thermal inertia is essential

One area in which development is already in progress, but in which it must continue, is optimisation of the thermal inertia of the designs. There is a contradiction in the facts that combustion requires the firebox to be insulated in order to provide acceptable emissions, while the heat required to raise the temperature of the firebox abstracts energy at the beginning of the firing process. The mass of the ceramic (or similar) material needs to be optimised to suit these opposing requirements, as does the volume of boiler water. A further factor that needs to be considered is the durability of the insulation. Experience of this aspect is hitherto limited, but it seems likely that the ceramic materials in present-day designs will need to be replaced two or three times during the life of the boiler. Development of new ceramic materials is underway. There is also a tendency towards designs that minimise or possibly totally eliminate the use of ceramics.

Today, development of equipment for pellets and briquette firing is in its infancy. Only one single type of burner can be said to be commercial and systematically marketed. Good availability of good combustion equipment is essential in order to make full use of the potential of processed biofuels.

Pellet firing is the most attractive

Hitherto, it has been primarily equipment for pellet firing that has attracted interest. The size of briquettes is such that they are less suitable for automated firing on a small scale. New methods are needed for transport and charging into the boiler, although if these problems can be solved, briquettes can become an interesting alternative for domestic applications as well. Boiler designs do exist that combine good combustion technology with a suitability for briquette firing. However, so far, there has been no systematic evaluation of this possibility.

Burners for pellet firing constitute an area of considerable activity. The objective is to arrive at product designs that can replace oil burners in traditional boilers. Today, the cost of converting an oil-fired boiler to pellet firing is about SEK 15 000 - 20 000, although this must be compared with installation of a log-fired boiler and hot water storage system, today costs about 50 000-70 000. With an energy price about half that of oil, the use of pellets is therefore highly attractive.

Burners for pellet firing must fulfil the following requirements:
- low-environmental-impact combustion,
- load control capability over a wide power range, and
- reliable operation, i.e. insensitive to slag formation and fuel feed etc.

Equipment for burning pellets and briquettes is beginning to reach maturity. It is essential to employ good combustion technology if the best use is to be made of processed biomass fuels.
Photographer: Tommy Olofsson, Mira

Reliability is the key

From all these aspects, promising development has started. The prospects for low emission levels are good as a result of continuous combustion and the high-quality fuel. However, further development is needed for a number of years. Problem areas relate primarily to air supply and control systems, both of which are closely linked to control of power output. It is essential to develop combustion systems with low excess air, while retaining good emission values over a wide operating range. This is an area, too, in which modern sensor technology and use of microprocessors should facilitate major advances.

A key aspect is the operational reliability of the entire system. Experience to date is limited, but this is a vital area as availability must be able to stand comparison with that of an oil burner, which is almost 100 %. However, the view is that, provided that development that has started is brought to a satisfactory conclusion, high availability will be achieved.

An alternative to the use of a pellet burner installed in the boiler is the pellet stove. These stoves are intended for installation in living areas of the house in the same way as a log-fired stove. This is a very interesting concept, e.g. for houses that today have direct acting electric heating. The pellets are loaded into a bunker in the stove, and are normally fed to the burner head by a screw feeder. A number of types of such stoves have been granted environmental approval and are commercially available. Combustion problem areas requiring further development are essentially the same as those for the burners.

Heat distribution technology needs further development

Efficient use of bio-energy, as of other fuels, requires that the heat released should be made available to the right place and at the right time, as required by the demand. This implies a latent conflict, as combustion equipment often works best at a particular power output level. As far as log firing in boilers is concerned, this has hitherto been resolved indirectly by the use of a hot water storage tank. This allows the boiler to work under optimum conditions, with distribution being varied to suit requirements. In this particular case, the distribution problem can therefore be regarded as largely solved. However, there is justification for further investigation of how the heat storage tank system should be optimised relative to the boiler characteristics and the building's heat requirements.

A few designs are available today in which heat can be distributed from a local heat source to other rooms via warm air ducts or via an in-built water heater for connection to the radiator system. However, these systems have not achieved a particularly wide market penetration, primarily for cost reasons. The development of cost-effective system designs for the distribution of heat from local heat sources is therefore an important development area.

The question of power control of local heat sources is intimately associated with heat distribution. Most of today's products are manually controlled. It would be desirable to have a simple system that controls output power by means of, say, a sensor in a suitable position in the room. Again, it is development of control technology in conjunction with combustion technology that is essential.

It is environmental aspects that have been the driving force behind development hitherto, and this will continue during the foreseeable future. Environmental aspects are inseparable from combustion processes, although they are also strongly affected by the type of fuel and the match between the heat source and the building's energy requirements.

Environmental aspects cannot be separated from combustion processes

In principle, bio-energy has major advantages from an environmental viewpoint, which should be emphasised. The net emission of carbon dioxide is almost zero, which is of strategic importance for the greenhouse effect. Emissions of sulphur are negligible, which is very important from an acidification viewpoint. NO_x emissions from small-scale combustion amount to about 0.5 % of total NO_x emissions in Sweden. All these factors mean that bio-energy is highly preferable, and should be encouraged to develop into a significant sustainable future energy resource. However, if this is to become reality, those environmental effects that nevertheless do exist must be eliminated.

Emissions of unburned hydrocarbons are the most important problem area. A first step, which has been most effective, has been taken with development of present-day environmentally approved products. Development needs to continue, aimed at a second generation of products, from which VOC emissions have been reduced. Questions such as determining the ratings and design of fireboxes, methods of supply and admixture of combustion air and - particularly - control technology need to be thoroughly considered. Research into the fundamental processes of biofuel firing is essential, and has started. Effective dissemination of the results achieved to manufacturing industry is of vital importance.

Lowest emissions from processed fuels

Processed fuels inherently improve emission levels. Development of combustion equipment for pellets and briquettes must be encouraged. A combination of good combustion technology and equipment and a good fuel provides the best conditions for low emission levels.

The conditions under which a combustion process operates clearly affect emission levels. It is therefore important thoroughly to investigate the interaction between equipment, power demand characteristics and user behaviour. This will enable the bottlenecks in the way of lowest pollution use of biofuels to be identified. This can be broken down into a number of problem areas, with the solutions being treated on a number of planes. Training of users of bio energy is a consideration that should not be neglected. At the other extreme is the development of equipment that operates under

carefully optimised conditions, and over which the user has no real control. Finally, system investigations of the relationships between combustion equipment and the building's energy characteristics are an important area that can contribute to lower future emission levels.

This chapter is based on material by Lennart Gustafsson, Combustion and Heating Technology, SP, and Bengt-Erik Lövgren, ÄFAB, Götene.

OTHER LITERATURE

Marknadsförutsättningar för biobränslekraftvärme och vindkraft (Market conditions for bio-fuelled CHP and wind power). NUTEK R1994:44.

Biobränslen för framtiden. Slutbetänkande av Biobränslekommissionen (Biofuels for the future. Final report from the Biofuels Commission). SOU 1992:90.

WIND POWER IS BEST IN OPEN COUNTRY

SUMMARY

The current international development of wind power started in the middle of the 1970s along two parallel lines: small plants for immediate commercial sale, and large plants, developed by national research programmes, intended to mature into commercial units in due course.

At the best sites, wind power is financially viable with present investment grants, when analysed by real rate of interest methods. An environmental bonus of 8.8 öre/kWh (SEK 0.088/kWh) gives a balanced result without an investment grant.

The most important areas on which further development of wind power should concentrate are:
- aerodynamic research, particularly within the stalled flow range and non-stationary aerodynamics,
- development of aerofoils,
- development of blade materials,
- wind measurements for load calculations,
- development of computer models for wind power plants,
- development of electrical systems for operation at variable speed and with directly-driven generators.

If wind power is to be used, it is important to map wind resources, to investigate environmental effects in more detail and to investigate operation in conjunction with the public power system, including methods of forecasting wind speeds.

Except in sparsely populated areas, literal integration of wind power in the built environment is not possible. Wind power plants are too large, and in any case they require open country and freedom from obstruction (as would be caused by buildings) in order to give access to the wind. The types of wind power plants that will be described in this review could more properly be regarded as built-environment-associated. They may be co-operatively owned installations, or be owned by distribution utilities having their own electricity production facilities that wish to spread ownership of wind power among their customers.

Current international development of wind power started in the middle of the 1970s along two parallel lines: small plants for immediate commercial sale (initially with power outputs of about 20 kW), and large plants, with outputs of about 2000 kW, developed by national research programmes, and intended to mature into commercial units in due course. In both cases, the power plants were intended to be directly connected to existing electricity grids.

Commercial development has subsequently proceeded in small steps, resulting in cost reductions due to the benefits of size and progressive development of the technology. Today, development has reached the stage that most wind power plants are sold, both in Sweden and in other countries, in the 200-600 kW range. The next generation of power plants, with outputs in the 1000-1500 kW range, is under development, eagerly awaited by the market. This means that the previous high-profile battle between 'large' and 'small' units has now been abandoned, in that the 'small' units have developed upwards to reach the megawatt class of the larger units.

High tip speeds

Almost all the medium-sized wind power plants now sold are of the horizontal axis high tip speed ratio type, with two or three turbine blades. In this context, 'high tip speed' means that, under rated conditions, the tip speed of the blades is 5-10 times higher than the wind velocity. It is this characteristic that is the key to the viability of wind power plants, in that it enables the turbine to abstract wind energy over the entire swept area of the disc, at best efficiencies of 40-50 % (the theoretical maximum efficiency of a horizontal-axis wind turbine being 59.3 %), despite the fact that the physical area of the blades themselves constitutes only a few percent of the swept area. The blade area and the turbine diameter are the factors that primarily determine the forces on the structure, and thus its weight and costs.

A few vertical-axis wind power plants have been manufactured, but have not been able to compete, probably ultimately because they require more materials in proportion to the amount of energy that they abstract.

Superficially, therefore, most wind power plants look much the same: a two-bladed or three-bladed turbine, a nacelle (with a means of yawing the turbine to face into the wind), a tower and a foundation. In the larger sizes, the towers are nearly always made of sheet metal, partly because they are preferred aesthetically, partly because they provide protected access to the turbine and nacelle and finally because they cost much the same as a lattice structure. Prefabricated concrete towers have been used, but they are too narrow to allow internal access and in any case are hardly any cheaper than steel towers. In-situ-cast concrete towers have hitherto been used only for large prototype installations.

Lighter and simpler

The cost of any design depends primarily on the amount of materials involved in it and on its complexity. Continued development of wind power generation is therefore concerned mainly with making wind power plants simpler and lighter, using as cheap materials as possible.

As the power of the wind increases in proportion to the cube of its speed, it must be possible to control a wind turbine so that the generator etc. is not overloaded once it has reached rated output at a typical wind speed of 14 m/s. Two main principles are employed for power limiting, **pitch control and stall control.**

Pitch control means that the blades are feathered, in the same way as in a variable-pitch marine or aircraft propeller. The result is that excess power is spilt. Pitch control is also used to assist starting and stopping.

Stall control involves the same effect as demonstrated by a landing aircraft progressively pulling up its nose so that the air flow over the wings comes increasingly from below. At a particular angle and/or speed, the air flow no longer follows the upper surface of the wing, but parts from it, greatly reducing lifting force and allowing the aircraft to settle on the runway. In the case of the wind turbine, it is the increasing wind velocity that results in the angle of incidence on the blades increasing, provided that the speed is kept constant. This is due to the fact that the wind flow experienced by a blade results mainly from the rotation. This component meets the leading edge of the aerofoil, while the 'wind' component meets the lower surface of the aerofoil. Increasing wind speed therefore causes the resultant wind direction to meet the aerofoil at an increasing angle. At a wind velocity of about 13-14 m/s, the blades begin to stall, preventing the shaft torque (and therefore the power) from further increasing.

Stall control increasing its dominance

Stall control results in a simpler system, despite the fact that, for emergency braking, it needs to be complemented by twistable blade tips (or possibly with a second mechanical braking system). In total, the two systems today are approximately equally common, although the picture is different if we look at the situation in Denmark alone. There, there is only one (although large) manufacturer (Vestas) that uses pitch control and which has manufactured about a third of the over 3000 type-approved Danish wind power plants. In the 500 kW class, the stall-control power plants produce somewhat more energy per m^2 (about 5 %) and cost somewhat less (5-13 %) per annual kWh[1]. Maintenance costs should be less as a result of the lower complexity. It therefore seems likely that stall control will further increase its dominance in the future.

Problems with stall control are associated primarily with calculating the turbine's maximum power at the design stage, and with ensuring that this power is developed stably, regardless of external effects such as turbulence or wind gradient. These problems are associated with present-day inadequate knowledge of air flow under stalled conditions. This is a situation that, during all normal flying, is avoided, which means that there has previously been no particular interest in research into it.

By optimising the aerodynamic profiles and the turbine as a whole for stall control, there is a theoretical potential for increasing the energy abstraction from a given turbine and generator size by about 5 %: strong justification, in other words, for research and development in this sector.

It pays to reduce the number of blades

Reducing the number of blades from three to two is generally cost-effective, because the reduction in blade cost exceeds the loss of energy (which amounts to about 3 %). However, two-bladed units are dynamically more difficult to control, which has hitherto restricted their application. Nevertheless, as reliable and easy-to-use computer models become generally available, it can be expected that they will become more common. Single-bladed units lose so much energy (about 10 %) that it is difficult to justify them.

Current Swedish wind power unit designs are two-bladed, although only three-bladed plants are manufactured in Denmark.

There is some resistance to two-bladed units in Germany and Holland on aesthetic grounds, with the claim that a three-bladed turbine is more pleasing. A rather simpler explanation might also be found in familiarity, in that it is usually the most common form that is preferred.

Designs are deliberately compliant

The traditional Danish wind power plants have been regarded as rigid designs, with resonant frequencies of the tower well above the turbine speed. In reality, such a slender design as a (larger) wind power plant can never be wholly rigid, in that the various components all have their own different resonant frequencies, of which some are likely to be excited in the various operating modes. By deliberately making the structure compliant, it can be substantially lighter and thus cheaper. However, a prerequisite is that it is possible to avoid couplings between the natural frequencies of the various components, which in turn requires the reliable and easy-to-use computer models as mentioned above.

Hinged hubs provide flexibility

A hinged hub is one way of deliberately incorporating an element of compliance in the design. It may be in the form of a teeter hub, in which both blades are rigidly connected to each other but hinged to the turbine shaft,

allowing the turbine to move in the same way as a seesaw. The second main type is the flapping hub, in which each blade is individually hinged to the turbine shaft. These two types are manufactured by Nordic Windpower and Zephyr Energy respectively.

Variable speed also provides flexibility

With a normal synchronous or asynchronous generator, directly connected to the electricity supply system, the turbine will always run at a fixed speed. However, a wind turbine operates at optimum aerodynamic efficiency if the tip speed of the blades is at a particular ratio to the wind speed (normally 6-8). This presupposes that the turbine speed can vary with the wind speed. Variable turbine speed also incorporates an element of compliance in the drive line, which can reduce the load on it. One way of permitting variable speed is to rectify and invert the resulting variable-frequency current from the generator.

There are a number of problems with the power electronic equipment for variable-speed operation. The relatively low efficiency means that the energy yield may be less than it would have been at fixed speed, despite the improvement in turbine efficiency. In addition, the equipment is expensive and generates harmonics on the electricity system. These harmonics can be reduced or eliminated by employing the most modern components, but this unfortunately reduces the efficiency for fundamental physical reasons.

In the case of stall-controlled units, the benefits of variable speed are not much used, as the turbine reaches full speed at about 25 % of full power. On the other hand, it is very valuable to be able to change the full-power speed of the unit when testing and commissioning a stall-controlled unit. Nordic Windpower's 400 kW and 1000 kW units (prototypes) incorporate variable speed operation, primarily for development reasons.

Directly driven (gearless) generators

In a traditional wind power plant, the turbine drives the generator through a speed-increasing gear which increases the speed from about 35 r/min (in a 400 kW power plant) to 1000 r/min or 1500 r/min (for 50 Hz machines). This gearbox is a relatively expensive and complicated component, which also introduces losses, amounting to about 3 %. There has therefore always been an interest in designing a directly driven generator that could be connected directly to the turbine without an intermediate gearbox. This also simplifies the mechanical design. However, a directly driven generator has a large diameter (2-4 m for 500 kW output at 35 r/min) and generally requires operation through an inverter.

A German design of directly driven 500 kW wind power generator is commercially available, of which about 100 had been made by the spring of 1994. Several EC projects are in progress for the development of directly-driven generators, including one for which Nordic Windpower is the project leader.

Attempts are being made in Denmark and elsewhere again to introduce commercial wind power plants in the 20 kW range, on the hypothesis that present-day improved knowledge, in combination with an extremely simplified design, would render them cost-effective. However, the remaining Danish wind turbine manufacturers (many having fallen by the wayside) today produce only plants of 150 kW and above. It is not yet possible to say whether the re-introduction of small wind power plants will succeed. However, it must be realised that even these 'small' wind power plants can be used only in sparsely built-up areas. Their size is too large to allow them to be integrated into normal urban areas. In any case, wind conditions in urban areas are too poor as a result of friction losses caused by buildings.

An investigation at the end of the 1970s[2] estimated that there were 20 000-40 000 permanent residences in Sweden in sites in which their own wind power units would be realistic. With, say, 10 000 units of 20 kW each, there would be a potential energy contribution of about 0.4 TWh/year.

If individual units are not financially viable, and for all those who do not live in locations that are suitable for wind power production, ownership of shares in a larger wind power plant is a logical alternative.

In about 5-10 years' time, it is likely that mains-connected wind power plants in the 200-2000 kW range will be being produced in quantity, in sizes ranging from 200 kW to 2 MW. In addition, there will also be small wind power plants for isolated operation, and attempts are likely to be made again to introduce commercial power plants in the 20 kW range.

Operating cost about 5 öre/kWh

The mean cost of present-day medium-sized wind power plants is about SEK 9000/kW, ready-installed. Power plants on the best sites have a utilisation time of about 2500 hours/year. This gives a specific investment cost of SEK 3.60/annual kWh of production capacity. Experience indicates an operating cost of about 5 öre/kWh. Length of life can be estimated as at least 20 years. Revenue from the sale of electricity has been set at 28 öre/kWh, which is equal to the maximum payment under the Swedish electrical utility rules. However, in connection with deregulation of the Swedish electricity market, the Swedish Parliament has decided that, during a transition period, payment for electricity produced by wind power plants shall instead be equal to that paid to normal domestic consumers, with certain deductions. What the effect of these rules will be cannot yet be decided.

A real rate of interest analysis employs the real rate of interest as the interest rate, and is arrived at by reducing the nominal interest rate by the rate of inflation. The calculations below employ a real rate of interest of 6 %. Historically, the real rates of interest have been less than this value, although during the summer of 1994 it was closer to 10 %. This method of analysis gives a picture of the operating costs over the entire life of the plant. If the result is positive, it represents a profit, over and above interest payments and repayment of capital. A negative result indicates that this objective has not been achieved.

Summarising, the real rate of interest calculations show the following results:

- Without a grant, the result is negative (-8 öre/kWh).

- With an investment grant, there is a net profit of 3 öre/kWh.

- With an environmental bonus subsidy of 9 öre/kWh, the net profit increases to 12 öre/kWh.

The real rate of interest calculation says nothing of cash flow variations with time. In the case of a nominally neutral result, there is normally a deficit at first, compensated by a corresponding surplus during the latter half of the plant's life. This is the result of inflation.

The average cost for a medium-sized wind power plant is about SEK 9000/kW, including installation. Running costs are about 5 öre/kWh, and life is about 20 years. Photographer: Bengt Olof Olsson, Bildhuset

A nominal cost analysis, on the other hand, provides a correct result for the cash flow during the first year. A corresponding nominal budget that includes both investment grants and environmental bonus indicates a return on capital of over 12 %.

The potential for Swedish wind power was most recently investigated by the Wind Power Commission[3], which was asked to find suitable areas for the construction of large wind power plants (3 MW) to give an annual production of about 10 TWh on land and 20 TWh at sea. The report presented results of 6.7 TWh and 2.9 TWh on land, depending on whether the closest distance to the nearest housing was 300 m or 500 m respectively. At sea, there was no difficulty in achieving the intended quantity of wind energy. A review of the rules governing wind power siting is presented in a report[4] published by the National Board for Industrial and Technical Development (NUTEK).

Working in parallel with the grid

Wind power is inherently intermittent. Although, over seasons and years, it is reliable, it can vary very widely over short periods of time. If it is operated in parallel with an existing electric power system - as is presupposed here - it is this variability that must be compensated. Sweden has a substantial hydro power generation base, which provides the first level of regulation as soon as demand or other production capacity changes. This means that water remains in the reservoirs if demand falls or other production increases, and vice versa. This would probably result in hydro power production being operated under less optimum conditions than would otherwise be the case, i.e. suffering from efficiency losses. A recent research report[5] states that construction of wind power plant to produce an energy contribution of up to about 2 TWh would not give rise to any such losses, but that a contribution of about 4 TWh would result in about 1 % loss (relative to the wind power production contribution) and that 7 TWh would give losses of about 1.2 %. This final figure, however, needs to be further checked. A loss of 1 % is equivalent to a cost increase of about 0.3 öre/kWh. In addition, the costs of transmitting the power contribution may be positively or negatively affected by the introduction of wind power, depending on where it is and how large it is.

Earlier investigations[6] found that up to 30 TWh/year of wind power could be operated in parallel with the grid. This would require thermal power production (coal-fired cold condensing production) to be regulated as well.

Shared ownership provides new prospects for green energy

From the above, it is clear that wind power can hardly be integrated into our way of life in the same way as, say, solar collectors or energy conservation. Wind power plants need to stand alone on open ground, within those parts of the country with sufficiently good wind conditions for their operation. What we can see, however, is a tendency towards individuals wanting to influence production of the electricity that they use, either to protect themselves against the effects of possible future price rises or because they want the electricity that they use to be produced with a minimum of environmental impact. These tendencies have manifested themselves in a certain degree of private ownership of wind power plants and, to a greater degree, through ownership of shares in such plants. It is possible that cooperatively-owned wind power plants might provide a significant proportion of electricity production in future. In Sweden, domestic electricity and electricity for space heating amount to about 50 TWh/year. If only a smaller proportion of households purchase shares in wind power plants, the effect will be significant.

Another aspect to be considered is that electricity users, whether individual s or companies, may directly request 'green' energy, i.e. require their electricity supplier to have access to wind power production equal to what they and other 'green' customers together require. For the supplier, this may resolve into a question of keeping or losing customers: from a cost point of view, there is little difference between wind power and any other form of new electricity production. Manufacturing companies that use a lot of electricity may feel themselves under pressure to improve their environmental credibility, as has been experienced, for example, very clearly by the Swedish forest industry, and can therefore also be expected to call for 'green' electrical energy. Tendencies of this type have been noted in the UK, Germany and the USA[7].

Continued introduction of wind power

It is clear that wind power will continue to be introduced in Sweden and the rest of the world, even without further Swedish research and development. As the objective for its work, NUTEK's Wind Power Consortium[8] has stated that it is working to improve knowledge in the wind energy sector to allow the development and manufacture of cost-effective wind power plants in Sweden and the cost-effective utilisation of wind power in the Swedish power system.

To this must be added that wind power must also be environmentally acceptable.

The first objective - that of developing and manufacturing cost-effective wind power plants - is essentially industrial. We need to be able to exploit the results of research and development in products that can find an international market. To some extent, it is also a matter of energy policy, as the improved and cheaper plants in which the work should result could lead to wider use of wind power than would otherwise be the case, both in Sweden and elsewhere. Bearing in mind the continuity of Swedish research into wind power, this is not entirely unrealistic.

The second objective, of utilising wind power cost-effectively in the Swedish power system, is concerned with making use of wind power in Sweden, regardless of where the actual wind power plants themselves are developed or manufactured. In this case, too, we need to conduct research in order to determine where the plants should best be sited, the requirements imposed on them and how they are to be integrated into the power system.

Important areas for wind power development

The following working areas are important if we are to be able to develop successful wind power plants:

- **Aerodynamics**, particularly under stalled conditions and non-stationary aerodynamics. This includes the development of aerofoils intended specifically for wind power plants, as well as finding methods of further reducing aerodynamic noise.
- **Data for load calculations**, in the form of year-long records of one-second values of wind velocity from relevant sites and heights. It has been found that the fatigue performance of wind power plants needs to

be determined on the basis of conditions that occur for only about 1 % of the time. Extreme wind gradients (i.e. with the wind speed increasing very rapidly with height) are an example of such a situation.

- **Computer models**, capable of easily and reliably modelling the interaction and effects of the hundreds of parameters that together define a wind power plant.
- **Blade materials**, primarily glass fibre composites and wood.
- **Electrical systems** for operation at variable speed and with directly-driven generators.
- **Control technology** for optimum operation of wind power plants.

In addition, we need to map wind conditions to provide a basis for siting decisions. There are models available today that operate relatively well in flat terrain, but are less successful in hilly areas. We also need more information on wind conditions at sea.

Environmental impact, in the form of such factors as noise, interference with telecommunications, effects on birds etc. need to be investigated. Finally, we also need to investigate interaction with the power system, including methods of forecasting wind speed.

Research institutions

The *Aeronautical Research Institute of Sweden* is active in the fields of aerodynamics, materials etc.

Development of design models is carried out in conjunction with *Teknikgruppen*.

The *Department of Meteorology at Uppsala University* is working on wind data for siting and design.

The *Department of Electric Machines and Power Electronics* at Chalmers University of Technology is investigating electrical systems for wind power production, in conjunction with the *Department of Control Technology*. Generators for wind power plants are also developed by the *Department of Industrial Electrical Engineering and Automation* at Lund Institute of Technology.

The *Department of Electric Power Engineering* at the Royal Institute of Technology is conducting research into the interaction of wind power and the power system.

Industrial base

Kvaerner Turbin AB in Kristinehamn (previously KMW, Kamewa) has developed the Näsudden I and II installations (2 MW and 3 MW respectively). Kvaerner is at present investigating a new generation of wind power plants, with the objective of effecting drastic cost reductions to achieve commerciality.

Zephyr Energy AB in Falkenberg has designed and manufactured three 250 kW units. The company is working at present on a batch of ten units, as well as developing a 750 kW unit.

Nordic Windpower AB, which is owned by ÅF-Industriteknik and Hägglunds AB, has developed a 400 kW unit and is preparing production of a batch of ten. A 1000 kW power plant, partly financed with money from the European Union, was erected at the beginning of 1995.

Vattenfall has acted as purchaser and performance specifier for Kvaerner and Nordic Windpower.

This chapter is based on material by Staffan Engström, MSc., Ägir Konsult AB, Lidingö.

REFERENCES

1   Basic data from Vindmølleoversigt, July 1993, Sustainable Energy Information Secretariat.

2   Small wind power units, National Swedish Board for Energy Source Development, 1978:4.

3   Sites for wind power. SOU 1988:32.

4   S. Engström: Legislation etc. for small-scale wind power. NUTEK R 1992:16.

5   L. Söder: Integration study of small amounts of wind power in the power system. Project 506 302-1, Integration of wind power. Royal Institute of Technology, Department of Electric Power Technology. 1994.

6   Wind energy in the power system. National Swedish Board for Energy Source Development, NE 1982:12.

7   Lars Hallén: Carrots replace the stick. Teknisk utblick, 25 August 1994.

8   Wind Power Consortium: Basic knowledge programme 940601. FFAP A-1023. The Aeronautical Research Institute of Sweden.

OTHER LITERATURE

Etablering av vindkraftverk på land (Siting wind power plants on land). National Board of Housing, Building and Planning, General Fact Sheets, 1995:1.

Kombinationen vindkraft och solvärme för grupphusområden (Solar heating and wind power in combination for residential areas). NUTEK Project Reports Wind-93/1.

SMALL-SCALE COMBINED HEAT AND POWER PRODUCTION MUST BE USER-FRIENDLY

SUMMARY

Application of small-scale combined heat and power generation directly within the built environment imposes severe demands on the reliability and user-friendliness of the equipment. Additional important characteristics are low emissions and low noise level, while wide flexibility in respect of fuels is also of value.

The most commonly employed prime mover at present is the gas diesel engine, although this requires good exhaust cleaning and efficient acoustic insulation. The Stirling engine, the gas turbine and the steam engine have clear advantages in respect of fuel flexibility, quiet running and low emissions.

With the present low electricity prices in Sweden, such decentralised small-scale CHP production is not economically viable. Cost conditions for small-scale CHP are completely different in some other countries, e.g. the UK and Denmark, which may affect conditions in Sweden as well.

Methods of determining ratings and new methods of exhaust cleaning need to be developed, while knowledge of operating conditions needs to be improved.

The fundamental underlying principle of CHP is that electricity and heat are produced together. This is an energy-efficient process, as most of the energy content of the fuel is used. The primary objective of the process is to produce electricity, as required, with the parallel production of heat being regarded as a secondary process, but with the heat being of such a quality (temperature) that it can be used for space heating purposes.

World-wide, the commonest form of electricity production is in cold condensing thermal power stations, producing only electricity. (More correctly, the plants also produce heat, but as there is no use for this heat [i.e. there is no heat sink available to which the heat can be sold], it has to be discharged to a water body or to atmosphere by cooling towers.) This applies naturally regardless of what fuel is used: coal, oil or nuclear fuel. By using, or finding a market for, both the heat and the electricity produced, the process becomes more profitable and also reduces environmental impact.

If combined heat and power production is to be integrated in buildings, power ratings will obviously be very much less than those used in public district heating systems, and so the process is referred to as small-scale CHP or micro-CHP. Plant is usually classed as small-scale if its electrical output is less than 10 MW, and sometimes if it is less than 3 MW. Micro-CHP is plant that produces electrical outputs of less than 1 MW, which is the output range concerned for applications in buildings or compact built-up areas.

Severe demands on the engines

The actual methods used differ somewhat and have different performance depending on the size of the plant and the fuel that is used. Important characteristics of engines to be used in locally-integrated CHP are operational reliability, low emission levels, fuel flexibility and - naturally - good cost-effectiveness in comparison with alternatives. For the plants as a whole, the critical parameters also include good overall efficiency, high operational reliability and low service and maintenance costs.

A combined heat and power plant produces both heat and electricity, which is thermally and financially efficient and also reduces pollution.

The gas diesel engine: the most widely used prime mover

Within the power output range of interest here - less than 1 MW - it is the gas diesel engine that is most commonly used to drive the electrical generator. This type of engine requires careful silencing, and is often built together with the generator and heat exchanger in a single package in a well-silenced enclosure. These packages are sold as standard units by a number of manufacturers around the world.

Natural gas is normally used as the fuel, as this is relatively cheap, although diesel oil and LPG may also be used. The engines are originally of diesel type, intended for industrial use or vehicle propulsion, but converted to allow them to run on natural gas. Part of this conversion involves fitting sparking plugs. Larger engines are also built in variants that can use both diesel oil and natural gas simultaneously to improve combustion performance.

The waste heat that is recovered comes mainly from the engine cooling water and the exhaust. About 45-55 % of the energy in the fuel can be recovered as waste heat: the higher proportion involves recovering heat from an intercooler that cools the charge air and providing a condensing heat exchanger for the exhaust gases.

The generator is usually of synchronous type, capable of operating synchronised to the grid or of producing power in a stand-alone mode, e.g. in the event of a power failure. About 25-35 % of the energy in the fuel can be obtained as electricity, depending on the size of the generator. Total efficiency of conversion of the energy in the fuel to electricity and heat is of the order of 80-90 %.

In addition to the engine, generator and heat exchangers, suitable control equipment is also needed, and is normally provided for internal control of the equipment. Other controls are required for external control, i.e. between the CHP unit and the grid or local electricity system. Operation at part load should be avoided: instead, it is better to operate the plant in an on/off mode.

New alternatives under development

Several alternatives to the gas diesel engine are being developed[1]. The most important of these are the Stirling engine, the gas turbine and the steam engine. All these engines employ continuous combustion, which increases the flexibility of fuel use and facilitates very low exhaust emissions.

The use of the Stirling engine is established in submarines, and development is in progress aimed at stationary applications in the 3-200 kW range. The engine is quiet and vibration-free and can, with further development of the combustion system and incorporation of exhaust gas cleaning, produce substantially less emissions than those possible from, say, a diesel engine. Efficiency, however, is somewhat lower than in a diesel engine. The Stirling engine is regarded as having the best prospects for commercial breakthrough as a prime mover for small-scale CHP.

The gas turbine, too, could become a commercially successful CHP prime mover. The most important arguments in its favour are its fuel flexibility and low emission levels. Development of machines with outputs in the range 30-300 kW is in progress.

At high load, small-scale steam engines have a lower efficiency than the other prime movers, but have high efficiency at low load[2]. This advantage becomes particularly valuable in stand-alone systems not connected to the public electricity grid, where operation at low load would be common. The steam engine also has the advantage of flexibility in choice of fuel, quiet running and low emissions. Hardly any development of the steam engine is being carried out.

Must be user-friendly

Technically, there are no particular problems in connecting a CHP unit to a larger building. However, connection does require high reliability on both the electrical and the heat sides. The unit will always be working in parallel with existing heating equipment and the existing electricity supply, and replaces purchased electrical energy.

If the method is to have a reasonable chance of spreading, it must be user-friendly. This is not something that can be taken for granted, as the equipment comprises relatively complicated components and is assumed to be installed in building having only ordinary caretaker personnel. One solution to this problem is the signing of a maintenance contract with the supplier.

Although energy conversion to electricity and heat is efficient, this alone is not enough: the unit must also generate a respectable surplus in order to pay back its capital cost. Operating costs consist of those for fuel and maintenance, with the fuel price generally being clearly known but difficult to influence. The cost of maintenance is more uncertain, particularly in Sweden where there is no fund of operating experience. This can substantially affect profitability in either direction. Keeping this cost down to a minimum level is of the utmost importance for the method's profitability.

Reduced cost of electrical energy

Revenue is not so much a positive income as a reduction in outgoings, in the form of reduced costs for electrical energy. Reduction in power demand can also contribute to profitability, depending on the tariff structure and on whether the unit is operated at high cost periods. However, in any case, it is most important that the unit should replace purchased electricity, which means that, electrically, it must be connected after the electricity meter on the subscriber's side. No electricity may be delivered to the distributor's system as long as prices for such electricity are as low as they are today. Nor may any heat production be dissipated by coolers solely to maintain electricity production over some particular period. (See the chapter on solar electricity.) Taken together, all these points (plus the fact that CHP technology is expensive) mean that particular care must be taken to determine the correct ratings of the equipment and systems. It is fatal, both for the equipment and for system cost-effectiveness, if too large a unit is supplied, so that electricity and/or heat power exceed the corresponding demands during the period when the unit is expected to be operating.

Electricity prices must rise before systems become profitable

A few small CHP units in the 100-400 kW power output range, produced in other countries, are in operation in Sweden. They have been installed by larger energy utilities and electricity producers, mainly for demonstration purposes and general acquisition of knowledge. In one case, performance has been more exhaustively monitored: Vattenfall, for example, has monitored the performance of two LPG-powered units, one of which incorporated lean burn technology while the other was fitted with a three-way exhaust catalytic cleaner, and compared their emissions. Several reports

and investigations have been written, describing systems and profitability.

The fact that this technology has made so little impact in Sweden is due solely to the country's price relationship between electricity and fuels. Several alternative energy technologies will become viable only if the price of electricity rises and there is a greater price gap between electricity and fuels. In the case of small-scale CHP, this is absolutely essential, as it is the savings in purchased electricity that are intended to pay the running and capital costs of the equipment. At present, the price of purchased electricity is too low for any operating surplus to be generated for payment of the capital costs.

Profitable technology in the UK and Denmark

The situation is different in, for example, the UK and Denmark. Natural gas in the UK costs about SEK 150-200/MWh, while electricity costs about SEK 300/MWh during the night, SEK 600/MWh during the day in summer and SEK 1000/MWh during the day in the winter. This provides a substantial gap between the prices of gas and electricity, with the result that small-scale CHP can be immediately profitable, although the lower price of electricity during the night generally means that the units will be shut down at that time. In Denmark, the size of the price gap is somewhere between that of Sweden and the UK, which does not fully justify local CHP. However, as there is strong political interest in increasing self-sufficiency in electricity supply, the government has reduced taxation on natural gas intended for CHP production, which has made the method profitable in Denmark as well.

Exhaust cleaning and rating methods are interesting areas of research

Small-scale CHP, using a gas diesel engine as its prime mover, is commercially viable in other countries. Interesting areas for further development are cleaning of exhaust gases and methods of determining necessary machine ratings. If the technology is to become reasonable widely used once it has become profitable, it will be essential that it does not pollute its immediate environment. Burning clean natural gas in an engine always forms various amounts of NO_x, while some

Photographer: Mikael Andersson, Mira

DEMAND-SIDE MANAGEMENT BECOMES INCREASINGLY IMPORTANT

SUMMARY

Several hundred different demand-side management projects have been performed in various countries and in Sweden over the last few years, mainly by energy utilities. Directly controlling the load by such means as restricting heating, domestic hot water or ventilation can have adverse effects on the occupants' comfort, and so the comfort requirements set limits for what can be done in respect of demand-side management.

Coming restructuring of the Swedish energy supply system will require improved knowledge of the power demand of various types of customers. Concentrating on the power aspect has been shown to be of considerable importance on several occasions when there has been a shortage of generating capacity in the Swedish electricity supply system. In future, power aspects will play an even more important part for both energy suppliers and users.

Measures introduced to curb power demand on the energy supply system apply mainly to users. In addition, there is a strong readiness on the parts of users to help to reduce power demand and energy use in buildings, that should be harnessed.

Knowledge of how it is possible sensibly to make best use of an energy supply system's capacity is referred to as demand-side management, and can be regarded as a particular area of work within the field of energy economics and planning.

Load management in buildings presents a highly complicated problem: many different factors affect the variations in power demand with time and make any links difficult to determine. This applies to climate factors, the structure of the building envelope, types of building services systems, user behaviour etc.

The aggregated requirements of energy users mean that energy suppliers must make sufficient capacity (= power) available on the energy supply system at any and every time. This applies to all types of energy supply systems, regardless of the type of energy carrier or type of user. In the case of the electricity supply system, which differs from district heating or gas supply systems by not having their inherent possibilities of energy storage, electricity must be produced in the same instant as it is used. It is therefore the total aggregated power demand (= after allowance for the effects of diversity) that determines the necessary production capacity that must be in operation. Capacity shortages on the electricity system quickly make themselves noticed in the form of voltage reductions, frequency reduction or load disconnection.

Calling for large quantities of energy over short periods of time results in greater costs for both the energy producers and users. Providing sufficient power capacity in the energy-producing plants to enable them always to be capable of meeting potential demand is capital-intensive and resource-intensive. This provides an incentive to restrict power demand. However, conditions and potentials for doing this are rapidly changing. 'Society' has set high environmental performance requirements and employed the taxation system and compulsory rules to adjust the relative prices of different energy forms. At the same time, politicians have sent various (and sometimes contradictory) signals to the interested parties, which have by no means facilitated decision-making in the energy sector. Financial conditions for changing the capacity of energy supply systems are constantly altering.

Load management in residential buildings and commercial premises is very complicated. The sheer number of different factors that are regarded as being capable of influencing variations of power demand in time, such as climate, construction of building envelopes, types of building services systems, user behaviour etc., mean that the picture of any relationships is very blurred. This applies particularly to detailed investigations at individual building level and for short periods of time. Over longer periods of time, and with the help of diversity, the effects of the various factors become less visible.

The various parties involved in the energy supply market, e.g. the bulk power producers, have always actually been aware of the power demand problem and monitored users' demand patterns, particularly in respect of aggregated loads on the energy supply system. The energy suppliers have created systems that provide financial incentives or apply direct load control to modify power demand. However, it is clear that the parties on the energy market would benefit from more exact knowledge of the variations of energy demand with time, of the factors that affect energy demand processes and/or the consequences that any changes in demand patterns might cause. This would improve the efficiency of use of existing production capacity and provide a better basis for future decisions in respect of short-term and long-term capacity additions. Development of guide measures intended either directly or indirectly to affect demand, e.g. in the form of more cost-effective tariffs or building standards intended to encourage energy conservation, also require greater knowledge in the field of load management.

Load management - controlling users' energy demands

Today, power demand limitation on the user side can be regarded as interwoven with the widely used concept of demand-side management (DSM). Demand-side management concepts involve primarily two types of parties - energy utilities and users. The energy utilities are responsible for energy production and distribution and can, by means of tariffs, contracts, load control, information and energy services, affect their customers' use of energy. For their part, the customers determine the magnitude of power and energy demand through such actions and means as their behaviour, their requirements and their investments. The objective of demand-side management measures is to bring together energy utilities and end users to encourage more efficient use of energy for the benefit of both parties - and for the benefit of society as a whole.

Several demand-side management projects in Sweden

Many demand-side management projects have been carried out by various energy utilities in Sweden: Sydkraft's EUFEMIA load control project can serve as an example. The objective of this project was to obtain a controllable demand buffer of 100 MW, mainly from industry, but also from residential users in order to postpone an increase in production capacity that would otherwise be needed to meet peak power demands. In detached houses and commercial premises, the load control facility allows electric heating to be reduced by 75 % over a maximum period of two hours, while immersion heaters can be disconnected for up to five hours. Communication employs FM radio transmitters/receivers[1].

Vattenfall's Uppdrag 2000 has also tested the possibilities of changing consumer demand. A brief description of one of the projects can give an idea of the results that power conservation can achieve.

Two different remote control systems were tested in two different detached house areas in Ösbydalen and Sylta in order to investigate the resulting power and cost savings from load control. One was intended for large customer groups and the other for small customer groups. The work was carried out jointly by Vattenfall, Värmdö Energi and Mälarkraft.

Ösbydalen and Sylta consist of 127 and 136 newly-built tenant-cooperative dwelling units in semi-detached houses and terrace houses built in 1988-90. The houses have waterborne electric heating and heat recovery by exhaust air heat pumps that supply heat to the domestic hot water and space heating system.

The electric boilers could be disconnected by remote control signals, transmitted either on the electricity distribution system or by radio. The objective of the project was to show how such remote control systems can deal with disconnection of electric heating in such areas, and what the magnitudes of the power savings are for the individual customer and as aggregated at local distribution substations.

Another important objective of the work was to investigate the effects of such remote control on the occupants. Consumers' incentive to take part in the scheme was tested by the introduction of a new three-level tariff in one of the areas. This consisted of a conventional time tariff, with a third electricity price during the controlled load periods. A red warning lamp, installed in the halls of the houses connected to the scheme, provided a further reminder of the price of peak load electricity.

Power savings of up to about 230 kW, as aggregated at the substation, or about 1.8 kW per house, were measured at ambient temperatures between about 0 °C and -2 °C. Extrapolating these results to an ambient temperature of -20 °C would give a power saving of about 340 kW at the substation, or 2.7 kW per house, which amounts to about 60 % of the theoretical heating power demand without load control. There was no measurable indication that the red peak load tariff warning light in the houses has had any effect on domestic electricity demand.

The 'recovery load', occurring when the electric boilers were reconnected after the disconnection periods, was almost the same as the power saving. Extrapolated to -20 °C, this indicated an increase of 308 kW (2.4 kW/house), relative to the reference periods.

The power reduction during the controlled periods of the colder days was large in proportion to the power variations over the day in the Ösbydal area. This reduction could be used to optimise the distributor's total load, which is relay the primary purpose.

The mean measured power saving, relative to the distributor's peak load charge, was estimated as about 192 kW (32 % of the maximum power demand in the area) for the 1990/91 heating season, based on measured ambient temperatures and extrapolated power savings. This would mean that the distributor would save about SEK 48 000/year through load control. In addition to the peak load tariff savings, it would also be possible to reduce the nominal rated power supply capacity in the long term, which would bring further savings. During colder weather, the savings should exceed those that were actually measured[2].

Sub-programme: energy-efficient buildings

The Swedish Council for Building Research (BFR) has initiated long-term research and development in the Energy-Efficient Buildings sub-programme. The programme includes a group of research workers at the Department of Heat and Power Engineering at Lund Institute of Technology, who are investigating electricity power demand in building-related energy supply systems.

To date, the following and other investigations have been carried out:

- Analyses of how various building services systems (heating and ventilation systems, domestic hot water production, lighting, domestic electricity) can affect power demand in various types of single-family houses[3].
- Analyses of the potential limits for load management by the distributor, without causing noticeable reductions in heating or living comfort[4].
- Analyses of the effect of ambient temperature on power demand in single-family houses[5].
- Energy and power demand in commercial premises.

The USA: lower electricity cost and a better environment

Various types of DSM programmes were introduced in the USA during the 1980s and 1990s, with significant power and energy savings as the results. However, reductions in power and energy demand are only part of the results effected by DSM programmes: probably the most important is the fact that, as a result of improved utilisation of generating capacity, the power utilities can supply electricity at a lower cost and also comply with more stringent environmental requirements.

In the residential sector in the USA, power utilities are offering energy surveys which in due course can result in energy conservation measures. The utilities offer discount incentives to persuade customers to buy more energy-efficient domestic appliances and lighting equipment. The utilities introduce indirect load management in the form of differentiated tariffs and direct load management using one-way or two-way communication. Domestic hot water immersion heaters, air conditioning equipment and swimming pool pumps can all be remotely controlled as necessary by the power utilities.

The American Electric Power Research Institute (EPRI) states that several hundred energy utilities are engaged in over a thousand DSM programmes, covering millions of residential subscribers[6]. A typical example of such a DSM scheme is that of the South Carolina Electric

& Gas utility that has instigated a programme of reducing its need for construction of additional generating capacity by 40 MW/year[7]. EPRI has developed an evaluation programme for DSM measures, and assembled a large database (the EPRI DSM Evaluation Database) for the storage, processing and evaluation of results[8].

Canada: reduced power demand

DSM programmes started to make their appearance in Canada towards the end of the 1980s[9]. The Ontario Hydro scheme can be seen as a typical example of changes that are occurring within the energy sector in Canada[9]. A wide range of differing programmes was introduced for various sectors, including the residential/commercial premises sector. Residential customers were offered energy surveys, with follow-up in the form of energy conservation measures. Both new and existing buildings were offered a range of attractive benefits in connection with the installation of heat pumps, low-energy lamps, power-efficient and energy-efficient domestic hot water heating and replacement of windows. As a result, total power demand, aggregated over all subscribers, fell between 1989 and 1992 by 865 MW, complemented by a further 1000 MW in interruptible supplies[10].

Hydro Québec, with a total installed power production capacity of 33.5 GW and about three million customers, has also started a DSM programme under the name of ECOKILO. Its objective is to reduce energy use by 9.3 TWh/year by 2000 and to reduce the maximum demand requirement by a total of 3 GW[11].

140 DSM projects in Germany

Today, almost half of all the energy utilities in Germany are operating some form of demand-side management. The commonest forms are load control and the provision of advisory services for subscribers. At present, 49 different energy utilities are operating a total of about 140 DSM projects[12].

The best known of these DSM programmes is KesS (Customer Service for Energy Efficiency Improvement), which was started in October 1992 by RWE Energie AG. The programme covers about 3 million private households, and operates primarily with information on efficient use of electricity over a wide front. The utility also encourages the purchase of energy-efficient domestic appliances through attractive credit terms and price subsidies. According to estimates made by Vereinigung Deutscher Elektrizitätswerke (VDEW), this campaign could result in an annual electrical energy saving of about 210 GWh from 1995 when the programme is concluded[13].

The UK's DSM programme at the development stage

The electricity supply industry in England and Wales was restructured in March 1990 as a first step towards privatisation and deregulation. The Office of Electricity Regulation (OFFER) was established to supervise this reorganisation.

DSM programmes are at a development stage. A report prepared for OFFER by LE Energy and SRC International[14] states that there is a substantial potential for DSM measures applicable to all types of users. Electricity use in the residential sector can be expected to be reduced by about 12 % per annum over the next 10 years, or by about 1990 GWh and 315 MW per year.

France: specific electricity use has fallen in homes

As far as DSM programmes for domestic subscribers are concerned, improvements have already been effected in the efficiency of electricity use for heating purposes. Over the last 20 years, power demand in electrically-heated houses has fallen from about 1.2 W/(m$^3 \cdot$ K) to about 0.75 W/(m$^3 \cdot$ K). The shape of the load curve has been changed by moving the power demand for domestic hot water heating in about 9 million households (out of about 22 million in total) to an off-peak time during the night. Specific use of electricity in dwellings has been reduced: e.g. in the Paris area from about 170 kWh/(m$^2 \cdot$ year) to about 95 kWh/(m$^2 \cdot$ year).

At present, trials are in progress with reducing electricity use by domestic equipment, air conditioning and lighting. During 1994, a new type of electricity tariff was introduced on trial with low-voltage subscribers. This tariff, known as the 'blue/white/red' tariff, divides the year up into periods with different electricity prices.

France is also widely promoting the Domotique system (Domestic Automation), in conjunction with other countries under the EHSA (European Home Systems Association) umbrella and as part of the EU ESPRIT programme. It is the intention that, in future, these systems should allow control of heating, lighting, ventilation etc. via the TV screen[15].

Denmark has introduced a time-differentiated tariff

Since 1990 NESA, with about 500 000 subscribers in the Copenhagen area, has implemented a programme for the introduction of a time-differentiated tariff for all customers using more than 20 MWh/year of electricity[16]. This programme has been carried out in parallel with other types of DSM activities such as the provision of advisory services, information meetings, brochures and consultations for non-residential customers.

The Danish Electric Utilities Association Investigation Department (DEFU) has carried out two projects involving the use of a control unit by the name of FLEXTAR[17]. This is a system that is based on two-way communication and has been tested by an electricity utility in west Denmark in 25 single-family houses to provide direct control of space heating and domestic hot water production and for indirect control through information on the tariff in operation at any given time. Another, later, investigation covered 50 houses and was intended to reduce the peak load at critical load times. Customers could restore the heating manually, but it would then cost them six times the normal tariff[18].

Deregulated electricity market in Norway since 1991

The electricity market in Norway was deregulated on 1st January 1991, with the introduction of free competition in electricity supply.

Norway's Energiforsyningens Forskningsinstitutt (EFI) has investigated energy and power demands of various types of users since the end of the 1980s, e.g. Livik & Feilberg[19] and Rismark[20]. These load investigations have been used as a basis for energy advisory services for office buildings, schools and homes[21].

Interesting CADDET reports

CADDET - the Centre for Analysis and Dissemination of Demonstrated Energy Technologies - was established by the IEA at the end of the 1980s with the objective of disseminating information and improving the exchange of experience from demonstration energy conservation projects with different types of end users in the OECD countries. In terms of efficacy, several of the investigations described in CADDET reports are interesting.

Abel et al.[22] summarise experience from projects carried out at the end of the 1980s concerning new types of heating and ventilation systems in office buildings.

Piette[23] has collected the results from 24 investigations carried out in six countries into the storage of heating and cooling as a means of improving electrical power conservation in homes and commercial premises. The results show that almost the entire heating demand in homes can be transferred to off-peak periods. The storage potential for heating and cooling in commercial premises also increases in step with the development of increasingly sophisticated control systems.

Aronsson and Nilsson[24] describe new energy-efficient lighting systems for commercial premises. Their report summarises experience from 17 large demonstration projects carried out in Australia, Holland, Sweden, the UK and the USA. The investigations have shown that replacing light sources and installing supervisory and control systems for the lighting systems can reduce energy and power demand by 20-80 %, with pay-off times of between one and eight years.

Piette[25] summarises the results of 15 investigations performed in five countries (Canada, Finland, Norway, the UK and the USA) of lighting control systems intended to reduce uncontrolled peak power demands on the electrical system and so reduce energy use. The results show that maximum power demand could be reduced by between 3 and 54 W/m^2. Power savings of between 20 and 24 % were noted in large refrigeration systems in three hypermarkets.

Power demand control and user acceptance

The majority of power demand control measures that have been applied in Sweden and other countries have been carried out by the energy utilities. However, direct load control in the form of reduction of heating, hot water supplies or ventilation can adversely affect user comfort, and so limits have been set for the maximum variation of the comfort requirements and of the degree of acceptance (particularly in respect of variations in indoor climate) by users. Assessment of thermal comfort should be based on the recommendations set out in the various rules and regulations.

Investigations performed by Sydkraft[26] and Uppdrag 2000[27] have shown that users have not experienced any loss of comfort as a result of a 50 % reduction in heating over a three-hour period.

Trials of a power demand control system in single-family houses having airborne heating systems[28] have shown that transferring heating power input to an off-peak period (22.00-06.00) results in excessive temperatures during the mornings, which the occupants regarded as an unpleasant change in their thermal comfort.

As indoor temperature can temporarily be allowed to fall below 20 °C, although not lower than 18 °C, or be increased to over 24 °C, but not higher than 28 °C, any load control system that results in reductions/increases of indoor temperature by not more that 3 °C over a 3-4-hour period should be fully acceptable[29].

Concentration on the power aspect

Experience shows that most research into power demand control is carried out by energy utilities or planned from their point of view. This means that there is a need of research that can cover the middle ground between the electricity suppliers and their customers, in order to defend customers´ interests.

At the same time, there is also a tendency for the energy utilities increasingly to modify their attitudes towards their customers from having been 'energy providers' to 'energy service companies', providing a broad spectrum of services. In its 'Scenario 2005', the Association of Swedish Electric Utilities' Technical Council's Development Standing Committee describes its views on the changes that it feels will most affect electricity distribution companies up to 2005[30].

All possible future structural changes will require greater knowledge of energy demand requirements, but particularly also the power demands of different types of consumers. Concentrating on the power aspect in particular has been shown to be of considerable importance on a number of occasions of power shortage in the Swedish electricity supply system. In future, the power aspect will play an even more important part, both for energy suppliers and energy users.

Deregulation (or primarily 'changes of regulation') of the electricity market in Sweden will also introduce completely new conditions for electricity use. Efficient utilisation of available capacity in the energy supply system will become even more important.

Application of research results

Experience from the various power demand control projects in buildings that have been carried out in Sweden and other countries have shown that constant

development and refinement of our knowledge of variations in power demand are essential for both energy utilities and users. Improved knowledge provides a means of guarding more surely against insufficient capacity in the production and distribution stages through operation of measures on the demand side. In turn, this results in improved ability to meet customers' power demands. More efficient utilisation of power capacity reduces the pressure for new investment in the production/distribution sides. More exact knowledge can provide more accurate rating of production and distribution facilities, together with improved planning as a result of more accurate assessment of expansion requirements. Power demand investigations facilitate analyses of potentials for improving power demand control on the part of users and in the distribution systems.

Future work

Power demand control does not concern only energy producers and energy distributors, as power demand control in energy supply systems primarily affects the end users. Knowledge is needed in order to be able to guard the interests of consumers. In addition, users have a strong incentive and desire to help to reduce power demand and energy use in buildings, and these interests should be utilised. General support by government for research into work on the power demand side is therefore justified and essential.

Future R&D work should concentrate primarily on:

- power demand analyses for different types of users, in single-family houses, apartment buildings and commercial premises,
- analyses of the feasibility of, and potential limits for, load management, either by the user or by the energy supplier,
- demand analyses at higher levels in centralised energy supply systems,
- development of 'user-friendly' load control concepts, and
- the consequences of various types of power demand control measures.

This chapter is based on material by Dr. Jurek Pyrko, Department of Heat and Power Engineering, Lund Institute of Technology.

Energy users are both involved in, and have an interest in, reducing their energy use.
Photographer: Bruno Ehrs, Bildhuset

REFERENCES

1 Ottosson, H., Söderström, M.: *Teknikstyrning av elanvändning* (Load management of electricity use). SEU, Sydkraft AB, 1990.

2 Levin, P., Wesslén, M., 1993: *Laststyrning i nya småhus med vattenburen elvärme* (Load control in new single-family houses with waterborne electric heating). Vattenfall, Uppdrag 2000, Stockholm.

3 Pyrko, Jurek, Qvistbäck, Per: *Installationer i bostäder och effektbehov - datorsimulering* (Building services systems in residential buildings and power requirements - computer modelling). Report LUTMDN/TMVK-3161-SE. Department of Heat and Power Engineering, Lund Institute of Technology, October 1993.

4 Pyrko, Jurek, Qvistbäck, Per: *Belastningsstyrning i bostäder - datorsimulering* (Load control in residential buildings - computer modelling). LUTMDN/TMVK-3167-SE. Lund Institute of Technology, October 1994.

5 Pyrko, Jurek: *Effekthushållning i bostäder* (Load management in residential buildings). PhD thesis. LUTMDN/(TMVK-1008)/1-120/(1991). Lund Institute of Technology, December 1991.

6 Gellings, C. W., Rabl, V. A., Chamberlain, J. H.: *Demand-side Management: the Winds of Change in the USA.* Revue de l'energie, No. 440, June/July 1992, pp. 367-377.

7 Isemo Jens, Johansson Jan, Johansson Nils: *Demand-side management in the USA.* STATT, Newsletter No. 3, September 1992.

8 North, Alan et al.: *Accumulating and Synthesizing the Results of DSM Evaluations: The EPRI Database Project.* 2nd Int. Energy Efficiency & DSM Conf. 'Customer Focus', 21-23 September 1993. Stockholm, Sweden.

9 Riley, Mark: *Energy-efficient Building Technologies: An Overview of the Trends and Opportunities.* Int. Conf. 'Next-generation Technologies for Efficient Energy Uses and Fuel Switching', 7-9 April 1992. Dortmund, Germany.

10 Fraser, Marion: *DSM and the Transformation of an Electric Utility and its Customers.* 2nd Int. Energy Efficiency & DSM Conf. 'Customer Focus', 21-23 September 1993. Stockholm, Sweden.

11 Ouimet, J. H., Waintroob, D.: *Achieving a Market Transformation with a Large-scale Residential Mail-back Audit Program.* 2nd Int. Energy Efficiency & DSM Conf. 'Customer Focus', 21-23 September 1993. Stockholm, Sweden.

12 Andersson, Jonas: Information from the Office of the Swedish Technical Attaché in Bonn. Telefax, 1994-02-03.

13 Decker, Erwin: *First Experiences with KesS, the Customer Energy-saving Service of RWE Energie AG.* 2nd Int. Energy Efficiency & DSM Conf. 'Customer Focus', 21-23 September 1993. Stockholm, Sweden.

14 LE Energy Ltd & SRC International ApS, 1992. *Demand-side Measures.* Report for OFFER.

15 Boivin, J-Y., Nicolas, C.: *EDF Involvement in the Development of Innovative Technologies for Energy Management in Houses.* 2nd Int. Energy Efficiency & DSM Conf. 'Customer Focus', 21-23 September 1993. Stockholm, Sweden.

16 Rahbek, T., Haase, N., Østergaard, S.: *A New Family of Services Based on a Tariff Computer Helps Customers Obtain the Most Efficient Use of Electricity.* Int. Conf. 'Next-generation Technologies for Efficient Energy Uses and Fuel Switching', 7-9 April 1992. Dortmund, Germany.

17 Kofod, Kasper: *Load Management by New Equipment and Software.* Int. Conf. 'Next-generation Technologies for Efficient Energy Uses and Fuel Switching', 7-9 April 1992. Dortmund, Germany.

18 Kofod, Kasper: *DSM of Electric Heating by New Equipment.* 2nd Int. Energy Efficiency & DSM Conf. 'Customer Focus', 21-23 September 1993. Stockholm, Sweden.

19 Livik, K., Feilberg, N.: *Energi- og effektforhold hos ulike kategorier sluttforbrukere* (Energy and Power Demand of Various Categories of End Users). EFI, Norway, Report TR 3998.

20 Rismark, O.: *Belastningskurver for bygg med forskjellige oppvarmingssystemer* (Load Curves for Built Environments with Different Heating Systems). EFI, Norway, Report TR 3726.

21 Livik, K., Feilberg, N.: *Individuell energirådgivning basert på belastningsmålinger* (Individual Energy Advisory Services Based on Load Metering). EFI, Norway, Report TR 3789.

22 Abel, E., Aronsson, S., Jilar, T. and Nilsson, P-E.: *New Technologies for Heating and Cooling Supply in Office Buildings.* CADDET Analyses Series no. 3, 1990.

23 Piette, M.A., *Thermal Storage - Managing Electrical Loads in Buildings.* CADDET Analyses Series no. 4, 1990.

24 Aronsson, S. and Nilsson, P-E., 1991: *Energy-efficient Lighting in Commercial Buildings.* CADDET Analyses Series no. 6.

25 Piette, M.A.: Controls to reduce electrical peak demands in commercial buildings. CADDET Analyses Series no. 7, 1991.

26 See Johansson, P., Ejeklint, L., 1990.

27 See Ottosson, H., Söderström, M., 1990.

28 Andersson, S.: *BORO AB:s lågeffekthus* (BORO AB's Low-power House). LiTH, IKP, Exam Project, LiTH-IKP-Ex-950, 1991.

29 See Pyrko, J., Qvistbäck, P., 1994.

30 *Scenario 2005 - En framtidsstudie av Tekniska Rådets utvecklingsutskott* (Scenario 2005 - A Futures Study by the Development Standing Committee of the Technical Council. Association of Swedish Electric Utilities, Stockholm, 1993.

OTHER LITERATURE

Effekthushållning i bostäder (Power demand reduction in residential buildings). Pyrko, J. Lund Institute of Technology, Department of Heat and Power Engineering, TMVK-1008, 1991.

Effektivisering och ersättning av el i direktelvärmda flerbostadshus (Improving efficiency and replacing electricity in apartment buildings with direct electric heating). Nilson, A., Hjalmarsson, C. and Walter, A. BFR R41:1990.

REDUCING ELECTRICITY USE THROUGH CORRECT EQUIPMENT

SUMMARY

About 34 % of Sweden's electricity use in 1993 went to homes, 22 % to commercial premises, 42 % to industry and 2 % to transport. There are major savings to be made from improving the efficiency of ventilation systems and using new lighting technology.

The purchaser's costs for any new technology are not restricted solely to the purchase price, but also include indirect costs for finding information on the technology, training and allowance for uncertainty concerning the performance. There are also financial and institutional obstacles that stand in the way of the spread of most new technologies. Behavioural science research, such as investigation of how we use electric equipment and of purchasing behaviour, would be helpful.

Ongoing evaluations and re-evaluations of the performance and market availability of the new technology are needed. Reasonable minimum values for electrically-efficient building services systems need to be determined. Domestic lighting, street lighting and lighting of parking places are important areas of research. Demand-controlled ventilation is another important area.

Fundamental investigations of the effects of waste heat from electrical equipment and services are needed. In addition, research is needed into the future development and application possibilities of low-voltage DC, into dose/response relationships for short-time exposures to high magnetic fields and into the effects of stray currents in four-wire (3-phase and neutral) electric power supply systems.

Electricity use in non-residential buildings, including electricity for heating, has increased by 6 % per annum since 1970, amounting to almost 140 kWh/m² in 1993. Total electricity use for operation of domestic appliances has remained almost constant over the last 15 years, despite increased ownership of domestic appliances[1].

We have long known a lot about how electricity can be produced and transmitted: the parties involved on the production side are few, but backed by substantial resources and facilities. There is also an adequate base of statistical material, together with statistics on the breakdown of electricity use by different sectors of society. However, knowledge of what electricity is actually used for is less comprehensive. Here, many parties are involved, most of whom are far from expert. As far as the efficiency aspect is concerned, no real research or systematic processing of available knowledge has previously been carried out for the user side. It is only in the last five years that any more systematic acquisition of knowledge has been applied. If the electricity use side has been neglected in terms of acquisition of knowledge, there is probably considerable potential for applying new knowledge to improve performance. As we increase our knowledge of what electricity is used for, we can ask ourselves how electricity might be used more efficiently in order to meet our requirements as well as, or better than, it does today. This applies not only to research workers or manufacturers of domestic equipment, but also to end users in connection with purchasing and operation.

The problem areas that begin to become apparent include the following:

Electricity use is a particularly differentiated technology area. It can be divided up into many different application areas, with the applications and technology within each area varying widely. Each particular technology can then be applied in many other contexts, under different conditions. It is often system aspects that determine the actual level of electricity use. Users of the technologies have varying levels of knowledge and behavioural patterns, which can also result in different levels of electricity use.

If we then wish to improve the efficiency of electricity use, we need not only more efficient technology itself (components and systems), but also knowledge of how this more efficient technology is to be distributed, which brings the efficiency aspect of the product or technology into competition with all its other characteristics and features.

The payback gap

The literature discusses the concept of a payback gap. It is not sufficient that some particular technology or method should be cost-effective: the purchaser's costs for changing to a new technology or method, as represented by training, obtaining information and for aspects such as general uncertainty of what the new performance will be, all create substantial market barriers. And it is not just information barriers that result in inertia: there are also cost and institutional obstacles. The person who orders the technology etc., for example, may not necessarily always be the same person who will subsequently have to pay the running costs. Knowledge of factors affecting the spread of a new technology or method is therefore an important element in the wider problem area of more efficient use of electricity.

Summarising, the problem area of more efficient use of electricity comprises the following knowledge areas:

- Knowledge of the existing technology or method in respect of aspects such as efficiency, how it is used (i.e. intensity and user behaviour) and how the present user behaviour results from the present technical characteristics.
- The technical potential available on the market today and technical development possibilities.
- Knowledge concerning the introduction of new technology and inertia of such introduction in respect of market acceptance.

How electricity is used

An understanding of what electricity is used for today is a necessary starting-point in order to be able to assess possible areas for efficiency improvements and to identify important working areas on which to concentrate. Figure 1 shows a breakdown of electricity use by sectors. The diagram also shows the proportion of electric heating used in homes and commercial premises. Electricity is also used in industry for space heating purposes as well as for process heating. Electricity for building services systems in apartment buildings is included in the column for commercial premises. (See also Appendix 1.)

Figure 2 shows a breakdown of domestic electricity use, amounting to about 14 TWh/year. This does not include electricity for powering common services (building services systems) in apartment buildings.

It can be seen from Figure 2 that food storage and lighting are the two main areas of electricity use. A further 2.1 TWh/year are used in apartment buildings for lighting of common areas, ventilation and utility room requirements. Distributions differ between electricity use in single-family houses and in apartment buildings, and particularly between individual households.

Electricity use for operation of building services systems constitutes a significant element of total electricity use in Sweden, amounting to over 19 TWh[1].

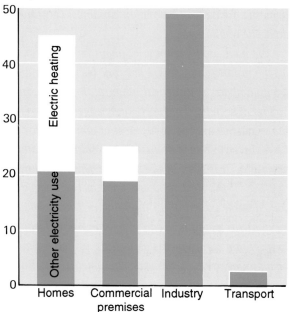

TWh/year

Figure 1. Electricity use in 1993.

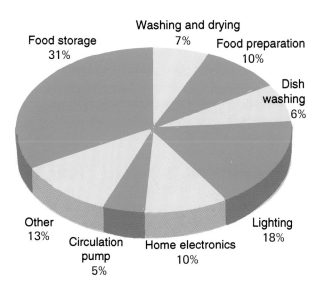

Food storage
31%

Washing and drying
7%

Food preparation
10%

Dish
washing
6%

Other
13%

Circulation
pump
5%

Home electronics
10%

Lighting
18%

Figure 2. Domestic electricity use in homes, 14 TWh. (Source: Statistics Sweden.)

This includes electricity for lighting, ventilation, climate cooling and other building services.

Interesting development for ventilation

A report by the Electricity Use Council (August 1992) estimates that the use of electricity for ventilation in buildings amount sto between 6 and 7 TWh/year, made up of 0.9 TWh/year for ventilation in residential buildings, 1.9 TWh/year for commercial premises and 3.2 TWh/year in industry.

On the basis of a larger empirical investigation of 110 ventilation systems in apartment buildings[2], the average total efficiency of ventilation systems in existing apartment buildings is estimated as amounting to about 20 %. The total efficiency of the two best fans in a recently completed field test of fans for use in residential buildings was over 45 %[3]. Further improvements in efficiency would require changes in the design and construction of ventilation ducts in order to reduce pressure drops, or entirely new system designs.[4 5 6]

The interesting development for ventilation in apartment buildings comprises the development of components for speed control (cheaper and less interference), acquisition of knowledge and system development in connection with demand-controlled ventilation and ventilation that responds to ambient temperatures, as well as new system designs that reduce the overall system pressure drops.

Today, ventilation systems in single-family houses and apartment buildings with small fans have a very low efficiency, often less that 10 %. Any improvement in this sector will require completely new designs of low-power motors (10-100 W), which in turn would require such large production quantities that development will have to be based on results from other application areas. In the longer term, we can foresee concepts based on DC motors, reluctance motors or variable-frequency induction motors.

There is also a substantial potential for improvement in the efficiency of ventilation systems in commercial premises, through demand control of ventilation systems, particularly as conventional designs are based on fixed air flow rates, often designed for the highest loading expected, whether in terms of number of persons or of temperatures. This is an area in which further demonstration installations and the feedback of experience are required in order to make details of good systems of this type more widely known. If ventilation systems for smaller room units are also to be demand-controlled at low overall costs, it will be necessary to develop cost-efficient designs for controlling air conditions in each room unit. Distributed intelligence may be one way of reducing wiring costs.

In the case of premises such as schools and industrial processes with high quantities of waste heat, there are thermal buoyancy effects that, under certain conditions, can be utilised to assist ventilation. However, such system designs are less attractive to the ventilation equipment manufacturers, and so may need more support from centralised building research organisations.

Comfort cooling (air conditioning) today tends to be installed on a somewhat hit-and-miss basis, i.e. the heating and ventilating consultant is simply told of a required cooling power capacity, or of a somewhat arbitrary internal heat load, in addition to solar heat input, that is specified for removal. There is no consideration of the effects of more efficient lighting, more efficient supply air fans or more electrically-efficient office equipment. The alternative, of installing more effective sunshades is not employed, and no use is made of the energy storage potential of the building structure, allowing heat to be stored from the daytime for release to the cooler night air.

More electrically-efficient cooling can be arranged by such means as employing 'free cooling' from waterways, evaporative cooling or absorption cooling. In certain cases, groundwater aquifers can also be used for storing heat and cooling.

More efficient refrigerators and freezers

The development of more efficient refrigerators and freezers provides a good illustration of what successful technology procurement can achieve in forcing the development of more electrically-efficient equipment. Figure 3 shows the improvement in electrical efficiency of the market's range of refrigerators/freezers since 1980.

Continued development towards more efficient equipment can be based on improved insulation methods, e.g. vacuum panels or silica gel. Another line

of development is concerned with more efficient compressors. However, developments on the control and motor sides require very large production volumes, as they must compete with production volumes of established technology, where prices have already been pressed. Variable-speed refrigerator compressors will probably make their first appearance in refrigeration equipment using larger unit sizes.

Food preparation/heating - little potential

Cookers, hobs and ovens do not constitute an area with any great potential for efficiency improvement with present user habits. Improved insulation of ovens, better matching of oven sizes to actual requirements, the use of microwave ovens for heating or the use of electric kettles for boiling water are all examples of methods that can result in modest electricity savings. Demonstration

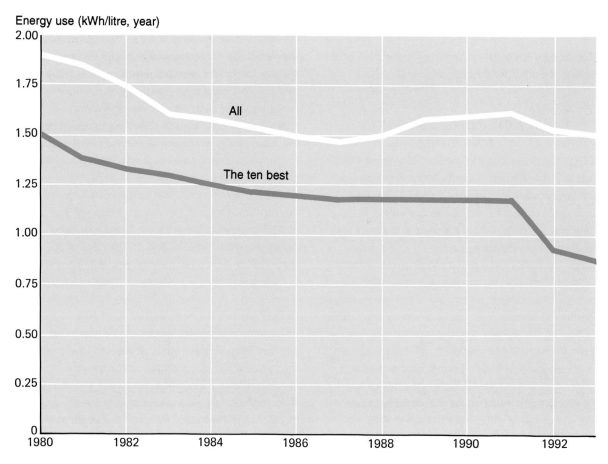

Figure 3. Energy efficiency of new refrigerators/freezers from 1980 to 1993. The upper curve shows the entire range available, while the lower curve shows the ten most efficient.

trials[7] of these various methods, coupled with replacement of older cookers, have indicated reductions of about 15 % in electricity use.

The use of induction heating for heating metal cooking pots/saucepans reduces the amount of waste heat and provides particularly rapid control. However, market acceptance of this particular technology is uncertain.

Clothes washing and drying - rapid development

This is another area in which there is rapid development towards more energy-efficient appliances. Reduced water volumes per load, together with lower washing temperatures, result in reduced electricity use. The greatest gaps in our knowledge relate not to the technology and its potentials, but to drying habits and how the needs and conditions for drying clothes vary from one type of dwelling to another. Apart from the use of an outdoor line, the most electrically-efficient method of drying uses a drying cabinet without any additional heating, connected to the building's exhaust ventilation system. Trials of such arrangements have started and are giving promising results[8]. An important information contribution for technology procurement is an investigation comprising in-depth interviews of 24 households performed by the Department of Consumer Technology at Chalmers University of Technology[9].

Domestic electronic equipment and office appliances

Wider ownership of electronic equipment increases the demand for electricity. At the same time, technical development has opened the way to higher electrical efficiency. Particularly important in this respect is the automatic power-down of computer monitors to a low-energy standby state. Figures 4 and 5 show possible trends in electricity use by office equipment[10].

The references to 'performance specification' in Figures 4 and 5 refer to the performance specifications drawn up by the National Board for Industrial and Technical Development (NUTEK) and the American EPA Energy Star Scheme. This trend towards more electrically-efficient office equipment will provide additional benefits in the form of reduced waste heat and thus improve indoor comfort in offices.

An investigation involving metering the power and energy requirements of 300 items of electronic equipment when in the standy state has shown that the average power demand of domestic electronic equipment is 4.5 W. Over the life of each item, this represents an additional cost for the household in electricity of SEK 200-300:-. Video tape recorders are the largest single electronic power users in the home. Domestic electronic equipment alone uses a total of about 1.4 TWh/year for the whole country[11]. If we subtract from this the energy that the equipment uses when in actual operation, we are still left with an energy

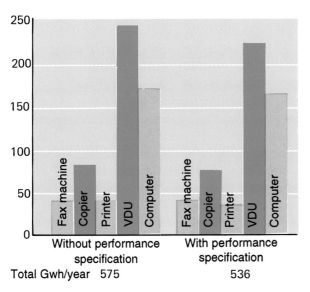

Figure 4. Electricity use for office equipment, 1994.

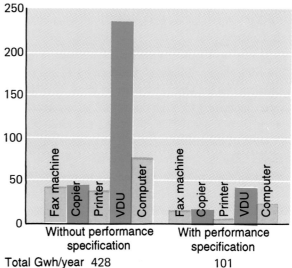

Figure 5. Electricity use for office equipment, 2000.

use level of 0.9 TWh/year, which is made up largely of pure losses.

Development of more efficient light sources

Lighting accounts for about 9 % of Sweden's electricity use, or about 13 TWh/year. Technical development in the lighting sector is extremely rapid: examples include the development of efficient luminaires for fluorescent tubes, high-frequency ballasts for fluorescent tubes and the development of compact fluorescent lamps as direct replacements for incandescent lamps, not forgetting the large number of conventional incandescent lamps that have been replaced by small halogen spotlamps. These halogen lights are more efficient than conventional incandescent lamps, but considerably less efficient that discharge lamps (fluorescent tubes).

Continued technical development embraces further development of more efficient light sources. Present-generation fluorescent tubes produce about 100 lumen/W, which can be compared with a theoretically possible maximum value of 235 lumen/W for artificial light. Research and development are being carried out internationally: examples of current development include high-efficiency metal halogen lamps and the use of fibre optics and light guides to convey light. Another example includes development of a small high-intensity (3000 lumen/cm²) light source, about the size of a cycle lamp, which will permit the use of small reflectors and is capable of competing with the popular halogen lamps, but which has a higher efficiency (86 lumen/W)[12].

A new light source, known as Solar 2000, and involving plasma technology, has been tested in a trial installation at the central hospital in Lund[13]. The lamp, with a rating of 3.4 kW, produces 400 000 lumen at an efficiency of about 100 lumen/W, after allowance for the losses in its microwave generator. The colour is that of daylight, but the lamp requires a special design of reflector in order to make best use of the intensive light. It is hoped to be able to increase the efficiency to about 150 lumen/W and also to develop lamps of lower power ratings.

There is still some technical potential for more efficient luminaires based on improved reflector design. This is an area in which there is still plenty to do for Swedish luminaire manufacturers.

Development on the component side includes more advanced control of lighting for better matching to actual requirements (occupation-sensing control, daylight control etc.). The use of distributed intelligence controllers, in particular, offers exciting potentials on the lighting side.

Lack of awareness

There are probably gaps in the knowledge of interior decorators, interior architects, property administrators, lighting consultants and electrical installation contractors concerning the possibilities of the new technology. Despite the use of more efficient luminaires, there is still a tendency to excessive installation density, thus giving greater lighting intensities than are really needed.

The lighting area covers many other different areas. The more rapid that technical development becomes, the greater the need for knowledge in adjacent areas, e.g. the use of daylight, optical transport of daylight and artificial light, the physiological effects of flicker, the value of individual controls for variation of lighting pattern and lighting intensity, lighting planning and the light-reflecting characteristics of paints and of wall and ceiling coverings. However, research must not be concentrated solely on areas relating to the work environment and commercial lighting. Other important lighting applications for which more electrically-efficient lighting is required include domestic lighting, street lighting, the lighting of parking places and other public areas.

Establish a new electrically-efficient building standard

It is a long way from development of a more electrically-efficient technology or method to its widespread market acceptance. By the far the greatest obstacle is the simple fact that, in the majority of cases, consumers do not even think about electrical efficiency when deciding on their choice of appliance or equipment. By, in one way or another, establishing a building standard that considers electrical efficiency aspects, we can accelerate acceptance of improved technology. Examples of areas in which standardisation is needed are:

■ The development of programme requirements for various technologies and application areas, e.g. for lighting in health care premises, schools, offices and industry[14].

■ Development of purchasing aids[15] that provide developers with help in formulating and formalising their requirements in respect of the electrical efficiency of building services systems so that they are rated and selected on the basis of true life cycle cost perspective.

'The Ventilation Guide - A Developer's Guide for Residential Ventilation - New Building'[16] which, in the same way as its follower, devoted to refurbishment, helps developers to describe their performance requirements - of which electrical efficiency is one - at an early stage, is already available. The Building Regulations, which specify overall requirements in respect of electrically-efficient building services systems[17], which establish recommended minimum standards for these areas, are also available. In addition, both the EU and the Nordic countries are discussing the value and feasibility of establishing energy standards for white goods[18]. However, in order to be able to establish a new standard, there must be a suitable technology/product/process that acceptably provides the required performance at a reasonable cost. Technology evaluation and methods for monitoring results and performance are important areas, as is knowledge of behavioural modification and customer acceptance. Today, there are also gaps in our knowledge in respect of proposals for reasonable minimum values of electrically-efficient designs of items such as pumps and comfort cooling. The worth or effect of these means of establishing new standards also needs to be monitored.

Waste heat and its value

The use of electricity in a building almost always results in the production of waste heat. This affects not only heating requirements, but also any artificial cooling requirements. When evaluating improvements in the efficiency of electricity use, whether for items of equipment, in energy standards, in technology procurement or as conservation potentials, we must always consider the value of waste heat from these items of equipment or apparatus.

Commercial premises today often have a surplus of heat, to the extent that any reduction in the quantity of waste heat reduces costs and energy requirements for comfort cooling. This, too, needs to be evaluated, as does the value of reducing waste heat in improving room comfort if there is no artificial cooling system.

This is not an easy area to work with. Is most of the heat removed by ventilation exhaust outlets at ceiling height, or does most of it radiate downwards into the room? What are the effects of the position of the source of waste heat in the room, of ventilation air change rates and of the type of ventilation?

In homes, the value of waste heat depends strongly on whether it is at high power or low power, whether it coincides with times of the day when other waste heat or free heat is available (insolation, activities of the occupants etc.) and of whether the waste heat source is in the kitchen or bathroom where ventilation air exhaust points are situated.

There are no thorough investigations into this problem area. The lack of sound basic knowledge also means that all computer and simulation models of building energy balances unavoidably include major uncertainty areas, as electrical equipment influences such a large part of each building's energy balance.

The value of electric heating

Energy conservation is not really concerned so much with saving kilowatt-hours as with saving money. In many situations, greater or lesser use of electricity in a building also affects the building's heating requirements. Installing a heat pump or heat recovery equipment saves thermal energy at the cost of some increase in use of electrical energy. A property-owner will evaluate the costs of different forms of energy carriers on the basis of their respective price levels.

Provided that taxes, levies and external environmental effects are correctly handled, a corresponding evaluation can be performed at the public economic level in respect of production and distribution cost calculations right through to the typical end user. This naturally increases the difficulty of making a correct evaluation. It is also difficult to evaluate the cost of electricity in a future electricity system, where marginal costs of electricity production can be expected to be considerably higher than they are now. This applies regardless of whether marginal electricity production is based on power produced in other countries, and imported by cable or transiting, or by production plant in Sweden.

What, then, should such an evaluation be used for? Today, the State influences energy use in new buildings through the Building Regulations. The present Building

Regulations assign equal values to electricity and other forms of energy, i.e. they are interchangeable in any energy balances. In practice, this means that, in many cases, savings of heat are replaced by greater use of electricity (e.g. by heat recovery requiring electrical energy amounting to 20-50 % of the energy saved). A combination of overall system analysis, linked to a political evaluation of future factors, is essential in order to perform such an analysis.

Behavioural science research is needed

Knowledge of electricity use behaviour by end users requires knowledge of purchasing attitudes, behaviour and use of particular appliances. This knowledge is needed for several reasons:

- To develop appliances so that they better accord with needs and with day-to-day use.
- To understand the effects of any technical improvement supplied.
- In order to disseminate knowledge and information intended to encourage users to behave more consciously and energy-efficiently.
- In order to understand how, and under which circumstances, a more efficient appliance will actually be bought.

Low-voltage DC systems in future buildings

A possible future scenario is that solar cell technology may achieve a commercial breakthrough and be integrated into the walls and roofs of buildings. This will provide a supply of low-voltage DC that will need to be combined with some form of storage (e.g. a battery). This electricity can be used for charging electric vehicles, as well as for lighting and many items of apparatus. Domestic electronic equipment, fans and refrigerator motors can all be powered by low-voltage DC. This is a perspective in which there is much to be gained by anticipating and starting work on acquiring appropriate knowledge at an early stage.

Health-related research

Epidemiological investigations into the health of children, relating it to living in environments subject to high magnetic fields, have indicated twice the normal level of certain types of cancers in the presence of magnetic fields in excess of 0.2 µT.

It has not been possible to establish any links between ill-health and low magnetic or electric fields in workplaces. There are, however, a number of individuals, known as electrical allergics, who exhibit severe reactions to various electrical environments. Both at work and in the home there are a large number of electrical appliances and systems that can produce significant magnetic fields, although field strengths from most of them decline rapidly with distance. No information is available today on the dose/response relationship for short-term exposure.

Another phenomenon, to which more attention has been paid, is that of stray currents as can occur in four-wire electrical supply systems that are commonly used in Sweden. These unbalanced currents can give rise to high magnetic fields of up to 5 µT, which decline only in proportion to the linear distance from the radiating conductor.

Smart systems

The 'intelligent building' has been a popular, but also quite spectacular, theme, although it has not yet achieved any wider acceptance in Sweden. Technology has opened new doors, but we are still uncertain as to what it will be used for, while costs have hitherto discouraged its development. There is no clear definition of what is meant by an intelligent building, although it often involves linking several intelligent functions together. The major growth area is in telecommunications and media communications into or out of the building over digital networks or links[19].

Considerable potentials for improvement are also opened up in respect of building services systems, in the form of improved control via more sensors, simplified signal communication and distributed intelligence. This will allow more intelligent functions to be installed and linked together, such as demand control of lighting. In the case of demand control of ventilation, air flow rates can respond to carbon dioxide levels, relative humidity, temperature, draughts and noise. These are parameters that, in many cases, would need to be correlated in order to provide the best possible indoor climate conditions, despite varying factors such as number of occupants, ambient air temperature and relative humidity.

This chapter is based on material by Eje Sandberg, MSc.,ESAN Energi AB, Sollentuna.

REFERENCES

1 *Lokalerna och energihushållningen* (Commercial premises and energy conservation). Vattenfall, Uppdrag 2000, U1991/70.

2 *Effektiv ventilation spar el* (Effective ventilation saves electricity). BFR T11:1994.

3 Measurements performed by AIB Installationskonsult AB. Not yet published (September 1994).

4 *Ventilation i lokaler - Exempel på genomförda projekt* (Ventilation in commercial premises - Examples of completed Projects). NUTEK.

5 *Ventilationsguiden Byggherrens guide för bostadsventilation - ombyggnad* (The Ventilation Guide - The developer's guide for ventilation of residential buildings - Refurbishment). BFR T18:1995.

6 *Ventilationsguiden Byggherrens guide för bostadsventilation - Exempel* (The Ventilation Guide - The developer's guide for ventilation of residential buildings - Examples). BFR T19:1995.

7 *Eleffektiva småhus* (Electrically efficient single-family houses). SIB TN:42.

8 *Eleffektiv användning i flerbostadshus: Kv. Tisaren 1994* (Efficient Use of Electricity in Apartment Buildings - the Tisaren Block, 1994). Stockholm Energy, Marketing Department.

9 *Tvätt i nöd och lust. En konsumentteknisk och en psykologisk studie om tvätten i våra liv* (Washing for better or worse: A consumer-technical and a psychological investigation of washing in our daily lives). NUTEK, Department of Energy Efficiency, 1993.

10 *I've Got the Message*, NUTEK, Department of Energy Efficiency, August 1994.

11 *Hemelektronik - Stora förluster i avstängt läge* (Domestic electronic equipment - Substantial electricity losses even when turned off. NUTEK 1994.

12 IEA - Future Building Forum Workshop, 1994. Marc Fontoynont.

13 *I Lund sprids det nya ljuset med unik teknik* (New technology for the new light in Lund.) Energimagasinet No. 5:94

14 *'Belysning i vården'*, *'Belysning i vårdlokaler'*, *Belysning i kontor'* and *'Belysning inom verkstadsindustri'* ('Lighting in health care', 'Lighting in health care premises', 'Lighting in offices' and 'Lighting in industry'). NUTEK, Department of Energy Efficiency.

15 *ENEU - 94. Anvisningar för energieffektiv upphandling* (ENEU 94. Notes for energy-efficient purchasing. Industrilitteratur AB, The Swedish Building Centre.

16 BFR T19:1993.

17 Report from the National Board of Housing, Building and Planning: *Eleffektiva installationer* (Electrically-efficient building services systems).

18 Standards for maximum electricity use by domestic appliances etc. NUTEK/National Board for Consumer Policies, March 1992.

19 *Intelligenta hus, state of the art* (Intelligent buildings, state of the art 1992), Anders Ewerman. BFR T30:1995.

OTHER LITERATURE

Hushållsel i småhus. Mätning av elanvändningen i 66 småhus och av konsekvenserna av att byta hushållsapparater (Domestic electricity in single-family houses. Metering of electricity use in 66 detached houses and the effects of replacing domestic appliances). NUTEK B1994:11.

Kyl- och frysapparater för hushåll. Energiförbrukning och -effektivitet (Domestic refrigerators and freezers: energy use and energy efficiency). NUTEK R1993:56.

PLAN, POSITION AND NUMBER OF HOURS OF SUNSHINE ARE IMPORTANT FOR ENERGY COSTS

SUMMARY

The position, the local climate, the micro-climate, direction, amount of sun, seasonal variations, vegetation, wind and building plan - all play important parts in determining the energy costs of a building.

A building's size and shape are two parameters that are closely related to energy demand. If energy use is to be minimised right from the planning stage, the plan of the building should be carefully thought out. Town houses are favoured because they have 30-40 % less external wall area than do detached houses. As far as terrace houses are concerned, some can even have a wall and roof area that is only 50 % of that of a town house. However, provided that the building is suitable, it is always the user who determines the final cost of heating.

Developments in the planning of buildings to take account of their energy economics resulted in designs that require only half the energy of equivalent buildings constructed solely in accordance with the Building Regulations, although these designs have only partly been absorbed into routine building. The most important areas now for research and further acquisition of knowledge are performance and user-acceptance monitoring and evaluation of the best research results and of the best implemented experimental buildings. In addition, existing knowledge needs to be processed and distributed for use by consultants, decision-makers, materials manufacturers and building developers.

Before starting to plan a building with the aim of achieving good energy utilisation, it is desirable carefully to investigate the external conditions that can affect performance. What are the external factors that affect the design of buildings?

The Nordic latitudes determine solar height and intensity during the year, and thus the length of the necessary heating period and the building's varying power requirements, which are normally at a maximum in January-February. Heat loss through exterior walls and roofs can be reduced by incorporation of suitable thermal insulation, of a thickness to suit the climate of the region. It is well worthwhile asking for advice at local level before planning a building development, as this is likely to be an excellent source of information concerning the local climate.

Local climates can vary

The local climate can vary from region to region at the same latitude depending on the distance from the sea and topography, e.g. whether the site is high up, in a deep valley or on level ground. The local climate can be noticeably affected in areas exposed to strong winds, particularly when this occurs during the winter. Inversions in river valleys, or cold air sinks in low ground, can sometimes result in undesired climate situations.

The proportions of clear skies and overcast skies - the percentage cloudiness - can have a considerable effect on the local climate of an area and on the true heating requirements of a building. Cloudiness varies throughout the year for any given site: examples are the increased cloudiness along the Swedish west coast during the summer or the effect of the large water body of Lake Vänern which provides more hours of sunshine for Karlstad, on the north coast of the lake, than for other towns well away from large water areas.

Microclimate can vary in much the same way as local climate, being noticeably better or noticeably poorer depending on the lee conditions of the immediate environment, sun conditions and the vicinity of large water bodies. The position and orientation of a building, or siting it in the lee of cold winds, can have a favourable effect on its energy requirements during the heating season. Microclimate conditions need to be investigated from case to case.

The direction in which a building faces is of major importance for solar heat input contribution, provided that most windows face in a sunny direction. Although an unshaded south-facing facade provides maximum solar input, facades facing south-east and south-west also receive worthwhile solar input, giving relatively substantial freedom in positioning the building. Buildings facing east or west receive only half as much sun as one facing south.

Availability of sun is the key

Availability of sunlight is the key to detailed planning of plots and buildings in respect of making best use of solar energy. When deciding on a site, it is important that tall coniferous forests, rock outcrops or buildings do not encroach too much on sunlight.

Solar altitudes for any time of the year can be determined from tables for any given latitude. Simple model investigations can determine when and how much of a building facade will be sunlit. The same information can also be obtained graphically from diagrams.

Achieving a good energy balance in a building requires consideration of seasonal variations based on solar altitude, solar intensity and sunlight/cloudiness conditions when determining the siting of a building and deciding on its window area.

The effect of vegetation on a building's heat balance should be utilised. During the summer, high deciduous trees close to a building can shade ground areas around the building but particularly shade south-facing windows and thus keep down indoor temperatures. During the spring and autumn, when there are no leaves on the trees, the trees act as a type of fully automatic sunshade to allow the greatest possible solar contribution to room heating. The reflection/absorption characteristics of ground close to the building can sometimes also be included in consideration of the effect of the immediate environment on the thermal balance of the building.

The cooling effect of the wind on a building can substantially affect its energy requirements: measurements and calculations have shown a 5 % effect during the winter. Screens of trees and/or the shelter provided by woodland against the predominant wind

direction can contribute to reducing the heating power requirement.

Size and plan related to energy requirements

The size and plan of a building are two parameters that are closely related to its energy requirement. A compact two-storey building, of more or less cubic shape, has the smallest surface area in total, relative to a compact single-storey building with the same floor area. A souterrain building can provide additional energy savings as a result of part of it being below ground level. Buildings with a non-rectangular shape present a larger surface area to their surroundings, which means they are less efficient in energy terms. Minimising energy requirements at the planning stage requires careful consideration of the plans to ensure that there are no undefined above-ground surfaces.

Terrace houses are particularly efficient in energy terms as the amount of roof and wall surface exposed to the surroundings is 30-40 % less that in an isolated house. Houses or apartments built in a row up a slope can also be regarded as terrace houses, but of souterrain type arranged on top of each other, which further reduced their exposure to the surroundings, depending on the slope of the ground. In special cases, it is possible to produce an envelop that is only 50 % the size of a corresponding terrace house.

Seasonally tuned houses store heat

A seasonally tuned house is one that is so designed that it receives and stores the thermal contribution from the sun during the spring, thus reducing the amount of artificial heating required. By as early as February and March, the sun can be making a valuable contribution to heating on clear days. What is valid for a 'spring' house is also essentially valid for an 'autumn' house. During the summer, the indoor climate can be controlled with sunshades or by suitably positioned deciduous trees and by ventilation. During the winter, external shutters could be used to cover the excess area of window surface required to capture solar heat during the spring. As a result, during the colder part of the year the house has an effective window area equivalent to that of a normal house. The occupants, after all, vary their clothing, food, recreational activities etc. to suit the seasons of the year.

Why should not the same apply in respect of their house? The measures that have been suggested are easy to understand and can be applied and operated by anyone.

Windows make excellent solar collectors

Windows are the most interesting components of a building. Besides providing daylight, views in and out and a substantial contribution to the impression of space, they also give life to the interior of a building and are effective as solar collectors. Short-wave radiation passing through the glass is re-radiated by the surfaces upon which it falls as long-wave thermal radiation. The number of panes affects both the transparency of the window and the amount of insolation passing through it. Ordinary window glass reduces insolation by 10-11 %, mainly as a result of reflection and refraction. Present-day triple-glazed windows have a low U-value of the order of 1.8-2.0 W/m² K. With appropriate coatings on the glass, and gas filling between the panes of sealed glazing units, the window industry has substantially reduced emissions through windows.

Quadruple-glazed windows, with coated panes, provide further reductions of the U-value down to 0.9-1.0 W/m² K, although the trade-off is in poorer transparency and light admittance. Four panes must be regarded as the limit of what is acceptable in terms of light quality and transparency.

The 2 + 2 window is one way of solving the problem of having an extremely low U-value when the weather is coldest but nevertheless providing good transparency and light admission during much of the year. This is a design in which the inner and outer casements are each fitted with sealed double-glazing units. The inner window is fitted from November to March: with the outer window alone being used during the rest of the year. The 2 + 2 window can be regarded as a building element to match the seasons.

The glazed veranda or conservatory, a solar-heated room for use during the spring and autumn, was developed around the turn of the century as a residential feature. It has become increasingly popular in new buildings since the energy crises of the 1970s. It has not generally been possible to demonstrate any direct energy savings, but it does generally improve living quality. This applies regardless of whether the glazed area is used as a traditional veranda or solely as a greenhouse.

Ducted solar preheaters - two sheets of glass, separated by plastic ribs to form vertical ducts between the sheets, and with the rear sheet painted black to absorb heat - fitted externally to wall sections below windows provide a cheap and very simple method of effectively preheating ventilation supply air. Glazed rooms in combination with these panels have been tested. However, the temperature in the room can easily reach 40-50 °C on a sunny day, which is unacceptable from a user viewpoint. It is therefore essential to incorporate bypass dampers in the panels below the windows and cross-draught ventilation through the provision of openable windows.

The concept of temperature zones

Zoning - dividing a building up into areas of different temperatures - can be one of several ways of saving heating. Zoning requires careful planning, grouping rooms and features to suit different temperature levels.

The association of kitchen-dining room-sitting room can, for example, form a unit with acceptable indoor temperature during most of the day, while another group of rooms, such as the bedrooms, or rooms for other purposes, can have lower temperatures during most of the day.

Zoning can also be employed to accommodate seasonal changes by changing the use of a room from one time of the year to another. The glazed veranda has already been mentioned as an example. When it is not being used for normal occupation during the coldest months of the year, it can normally serve to provide temporary winter storage or as a type of temperature lock (analogous to an airlock) if it is arranged around the entrance to the house. A general concentration of activities in a building in an inner 'core' during the winter can be seen as an extension of this argument.

Heat storage capacity varies

The heat storage capacity of a building - its ability to absorb and release heat - affects mainly the indoor climate comfort. Massive building materials reduce

Windows provide daylight, views out and views in. They create an impression of light and space, and are also excellent solar collectors. Photographer: Lars Hesselmark, Mira

temperature fluctuations resulting from changes in insolation and ambient temperature. They release absorbed heat partly by radiation and partly by convection.

Different building materials have different heat storage capacities. Concrete has the greatest storage capacity, while brick stores about half as much and lightweight concrete stores considerably less.

To benefit from the thermal storage capacity of building materials, it is necessary to consider not only the relative quantity of such materials but also how they are placed in relation to the air in the room and/or incident solar energy. Exposure of the material is an important factor. The application of even a very thin insulating layer, e.g. carpets, wooden panels, parquet flooring etc., is sufficient to interfere with the thermal storage function.

Water or appropriate salts have considerably greater thermal storage capacity than concrete if some other medium is to be used for energy storage.

Heat from the occupants and waste heat from domestic appliances have always provided a contribution to the total heat input. Kitchen equipment, with heat contributions from freezers and refrigerators, as well as that from cookers, ovens and dishwashers etc., provides a substantial heat input to buildings. To this must be added heat from lighting, television, radios etc. Taken together, all these sources of additional heating should be seen as an important item in the energy balance.

User habits determine the results

Even if a house has been planned to make best use of its heat, the actual end result will depend on the occupants. The way in which they live with a house and utilise its features is very important, i.e. of making best use of solar heat contributions, opening windows to best effect, suiting room temperatures to activities, making best use of waste heat, adjusting to the seasons, saving domestic hot water by showering, defrosting refrigerators and freezers regularly and so on.

Two families of the same size, living in identical detached houses or terrace houses, can have energy demands that can vary so widely that one family uses twice as much as the other, despite the fact of living in identical houses.

Research results must be disseminated

In the best cases, research into energy-efficient building during and after the energy crises resulted in simple houses, easy to live with and with energy use levels half that of other buildings that simply complied with the Building Regulations. Swedish research has achieved excellent results in an international perspective, with some of them finding their way into the built environment.

Even in the refurbishment sector, it has been possible to reduce energy use substantially by such means as additional insulation of roofs, basements and exterior walls, upgrading of windows, modification of heating systems and adjustment of temperature control systems.

The objective of continued research in this sector should be to obtain performance and user acceptance monitoring of the best research results and/or of the most successful experimental buildings. Assessment and processing of the information should provide valuable knowledge that should be disseminated to consultants, decision-makers, materials manufacturers and building developers.

Future research needs to be concentrated on reducing the complexity of energy systems, aiming at simple, reliable and easily understood systems for both users and building administrators. If we can achieve this objective, prospects are good for an improved society with fewer emissions as a result of a substantial reduction in heating requirements.

This chapter is based on material by Professor Bengt Hidemark, of Bengt Hidemark Arkitektkontor, Stockholm.

REFERENCES

Lyberg, M. D., *Building thermal performance, Techniques for analysis, auditing and monitoring.* Swedish Institute of Building Research, SIB, Gävle, 1993.

Olsson, C. H., *Strategies for energy intelligence in building design. Research plan and state of work.* BFR Report 900499.

Sexton energisnåla sunda hus. Presentation av förslagen i Stockholms stads markanvisningstävling för energisnåla sund hus (16 low-energy healthy buildings. Presentation of entries in the Stockholm City competition for low-energy healthy buildings). Byggdok Mono 90-1002.

Lundborg, H. and Göransson, A., *Areabegrepp vid bestämning av byggnaders specifika energianvändning* (The area concept in determining specific energy use of buildings). BFR R63:1990.

Krupinska, J., *Bra klimat - en formgivningsfråga? Fallstudie av danska naturligt ventilerade nybyggda skolor* (Good climate - a question of planning? Case studies of newly-built naturally ventilated Danish schools). Royal Institute of Technology, Division of Form and Environment, TRIFA-FL-4124.

Building and planning in Sweden with consideration to climate and energy. EFEM Arkitektkontor, BFR Report 860975.

Bratsberg, G. *Inneklima- og energiriktige boliger* (Indoor climate and energy-efficient homes). SINTEF Report STF 15 A93041, Trondheim, 1993.

Kanstad, T. *Arkitektur og energi* (Architecture and energy). Norwegian Architects' Association, NAL, NAL seminar on buildings and the environment. Oslo, 1992.

Blom, P., Stenstad, V.,Dahlseen, T. *Energiøkonomisk prosjektering av bygninger* (Energy-efficient design of buildings). Norwegian Building Research Institute, Handbook 37. Oslo, 1988.

Jacobsen, T., Raaen, H., Hestnes, A. *Effekt- og energiriktig bolig - formstudie* (A power-efficient and energy-efficient home - a feasibility study). SINTEF, Department of Architecture and Constructional Engineering. Report STF62 A88004, Trondheim, 1988.

Moltke, I. *Energi i arkitekturen* (Energy in architecture). Danish Institute of Technology, Department of Energy Technology, Tåstrup, 1990.

OTHER LITERATURE

Byggnadsutformning. Kunskapsbas Hus och Hälsa (Building planning. A knowledge base, House and Health). National Board of Housing, Building and Planning and BFR, U8:1992.

Klimatstudier som underlag för bebyggelseplanering [Diss] (Climate investigations as a basis for building planning [Diss]). Glaumann, M. SIB. Research Report TN:33, 1993.

INSULATION, WINDOWS AND WEATHERPROOFING – ELEMENTS OF GOOD ENERGY CONSERVATION

SUMMARY

A building envelope must not only fulfil its desired purpose at the time of construction, but must maintain this performance throughout the lifetime of the building. Durability and length of life are therefore important aspects of materials used in building envelopes. For many years, Swedish building has complied with detailed rules on **how** buildings are to be designed and constructed. These rules have now been changed to define **what** the building is to do, i.e. performance requirements. This change to performance requirements will increase the pressure for adopting an overall view of a building, i.e. that materials, design and building services systems together provide an operative solution. There is a long tradition of research in these fields, but several important areas for continued R&D can nevertheless be identified:

- Determination of correct and reliable values of U/ ratio for most types of materials and designs.
- Continued research into thermal bridges.

- Development of materials and methods for airtightness.
- System investigations into the interaction between building envelopes, heating and ventilation systems.
- Development of methods of evaluating the ageing performance of foamed plastic products.
- Continued development of methods for determining the settling characteristics of loose-fill materials.
- Development of window features.

As a result of the 1970s energy crises, requirements in respect of buildings' energy conservation performance were substantially tightened up. Examples of measures taken to reduce energy losses include increased insulation thicknesses in walls and roofs, reduced uncontrolled ventilation by making buildings more airtight, a change from double-glazed to triple-glazed windows and selective coatings on window glass. Although all these measures were largely based on known methods and technology, various questions still arose. How efficient is thick insulation? What do occupants think of coated windows? What is the link between airtight buildings and sick buildings? These are some of the questions that initiated research and development projects in a wide range of areas.

Investigations into the performance of substantial thicknesses of insulation during the 1980s and 1990s have increased our understanding of building physics relationships in highly insulated wall and roof structures, and have also shown the need to revise the method of calculating coefficients of heat transfer. The high performance requirements in respect of thermal insulation, and thus the resulting substantial thicknesses of traditional insulation materials, have also generated a certain amount of increased interest in new materials and designs, such as vacuum insulation.

A building envelope must not only fulfil its desired purpose at the time of construction, but in many cases must maintain this performance throughout the lifetime of the building. Durability and length of life are therefore important aspects of materials used in building envelopes.

Windows are that part of a building which, in certain cases, accounts for by far the greatest losses of energy but which, in other cases, results in difficulties in dealing with excess temperatures resulting from insolation. It is therefore natural that considerable interest should be devoted to the thermal balance of windows.

A new method of calculating coefficients of thermal conductivity

The amount of thermal insulation in buildings envelopes has been increased substantially over the last 20 years. In the case of roof space insulation in single-family houses, for example, 150 mm was a common thickness in 1975, while the corresponding value today is about 500 mm. However, as the thickness of insulation has increased, a debate has arisen around the efficacy of such thick layers. What is clear is that these massive thicknesses, with their resulting low heat flows, are more sensitive to shortcomings in the standard of workmanship than earlier designs. This has necessitated the development of a new method of calculating coefficients of thermal conductivity, U-values.

From the point of view of thermal performance, designs are never perfect. This means that a coefficient of thermal transmittance, U, calculated on the basis of measured coefficients of thermal conductivity, λ, of the materials, does not normally give a true representation of energy flows through the relevant parts of the building. As a result of shortcomings, such as gaps between insulation and studs in a wall, there will be a greater transport of energy through the structure than as indicated by calculations. Until 1989, Swedish building practice employed a correction for this uncertainty by using a system known as 'practical applicable thermal conductivity' when calculating the U-value of a design. This system - which is still the system most commonly used in most countries - employed a value of classed thermal conductivity that was normally about 10 % higher than the measured thermal conductivity. The system was well developed and provided a relatively accurate picture of the thermal insulation performance of a building. However, problems occurred when we started to apply the method to more highly insulated structures, i.e. those having low U-values. The method involving an increase in the value of thermal conductivity, resulted in a percentage increase in the coefficient of thermal transmissivity, U, and thus a lower increment for a lower U-value. However, in real structures, a gap transmits the same quantity of energy whether the walls is thin or thick, i.e. it results in a constant increment to the U-value.

The system of a ΔU increment[1] that has been developed in Sweden is now being distributed throughout Europe by CEN. However, intensive research will be required in future in order to determine correct values of the ΔU increment for different types of structures and different production conditions.

Results depend on quality of workmanship

Although a number of projects aimed at determining ΔU increments are already in progress, it is extremely important that further research projects should be started. The principle of ΔU increments was developed in Sweden at the end of the 1980s, and it is important that the rest of Europe should now accept the method. It will presumably be a requirement that correct, reliable values of ΔU increment can be given for most types of materials and designs.

Projects with the objective of determining the effects of workmanship on thermal transmissivity of various types of designs are now in progress at a number of places throughout the country. A project financed by the Swedish Council for Building Research (BFR) and Swedisol, entitled 'Heat and air flows through thick layers of insulation', is in progress at the Lund Institute of Technology[2]. A BFR-financed project, entitled 'Natural and forced convection in loose mineral wool insulation'[3] is being carried out at Chalmers University of Technology. Projects aimed at direct measurement of the thermal resistance of ceiling/roof structures, insulated with various types of loose-fill materials, are in progress at the Swedish Testing and Research Institute (SP) in Borås[4]. In parallel with these measurements, SP is measuring thermal conductivity of corresponding materials under laboratory conditions[5].

A joint project is in progress in Denmark between Rockwool International and the National Research Council of Canada, investigating the performance of stud walls insulated with mineral wool[6]. Walls have been built, incorporating various degrees of carefully defined 'defects', and their performance investigated at different ambient temperatures. A major effect on the thermal transmissivity of low-density insulation materials has been found if the temperature difference across the structure is high.

Thermal bridges

The principle of an increment added to the coefficient of thermal transmissivity has been used for a long time in the context of thermal bridges. L-E Nevander published values of the extra heat flow per unit of length through a thermal bridge, i.e. essentially a ΔU increment, for a number of typical design details, as long ago as 1961[7]. Research in this field has been continued, so that we can now calculate the performance even of extreme thermal bridges such as steel elements in high-performance insulation materials. The practical value of this research can be seen in examples such as the aluminium joists that have been developed in recent years, where suitable design of slits in the webs of the studs has substantially reduced their thermal bridging performance.

Standardisation work in the field of thermal bridges is being carried out by CEN/TC 89, 'Thermal Performance of Building Components, WG2, Thermal Bridges and Surface Condensation'. This standard will describe how to calculate the effects of thermal bridges, but will not specify that such calculations must be made, e.g. in connection with applications for building permission.

It is important that Swedish scientists should be involved in research into thermal bridges. Sweden was well advanced in this work at any early stage, e.g. as manifested by the publication of a Swedish standard[8], but it is important that this knowledge is now not only employed in international standardisation work but is constantly consolidated by means of new research projects.

Airtightness - insufficient knowledge of durability

In connection with the energy crises of the 1970s, the question of airtightness of building envelopes became of considerable interest. The Building Regulations specified requirements in respect of airtightness for the building envelope as a whole and for individual components. This resulted in research and development into these areas, while specific solutions for the building envelope in respect of choices of materials and the design of joints, connections etc. were investigated. Weatherstripping of windows and doors was investigated, together with ways of applying such weatherstripping.

In recent years, there has been little research and development activity in this sector: it has been felt that there was sufficient knowledge to be able to fulfil the requirements of the Building Regulations. However, we still do not know enough about the durability of the airtightness of buildings, even though experience from 5-10 year-old buildings does not indicate any significant deterioration.

It is likely that the need for airtightness of the building envelope will increase in future. Total control of air flows is needed in order to be able to control and vary ventilation as required, and in order to be able to recover heat from ventilation exhaust air. Such total control requires a very airtight structure. Further development of materials, design and working methods and inspection will be essential.

Alternatively, the trend towards a return to natural-draught ventilation or 'fan-assisted natural-draught ventilation' could instead require less airtightness and deliberate diffuse leakage of air through the building envelope. Another line of development is 'dynamic insulation', which involves reducing the heat flow through a structure by arranging for the ventilation supply or exhaust air for the building to flow through the insulation. The principle is based on the concept of the insulation itself acting as a heat exchanger, and possibly also as an air filter. A number of experiments have been carried out using contra-flow insulation of ventilation supply air through walls and ceilings. (The performance of the Skantera-Optima system has been evaluated at Lund Institute of Technology[9].) From an energy point of view, the design operates well. However, there are difficulties in achieving a uniform air flow rate through the insulation and achieving a sufficiently airtight structure.

Several of these questions are related to building services systems, and need to be seen in relation to the interaction between the building envelope, the heating system and ventilation system. In these contexts, it is important to study the required performance of the particular part of the building in the building as a whole. Discussions have arisen at times into the suitability or correctness of particular design solutions, e.g. into the need for plastic film vapour barriers in walls. In certain cases, it has been claimed that there is no need to use plastic if the insulation material is hygroscopic, e.g. cellulose fibre. Attention is concentrated on the effect of the plastic film on moisture distribution through the wall, although the interesting question instead should perhaps be whether sufficient airtightness can be achieved in the wall and its joints in order to ensure that the ventilation system works as intended.

Vacuum insulation panels - very low pressures required

If a vacuum can be produced in a gap, the thermal insulation performance of the gap will be excellent, as heat transfer by both conduction and convection will be eliminated. However, the difficulty with vacuum insulation is to find a design that will maintain the low pressure throughout the life of the structure. It should be noted that the pressure must be extremely low (of the order of 0.01 Pa) before there is any benefit from pressure reduction in a clean airgap. Such low pressures can be achieved in special materials and shapes, e.g. vacuum flasks, but are hardly realistic for flat panels and ordinary building materials. Reduction of the air pressure from the normal 100 kPa to, say, 1 kPa is of no interest in terms of thermal performance.

Flat insulation panels must contain some type of spacer to keep the surfaces apart at these low pressures. These spacers need to withstand relatively high stresses, but at the same time must not consist of materials having high thermal conductivity, as they will otherwise increase the thermal transmission of the entire panel. The most realistic solution is presumably some form of extremely fine-celled material, which at the same time acts as both a spacer and radiation limiter.

Reducing radiation is extremely important, as about 70 % of the heat transfer across a normal air-filled gap is by radiation. It is not until this component has been minimised, either through the use of some appropriate material in the gap or by low coefficients of emission of the facing surfaces, that it becomes of interest to minimise heat transfer by air conduction.

The introduction of an extremely fine-celled material would bring benefits not only in terms of radiation reduction, but would also mean that the effect of low pressure would start to become effective far sooner than would be the case in a completely empty gap. At a pressure where the free median wavelength of the air's molecules is very much greater than the cell size, the thermal conductivity of the air approaches zero. A total coefficient of thermal conductivity of the order of 0.005 W/m^2, K can be achieved at a pressure of 1 Pa with certain forms of fine-celled structures[10].

No larger-scale use of such low-pressure insulation in the building envelope is likely within the foreseeable future, as both the costs and durability are very doubtful. An interesting use might be in refrigerators and freezers, where the small sizes and performance of vacuum insulation systems are interesting.

Special walls - transparent materials

Using transparent materials for external insulation allows the outer surface of the building to be warmed and thus reduces heat losses. Systems such as these, for passively utilising solar energy, are being closely investigated in a number of countries, e.g. Germany (LEGIS).

Foils with low emissivity (aluminium or coated plastic films) can be used in an airgap in order to reduce radiation losses and convection. Parallel foils are needed in order to minimise heat flow. The USA is one country in which this type of insulation system is being investigated.

There has been little interest in methods of these types in Sweden, probably because of the difficulty of producing systems that can provide equivalent cost and physical performance with that of conventional systems.

Ageing of cellular plastics changes their thermal conductivity

The thermal conductivity of cellular plastics that have gases other than air in the pores of the material, e.g. XPS and PUR, changes with time. This is a problem that has been recognised for a long time, and became particularly prominent when the debate on CFCs and their influence on the ozone layer took off in the 1980s. Producers changed the mixture of gases in their materials, and it became important to develop methods to evaluate the effect on thermal conductivity of changes in the gas content with time. The Swedish National Testing and Research Institute and Chalmers University of Technology developed a method based on sawing the material into thin slices, about 10 mm thick[11]. Further investigations[12] have shown that the method produces reliable results.

The method is now accepted by Nordtest, ASTM and ISO. CEN employs the slice method for XPS, but uses a thermal ageing method for other plastics (PUR and PF).

At present, virtually no research is being conducted within this sector in Sweden. For environmental reasons, the presently known gases with low coefficients of thermal conductivity are no longer acceptable, while the method of performance evaluation is well established. However, there is still a need to develop a method of evaluation for cellular plastic products having different types of surface coatings and surface layers.

Tendencies to settling of insulation materials

Loose-fill insulation materials have a tendency to settle with time. Organic fibres are particularly sensitive in this respect, although inorganic fibrous material also settles. The main driving forces are gravity, vibration and varying moisture and temperature conditions. It is important to be able to forecast the future settlement of such materials in order correctly to determine the amounts of materials required.

A method has been developed at the then Swedish Institute for Building Research (nowadays the Department of the Built Environment [at the Royal Institute of Technology]) in Gävle and the Lund Institute of Technology for laboratory determination of various materials' tendency to settle[13]. The method is promising, but needs further development. An analytical model of the settlement process would be valuable in order to be able correctly to determine and quantify the relevant parameters that affect settling of the material for accelerated ageing testing. There is substantial interest on the international plane in solving these problems. However, not much research is at present in progress. As greater use of loose-fill insulation can be expected in both horizontal and vertical elements of buildings, it is most important to develop reliable methods of evaluation and determination of necessary quantities.

The effects of moisture

Two aspects of moisture are considered here; namely, the effect on thermal resistance and the effect on durability.

The principle for the effect of moisture on thermal resistance, and various methods of evaluation thereof, are described in ISO 10 051. Moisture affects temperature distribution and heat flow through the material partly by its presence as such and partly through moisture transport and phase changes. The performance determination principles that have been developed are based on laboratory determination of the effect of the presence of moisture as an incremental increase in the thermal conductivity ($\Delta\lambda$) and of determination of the effect of phase changes by calculation. Concrete methods for determination of $\Delta\lambda$ have been developed for fibrous materials[14], but further work is needed for cellular plastics and wall materials.

In addition, mathematical models are needed that allow for the effects of phase changes.

Extensive work is in progress within IEA Annex 24 HAMTIE (Heat, Air and Moisture Transfer in Insulated Envelopes Parts) on investigation of such aspects as the effect of moisture on well-insulated parts of buildings. This work is due for completion and final reporting in 1995.

Uncontrolled moisture conditions can give rise to damage such as mildew, rot, corrosion, dimensional changes and frost damage. It is therefore essential for the good thermal insulating performance of the building envelope that it should be designed to withstand moisture loads that are likely to be encountered. This is an area in which work is in progress both nationally and internationally.

'Ecological building' requires agreement in the building sector

There is a strong interest in Sweden at present in 'ecological building'. This manifests itself in such ways as the use of old materials and old design principles, on the basis of "things were better in the old days". In some cases, this approach is perfectly correct and results in improved conditions, but in other cases the principles were faulty and put environment and conditions at risk. Today, many of those involved in the building sector are uncertain of what is right or wrong. Substantial effort is therefore needed to develop methods of evaluation and to assess these 'rediscovered' building methods. A common view of these aspects within the building sector is an important prerequisite for low-energy environmentally acceptable building in future.

Many requirements in respect of windows

In addition to good thermal insulation, windows must fulfil many other different requirements, such as the ability to be opened, admission of sunlight, the provision of light in general, contact with the surroundings and so on. Windows are often presented as the weak points of a building, as their thermal insulation performance is considerably poorer than that of walls. However, net heat losses through windows can be significantly reduced through efficient utilisation of incident solar radiation. In order not to create excessive indoor temperatures or require unnecessary use of energy for cooling it is desirable to be able to regulate the admission of light and heat.

The quality of light in buildings has a considerable

Windows are the weak points of buildings, as they provide poorer thermal insulation than walls. From a thermal performance point of view, their design can never be perfect. Intensive development has been concentrated on achieving high thermal insulation performance and good transparency.
Photographer: Esko Männikkö, Mira

significance for general well-being and health. It is therefore important that windows should admit the correct spectrum of daylight, which should be considered when deciding on the number of panes, the quality of the glass and the types of coatings.

Developments in creating high-insulation-performance transparent panes has been intensive, with many different approaches within materials research in particular. Basic research into materials and the design of windows is being carried out under the auspices of IEA[15].

In order to encourage the development of windows having good thermal insulation properties, the National Board for Industrial and Technical Development (NUTEK) has carried out a number of programmes intended to accelerate market introduction of high-performance windows. The main objective of this technology procurement programme has been to bring present-day designs up to existing knowledge and technical capabilities levels. It should therefore be possible to find windows with U-values about 1.0 W/m²,K among the product ranges offered by window manufacturers[16].

The following U-values for the centres of windows illustrate the improvements that can be made in their thermal insulation performance.

	U-value (W/m²,K)
Single glazing	5.7
Double glazing	2.8
Triple glazing	1.9
Sealed triple glazing unit with low-emission coating	1.4
Sealed triple glazing unit with low-emission coating and argon filling	1.2
Sealed triple glazing unit with two low-emission coatings and argon filling	0.8
Vacuum window (high vacuum)	0.5
20 mm aerogel window (low vacuum)	0.3

Work is in progress within CEN aimed at the development of European standards for determining the U-values of windows in a consistent manner and the simplification of methods of calculation.

Different types of coatings

Various types of coatings (low-emission layers) have been developed in order to reduce heat losses or to control inward radiation of light and heat. Thermal insulation can be improved through soft coatings, which must be used in sealed glazing units, and by hard coatings, which can also be used as single panes. There are therefore substantial possibilities for improving both existing and new windows.

Electrochromic, thermochromic and photochromic coatings for the control of incident radiation are available. Of these, the electrochromic systems seem to offer the most interesting potentials. A voltage applied across them can substantially change their transmittance characteristics. It is expected that practical application will have been tested and demonstrated in the near future, so that windows can actively control the admission of light and heat. Research within this area (into what is known as 'smart windows') is being carried out primarily at Uppsala University[17].

Vacuum windows

This is an area in which research is in progress in order to learn to control the life of the vacuum, thermal bridges (spacers) and manufacturing technology. Heat losses are reduced partly through evacuation of the inter-pane space to a pressure of about 0.01 Pa (10^{-7} atmospheres) and partly by the use of low-emission coatings. The potential possibilities for future better utilisation and new applications of passive solar heating are increased by combinations of evacuated glazing and selective coatings. Development of evacuated glazing units is supported by the BRITE EURAM EC programme[18].

Aerogel - both as sheets and loose spheres

Aerogel is an interesting material, having a silicate (SiO_2) cell structure, with cell sizes less than the mean free path length. This results in an extremely low value of the material's thermal conductivity (lower than that of

air). If it is combined with a negative pressure of about 100 Pa (0.001 atm), thermal conductivity can be further significantly reduced. The EC JOULE project is conducting research into aerogels and aerogel panes. The material is at present available both as sheets and as loose spheres[19].

The drawbacks of the material are that it is not completely transparent and that it is expensive. Nevertheless, highly interesting applications for the material can include windows for daylight admission and windows/wall elements for solar energy utilisation. The material can also be used for thermal insulation of appliances such as refrigerators/freezers and hot water tanks.

Sealed insulating units

Gases with low thermal conductivity can be used in sealed glazing units, possibly also in combination with plastic films for reducing convection. These plastic films can, in turn, also be coated with low-emission layers. The films need to be permanently stretched in order to prevent the formation of wrinkles that interfere with clear vision.

Spacers at the edges of sealed glazing units are often made of metal and therefore act as thermal bridges along the edges. The materials industry is working to improve the thermal characteristics of these spacers, and several different types of solutions have been proposed. It is important that the durability of various different types of spacers is thoroughly determined. Seals must prevent any gas filling (e.g. argon) from leaking out or water vapour from diffusing inwards to produce condensation on the interior surfaces of the glass.

As far as special designs of windows are concerned, trials have been held of windows through which fresh ventilation air or ventilation exhaust air flows. The major limitations seem to be those connected with integrating the windows into the building to provide good performance at a cost-effective price.

Frames and casements need further study

As the thermal insulation performance of the glazed area of windows can be significantly improved, it is important that the thermal insulation performance of other parts should be equivalent. Edge losses around the glazed area and the design of frames and casements need further study. The use of two-dimensional computer programs provides an excellent means of investigating heat flow through frames and casements, thus opening the way to better use of materials and improved designs.

To produce a really high-performance casement/frame design requires the use of high thermal insulation materials. Interactions between different types of materials create new problems in respect of durability, strength etc. Development of such designs is still at a very early stage.

Large areas of glazing often use more traditional approaches. It is extremely important that these large glazed surfaces should be regarded as part of the building as a whole, so that heat losses, energy for cooling and daylight admittance are all optimised[20].

Insulation of pipes and duct systems

Thermal insulation is used within a building for insulation of pipes and duct systems. Whether the insulated systems are cold, warm or hot, it is essential to limit the heat flow to the cells from the medium in the system. Moisture flows must be limited in order to ensure that the insulation of cold items operates properly. Today, insufficient is known about the costs and effects of moist pipe insulation, and more research is needed.

'European' building methods differ from Swedish methods

Sweden often uses multi-layer designs in its building envelopes. Each layer of material serves a particular purpose: cladding protects against precipitation, a wind barrier prevents forced convection in insulation material behind it, a sealing layer (often a plastic film) ensures the total airtightness of the building while also preventing moisture from the interior of the building penetrating into the wall structure, and finally a sheet material protects the wall from damage etc. from the inside. More massive constructions are used in many other parts of Europe: a brick wall, for example, may serve several of the above purposes. An open building market in Europe will require well-documented solutions in terms of performance and durability. Research is needed in order to develop methods of testing and evaluation and to provide the necessary knowledge on which proper

decisions can be made when choosing between different design alternatives.

Performance requirements instead of rules

For many years, Swedish building work has been based on compliance with detailed rules for how buildings are to be designed and constructed. In future, the requirements will instead be in the form of performance requirements, while legislation will be changed to make the developer responsible for ensuring that the building fulfils legal requirements. Performance requirements can be expressed in respect of the function of the entire building, e.g. its indoor climate or its energy conservation, as well as at more detail levels for building components and materials. The change to performance requirements will increase the pressure for regarding a building as a whole, i.e. that materials, designs and building services systems should together provide a coherent operating solution. This will require intensified research into system relationships between the building envelope, design and building services systems, as well as with the resulting indoor climate.

This chapter is based on material by Dr. Jan Isberg, Department of Building Design and Construction, Chalmers University of Technology, Per Ingvar Sandberg and Bertil Jonsson, Building Physics, Swedish National Testing and Research Institute.

REFERENCES

1   The National Board of Housing, Building and Planning. *Värmeisolering. Värmegenomgångnskoefficienter för byggnadsdelar och köldbryggor, tjälfria nivå* (Thermal insulation. Coefficients of thermal transmissivity for parts of buildings and thermal bridges, frost-free level). Allmänna Förlaget Gotab, 1989.

2   Roots, P. *Värme- och luftströmning i välisolerade väggar* (Heat and air flows through well-insulated walls). Lund Institute of Technology, Department of Building Physics, Report TVBH-3022. Lund, 1994.

3   Serkitjis, M. *Natural convection heat transfer in a horizontal thermal insulation layer beneath an air layer.* Chalmers University of Technology, Department of Building Design and Construction, Gothenburg, 1995.

4   Löfström, R., Johansson, C. *Lösfyllnadsisolering på vindsbjälklag - Bestämning av värmemotstånd* (Loose-fill insulation in ceiling/roof structures - determination of thermal resistance). Swedish National Testing and Research Institute, Department of Building Physics. SP Report No. 1992:62. Borås, 1992.

5   Jonsson, B. *Lösfyllnadsisolering - Laboratoriemätning av värmemotstånd* (Loose-fill insulation - Laboratory measurements of thermal resistance). Swedish National Testing and Research Institute, Department of Building Physics. SP Report No. 1993:22. Borås, 1993.

6   Rasmusen, J., Brown, W. C., Bomberg, M. T., Ullett, F. M. *Measured Thermal Performance of Frame Walls with Defects in the Installation of Mineral Fibre Insulation.* Proceedings of the 3rd Symposium on Building Physics in the Nordic Countries. Thermal Insulation Laboratory, Lyngby, Denmark, 1993.

7   Nevander, L-E. *Köldbryggor i ytterväggar* (Thermal bridges in exterior walls). Royal Institute of Technology, Department of Building, Note No. 61. Stockholm, 1961.

8   SS 02 42 30. *Värmeisolering - Plåtkonstruktioner med Köldbryggor - Beräkning av värmegenomgångskoefficienten.* 1983 (Thermal insulation - Metal sheet structures with thermal bridges - Calculation of coefficient of thermal transmissivity).

9   Roots, P. *Skantera-Optima* (Skantera-Optima). Lund Institute of Technology, Department of Building Physics, Report TVBH-7165. Lund, 1994.

10 Kodama, K., Yuge, K., Masuda, Y., Tanimoto, Y. *Development of Micro-cellular Open Cell Rigid Polyurethane Foams.* Polyurethanes World Congress 1993, pp 140-145. Technomic Publishing Co.

11 See, for example, Isberg, J. *Thermal Insulation - Conditioning of Rigid Cellular Plastics Containing a Gas with Lower Thermal Conductivity than Air Prior to Determination of Thermal Resistance and Related Properties.* Nordtest Project No. 603-86. Chalmers University of Technology, Department of Building Design and Construction, Publication 88:3. Gothenburg, 1988.

12 Isberg, J. *Conditioning Method for Cellular Plastics Verification of the 'Nordtest Method'.* Chalmers University of Technology, Department of Building Design and Construction, Publication 92:4. Gothenburg, 1993.

13 Svennerstedt, B. *Settling of attic loose-fill thermal insulation - Development of laboratory method.* Lund Institute of Technology, Department of Building Physics, Report TVBH-3018. Lund, 1992.

14 Sandberg, P. I. *Metod för bestämning av fuktens inverkan på värmekonduktiviteten i värmeisolering av cellulosafiber och mineralull* (A method for determining the effects of moisture on the thermal conductivity of cellulose fibre and mineral wool thermal insulation). Swedish National Testing and Research Institute, Building Physics, SP Report 1992:26. Borås, 1992.

15 IEA Solar Heating and Cooling Programme Task 18: Advanced glazing and associated materials.

16 NUTEK. *Teknikupphandling av energieffektiva fönster* (Technology procurement of high-performance windows). Stockholm, 1992.

17 Granquist, C. G. *Energy-efficient windows. Options with present and forthcoming technology.* Pp 89-123, Lund University Press. Lund 1989.

18 Molke, I. *EFP-90 Reviews on vacuum windows.* DTI, Taastrup, Denmark, 1992.

19 Herman et al. *Aerogels - a foam alternative.* H & V Engineer, Vol. 66, No. 722.

20 Gunnarshaug, J. *Glass and window technology for the 1990s.* SINTEF, Trondheim, Norway, 1991.

OTHER LITERATURE

Möjligheter med installationssystem och energieffektiva fönster. En vägledning med hänsyn till teknik, komfort, energi och kostnader vid val av installationssystem och energieffektiva fönster. Tema: flerbostadshus (Potentials of building services systems and energy-efficient windows. A guide to technology, comfort, energy and costs when selecting installation systems and energy-efficient windows. Theme: apartment buildings). Eneström, E. NUTEK T1993:4.

BUILDING SERVICES SYSTEMS – HEATING, VENTILATION AND COOLING NEED TO BE PLANNED FROM A PERFORMANCE VIEWPOINT

SUMMARY

The most important task of building services systems in an energy context is to establish and maintain a desired indoor climate.

Heat surpluses and heat deficits are very different in residential buildings and in commercial (and similar - i.e. schools, hospitals, child day-care centres etc.) premises. There are only very modest heat surpluses in residential buildings, and thus no need of artificial cooling systems. Commercial premises, on the other hand, can have very substantial heat surpluses

during much of the year, so considerable care needs to be invested in the design of their climate maintenance systems. It is therefore important that the purchaser specifies the performance requirements on the basis of well-defined needs, rather than attempting to specify the requirements in the form of physical designs.

Alternative system designs must be analysed on the basis of the specified performance requirements, with this analysis being based on investigations of the interaction between the building, the

activity carried on therein and the climate maintenance system.

Today, the most important research requirements are to identify relevant factors for describing the indoor environment, to quantify these factors, to develop methods of formulating requirements so that they can be converted to reliably operating physical solutions and to develop methods of improving existing design tools for modelling buildings and their energy supplies.

It is a delicate task to design a building so that it is genuinely energy-efficient while also working well in the long term. A building must fulfil in all respects the requirements in respect of aspects such as indoor climate specified by the occupants of the building or as required by the activity for which the building is used. It is primarily the design stage that determines whether a building (or a refurbishment) is energy-efficient and if it works well.

The purchaser must, right at the beginning of the design process, define the requirements to be fulfilled by producing performance specifications. Before they are finally settled, the purchaser must have understood the effects of the specified requirements. It is not, for example, possible to maintain indoor temperatures within narrow limits and at the same time to expect that this can be done by a simple climate control system. The consequences of the requirements that have been specified depend on the interaction between the body of the building, the climate outside it and the activities carried on within it. Once the performance specifications have been agreed, it is the job of the designer to produce technical designs that can fulfil the

performance requirements with the greatest possible energy efficiency.

The first and foremost requirement in respect of indoor climate in a building is that the temperature shall be comfortable, regardless of the weather outside. It must not be uncomfortably cold indoors during the winter, nor may it be unbearably hot during the summer. In addition, the indoor air must be acceptably clean, lighting must be good, installations and apparatus must not produce irritating noise etc.

As soon as the outdoor temperature is lower than the indoor temperature, heat flows out from the building to its surroundings as a result of thermal transmission and air leakage through the building's walls, windows, doors and roof. As the indoor temperature is usually required to be held at +20 °C, or somewhat higher, and as it is only for a very limited time of the year that the outdoor temperature reaches this value, the building loses heat to the surrounding air throughout nearly all the year. However, heat is also given off by the occupants of the building and by electrical apparatus and equipment in it. Further heat is received by insolation during the day, contributing to internal temperature build-up.

The balance temperature
- an important concept

Somewhat simplified, we can say that, at a certain ambient temperature, the outward losses of heat are balanced by internally generated heat. This ambient temperature is defined as the building's **balance temperature**. In commercial premises, the balance temperature differs for daytime and night-time, as the internally generated heat is usually considerably less during the night as the occupants go home, lighting is extinguished, there is no insolation contribution through the windows etc. When the ambient temperature is lower than the balance temperature, it is necessary to supply heat to the building in order to prevent the indoor temperature from falling. If the ambient temperature exceeds the balance temperature, heat has to be removed from the building in order to prevent the indoor temperature from rising.

The balance temperature of residential buildings is considerably higher than that of commercial premises. This is due to the fact that, in commercial premises, the amount of internally generated heat is normally much greater than in residential buildings.

Residential buildings
and commercial premises are very different
from an energy viewpoint

In a residential building, internal heat generation is normally relatively limited, with the result that its heat losses exceed the amount of heat released indoors for much of the year. The building thus has a *heat deficit* for much of the year, which has to be compensated by the supply of heat via the building's heating system.

For a relatively limited portion of the year, internal heat development in residential buildings actually exceeds the heat losses, to produce a heat surplus. It is generally sufficient to open windows to get rid of this surplus heat, or simply to accept that the indoor temperature will rise. Residential buildings therefore normally require no special physical systems to remove surplus heat. However, they always require a heating system that ensures that the indoor temperature does not fall when the heat losses from the building exceed internal heat release.

In commercial premises and industrial buildings, internal heat release is often relatively high. Building technology has developed, so that these buildings are nowadays well insulated and airtight, with the result that their heat losses are low. As a result, new office buildings, department stores, hospitals and other commercial and industrial buildings often have a significant quantity of surplus heat during working hours throughout most of the year. Only at night-time and weekends, when internal heat release is much less, do the heat losses during cold weather become so high that there is a net heat deficit and a heat input is required. It is not uncommon, for example, for new office buildings to have a balance temperature that is as low as -10 °C during the daytime.

The high standard of thermal insulation has its origin in the residential sector, where it fills a purpose and is strongly justified. However, in the commercial premises sector, with its low balance temperatures, it means that less of the surplus heat can be released to the surroundings through the building envelope, with the result that a greater proportion of the surplus heat must be dealt with in some other way.

It can be seen, from the above, that it will become important in future to distinguish between residential buildings and commercial buildings in respect of their insulation standards and any proposed changes to them.

Specify what,
not how

Wishes in respect of the indoor climate and restrictions in respect of noise etc. from the building services systems can be expressed in the form of requirements that define the *function* that is sought. When formulating function requirements, it is essential always to understand that it really is a function that is being specified and not one of several possible measures or physical solutions that can effect the required function. It is necessary, in other words, to identify the function, which must then be expressed so that it is clearly defined and clearly quantifiable.

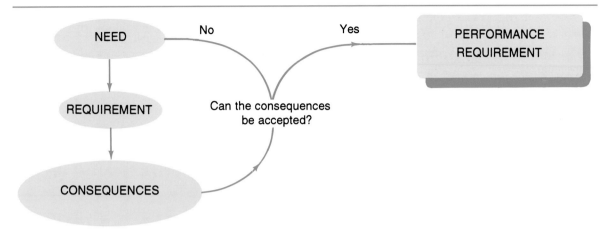

Figure 1. The performance requirement relationship.

As an example, consider the function requirement that the indoor air must be clean, i.e. that the concentrations of pollutant gases and particles must not exceed specified levels. In rooms in which persons work, this requirement is often specified by defining the highest permissible carbon dioxide concentration. This is a relatively coarse way of defining the function, although it is perfectly sufficient in many case.

In order to maintain the carbon dioxide concentration below the maximum permissible level, we ventilate the room with a sufficiently high air flow rate to prevent the carbon dioxide concentration rising above the permissible limit. Ventilation with this air flow rate is the physical solution that has been chosen to fulfil the performance requirement. A requirement calling for a particular air flow rate is thus not a performance requirement, as the air flow is the physical solution intended to bring about a given performance, in this case that of air quality. In any case, for the occupants of the room, it is essentially immaterial whether the air flow rate is high or low, as long as the air quality in the room maintains the required cleanliness.

The same applies for other parameters that can be related to physical solutions. It is important for the occupants of a room that the air is maintained sufficiently clean, that the temperature is held at the required level and that the ventilation system does not disturb through noise, draughts etc. However, it is essentially immaterial by which means these requirements are fulfilled, i.e. how great the air flow rate is, how the ventilation air is treated, how and whether the air flow rate varies or how the air is supplied to or removed from the room. Nevertheless, these aspects are of the greatest importance when deciding on the physical design to fulfil the specified requirements, but they must not be expressed as performance requirements.

Unfortunately, it is all too common for discussions on climate control systems to concentrate on the means, i.e. on the physical arrangements, instead of on the performance, i.e. on what the physical arrangement is to effect. In many cases, this can result in a somewhat strange discussion, complemented by arriving at (or retaining) solutions that are not ideal from a performance point of view.

Some physical designs, however, may be well-proven: we know that if we select a particular design, it will fulfil a particular performance requirement. Under such circumstances, it may be permissible to specify this particular arrangement as a requirement, but it is then important to be quite clear that it really is the question of the most suitable solution and not just of one solution among several possible.

Figure 1 describes a planning procedure: *What are the needs - What requirements must be specified - What will be the effects of the specified requirements?* It is extremely important that the purchaser, before finally freezing the performance requirements, understands what their effects will be in practice.

Physical solutions
- the designer's responsibility

It is not until the performance requirements have been agreed that it is possible to start to decide on the choice of the appropriate climate maintenance system, as it is the specified performance requirements that must provide the basis for the choice and design of the physical solutions. There should be a well-defined chain of responsibility between formulation of the requirements and the design of the physical solutions.

The process of selecting a climate maintenance system on the basis of specified performance requirements can be illustrated as shown in Figure 2.

Alternative system designs must be analysed on the basis of the specified performance requirements. This analysis must be based on investigations of the interaction between the building - activities - the climate maintenance system. Analysis must consider the consequences of the choices of various system designs in the form of plant cost, operation and maintenance costs, life cycle costs, generality, flexibility etc.

It is at the system design stage that the plan of the building and all essential points of its performance are decided. The actual work content at this stage normally constitutes only a relatively small proportion of the total work in designing a building, often somewhere between 10 and 20 %. The subsequent detailed design can certainly involve a significant quantity of work, but is essentially only technical implementation of the design principles that have been determined at the system analysis stage.

The major opportunities of influencing the energy requirements are thus during the process of specifying the performance requirements and during the process of choosing the building services.

Physical installations form a system whole

During the performance-based design of a building, as discussed above, the building services systems are divided into *climate control* and *physically serving* building services, which differs from the classification normally applied in practice. Here it is common to start instead from whether the systems handle a flowing medium such as air or water, or whether it is electrical energy that they handle. It is then natural to divide the various parts up into the main physical areas of Heating, Ventilation, Sanitation and Air Conditioning or into electrical installations.

The technical installations are characterised by

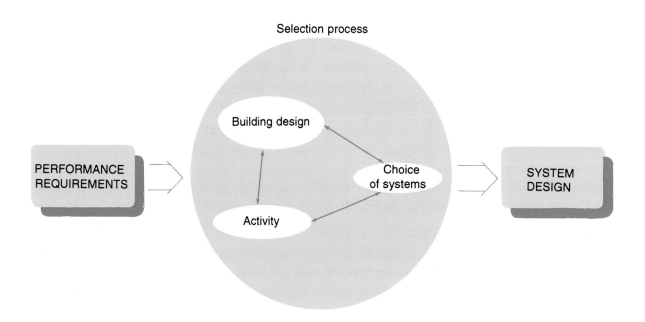

Figure 2. Selecting a climate maintenance system.

Table 1. Traditional classification of building services systems.

HVAC installations:	Electrical systems:
■ *heating system*	■ electricity for power requirements
■ *air conditioning and ventilation*	■ *lighting systems*
■ water and sewage systems	■ telecommunication systems
■ gas systems	■ data communication systems
■ fire-fighting systems (sprinklers etc.)	■ transport systems

Control and supervisory systems:
■ *control system*
■ supervisory system
■ protective and safety systems

forming systems consisting of various different types of apparatus. If these systems are to operate, they require control systems and control strategies. We thus arrive at the common classification which, for the sake of clarity, is shown in more detail below.

Of the building services shown in Table 1, it is only those shown in italics that can be related directly to the climate control systems from a performance viewpoint (i.e. heating systems, air conditioning and ventilation systems, lighting systems and control and supervisory systems).

As previously pointed out, the need for physical systems differs considerably between different types of buildings and different types of activities. One of the ways in which this can be clearly seen in shown by the proportion of the construction costs accounted for by the building services systems in different types of building projects. The following general presentation shows the magnitude of this proportion for a number of types of buildings (Table 2). The table also shows that, within the commercial premises sector, it is the building services systems that account for a very large proportion of the total cost. The figures shown are typical of building projects during the 1980s, and are largely representative of what is built today. Note, however, that it is the relative cost that is shown: absolute cost levels have fallen during the first years of the 1990s.

We have hitherto discussed the climate maintenance physical systems on the basis of what should be considered during planning and design and of how they interact in climate terms with the building and its activities. The following pages will describe the climate control services and building services systems in somewhat more detail. As residential buildings and

Table 2. Proportion of building costs accounted for by building services systems for different types of buildings.

Building type	HVAC, electricity and control systems - proportion of total building cost
New residential buildings	about 20 %
New offices	about 35 %
New laboratories	about 45 %
New industrial buildings	35-50 %
Refurbishment, residential buildings and commercial premises	40-60 %

commercial premises are so different in energy terms, they will be considered separately.

Falling heating requirements for residential buildings

As already mentioned, residential buildings need to be heated during the winter, although the heat requirement in new residential buildings is very low as a result of extremely well-insulated structures with triple-glazed windows and little air infiltration. This is fine, as long as it does not result in creating so much surplus heat that it is no longer sufficient merely to open windows during the hottest parts of the year.

A heating system consists of two parts: a supply system that supplies heat and a system that distributes the heat throughout the building and releases it in the rooms that need to be heated. We can summarise these two systems as shown in Table 3.

The presentation in Table 3 covers the heating systems that will generally be encountered. However, for each individual building, there will always be a number of specific factors that restrict the choice of system or mean that some particular type of system is most suitable. It is not necessary to discuss appropriate system choices in more detail here, although it is justified to emphasise that the choice of possible supply systems is restricted as building heat requirements fall.

In the 1960s, a single-family house usually had a heat requirement in excess of 30 MWh/year, while apartment buildings required 250 kWh/m², year or more. Single-family houses being built now often have a heat

requirement less than 10 MWh/year, while the specific heat requirement of apartment buildings is less than 100 kWh/m², year. With the modest heating requirements in modern homes, the total heating cost (capital cost + energy cost) can become unreasonably high if a heating system is chosen that is expensive to install, even though the annual running costs may be low. In addition, an expensive heating system is often complicated, and it is difficult to get complicated systems to operate satisfactorily in buildings with low heating requirements. This means that, in new homes, there is less scope for advanced heating systems, such as heat pumps or solar heating systems, no matter how much they may reduce the annual running costs. The same applies for larger centralised systems such as district heating and gas systems. In most cases, connection of detached houses to district heating systems is hardly realistic nowadays, as a result of the mains costs, while the mains losses are high in proportion to the small amount of heat that the houses require.

Table 3. A general view of heat supply and distribution systems.

SUPPLY SYSTEM	DISTRIBUTION SYSTEM
■ OWN BOILER Oil, biofuels	■ WATERBORNE HEATING Radiators
■ OWN BOILER Electricity	Floor heating Ceiling heating
■ OWN BOILER Gas	■ AIRBORNE HEATING
■ DISTRICT HEATING	■ DIRECT ELECTRIC HEATING
■ HEAT PUMP Airborne heating + top-up heating Surface earth heating Rock heating Exhaust air heat recovery (domestic hot water heating)	
■ SOLAR HEATING With 24-hour heat store (domestic hot water) With seasonal heat store (space heating)	

Ventilation must remove pollution

It is not, however, sufficient for the room temperature to be maintained at a comfortable level: the indoor air must also be acceptably clean. Air cleanliness is usually referred to as air quality, and the air quality is good if the air is clean.

It is practically impossible to have insufficient oxygen in a room, but it is possible to have excessive concentrations of carbon dioxide and other pollutants in the form of gases and particles. The purpose of ventilation is therefore not primarily to provide new oxygen but to remove the pollutants that are released to the air. This is done by replacing the polluted air with cleaner air by abstracting air from the room and supplying it with cleaner make-up air. There are two main principles of doing this.

The air may be evacuated from a room either by natural ventilation or by a fan-powered exhaust air system. The make-up air is drawn in directly from the outside, in principle at the ambient temperature, through leaks in the building envelope and ventilation openings in the walls or windows. Such systems are referred to as natural-draught systems or mechanical exhaust systems, depending on whether it is thermal chimney effects or a fan that powers the air flow in the exhaust air duct.

In a balanced ventilation system, make-up air is supplied via a make-up air system, with the air being preheated as necessary and supplied to the various rooms through ducts and supply air fittings. Such systems are referred to as balanced ventilation systems or balanced ventilation systems with heat recovery, if the heat in the exhaust air is recovered and used to warm the supply air.

Not many air leaks

Buildings constructed today have few air leaks through their walls and windows. With natural draught or mechanical exhaust ventilation systems, virtually all the supply air must be taken in through special inlets. This is perfectly satisfactory for ventilation air flow rates equivalent to air change rates of up to 0.5-0.6 air changes/h. At higher air flow rates, this will result in cold draughts and troublesome temperature differences. At ambient temperatures of around 0 °C or below, these problems will become noticeable.

If we need a ventilation air change rate higher than 0.6-0.7 air changes/h, even when it is cold outside, it is necessary to install a supply air system, i.e. to produce a balanced ventilation system. This results in a significant complication of the ventilation system, and is an example of the procedure shown in Figure 2. In order to be able to fulfil the specified performance requirements with a particular building design and for a particular activity or occupancy, it is necessary to resort to particular physical solutions. If we wish to have a simpler physical arrangement, it will be necessary to sacrifice performance requirements and/or modify the design of the building and/or the purpose for which it is to be used.

A detached house works perfectly well with a natural draught ventilation system if the building has a number of points through which air can enter, does not contain materials that can release hazardous pollution that requires ventilation air flow rates in excess of about 0.5 air changes/h, and is not too close to streets with heavy traffic.

This also applies for a mechanical exhaust ventilation system. From a technical point of view, an exhaust air fan is a simple and reliable piece of apparatus with a very low electrical energy requirement. It involves only an insignificant complication of the system but, in comparison with natural draught systems, provides better performance with considerably reduced space requirements.

If the purpose for which the building is used is such, if the building is so designed and if the requirements are such that ventilation air flow rates in excess of about 0.6-0.7 air changes/h are required, it is necessary (as already mentioned) to install both a supply air system and an exhaust air system. This will require a supply air handling unit with a heater, control equipment, filters etc., and normally also equipment for heat exchange between the supply and exhaust air flow rates for recovering heat from the exhaust air. The building also requires a duct system for distributing the supply air, together with supply air fittings in the individual rooms, designed and positioned so that they will not give rise to troublesome draughts. The end result is a system that, in technical terms, is on a completely different level from the simple natural draught or mechanical exhaust ventilation systems.

A common misunderstanding today is that the difference between a simple ventilation system and a complicated one is the absence or presence of fans. However, it is not the exhaust air fan that distinguishes the simple system from the complicated system: it is the need for a greater air flow rate than can be provided by a simple natural draught or mechanical exhaust system, together with the resulting need for a supply air system, that takes the step into a complicated system.

Commercial premises require more complicated installations

Commercial premises are regarded as being virtually all buildings that are not residential buildings or industrial buildings. In commercial buildings such as offices, department stores and hospitals, the activity necessitates complicated and space-demanding installations. In addition, present-day modern offices incorporate very much more electrical equipment. Yesterday's typewriter has been replaced by PCs on virtually everybody's desk. The use of copiers, fax machines etc. has increased greatly. All this has resulted in higher heat release indoors which, in turn, has further contributed to increasing the quantity of surplus heat.

In more modern commercial buildings, the heat

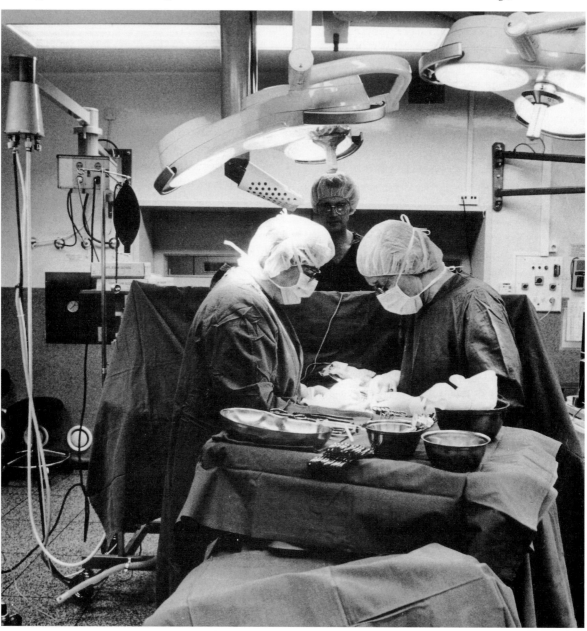

Building services systems in health care premises are often relatively complicated and are dictated largely by the requirements of particular activities. Photographer: Bo Dahlin, Bildhuset

requirement during the year is actually often so small that only simple heating systems are needed. What these buildings do require, however, are systems to deal with the large quantities of surplus heat to prevent the indoor temperature from becoming unacceptably high during working hours. In most cases, these climate control systems are absolutely essential if the building is to be used for its intended purpose.

Today, there are many manufacturers of office equipment and computers who are developing equipment with reduced electricity requirements and less heat release. Taken in combination with increased awareness that it is necessary to restrict internal heat release, this probably means that the development to date towards steadily increasing internal heat release in the buildings of the commercial sector is likely to be interrupted. However, the large quantities of excess heat during working hours, necessitating the use of climate control equipment with high cooling capacity, will remain, although at a somewhat lower level.

Problems of substantial surplus heat quantities

The capacity of a climate control system is determined primarily by the quantity of surplus heat with which it is required to deal. In addition, it is generally the case that the greater the quantity of surplus heat, the more difficult it is to ensure a good indoor climate in all respects. It is therefore important, when designing commercial premises, to attempt to arrive at designs that result in as little surplus heat as possible. This requires an overall view of the building and its climate control system, both when designing new buildings and in connection with refurbishment.

The most difficult task for the climate control system is generally to deal with surplus heat so that indoor temperatures do not become excessive when the building is in use, rather than in maintaining good air quality. As already mentioned, the balance temperature during working hours in more modern commercial premises is often below -10 °C, i.e. there will nearly always be surplus heat during working hours. As a result, the climate control system will have three duties:

■ to supply heat when the rooms have a heat deficit which, in more modern buildings, generally occurs only during the night and at weekends during the winter,

■ to remove surplus heat, which will be necessary at almost all times when the building is in use, i.e. during working hours, and

■ to remove airborne pollutants to maintain good air quality.

The flows required to remove surplus heat are often considerably higher than those needed to maintain air quality. Increasingly, it is becoming necessary to employ water cooling systems, having cold surfaces or fan coolers in the rooms, in order to deal with temperature maintenance.

Research is needed

If the performance requirements are to form the foundation of a properly operating physical solution they must not only be relevant, but also be formulated so that it is possible to convert them to properly operating physical solutions.

Research into indoor environment requirements is linked primarily to medical science and behavioural science, and can be divided into three sub-areas:

■ *Identification of relevant factors*, e.g. of which factors that involve problems in the indoor environment,

■ *Quantification of these factors to the extent that this is possible*, e.g. which concentrations of various gases or combinations of different gases that can be accepted in indoor air without risking its quality,

■ *Formulation of requirements*, e.g. how requirements are to be expressed in order to be able to serve as a basis for physical solutions, and how fulfilment of the requirements is to be checked in the completed buildings.

As far as physical building services systems are concerned it is always a matter of systems, which means that research needs to be clearly system-orientated. A system approach needs to be present in the background if it is a question of research aimed at any part of a system or concerned with an isolated problem within the sector, as well as with research.

In the case of climate-controlling physical systems, it is also so that the thermal climate and the air quality are the results of an often complex physical interaction between the climate control system, the design of the building and the work carried on therein. The emphasis of research needs to be concentrated on steady improvement of our knowledge of how we are to design systems, on the basis of the original performance requirements specifications, in order best to ensure the required final performance.

There are also important stages in the actual interaction between the climate control system and the building structure. For example, it is necessary to ensure that the climate control system works in such a way as not to involve any risk of damaging the building structure over a longer period of time. In the same way, it is necessary to ensure that the building structure does not contain any elements, materials or design features that substantially increase the load on the climate control systems.

A prerequisite for being able to perform system analyses is that there should be adequate calculation aids. If we start from the actual conditions at the time of carrying out initial design of buildings, it is possible to distinguish a number of terms that any such calculation model must fulfil:

- *The model must have a good correlation with reality.*
  The model must be inherently correct, and it must be possible for the building and its design to be correctly represented by the model.
- *It must be possible to perform model calculations with only a reasonable work input.*
  It should be possible to model the particular building, prepare the input data files and check that no faults have found their way into it in one or not more than two working days.
- *It must be possible to perform the calculations without a high level of special knowledge.*
  It must be possible for a well-trained design engineer, with normal computer familiarity, to be able to model a building and perform the desired calculations without excessive preparations.
- *It must be easy to investigate the effects of alternative physical designs.*
  It must, for example, be straightforward to investigate the effects on heat requirements and heat surplus throughout the year of factors such as wall designs and insulation levels, window sizes and window types, alternative methods of providing sun screening, lighting levels, types of lighting systems etc.
- *The results of the calculations must be suitable for use as*

a basis for determining physical system designs, and must be clear and easily understood by all those involved in the design process.
Interpretation of the results must not require special knowledge or a particular technical background.

We have not said much here about the development of new technology or new physical designs. There is naturally a need for development of new types of climate control systems and new apparatus, but it is primarily within the field of system development and system application that the major development needs are to be found.

Seeing the whole is the key

The important element is therefore to design the building, to fit it out and to use it in such a way that the whole - the building and its climate control system - operates as well as possible. This is generally synonymous with the whole being as physically and technically simple as possible. However, this does not mean that we can manage without relatively extensive climate control systems in hospitals, laboratories, department stores and offices, but it does mean that these systems will be simpler, and operate better in the long term, if an overall view is taken during the planning stage.

This chapter is based on material by Professor Enno Abel and Dr. Per-Erik Nilsson, Department of Building Services Systems, Chalmers University of Technology.

REFERENCES

Energiansvar - Sju experter om effektiv energianvändning i bebyggelse (Energy responsibility - Seven experts of efficient energy use in the built environment). Swedish Council for Building Research, T29;1992.

Installationer i byggnader (Building services systems in buildings); future BFR publication (Project No. 910389-7).

OTHER LITERATURE

Effektiv ventilation spar el. Undersökning av eleffektivitet i flerbostadshus (Efficient ventilation saves electricity: an investigation of electrical efficiency in apartment buildings). Isaksson, H. and Sandberg, E. BFR T11:1994.

SUBSTANTIAL POTENTIALS FOR ENERGY CONSERVATION IN RESIDENTIAL BUILDINGS

SUMMARY

Ever since the first energy conservation standards came into force in 1978, energy conservation in residential buildings has been largely regulated by standards and by mortgage rules. However, a feature of the Building Regulations is that they imposed requirements only on buildings' heat requirements, and not on their electricity use. It is urgent, both now and in the future, to attach considerable importance also to limiting the use of electricity in our buildings.

In many cases, interaction effects between buildings and their building services systems have been inadequately investigated. Major energy savings could probably be achieved if building technology and building services systems technology could be more closely integrated and made to work better together. It can also be noted that reduction of thermal bridges is becoming increasingly important, that new types or principles of insulation are being applied on a large scale without prior testing, that energy-efficient buildings are tending to become excessively complex and difficult to understand, and that it takes a long time to disseminate information on energy-efficient building to the entire building sector. It is therefore important that there should be a plan for continuous development training of the various parties involved in the building sector and of building occupants. Research and development are needed if the available relevant knowledge is to be put to use in the building process as a whole.

Experimental and demonstration buildings are important in order to disseminate knowledge and to test new designs under realistic conditions.

Heat exchange and heat pump systems, solar input contribution, appropriate ventilation quantities, physical designs for improved windows and the effects of the recycling concept are just some of the points that need to be investigated more closely in a research context.

Both building technology and building services systems technology have become increasingly complex over the last few decades. This is accompanied by a greater sensitivity to mistakes and defects. Many new building designs and methods have appeared. Buildings are generally designed so that there are many different materials in each part of the building, each having its own particular purpose. Examples of such materials are thermal insulation, wind barriers, air seals, internal and external surface coverings and so on. Shortcomings in the design and/or workmanship of any layer can then result in a serious threat to the performance of the structure. Failure in draughtproofing, for example, can result in draughts, a substantial reduction in thermal insulation performance or an increase in the risk of moisture problems. The relatively complex designs also result in difficulties in arranging connections between different parts of buildings. It may be difficult to ensure continuity of thermal insulation, draughtproofing and wind protection while at the same time transferring loads, assuring fire protection and preventing noise carry-over between apartments.

The building services systems in a building must work together with the building structural systems in controlling and maintaining the interior building climate. If the heat losses through the building envelope are reduced, problems can arise in controlling the indoor temperature, which can in turn result in excessive indoor temperatures and other problems. If the building services systems includes heat exchangers, heat pumps, solar collectors etc., it becomes increasingly difficult to ensure that the building operates satisfactorily as a whole. The overall view that is needed in order to ensure optimum cooperation between the building and its building services is often lacking.

Methods for reducing heat requirements for space

heating and domestic hot water production in new residential buildings have been primarily:

■ improved thermal insulation and draughtproofing of the building's envelope,
■ mechanical ventilation with heat recovery - using either air heat exchangers or heat pumps,
■ efficient heating systems.

Other factors that can affect heat requirements are:

■ window sizes and orientation,
■ the use of glazed external areas, and
■ water-conserving installations.

New, well-insulated buildings require very little heating energy to maintain required indoor temperatures. To a much greater extent than was previously possible, heat requirements can now be met by free energy from the sun and occupants, or from domestic appliances and equipment in the houses or apartments. However, this in turn imposes very high performance requirements on control of the heating system if the supply of unnecessary heat to the room or apartment is to be avoided. Average indoor temperatures in new buildings have become very high, which can hardly be explained by requirements in respect of comfort but must partly be seen as a result of inadequate systems.

Criticism of the complexity of the new systems has also resulted in both architects and many property-owners specifying a return to older technology, such as natural-draught ventilation. Several voices have also been heard, calling for a return to older building methods, which are sometimes even presented as tomorrow's building methods. New technology has not always lived up to expectations, and so some criticism is justified. However, naive criticism must be regarded as a serious threat to continued successful energy conservation, whether in new or existing residential buildings.

Insufficient knowledge on the parts of those involved

Are poorly performing buildings the result of a general lack of knowledge at the design stage? In some cases, it can be said that the knowledge simply did not exist - perhaps it still does not exist even today. However, knowledge was generally available to enable us to build low-energy houses with a good indoor climate. This knowledge was apparently not, however, spread throughout the building sector.

As far as existing buildings are concerned, knowledge of the function and performance of various systems and of their operation and maintenance will play a major part in the conservation potential. There is no formal organised training structure: materials manufacturers and building contractors have a large part to play here. Easily understood system descriptions, operating instructions and maintenance instructions should be demanded.

Occupants' and users' influence on energy use in buildings, particularly in detached houses, has been investigated by a number of workers[1,2,3,4]. Sixteen 'ecological' residential apartments in Tuggelite, near Karlstad, were also investigated[5]. Other work has shown that, within a given detached house area comprising apparently similar houses, energy use can vary by a factor of two. All this work should be considered when investigating how 'wasters' can be converted to 'savers' without having to sacrifice thermal comfort.

Standards and mortgage rules set the framework

Ever since the first energy conservation issues of the Building Regulations[6], standards and mortgage rules have had a very considerable effect on energy conservation in residential buildings. When the standards were introduced in 1978, they included specific requirements in respect of the insulation performance of the various parts of buildings. Only exceptionally was the compensation calculation procedure utilised that permitted the insulation of one part of a building to be reduced if another part was better insulated. The 1980 edition of the Building Regulations introduced a substantial improvement of the rules framework, ushering in rules that in practice specified limitations of the heat losses of the building as a whole. A notional reference building, constructed in accordance with the minimum requirements for the various parts of the building, provided a value for the maximum heat requirement of the building. The real building could than be designed in some other way, provided that the total heating requirement did not exceed that calculated for the reference building. The regulations thus opened the way for new, unconventional design solutions, although this possibility has been utilised to only a limited extent.

The 1988 Building Regulations for new buildings

introduced somewhat stricter requirements in respect of heat conservation. A somewhat different way of calculating the permissible heat losses was introduced, with the rules prescribing a maximum permissible average coefficient of heat transmittance. These changes have further assisted a wider design choice. Costs, for example, might dictate that a wall should be better insulated instead of using better-insulated windows. In other words, it is now possible to place the insulation in the building where it gives best value for money. As an alternative to low heating requirements, it is also permissible to supply energy from renewable energy sources, e.g. from solar collectors. However, this is a possibility of which little use is made.

The 1978 airtightness requirements

The 1978 Building Regulations introduced not only requirements in respect of thermal insulation but also, for the first time, requirements in respect of the airtightness of a building. At the same time, an upper limit of ventilation air flow rate was introduced in order to limit ventilation heat losses. The new rules had two effects. Firstly, all apartment buildings and most detached houses had mechanical ventilation with some type of heat recovery - either a heat pump or a heat exchanger. Secondly, the airtight buildings meant that there was no safety margin in the form of air leakage to provide additional ventilation if the ventilation system could not maintain the required air flow rate. As it is very difficult to construct a ventilation system that can provide the minimum ventilation air flow rate needed for good indoor air quality and, at the same time, the maximum to avoid waste of heating energy, the result has been far too many cases of insufficient ventilation, partly as a result of attempts to conserve heat. In addition, inadequate maintenance can result in lower air flow rates due to dirt deposits in the ducts, room fittings and air filters. This can also result in poor ventilation performance or uncontrolled air leakage. This has resulted in the requirements for average air flow rates having been increased somewhat in subsequent editions of the Building Regulations. The ELIB investigation clearly documented lower air flow rates than as prescribed in the Building Regulations.

There are very few clearly defined requirements in the building regulations in respect of air quality: it is only carbon monoxide values, mean annual values of radon daughter concentrations and maximum permissible values of formaldehyde that are expressed in quantifiable units. Apart from this, the Regulations give only general guidelines for air quality and values for the minimum permissible supply air flow rates. Bearing in mind the fact that new buildings contain many materials that emit substances which, either alone or in combination, can be health-hazardous, it most important that further research should be carried out with the aim of obtaining improved design data.

No requirements in respect of electricity use

A feature of the Building Regulations to date is that they have expressed requirements in respect of only the heating needs of a building. In practice, there are no requirements in respect of electricity use in residential buildings, whether for domestic electricity or for electricity for common services. This may have been quite correct during the early 1970s, when the country had a high dependence on oil and it was important to reduce the use of oil. With hydro power and nuclear power, Sweden has had a plentiful supply of cheap electricity.

The Building Regulations deal with electricity use in such a summary manner that they have hardly any guidance effect. In fact, up to now, the Regulations have more or less encouraged high electricity use: they have, for example, encouraged heat recovery by heat pumps or heat exchangers without considering that heat requirements have been reduced at the cost of higher electricity use. It will probably be essential to limit electricity use in buildings in future.

Inspection of ventilation systems now required by law

An important change in the rules in recent years was the introduction of obligatory inspection of ventilation systems. The objective of this is that property-owners will now be required to carry out regular maintenance of ventilation systems. In the longer term, this requirement will also result in improved designs in new installations: it will have to be easier to inspect and clean the systems. Many systems will probably be fitted with monitoring and inspection devices right from the time of building.

In addition to the Building Regulations and standards, the rules governing the provision of

Consumers have started to become more demanding in terms of what they get for the money they pay in rent or running costs of their homes. Building companies can no longer concentrate solely on low production costs, but must also start to think about low running costs, i.e. the costs of energy use during the life of the building.
Photographer: Tomas Södergren, Mira

mortgages have had a great effect on the size, physical design and choice of physical installations of houses.

Growing consumer influence

As described above, the general design of houses has been substantially influenced by the rules framework, while living costs or rent levels have been strictly controlled and subsidised. The housing 'consumer' has had only a limited influence on the design and quality of housing.

Today, the situation has changed. The regulations framework and mortgage rules no longer have such a strong influence on the design of housing: the consumer is acquiring greater influence on the design of the product. The reduced housing subsidies result in higher costs, which in turn means that the consumer has more demanding requirements in terms of what he/she gets for his/her money. Summarising, this means that the building companies are now more interested in building for the tenant/occupier than they were previously. Instead of concentrating solely on low production costs, they are now also starting to consider low running costs. Energy costs during the life of the building can become increasingly important.

Healthy buildings have also become a means of competition. Healthy buildings generally also provide a high standard of comfort. Good building comfort includes excellent insulation performance, allowing the entire volume of the building to be used. It should be possible to extend the occupation zone right out to the exterior walls. There must be no cold downdraughts from windows, and no cold floors as a result of thermal bridges. In other words, the building needs to be extremely well constructed in order to meet high comfort requirements. High comfort also includes a ventilation system that provides the right amount of clean air, without draughts or cold supply air.

The consequences of the deregulated electricity market may encourage energy conservation if the price of energy becomes the controlling factor. However, in new buildings, energy costs are still so low that the price of energy does not, as yet, provide any great incentive towards the construction of low-energy residential buildings.

Through the State and local authorities, society has a very strong ownership interest - almost a monopolistic interest - in heat and power utilities. This means that, in turn, it has a major responsibility for the use of finite energy resources. Tariff systems with very high fixed costs and relatively low variable costs hardly encourage low energy use.

New buildings
- a characteristic of present-day technology

Some of the features developed in experimental buildings from the 1980s are now being employed as standard in the production of apartment buildings. Their primary objective is to achieve low energy use for space heating in order to fulfil the Building Regulations requirements. However, the risks associated with the new methods and systems are that they are too complicated to commission, look after and maintain[7]. Competence to look after the systems properly is largely lacking on the part of building administrators and operators. Instead, they attempt to avoid the use of complicated systems by prescribing simple solutions, e.g. mechanical exhaust ventilation.

Building developers and contractors are acting rationally in relation to the regulations and cost conditions applicable at the time of constructing the building. Budgets are largely based on mortgage rules and low capital costs. The methods used are not particularly well suited to life cycle cost analyses or to future energy systems. Seen in a longer perspective, energy use breaks down to not more than 15 % during the building stage (including the manufacture of materials and transport) and at least 85 % during the occupancy and use stage.

Very little interest is still attached to electricity use in buildings: only in exceptional cases are details given of expected electricity use or of alternative designs that could encourage electricity conservation.

Greater importance has been given to thermal bridges. Although research has resulted in better knowledge of the effects of thermal bridges and in well-documented computer programs, little use is made of either. It is important that this knowledge should be used. As an example, we can consider the three winning entries for the Stockholm City Council's and BFR's Majrovägen competition, which was intended to provide an opportunity for the construction of apartment blocks carrying forward the energy conservation advances made in the earlier Stockholm Project. Although the extra heat losses resulting from thermal bridges across connections to structural beams, balcony supports and connections to the ground amounted to between 5 % and 39 % of the total heat transmission losses, the entries were better designed than is normal for new buildings. Nor do the current Building Regulations require consideration of the effect of constructive thermal bridges when calculating the heat requirements of buildings.

Low energy use but higher electricity use in new residential buildings

Energy use that is low in relative terms is achieved in present-day new apartment buildings through the use of good quality building envelopes and ventilation air heat recovery systems. However, electricity use for powering these systems increases, partly as a result of the heat recovery systems. Figure 1 shows a breakdown of energy use (as of 1989) for apartment buildings of various ages in Stockholm[8].

Monitoring the performance of three concrete apartment buildings in Örserum, designed for good thermal performance, and containing four apartments each, showed that energy use for space heating and domestic hot water production for the 1982-83 heating season amounted to only 53 kWh/m^2 per statistically average climatic year. The buildings contain heat exchangers for ventilation air and a heat pump for domestic hot water production and preheating of ventilation supply air in each apartment. Total energy use amounted to about 100-110 kWh/m^2, year, equivalent to the calculated values for these experimental buildings[9].

The Stockholm Project

The Stockholm Project is the name of six energy-efficient experimental apartment buildings in Stockholm, constructed between 1982 and 1985, and incorporating well-proven energy-efficient technology in combination with a number of new design features. The buildings are described in 'Energy in the built environment'[10]. The theoretical total energy use of these buildings was about 100 kWh/m^2, year, but the actual measured energy used was considerably higher. Much of the difference between the theoretical and actual values can be accounted for by the fact that electricity used for common purposes was much higher than had been assumed in the calculations.

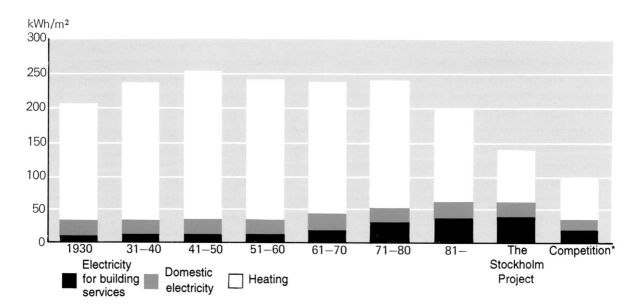

*for low-energy buildings, calculated values for the winning properties

Figure 1. 1989 energy use for apartment buildings in Stockholm, converted to a statistically average climatic year. The right-hand column shows expected values for entries in the Majrovâg competition arranged by Stockholm City Council and the Swedish Council for Building Research in 1990.

The most important conclusions of the Stockholm Project were:[11]

■ The buildings have low heating requirements in respect of space heating, ventilation and domestic hot water. However, total energy use is relatively high - 120-155 kWh/ m², year of purchased energy - as a result of excessive electrical energy for operating building services.

■ All values of measured energy use were higher than the theoretical values. Some of the reasons for this were that the indoor temperature was higher than the value of 20 °C as used for the calculations, the control systems did not work with the precision foreseen in the calculations, insufficient consideration was given to thermal bridges, the actual performance of heat exchangers and heat pumps was lower than expected and insufficient consideration had been given to the amount of electricity used for running fans.[*]

■ Much work was needed to inspect and commission the building services systems. There were far too many problems with standard components.[*]

■ If the occupants are to assist in looking after any of the building's physical systems, they need to be simple to look after and must be arranged with clear, easy to understand controls and instructions.

■ Thermal bridges resulted in substantial additional heat losses and locally low surface temperatures, particularly of floors adjacent to exterior walls.

■ Most of the buildings were very airtight, with the result that ventilation rate depended almost entirely on the ventilation systems and was almost independent of the weather. Air change rate depended entirely on correct adjustment of the ventilation system.

■ The glazed areas did not provide the expected energy contribution.

■ Although the occupants appreciated their glazed courtyards, they did not use them as often as had been thought when they were designed.

■ The low-energy buildings had better indoor climate than was common in ordinary newly-built property.

■ Occupants wanted an indoor temperature of about 22 °C and the ability to control it themselves.

■ It was difficult to arrange draught-free ventilation.

■ Fan noise and other noise from building services systems was often regarded as troublesome.

[*]See also **A case example from reality** in the chapter entitled **Occupants before technology (in The Building And Its Occupants section)**, for a more detailed description of the problems encountered.

The Majrovägen Project

Experience from the Stockholm Project was used when announcing the rules for the Majrovägen Development Competition, arranged by the Stockholm City Council and BFR in 1990. All 16 entrants are described in a publication available from the Stockholm City Council Housing Department[12].

Another starting point for the Majrovägen competition was the Building Regulations for new buildings. The theoretical total energy use for the competition entries was about 30 % lower than for corresponding buildings constructed in accordance with the 1980 Building Regulations. A major contributory cause of this low energy use was the reduced use of electricity for building services systems and common services. Another reason was to be found in the special requirements defining the design of connections to avoid thermal bridges. Unfortunately, the economic recession and the housing market situation at the time meant that none of the buildings was actually erected. No monitoring of buildings constructed in accordance with the new Building Regulations has been carried out to date.

Few documented energy-related experimental building projects for new detached houses have been carried out since Energy in the Built Environment[10] was published. A few small-scale experiments - some of which are commercially financed - are in progress, involving various new building systems, new thermal insulation materials, ventilated (heat-exchanging) floor/ceiling structures, heat recovery without special apparatus and the use of sub-floor crawl spaces to provide space for installing building services equipment. Some reports have been published, but there have been no claims of any dramatic reduction in energy use.

The Institutes of Technology Project

The country-wide investigation under the name of the Institutes of Technology Project was a major statistical investigation of the effects of various energy conservation measures in a large number of detached houses and apartment buildings. The results show that, on average, the expected savings have been achieved[13,14]: see Table 1. However, there are major differences between measured and calculated savings in individual buildings, as well as in savings from building to building. The project indicated that measured savings resulting

Table 1. Summary of energy savings achieved per statistically average climatic year in apartment buildings resulting from measures in the Institutes of Technology Project.

Conservation measure	Average apartment size, m²	Saving, %	Measured pre-improvement energy use, MWh/apt.	Measured energy saving, MWh/apt.	Expected energy saving, MWh/apt.	Savings cost, öre/kWh
Window improvement	112	9 %	14.8	1.3	1.3	84
Roof insulation	101	5 %	15.0	0.7	0.8	10
Group of measures (larger structural and other larger measures), average[1]	92	14 %	15.2	2.1	2.1	38
District heating connection	112	24 %	20.0	4.7	2.4	10
Control measures average[2]	111	4 %	16.8	0.7	0.5	23

1.   The various conservation packages resulted in the following savings:
      Mainly building services, window replacement, 11 %
      Mainly building services, roof or exterior wall insulation, 11 %
      Mainly building measures, 14 %
      Mainly building services, replacement of boiler or oil-burner, 16 %
      Mainly building services, new heating system, 28 %

2.   Group 1:   Thermostat valves, adjustment, weatherstripping, 8 %
      Group 2:   Radiator valves, adjustment, -3 %
      Group 3:   Thermostat valves, adjustment, boiler or burner replacement, 8 %

from upgrading of window performance in detached houses were less than had been expected, at 1.6 MWh/apartment, year as against 2.7 MWh/apartment, year. Much of the explanation for this is that the calculations had assumed that the indoor temperature could be reduced by 0.5 °C, and ventilation by 0.05 air changes/h, which was not achieved.

In addition to additional insulation of various parts of the buildings, combinations of additional insulation in walls, roofs and windows were also investigated. This involved a total of 29 detached houses, with the average result being 6.0 MWh/dwelling unit, year, as against a calculated value of 8.3 MWh/dwelling unit, year.

The savings effect of heat pumps was investigated in 59 detached houses and 20 apartment buildings, as shown in Table 2. The following heat sources were used:

1. Surface earth or lake water.
2. Rock or groundwater.
3. Outdoor air.

The annual coefficient of performance for Group 1 was measured at 2.3 in the three investigations, with a 95 % energy coverage. In Group 2, the annual COP was 2.3, with an annual energy coverage of 93 %, while in Group 3 the results were 2.1 and 70 % respectively. Investigations of the effects of heat pumps have also been carried out by SP in 1985[15] and Vattenfall in 1986[16]. The investigation also looked at conversion of heating

Table 2. Results of heat pump installations in buildings in the Institutes of Technology Project.

APARTMENT BUILDINGS

	Average apartment size, m²	Saving, %	Annual COP		Cost of savings, öre/kWh
			As measured	Brochure claim	
Heat pump installation, average	111	48			
Classified by heat sources:					
Surface earth and lake water		46	2.0	2.7	
Rock, wells and groundwater		54	2.9	2.9	17
Outdoor air		42	3.1	2.4	
Heat pump and one other smaller improvement		37			

DETACHED HOUSES

	Average house size, m²	Saving, %	Annual COP		Cost of savings, öre/kWh
			As measured	Brochure claim	
Heat pump installation, average	293	52			
Classified by heat sources:					
Surface earth and lake water		60	2.4	2.6	16
Rock, wells and groundwater		64	2.3	2.6	19
Outdoor air		37	2.0	2.6	23
Heat pump and one other smaller improvement		56			

systems from oil to electricity. The measured saving, comparing fuel energy and electrical energy, was 22 %, which results from the improved annual efficiency and savings resulting from an improved control system.

Conclusions from the Institutes of Technology Project

General conclusions from the Institutes of Technology Project were:

- The improvement measures resulted in statistically confirmed energy savings.
- For entire groups of houses/buildings, the average savings amounted almost to the expected values.
- There was a major variation in savings results from house to house.
- The greatest energy savings were found in houses/buildings having high pre-improvement energy use.
- Indoor temperatures did not fall after implementation of the improvement measures. However, it was felt that it would be possible to reduce the temperatures without excessive comfort losses in houses/buildings having additional insulation.
- Existing heating equipment was often in poorer condition than had been expected.
- The large spread in energy savings from one house to another indicated that the conservation measures were not always being correctly applied or designed.

Careful inspection of the quality of workmanship was recommended.

■ Even when considering only the savings to the property-owner, roof insulation, improvements to control systems, connection to district heating supplies and the installation of heat pumps were all very cost-effective. Profitability can be further improved by performing such work in connection with refurbishment or maintenance work,

The average savings were close to the calculated theoretical savings, although there were significant variations around the mean value of measured savings. The conclusion is that it is possible to achieve a calculated savings, but that this is often not actually done in individual cases. This may be due to occupants' living habits, or also to poor workmanship or inadequate design data. There is a general lack of long-term experience of energy conservation measures in existing residential buildings.

Other investigations carried out in Sweden, Norway and the USA show approximately the same patterns as above.

Conservation measures in buildings with direct electric heating

Particular interest has been devoted to directly electrically heated single-family houses, and a number of projects have been carried out by BFR, Vattenfall, the National Board for Industrial and Technical Development (NUTEK) etc. The common objectives of improvement measures can be said to be:

■ to improve the efficiency of electricity use, preferably bringing it up to the level of efficiency in present-day new buildings,
■ to shift electricity demand from daytime to night-time, and
■ to replace the use of electricity by some other fuel.

A BFR project entitled 'Electrically-efficient Single-family Houses' carried out a variety of more extensive or less extensive building and building services conservation measures in 37 houses constructed between 1966 and 1976 in four towns in Sweden. Particular attention was paid to how much domestic electricity might be reduced by changing to low-energy white goods appliances. Reductions in electricity use of between 25 % and 35 % were noted. However, during the winter, it was necessary to supply more heat from the heating system

in order to compensate for the loss of waste heat[17].

An experimental building project from 1990[18], performed by Rockwool AB and Enertech AB, demonstrated a substantial energy saving in four existing directly electrically heated single-family houses. Their building envelopes were improved and windows upgraded with a third pane, with heat recovery being effected by means of heat exchangers in two houses and by heat pumps in the other two. Three of the houses retained their electric heating, although distributing it by an airborne heating system, with the electric heating in the fourth house being complemented by oil-fired heating at times of expensive electricity.

In the Österåker Project, which was part of Vattenfall's larger Uppdrag 2000 Project, the overall objective was to provide a basis for assessing how heating systems might be converted from electric heating or to ascertain how the efficiency of electric heating might be improved, in a typical group of older houses having direct electric heating[19]. Various measures were applied in 14 houses built between 1967 and 1970.

The effects on electricity use in the Österåker Project varied from an increase of 1500 kWh/year to a decrease of 9000 kWh/year. Expressed in cost terms as of November 1990, the corresponding cost savings varied between SEK 400 and SEK 4300 per year - in other words, even in those cases in which electricity use increased as a result of the modifications, there was still a net cost saving. Cost savings as a result of transferring electricity use from daytime to night-time were noted. Houses with the capability of using either oil or electricity were able to maintain over 90 % of their electricity use on an off-peak tariff.

In terms of comfort, the occupants felt that the new heating systems were an improvement on the old direct electric heating system. Some minor problems of noise from the equipment, resulting from faults or teething troubles associated with new products, were noted and have been rectified. Measures that resulted in an improvement of ventilation were regarded most positively.

The results from these single-family house projects are all in agreement, and can be summarised as follows:

■ Existing single-family houses can be improved so that their energy performance is similar to that of newly-built houses.
■ The long payback times mean that the costs of the various measures, however, are very difficult to justify from the owner's point of view.

■ Measures carried out in connection with normal maintenance are more profitable.

Some conversion measures have been carried out in directly electrically heated apartment buildings. Two buildings in Furulund, built in 1973 and each having ten apartments, had waterborne and airborne heat distribution systems installed together with mechanical balanced ventilation systems with heat recovery. Post-improvement energy use was measured as being essentially the same as pre-improvement use, although the work had a very favourable effect on air quality in the apartments[20].

The regulations must encourage sustainable building

In future, both new building and refurbishment/-modernisation must pay more attention to the recycling/re-use approach. Sustainable building involves conservation of finite resources and elimination or substantial reduction of emission of pollution. Considerable research is needed in order to develop effective guide measures, which may be administrative (legislation), financial or behaviourally-related. It is important that financial guide measures are so constructed that low operating costs are favoured rather than low capital costs. Operating costs need to be loaded with pollution costs, e.g. for emission of carbon dioxide or as a levy for the storage of nuclear waste. A long-term sustainable and globally ecologically responsible economics system is needed for sustainable building.

Integration of building services is important

A review of the results of research from recent years shows that excellent building and building services technologies and methods are available, but are not fully utilised in new production. Substantial energy savings could probably be achieved if building services systems and the buildings and/or building methods themselves could be better integrated. System aspects need to be considered at an early stage of the work, when preparing the general design.

For every new building project, there is good reason to ascertain what technical/physical and human resources are available, in order to determine the appropriate levels of building technology and building services systems. There is also reason to start planning for operation and maintenance at the design stage. In addition, it is necessary to allow for the competence of caretakers and likely competences of future personnel. There are also cost aspects to be considered. A main question for research is therefore how the results of available knowledge can be implemented in the building process as a whole: this also includes determining how advanced technology can be applied on a large scale.

It is becoming increasingly clear that the most fruitful advances in research can be achieved in the boundary zones between established research disciplines. Experimental building projects are extremely important in enabling such areas to be identified and investigated: it is only in full-scale experiments that system aspects can be properly investigated. In addition, they enable various specialists to work together in carrying out careful investigations and evaluations.

As new, modern technology is often very complicated, risks of faults or mistakes can arise. It should be possible to deal with these systematically through application of some form of risk analysis. It is not entirely unthinkable that the end result might be better if less advanced technology was correctly used, rather that if excessively complex technology was incorrectly used: results from the most advanced experimental buildings indicate that this might well be the case. However, research into the introduction of new technology should result in the development of technologies and methods that fulfil expectations in the form of robust, reliable designs.

Combine refurbishment with energy conservation measures

A key question for energy conservation in residential buildings is how far energy conservation measures should go. Extremely low levels of energy use can be achieved, but this is generally at the price of complicated technology and difficulty in monitoring overall performance of the systems. This is a difficult question, both for new building and for existing buildings, and is closely related to both the levels of knowledge of different parts of the building sector and to occupants' knowledge and interest.

The switch from fossil fuels and nuclear power to sustainable energy sources is an enormous problem, towards the solution of which we can today present little other than visions. Regardless of when nuclear power is phased out, it will have to be replaced eventually. This may mean that the use of electric heating has to be replaced by heat from fossil fuels, with resulting accompanying increase in carbon dioxide emissions. This is in contravention of Agenda 21 of the Rio Agreement, by which Sweden and other countries agreed to reduce their emissions of carbon dioxide. Against this background, there is every justification for attempting to reduce heating requirements of the building sector.

Within the foreseeable future, energy use accounted for by older housing stock will totally dominate other energy use. It is therefore of the greatest importance that measures should be taken that can substantially reduce total energy use in existing buildings. Sooner or later, buildings need to be repaired or converted. These occasions provide unique possibilities for combining renovation/refurbishment with energy conservation measures. Present-day knowledge of how energy conservation can be implemented is good, and it is important that this knowledge should be widely spread. However, this is difficult, as so many parties are involved in the refurbishment process, all of whom must possess the relevant knowledge of what can and should be done, and of how it can be done.

Good liaison and improved knowledge are needed

Improving the quality of building envelopes of existing apartment buildings is very important in the interests of reducing environmental impact. It is important that the correct measures should be applied, and be of sufficient extent, when carrying out refurbishment. Today, for example, we can see that many additional insulation projects from the 1970s had far too little insulation. Further improving such insulation is almost always uneconomic. For most buildings, the current new building standards should be aimed at when carrying out more extensive refurbishment. Correctly applied measures can also substantially improve comfort and provide an opportunity for simplifying heating systems. Correctly applied measures to the building envelope will continue to be effective and to provide savings throughout the remaining life of the building.

Many architectonic, structural and building services problems must be resolved through appropriate cooperation between the various specialists, and comprehensively performed and evaluated experimental

building work is of great assistance in doing so. Good examples can constitute the basis for successful energy conservation.

Energy conservation measures should be evaluated in the light of the following considerations:
- Existing and future maintenance requirements.
- Possible savings in running costs.
- Suitable longer-term heating systems.
- Practical installation aspects.
- Reductions in environmental impact.
- Improved indoor climate (more healthy, better working climate).
- More efficient use of rooms and premises.

Improved knowledge of the technical standards of existing buildings is needed across a wide front if we are to be able to select the most suitable energy conservation measures. We also need to be aware of the need to improve indoor climates, as well as carefully monitoring the effects of various measures on indoor climate.

Improved production methods needed

It is important to investigate why expected energy savings do not always materialise. It should be possible to apply most of the planned improvement measures in order to achieve the calculated savings in practice. It is important that improved and more effective methods of production should be developed to reduce the costs for insulation and building services improvements. Particular attention should be paid to the use of electricity in existing buildings. After refurbishment, electricity use should not be allowed to increase unless such an increase has been previously supported by a careful budget analysis.

It is well documented that new building technology, in combination with modern building services systems, can produce very healthy and comfortable buildings - buildings having very low energy requirements for space heating, domestic hot water production and operation of building services systems[21]. One of the most important tasks must therefore be to ensure that appropriate knowledge of these good methods is generally applied. There is also every reason to improve technologies so that they become more robust and less prone to problems. New methods and technologies must not produce their own problems of noise, draughts or other irritants.

More training needed in all sectors

More training in all aspects of energy conservation work is presumably even more important in respect of improvement measures in existing single-family houses, as such measures are often carried out by smaller builders and craftsmen, with no real planning work being likely.

The need for continued training has often been emphasised, as has the need for improving the general level of competence in all aspects of the building process. This is why we need to take a more overall approach.

We cannot separate university education from high school education, engineering training, training of supervisors, training of craftsmen, training of caretakers etc. An investigation to determine the knowledge status of the various sectors, with proposals for improvements in training methods, is essential.

This chapter is based on material by Professor Bo Adamson, Department of Building Science, Lund University, Professor Arne Elmroth, Department of Building Physics, Lund University and Dr. Per Levin, Department of Building Technology, the Royal Institute of Technology, Stockholm.

REFERENCES

1   Gaunt, L. *Bostadsvanor och energi* (Living habits and energy). SIB M11:1985.

2   Lundström, E. *Occupant influence in energy consumption in single-family dwellings*. BFR D5:1986.

3   Palmborg, C. *Social habits and energy consumer behaviour in single-family houses*. BFR D24:1986.

4   Lundgren, T. *Bostäder som brukarstyrda energisystem* (Homes as user-controlled energy systems). BFR R7:1989.

5   Tidäng, K. *Att bo i Tuggelite* (Living in Tuggelite). BFR T19:1992.

6   1975 Building Regulations, Supplement 1. Energy conservation etc. (with effect from 1st January 1977).

7   Johansson, H-E. et al. *Energiförbrukning i flerfamiljshus* (Energy use in apartment buildings). BFR R74:1989.

8   Fyrhake, L. *Nya friskare hus med lägre elbehov* (New, healthier buildings with lower electricity requirements). Byggforskning 92.6 Stockholm.

9   Södergren, D., Elmroth, A. *Betonghus med extremt låga energibehov. Flerbostadshus i Örserum, Gränna* (Concrete buildings with extremely low energy requirements: apartment buildings in Örserum, Gränna). BFR R30:1991.

10 *Energi i byggd miljö. 90-talets möjligheter* (Energy in the built environment. The way forward to the 1990s. BFR G16:1988.) BFR G16:1987.

11 *Unika resultat från sex energisnåla hus* (Unique results from six low-energy buildings). EHUB. BFR T14:1989.

12 Stockholm City Council Housing Department, 1990. *Sexton energisnåla, sunda hus. Presentation av förslagen i Stockholms stads markanvisningstävling för energisnåla, sunda hus* (Sixteen low-energy healthy buildings. A presentation of the entries in the Stockholm City Council development competition for low-energy healthy buildings). Energi och miljö, Box 8311, S-104 20 Stockholm.

13 Elmroth, A. et al. *Effekter av energisparåtgärder i bostadshus* (Effects of energy conservation measures in residential buildings). BFR R107:1989.

14 Elmroth, A. et al. *Energisparåtgärder i bostadshus* (Energy conservation measures in residential buildings). BFR T13:1991.

15 Swedish National Testing and Research Agency, 1985.

16 Vattenfall, 1986.

17 Kronvall, J. et al. *Eleffektiva småhus - möjligt men olönsamt* (Electrically-efficient single-family houses - Feasible but unprofitable). Journal of Swedish Council for Building Research, 1994.5.

18 Stadler, C-G. and Åkerblom, B. *Hur man skapar låg energianvändning i äldre direktelvärmda småhus* (How to reduce energy use in older directly electrically heated single-family houses). BFR R8:1990.

19 Levin, P., Isaksson, T., 1991. *Österåkersprojektet - Pilotprojekt för konverteringsteknik för direktelvärmda småhus* (The Österåker Project. A pilot project for conversion technology for directly electrically heated single-family houses). Vattenfall Uppdrag 2000, Stockholm (Additional Report 1993).

20 Dahlberg, L. *Konvertering av direktelvärme i flerbostadshus. Installation, mätning och analys* (Conversion of direct electric heating in apartment buildings. Installation, performance metering and analysis). Furulund. BFR R49:1993.

21 Fyrhake, L. et al. *Godbitar: Ur tävlingsförslag om sunda och energisnåla hus* (The best bits: From competition entries for healthy, low-energy buildings). BFR T10:1994.

OTHER LITERATURE

Berättelsen om ett energiekonomiskt småhus. Ett systemtänkande baserat på enkla lösningar (An energy-efficient detached house. The system approach, based on simple solutions). Eriksson, G. BFR T22:1991.

Bostadsbeståndets tekniska egenskaper (The technical features of Sweden's residential building stock). ELIB Report No. 6. Tolstoy, N., Borgström, M., Högberg, H. and Nilsson, J. SIB. Research Report TN:29, 1993.

Energieffektiviseringshandbok, Del 3: Småhus (The energy efficiency manual, Part 3: Detached houses). Ställborn Werner, C., Morelius, P. and Öberg, P. Stockholm Energi, 1992.

Energieffektiviseringshandbok, Del 2: Lokaler och flerbostadshus (The energy efficiency manual, Part 2: Commercial premises and apartment buildings). Ställborn Werner, C., Morelius, P. and Öberg, P. Stockholm Energi, 1992.

MAJOR POTENTIALS FOR ENERGY CONSERVATION IN COMMERCIAL PREMISES

SUMMARY

An analysis of heating and electricity use in commercial premises during the 1980s shows that, while the amount of heating energy used has decreased, total use of electricity has increased. New commercial premises have lower total energy use than older premises, but a greater percentage of electricity use.

When improving the efficiency of electricity use, there is a substantial risk of simply transferring some of the load from electricity to heat. Avoiding this requires greater knowledge of various system relationships and an overall view of the building and its building services, both during the design of new premises and in connection with refurbishment/renovation of older premises. Knowledge of system aspects in general also needs to be improved. We need refined methods that are capable of considering the energy aspects at an early stage of design. It is also important to adjust the concept of life cycle costs to suit the practical requirements of the building sector.

Major savings can be made by reviewing operating strategies and persuading users to change their habits in respect of lighting, use of computers etc., as well as by changing the actual physical sectioning of lighting. It is also important to consider the tariff structure when investigating the viability of various efficiency improvement measures.

Within industry, improvements in energy efficiency are often effected in connection with changes to production processes. In future, the link with companies' environmental images will become important.

The concept of 'commercial premises', as used in this article, relates to buildings for all purposes except residential buildings and except those used for industrial production. As a result, the spread in respect of the types of administration, purposes of use, physical status and energy use for heating and electricity is therefore very wide.

Published statistics show that the total energy use for much of this building stock has fallen during the last decade[1].

A simultaneous analysis of heat and electricity use during the 1980s shows that, while the use of thermal energy has fallen, the use of electricity has increased[2,3], as shown in Figure 1.

It therefore appears as if the reduction in the use of heat has occurred at the cost of greater use of electricity. There has been a change in the relative proportions of these forms of energy carriers, both in new buildings and after refurbishment. There is also a corresponding tendency for the country's apartment building stock. Some factors that have probably affected this development are:

■ Poor awareness of electricity use.

■ Greater use of office machinery (computers, copiers, fax machines etc.).

■ The concentration of the Building Regulations on heating requirements.

■ Uncritical transfer of knowledge from the residential sector to the commercial premises sector.

■ (In many cases) short-term cost attitudes.

■ Inadequately developed knowledge of system relationships and tools for system analysis.

■ Unclear signals from Government and authorities concerning future energy policy.

In connection with production of its review document, 'Energy in the built environment'[4] in 1987, the Swedish

Space heating and domestic hot water production (net),
kWh/m² and year (including electricity for space heating)

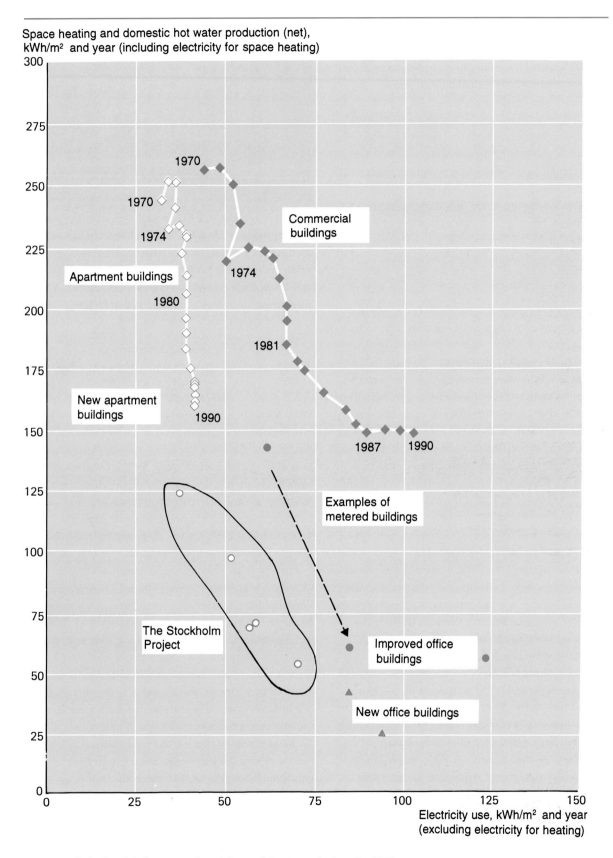

Figure 1. Relationship between electricity and heat use during the 1980s.

Council for Building Research and other parties on the market started to observe the above tendencies. The review presented the following examples of important areas for continued research and development:

- Analysis of the reasons for higher electricity use.
- Development of methods and systems for balancing cooling and heating requirements, with the emphasis on minimisation of electrical power and energy demands.
- Development of efficient operation and supervisory systems.
- Investigation of the effects on the heat balance and energy use of commercial premises of the introduction of energy-efficient lighting and electrical equipment.
- Simulation studies of efficient use of daylight in various types of commercial premises.

Several R&D projects have therefore been carried out over the last 5-10 years into energy use of important parts of the country's commercial buildings stock. This is an area in which the link with indoor climate is important, not least in respect of the energy conservation measures to be proposed. Several other parties, such as energy distributors, energy utilities, larger property-owners etc. have also been active in this area in recent years.

The main emphasis of the Second Office Project has been to improve the efficiency of electricity use and to analyse the building services systems technology relationships. The project was carried out in four office buildings owned by insurance companies. The picture shows WASA's building in Gothenburg.

Office project I

During the middle of the 1980s, a larger energy conservation project for office buildings, with the working name of Office Project I, was performed with support from the Swedish Council for Building Research (BFR)[5,6.] The work was carried out in conjunction with the larger Swedish insurance companies, and covered five buildings, erected between the middle of the 1950s and the beginning of the 1970s, in different parts of the country.

The objective of the work was to apply larger energy conservation measures and, through extensive before-and-after measurements, determine the savings, calculate the capital costs and analyse any problems. The main thrust of the work was on heat conservation, primarily through various types of building services systems improvement measures. The actual financial viability of the improvements varied widely from building to building, although was good in most cases.

Office Project II

Work has since continued in conjunction with the insurance sector during the end of the 1980s and beginning of the 1990s through a second larger project with BFR support, Office Project II. The emphasis of the work has been mainly on improving the efficiency of electricity use and determining and analysing the technical relationships between systems. Here, the interaction between thermal energy and electricity use has been central.

This project[7], which has been carried out in four office buildings owned by the Folksam, Trygg-Hansa, Wasa and Skandia insurance companies, is at present in its closing stages. These four buildings are representative of different ages (prior to 1980 and after 1985), and also partly have different designs of building services systems and the way in which they are used. Three of the buildings are situated in Gothenburg, and one in Stockholm. Table 1 shows the main features of the four properties.

Measurements, analyses and computer modelling have improved our knowledge of such factors as the structure of electricity use in typical office buildings, its spread among different applications, control of building services systems, aggregation of various internal heat loads and their effect on design electrical power ratings.

It has been possible to analyse the interaction between heat and electricity use in response to different

Table 1. *Main features and performance parameters of the buildings in Office Project II.*

	Folksam	Trygg-Hansa	Wasa	Skandia
Electricity supply	Low voltage	Low voltage	Low voltage	Low voltage
Main activity	Offices Shops	Offices Apartments Restaurant	Offices Shops	Offices Restaurant
Measured floor area [m²]	609	655	664	356
Total installed electrical power [kW]	26.3	24.4	28.7	11.5
Specific installed electrical power [W/m²]	43	37	43	32
Total installed lighting power [kW]	9.1	13.9	12.4	4.2
Specific installed lighting power [W/m²]	14.9	21.2	18.7	11.8
Specific installed lighting power in office areas [W/m²]	16.9	22.1	17.0	12.6
Illuminance in office areas [lux]	200	300	350-400	320
CO_2 concentration [ppm]	410 - 830	385 - 510	510 - 600	560 - 750
Ventilation	Balanced with heat recovery	Balanced with heat recovery	Balanced with heat recovery	Balanced with heat recovery
Comfort cooling	Indirect, Fan-Coil	Direct [heat exchange]	Indirect, ISAC	None[1]
Computerised control and supervisory system	Landis & Gyr, Visonik 400	None	Landis & Gyr, Visonik 400	TA, System 7 Midi

[1] Only central computer cooling for the high-rise block.

types of electrical energy efficiency improvement measures through extensive computer modelling, using the American DOE2 model[8].

Suitable efficiency improvement measures within the fields of ventilation, cooling, control technology, lighting, office equipment etc. have also been developed, and their cost-effectiveness analysed. This has been carried out as part of the work of a continuation project supported by the National Board for Industrial and technical Development (NUTEK) and the insurance companies. Some of the work has been financed by grants from NUTEK. The results have assured good knowledge dissemination.

The extensive measurements have greatly improved our knowledge of power demand and its make-up and variation in daily, weekly, monthly and annual terms.

Key indicators for power and energy demands for the various subsystems have been determined, and are shown in Table 2, as is the total energy use for various purposes: heating, larger items in building services systems (fans, cooling, pumps, lighting etc.) and larger items of occupants' electricity use (lighting, office equipment etc.).

Figure 2 is an example of how electricity use is apportioned between different applications in an office building constructed during the middle of the 1980s.

The aggregation of internal heat loads on typical office floors, in the form of lighting, computers, copiers etc., is larger than had been expected. The aggregation is expressed as a load factor (the quotient of measured and installed power capacities), and varies between 40 % and 60 % in these buildings, depending on such factors as load control and sectioning. Similar results have also been obtained in other office buildings.

If the measurements had extended to the entire buildings, it is probable that the aggregation had been even larger (= lower load factors). This is an area in which we need more knowledge that can result in improved design data for dealing with diversity effects when determining the ratings of air conditioning cooling equipment etc. This could result in lower capital and running costs, as well as more efficient use of energy through improved matching of the capacities of cooling equipment to actual heat loads (part load characteristics).

Results from simulation using the DOE2 model clearly show a relationship between various subsystems and how, for example, substantial savings in electricity for lighting can be partly offset by greater use of district heating.

The well-known rule in energy conservation circles that every building is unique still applies. As a result, simulation results of the magnitude of total energy savings cannot simply be uncritically transferred to other similar buildings, where pre-improvement conditions and control conditions are perhaps completely different. As a result, the interaction between electricity and heat varies from case to case, but is always there.

Training and information campaigns[9] have disseminated the results to the sector, but further work is needed. Results have also been published in the international trade press[10,11].

The Råcksta Project (Vattenfall's headquarters, Stockholm)

Vattenfall's headquarters complex in Råcksta, Stockholm, is a good example of a building in which, at the end of the 1980s and the beginning of the 1990s, a major programme of improving the overall efficiency of energy use was carried out[12]. The building, with a floor area of about 100 000 m², was erected at the beginning of the 1960s and contains offices, restaurants, large computer centres, parking garages etc. By the end of the 1980s, the various building services systems were in substantial need of upgrading.

If wide-ranging measures aimed at improving the efficiency of energy use are to be undertaken, it is generally the case that this must be done in combination with building conversion work or more substantial refurbishment, as this allows the capital costs to be charged to both energy and maintenance, simplifying the underlying investment decision.

The following efficiency improvement measures were carried out:

- Upgrading of induction units.
- A new operating strategy for heating and ventilation.
- Electrically-efficient fans and control strategies, with merging of plant into larger units.
- Installation of Sweden's first large-scale high-frequency lighting system, with occupation and day light sensors, in a 700 m² office area.
- Heat recovery and condenser heat recovery from the cooling systems heat pumps.
- Computerised control and supervisory systems.

The savings achieved can be summarised as follows:
- District heating requirements have been more than halved, in terms of both power and energy.
- Electricity use for ventilation has been reduced by about 60 %.
- Electricity use for lighting has been reduced by about 70 % on the experimental floor, with a particularly marked reduction in power.
- Improved indoor climate.
- Substantially improved operational and maintenance

Table 2. Some key indicators for the four office buildings.

	Folksam	Trygg-Hansa[1]	Wasa	Skandia
Approximate net floor area [m²]	8900	9800	12000	23000
Total energy: [MWh/year]	1285	1755	1410	2900
of which electrical energy	750	1205	1270	1940
f which heating energy	535	550	140	960
Specific energy use [kWh/ m², year]				
total	145	179[172][2]	117	126
of which electrical energy	85	123(100)[2]	105	84
of which heating energy	60	56(72)[2]	29	20
Metered maximum power demand				
[kW]	169	253(278)[2]	353	462
[W/ m²][3]	19	26(20)[2]	29	20
Specific fan power for office units [kW/(m³/s)][3]				
Rated data	3.7	3.6	5.2	2.9
Measured	2.2	2.6	4.6	2.8

[1]Excluding residential apartments.
[2]Values in brackets include residential apartments.
[3]For all units for the entire air distribution system to the office floors.

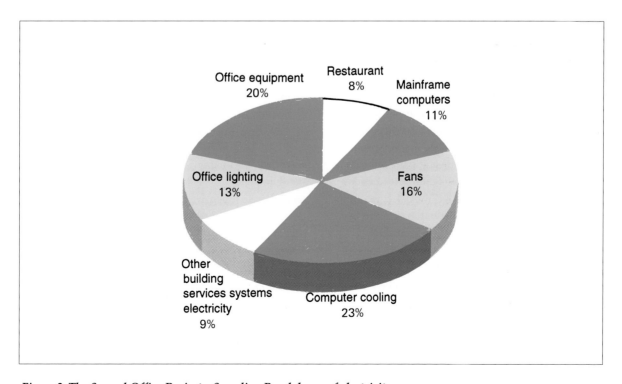

Figure 2. The Second Office Project - Scandia. Breakdown of electricity use.

potentials and facilities, together with improved operational reliability.

The high-frequency lighting installation, which was the first large-scale genuinely efficient installation of its kind in Sweden, incorporates a number of special features, including sensors to respond to occupation of rooms and to daylight. It was commissioned at the beginning of 1990. Experience from it, both favourable and adverse, has meant much for the subsequent rapid technical development of lighting systems in Sweden. Today, high-frequency lighting is more or less standard in connection with larger conversions and new building of offices, schools, shops and health care facilities. The system has excellent prospects, but does require a higher degree of knowledge for design, installation and maintenance.

Projects with other parties

During the last five years, several other parties among the energy distribution utilities have been actively engaged in the field of improvement of efficiency of energy use; mainly in the field of electricity use. The Råcksta Project, mentioned above, is an example of one such scheme.

Stockholm Energi AB has performed several investigations into improving the efficiency of energy use of various applications, including buildings in the commercial premises sector. These investigations - with the Nordbank headquarters and the Bank of Sweden being typical examples - have been concerned primarily with status surveys in combination with suggestions for improvements. In 1992, Gothenburg Energi AB carried out a larger project in six office buildings of varying ages, having different owners and different types of building services systems for ventilation, lighting etc. Besides increasing the utility's knowledge, the objective of the work was also to obtain a picture of the situation in various buildings and to assess the potential for efficiency improvements and the cost effectiveness of various measures. This work, too, concentrated mainly on electricity use, although the interaction between electricity and heat use in all the buildings was a central element.

These projects are examples of the way in which energy utilities have changed, in that they now market themselves as energy service utilities. In both cases, these energy service utilities have concentrated primarily on their larger customers, and then often on high-voltage customers or those who would be expected to take supplies at high voltage.

With BFR support, the National Board of Public Building has also conducted surveys of three different office buildings, concentrating primarily on the amount of electricity use and its breakdown for various purposes[13,14,15]. Certain simpler metering work has also been included. One of these buildings, the Rosteriet block, has also been modelled in other BFR projects using the American DOE2 model.

The Kristallen block

The Kristallen block is a newly-built office building in Uppsala which has been designed to make maximum use of daylight. The use of a glazed atrium ensures good lighting conditions in all rooms.

Design of the building included analyses of daylight conditions and the effects of passive solar energy, as well as minimisation of electricity use for lighting. Alternative systems for controlling the lighting system have also been investigated.

Unfortunately, as a result of the property crash at the end of the 1980s, the Kristallen block was not built fully in accordance with the original plans as far as an energy-efficient lighting system was concerned. However, as at present only half of the building is occupied, there has been no follow-up monitoring of energy use despite some international interest[16].

Computer simulations using the DOE2 model

To measure is to know. However, detailed metering and measurement in the field over a period of several years is usually quite expensive. It is therefore important to develop simpler methods that can provide acceptable accuracy. Other ways involve using validated computerised simulation models, e.g. the American DOE2 model. A number of investigations have been carried out in Sweden over the last five years, using this model[17,18,19,20]. The first of these was performed by an American team of scientists, working with a Swedish advisory group. It was concerned with modelling the effect of various energy efficiency improvement measures in a typical Swedish office building.

In a subsequent continuation investigation, with BFR

support, corresponding simulations have been run, using input data and other parameters that are more typical of Swedish conditions, studying the effects of different designs of air handling systems, lighting etc. The efficiency improvement measures have been harmonised with those covered by NUTEK's outline agreement with larger property owners in the commercial buildings sector. Important schemes for the use of lighting, lifts and office equipment have been modified to bring them into line with Swedish conditions. Much of the input data has been taken from measurements made by the Office Project II investigation.

Alternative designs of windows in respect of differing U-values, daylight admission characteristics and so on have been analysed by DOE2 modelling for the same office building as described above. The various window designs were combined with different types of lighting systems, heat losses from office equipment etc. All combinations were analysed in respect of their total energy use, power demand and utilisation of daylight. Life cycle costs were also calculated for all system combinations. The work was carried out with support from both BFR and NUTEK. The results will provide improved knowledge of complicated system relationships in a typical Swedish office building. They will also provide a basis for correct design and selection of windows, including their effects on the life cycle cost. This is particularly important at early design stages.

Borås Hospital - more electricity and less district heating

Building services systems in hospital premises are often relatively complicated, with performance and specifications being determined largely by the type of activity (surgery, wards, laboratories, kitchens etc.). Ventilation air flow rates are determined by the combined requirements of excellent air quality and a good thermal indoor climate, as opposed to office buildings where it is essentially only the thermal indoor climate (cooling requirements) that determines the design and performance of the system.

Another factor that strongly affects the potential for energy efficiency improvement, together with the cost-effectiveness of improvement measures, is the duration of the system operating time. In hospitals, the ventilation system often runs for most of the day.

A project has been carried out at the Borås Hospital[21]

to investigate the potentials within this sector for improving air quality and the thermal indoor climate while also improving the efficiency of electricity use for fans and lighting. Some of the results from this work have already been used as a basis for improvement measures in connection with major changes in the work of the hospital and associated rebuilding.

With its 800 beds, energy use in this hospital is probably quite representative of that in other Swedish hospitals. This investigation (and others) shows that electricity use increases and the use of district heating decreases in more modern hospital buildings. As far as energy use is concerned, the results from the Borås Hospital are relatively good in relation to the average for hospitals throughout the country.

As far as the building services systems are concerned, the points noted included a lack of operational analysis, complicated systems and problems with attempting to superimpose new control equipment on older systems. New medical equipment, the use of PCs etc. can result in high indoor temperatures or a greater use of electricity for cooling.

To improve the overall operating strategy, it has been suggested that set values should be reviewed and analysed for each building, total operating times should be checked and individual control provided for each ventilation unit. This is important for a number of reasons, not least bearing in mind the fact that activities in a particular part of the building can be quickly changed. Cost-effective improvement measures cover the areas of ventilation, heat recovery systems, lighting, transformers, refrigeration equipment and kitchen equipment.

A continuation project at the Borås Hospital, involving life-cycle-cost-based optimisation, particularly of the central kitchen facilities and their supply systems, has recently been concluded[22].

The largest statistical investigation

The information for the following comparison factors is based mainly on the largest statistical investigation of the commercial premises sector that has hitherto been performed in the country. This was part of Vattenfall's Uppdrag 2000, under the name of STIL[23,24]. On the basis of the results from the investigation, the country's commercial premises building stock has been divided into four groups, depending on their level of electricity use (Table 3).

It can be seen that the average total electricity use in the commercial sector is about 130 kWh/m², year, of which 30 kWh/m², year is used for various types of space heating and for domestic hot water production. Office buildings are close to the mean value for the entire sector, both in terms of total electricity and breakdown for various purposes. However, it is important to remember that there are wide variations, not least in the proportions between different applications. Every building is unique!

Lower energy use in new buildings

Figure 3 compares specific energy use in a homogeneous group of 17 office buildings in which energy use has been comprehensively analysed[25]. The key indicators in this investigation relate to total energy use broken down into heating and electricity for climate control, lighting and office equipment.

The STIL investigation obtained a value of electricity use of the same order for a comparable, relatively homogeneous group of office buildings, i.e. total mean average electricity use of such buildings in Sweden is about 120 kWh/m², year, excluding the possible use of electricity for domestic hot water production.

In all cases, the total area of the items in Figure 3 has been defined in one and the same way. These various items represent different ages, sizes, siting and types of systems for climate control etc. It can be seen from the figure that there is a clear link between the age of the building and total energy use. New buildings use less energy in total but a much higher proportion of electricity. New buildings often have a total value of energy use that is close to 150 kWh/m², year, while older buildings can often be almost twice this. The average proportion between electricity for common services/building services systems and that used by the occupants of the 17 office buildings is 45/55 %.

The relationship between electricity and district heating energy is about 50/50 % in older buildings, while in newer buildings it is closer to 70/30 %. In some cases, so little district heating is used in newer buildings that connection to a district heating supply is fundamentally doubtful.

A comparative analysis of a large number of demonstration projects shows that the requirements in respect of the indoor climate and the effect of internal loads and insolation seem to have a greater effect on annual energy use than do the choice and design of the climate control systems[26].

Major potential for efficiency improvement

The STIL investigation shows that, with present-day electricity prices, improving the efficiency of electricity use is cost-effective and technically feasible in no less that 80 % of Sweden's commercial buildings. Depending on alternative possible energy pricing scenarios, the magnitude of the potential savings is probably 10-15 %.

Table 3. *Comparison figures for electricity use in four different groups of commercial premises.*

Group	Electricity for operation	Electric heating incl. domestic hot water	Total electricity use
	kWh/m², year	kWh/m², year	kWh/m², year
I	270	30	300
II	140	40	180
III	75	35	110
IV	50	10	60
All	100	30	130

Group I: Grocery shops.

Group II: Restaurants, hotels, workshops and sport.

Group III: Child day-care centres, stores, offices, banks, meeting halls, accommodation and health premises.

Group IV: Education.

Energy use, kWh/m² and year

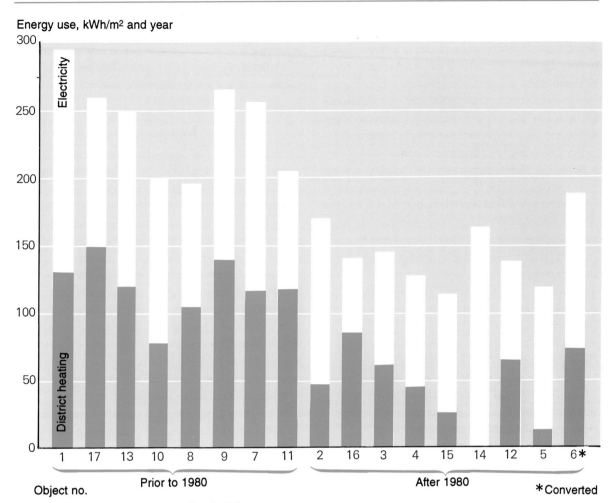

Figure 3. Specific energy use in office buildings.

On average, it is necessary to apply 3-4 improvement measures in each building in order to achieve the theoretical potential, as most such measures result in only a relatively small individual improvement. Half of the potential savings can be achieved by carrying out improvement measures that require no cost investment at all.

If electricity prices increase by 30-40 %, the proportion of commercial premises in which it will be cost-effective to improve the efficiency of electricity use will rise to 90 %.

By far the largest savings, in absolute terms, can be found in the lighting side. This is followed by improvement measures for ventilation and refrigeration/freezing of foodstuffs. However, when applying such improvements, it is important always to consider the overall view, as the entire building constitutes a single, active system.

As far as indoor climate is concerned, it has been found that about 85 % of offices and health care premises have good or acceptable carbon dioxide concentrations (below 1000 ppm). However, carbon dioxide concentration is only one of many indicators of indoor climate quality.

A risk of sub-optimisation

New commercial premises today often employ VAV ventilation systems. This provides an energy-efficient way of adjusting the ventilation to varying loadings in different parts of the building. Modern cooling systems are normally designed as indirect systems[27,28.]

Internal heat loads are minimised through the use of new window designs and energy-efficient high-frequency lighting systems, controlled preferably by occupation sensors, but alternatively by daylight control. Combined systems, using both occupation sensors and daylight control, are uncommon, due to high price and because lighting levels have already been reduced to 10 W/m² or less in typical office rooms.

Development trends for hospital buildings today are relatively similar, except for the very special requirements dictated by the purposes of the rooms or buildings.

If allowance is not made for the overall view, there is a serious risk of sub-optimisation. If a building already has an energy-efficient VAV ventilation system and a low specific power lighting system, the physical and cost potentials for further efficiency improvements are very marginal. The strategy to be employed should be analysed by computer modelling and application of the life cycle cost principle.

In recent years, awareness of aspects involving electricity use etc. has substantially improved.

Electricity conservation in industrial premises

Vattenfall's Uppdrag 2000 also performed a number of projects in the industrial sector[29]. These projects investigated the energy conservation potentials with present-day technology in the existing built environment and existing installation in non-electrically-intensive industry. The electricity conservation potential was estimated on the basis of surveys and trials of actual improvement measures. The estimates were based on measures that could be justified on cost efficiency grounds in comparison with the alternative costs of new electricity production.

It is natural that the results are strongly dependent on the required profitability. However, with a profitability requirement of a three-year straight pay-off time, the electricity conservation potential in the country's non-electrically-intensive industry was estimated at about 1.5 TWh, or 8 % of the present total electricity use of 14 TWh.

Experience also shows that electricity conservation in the non-electrically-intensive industry can generally be achieved through better use of existing technology and modification of various types of equipment to suit actual conditions. Much electrical equipment is oversized, e.g. electric motors[30]. In addition, taking the overall system view, together with preparation of careful operation and maintenance instructions, is of considerable importance.

Improving the efficiency of energy use in industrial buildings is often carried out in connection with modifying a production process in one way or another. Flexibility is important in the light of the need to be able to change production conditions relatively quickly.

Incomplete statistics for the industrial sector

Although a good range of statistics concerning energy use is available for apartment buildings and commercial premises, the information available for the industrial sector is very poor. In recent years, the industrial statistics presented by SCB[31] have become very poor. This is an area in which future work is needed.

In one of the few statistical investigations of Swedish industrial buildings[32] and their characteristics and composition, there is unfortunately only little information that relates to energy use. The country's industrial building stock is very heterogeneous, which presents severe problems in obtaining specific figures for different types of industrial buildings for comparative analyses. As a result, the possibility of making even a rough estimate of the savings potential is very slight.

Comparison indicators, as given for commercial premises, can be used for some industrial premises. Similarly, conservation measures and savings potentials for various application areas, such as lighting, fans, pumps etc. can be based on experience from the commercial premises sector.

Although industry often has more demanding requirements in respect of rates of return than does the commercial premises sector, there are still substantial potentials for savings. However, knowledge of overall system aspects needs to be developed further.

The link to environmental image

Coordination of many small measures to produce an extensive packet of measures, including those intended to improve the efficiency of both heat and electricity use, is not uncommon. In the long term, the link to a company's environmental image is expected to become more important than hitherto. A good environmental image requires energy conservation.

In order to be able to design and purchase energy-efficient equipment and machinery with good long-term profitability, the Association of Swedish

Engineering Industries has prepared a design and purchasing guidelines document under the name of ENEU 9433. It is based on a general approach, using the life cycle cost concept and an associated bonus and penalty system. Purchasing negotiations based on it are at present in progress, and their performance and results will be appraised from a number of aspects.

Experience from the positive development of energy-efficient fans and lighting systems within the commercial premises sector is now finding many obvious applications in industrial premises. NUTEK, for example, has prepared a model performance specification for lighting in the engineering industry[34].

Poor follow-up

Knowledge of energy use, and particularly of electricity use in the commercial premises sector, has been substantially improved over the last 10 years. Nevertheless, it can be stated that monitoring of energy use, i.e. of both electricity and heat, is still poor, and not least with respect to electricity. This is the result more of such aspects as attitudes and the formulation of contracts rather than of any lack of modern aids for energy statistics in the form of computer programs etc.

A need for continued research and development

Over the next ten years, the commercial premises sector will almost certainly be dominated by conversion and refurbishment. The present large numbers of empty commercial premises will result in greater competition for new tenants, with the standards, flexibility and sites of premises being important competition parameters.

Several larger investigations and well-documented individual projects have shown that, both technically and financially, there is a relatively large potential for improvement in much of the country's commercial premises stock. However, it is important that system knowledge should be increased and widely spread in order to avoid the risk of an undesirable and uncontrolled change back from electricity to heat.

It is important to apply greater consideration of systems as a whole in order to be able to apply the essential whole view of the entire field of improving the efficiency of energy use. Such a system approach is also required in order to enable attention to be focused on other important working areas, and not simply on individual components and apparatus.

Greater awareness and application of the life cycle cost concept when deciding on the choice of systems is most important. Good examples from industrial applications and elsewhere should serve as models for the building sector in general.

Today, far too few parties think of, or can treat, buildings from the perspective of the whole. Increasing this approach requires a greater information input and good examples of successful approaches through demonstration and/or experimental building projects. This also includes the need for improved design data in respect of such factors as aggregation of various internal loadings[35].

Experimental building projects need to be carried out, employing knowledge already obtained in the fields of system interrelationships, utilisation of daylight, lighting control etc. Simple, cost-effective and reliable methods of field collection and processing of detailed measured data in the energy sector need to be developed. We also need to refine methods that can be used in the early design stages in order to take better account of energy aspects. Aids for energy-efficient purchasing of building services systems etc. need to be further developed. This work should build on what has been started by the Swedish Association of Engineering Industries in its ENEU 94 project for industrial purchasing of equipment of this type[36].

This chapter is based on material by Anders Nilson, MSc. Eng., Bengt Dahlgren AB, Gothenburg.

REFERENCES

1 Abel, E. *Use of electricity in commercial buildings*. Electricity. End-use and new generation technologies and their planning implications. Editors, Johansson, T. B., Bodlund, B. and Williams, R. H. Lund University Press, 1989.

2 See Abel, 1989.

3 Nilson, A. and Hjalmarsson, Ch. *Elanvändning i fyra kontorsbyggnader. Mätning, analyser och erfarenheter* (Electricity use in four office buildings. Metering, analyses and experience). BFR Report R56:1993, Stockholm.

4 *Energi i byggd miljö 90-talets möjligheter* (Energy in the built environment - the way forward to the 1990s. BFR Publication G16:1988). BFR G16:1987.

5 Sundbom, L., Nilson, A., Munther, K. *Energisparpotentialen i lokaler. Energieffektivisering av fem kontorsbyggnader genom energiteknisk upprustning* (The energy conservation potential of commercial premises. Improvement of energy efficiency in five office buildings through modernisation of energy equipment). BFR Report R27:1987, Stockholm.

6 Swedish Council for Building Research. *Energianvändning kan halveras i kontorsbyggnader* (Energy use in office buildings can be halved). Publication G22:1987, Stockholm.

7 See Nilson & Hjalmarsson, 1993.

8 *DOE2 BASICS*. Simulation Research Group, Centre for Building Science, Applied Science Division, Lawrence Berkeley Laboratory, University of California, Berkeley, CA 94720 (August 1991).

9 *Energisyn - lokaler. Minskad tillförsel ger ökat utbyte.* (The energy view - commercial premises. Reduced supply results in greater yield). NUTEK/Folksam/Skandia/Trygg-Hansa/SPP and Wasa. Training Binder.

10 Nilson, A. and Hjalmarsson, C. *Energy use in Swedish office buildings*. European Directory of Energy-efficient Building 1994. James & James Science Publishers Ltd., 5 Castle Road, London NW1, UK.

11 Jagemar, L. *Learning from experiences with energy-efficient HVAC systems in office buildings*. CADDET Analysis Support Unit. Final draft, 30 January 1995.

12 Nilson, A., Hjalmarsson, C., Uppström, R., Hedenström, C. et al. *El-, belysnings- och värmeeffektivisering för Vattenfalls kontor, Vällingby* (Improving the efficiency of electricity, lighting and heat use in Vattenfall's offices, Vällingby). Vattenfall, 1993, Stockholm.

13 Göransson, P. and Qvist, B. *Elanvändning i ett kontorshus. Mätning och analys, kv. Gamen, Stockholm* (Electricity use in an office building. Metering and analysis, the Gamen block, Stockholm). BFR Report R62:1990, Stockholm.

14 Kamjou, P. and Jung, R. *Mätning och analys. Kv. Rosteriet, Stockholm.* (Metering and analysis, the Rosteriet block, Stockholm). BFR Report R57:1991, Stockholm.

15 Nordling, B. *Mätning och analys av elanvändning i kontors- och laboratoriebyggnad vid Statens Provningsanstalt* (Metering and analysis of electricity use in an office and laboratory building at the National Research and Testing Agency). Report SP-AR 1990:25, Energy Technology, Borås, 1990.

16 *The Kristallen block. New ideas of the office building in the future.* 920304 BYGGDOK, Stockholm.

17 Holtz, Michael. *Electrical energy savings in office buildings*. BFR Document D17:1990, Stockholm.

18 Nilson, A. and Hjalmarsson, Ch. *Kv. Rosteriet, Stockholm. En jämförelse av uppmätt och simulerad el- och värmeenergianväding i ett kontorshus (1992-01-22)* (The Rosteriet block, Stockholm. A comparison of as-measured and simulated electricity and thermal energy use in an office building). BYGGDOK, 1992, Stockholm.

19 Nilson, A. and Hjalmarsson, Ch. *Simulerad el- och värmeenergianvändning i en ny kontorsbyggnad* (Simulated electricity and thermal energy use in a new office building). BYGGDOK, 1994, Stockholm.

20 Nilson, A., Hjalmarsson, Ch., Ziegler, M., Öfverholm, I. and Pertola,

P. *Energianvändning och livscykelkostnader för en kontorsbyggnad med alternativa utföranden av fönster. Simuleringar och analyser* (Energy use and life cycle costs for an office building with various window designs. Simulations and analyses). NUTEK, Stockholm, 1995.

21 Larsson, R. and Blomsterberg, Å. *Eleffektivisering och förbättring av inneklimat i sjukhus - Borås Lasarett* (Improving the efficiency of electricity use and improving the indoor climate in hospitals - the Borås Hospital). SP Report 1993:40, Energy Technology, Borås, 1993.

22 Nilson, A., Uppström, R. and Blomsterberg, Å. *Energieffektivisering och förbättring av inomhusklimat i storkök - LCC-baserad driftoptimering vid Borås Lasarett* (Improving the energy efficiency and indoor climate in a central kitchen: a life-cycle-cost-based operational optimisation at the Borås Hospital). Bengt Dahlgren AB and the Swedish National Testing and Research Institute. NUTEK, 1995.

23 *Från krog till kontor. Slutrapport för lokalsektorn inom Uppdrag 2000* (From pub to office. Final report for the commercial premises sector of Uppdrag 2000). Report No. U1991/50, Vattenfall, Stockholm.

24 *Lokalerna och energihushållningen* (Commercial premises and energy conservation). Report from the STIL investigation in Uppdrag 2000. Report No. U1991/70, Vattenfall, Stockholm.

25 See Nilson & Hjalmarsson, 1993.

26 See Jagemar, 1995.

27 Nilson, A., Bergh, U. and Walter, A. *Energiteknisk standard i nybyggda lokaler.* (Energy standards in new commercial premises). Summary PM, 1990-05-15, Vattenfall, Stockholm.

28 Nilson, A. and Uppström, R. *Energimätning i nybyggda kommersiella lokaler* (Energy metering in new commercial premises). Information report from Bengt Dahlgren AB, Gothenburg for Vattenfall, Stockholm, 1993.

29 *Från idé till investering. Slutrapport från Uppdrag 2000: Industrisektorn* (From idea to investment: Final report from Uppdrag 2000, the Industrial sector). Report U 1991:48, Vattenfall, Stockholm.

30 *Reducerade kostnader genom rätt motorvarvtal. Resultat från en studie av elmotordrifter vid kulsinterverket hos LKAB i Kiruna* (Reduced costs from correct motor speed. Results from an investigation of electric motor drives at the LKAB sinter works in Kiruna). Vattenfall, Uppdrag 2000. Report No. 2000 91 1202, Stockholm, 1991.

31 Statistical Notice E 14 SM9301. *Energistatistik. Förbrukning av elenergi och inköpta bränslen inom industrin år 1991* (Energy statistics. The use of electrical energy and purchased fuels in industry in 1991).

32 Lindgren, H. and Wilhelmsen, A. M. *Sveriges industrihus. Beståndets egenskaper och sammansättning* (Sweden's industrial buildings: Characteristics and composition). Report R26:1993, BFR, Stockholm, 1993.

33 ENEU 94. *Anvisningar för energieffektiv upphandling av utrustning och maskiner inom industrin* (Directives for the procurement of energy-efficient equipment and machinery for use in industry). Prepared by Bengt Dahlgren AB on behalf of the Swedish Association of Engineering Industries. Förlags AB Industrilitteratur, 1994, Order No. V060007.

34 *Belysning i verkstadsindustrin. Programkrav för god och energieffektiv belysning i verkstadsindustrin* (Lighting in the engineering industry. Model performance requirements for good and energy-efficient lighting in the engineering industry). NUTEK, Department of Energy Efficiency, 1994.

35 See Nilson & Hjalmarsson, 1993.

36 See ENEU 94.

A STATISTICAL PRESENTATION OF ENERGY USE IN THE BUILT ENVIRONMENT

Energy use in the built environment accounts for about 40 % of Sweden's total energy use. Despite access to extensive, high quality public statistics, there are still substantial gaps in our knowledge of energy conservation in the built environment. However, international comparisons indicate that the Swedish built environment has a relatively good energy status, i.e. low energy use in relation to our climate.

*The diagrams on the following pages provide information on Swedish building stock, both in quantitative terms and in respect of energy performance. The figures have been obtained by processing public statistics and consumption statistics. The material is an updated selection of previously presented work, namely **Energy use in residential buildings and commercial premises, 1970–1990** (Carlsson, L-G.: Swedish Council for Building Research R30:1992, in Swedish) and **Data from the built environment for energy planning** (Göransson, A., Wennerhag, P. et al.: Swedish Council for Building Research, R152:1984, in Swedish).*

Quantitative statistics on the built environment

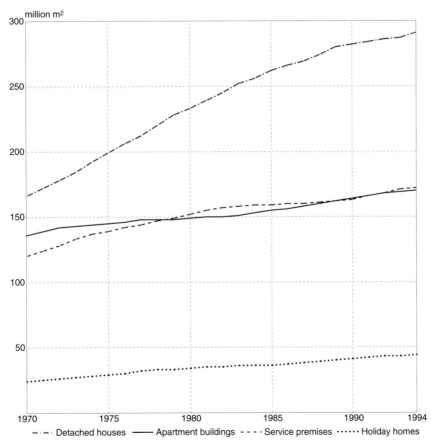

Figure 1. Growth of the total heated floor area in detached houses, apartment buildings, holiday homes and service premises since 1970.

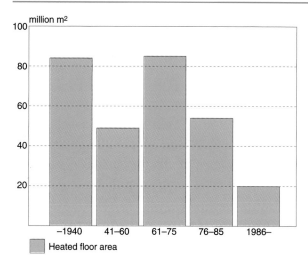

Figure 2. Heated floor area in detached houses, classified by year of completion.

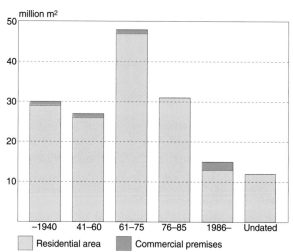

Figure 4 Heated floor area in service premises, classified by year of completion.

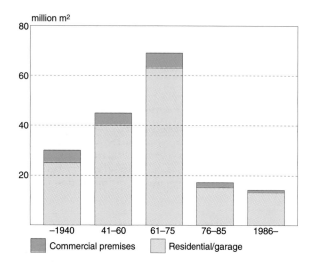

Figure 3. Heated floor area in apartment building stock, classified by year of completion.

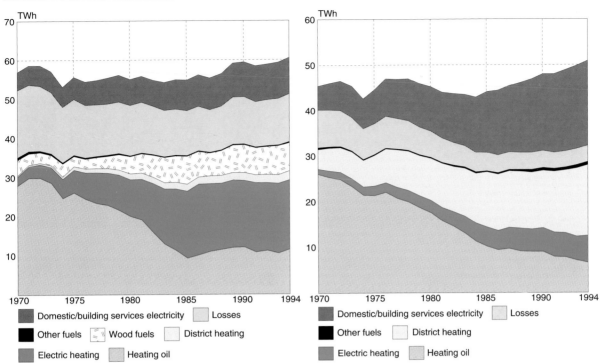

Figure 5. *Energy use in detached houses by category of energy carrier (district heating, electricity, oil etc.). Energy use for heating purposes has been corrected to a statistically average climatic year. 'Losses' represent the difference between gross and net energy use for heating purposes.*

Figure 7. *Energy use in service premises by category of energy carrier (district heating, electricity, oil etc.). Energy use for heating purposes has been corrected to a statistically average climatic year. 'Losses' represent the difference between gross and net energy use for heating purposes.*

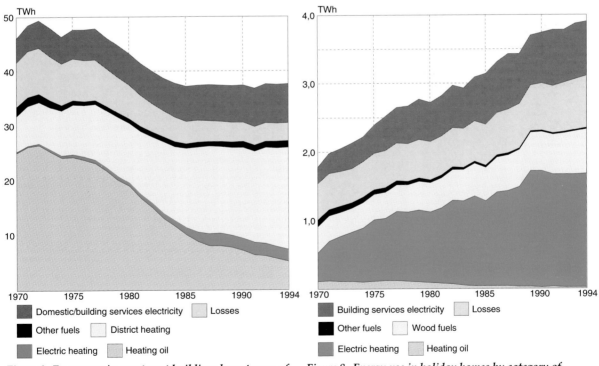

Figure 6. *Energy use in apartment buildings by category of energy carrier (district heating, electricity, oil etc.). Energy use for heating purposes has been corrected to a statistically cally average climatic year. 'Losses' represent the difference between gross and net energy use for heating purposes.*

Figure 8. *Energy use in holiday homes by category of energy carrier (wood fuels, electricity, oil etc.). Energy use for heating purposes has been corrected to a statistically average climatic year. 'Losses' represent the difference between gross and net energy use for heating purposes.*

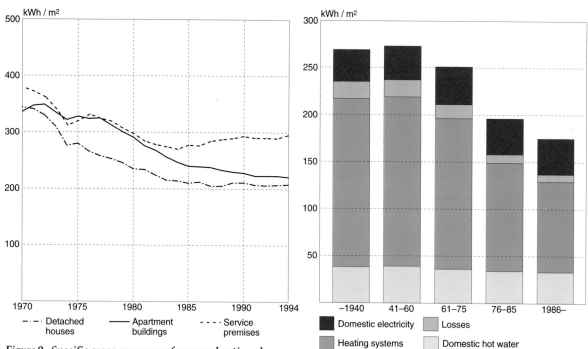

Figure 9. Specific gross energy use for space heating, domestic hot water and domestic electricity/electricity for building services as kWh/m², year in detached houses, apartment buildings and service premises, after correction to a statistically average climatic year.

Figure 11. Specific energy use in terms of final use in apartment buildings, by year of construction, after correction to a statistically average climatic year.

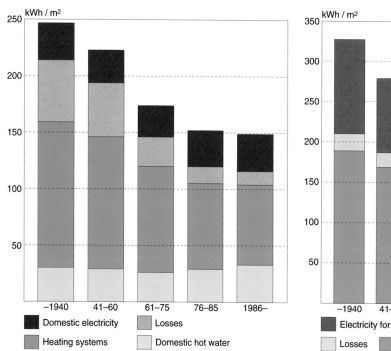

Figure 10. Specific energy use in terms of final use in detached houses, by year of construction, after correction to a statistically average climatic year.

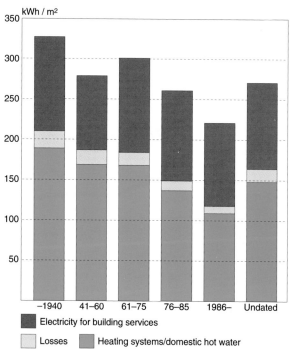

Figure 12. Specific energy use in terms of final use in service premises, by year of construction, after correction to a statistically average climatic year.

Figure 13. *Energy costs per m² (including tax and fixed charges) in detached houses. Prices have been calculated as mean prices at 1990 price levels.*

Figure 15. *Energy costs per m² (including tax and fixed charges) in service premises. Prices have been calculated as mean prices at 1990 price levels.*

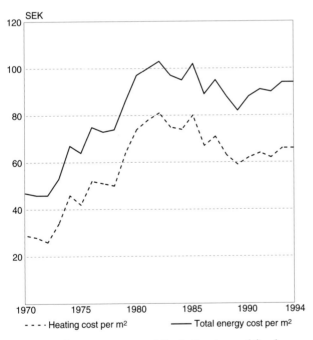

Figure 14. *Energy costs per m² (including tax and fixed charges) in apartment buildings. Prices have been calculated as mean prices at 1990 price levels.*

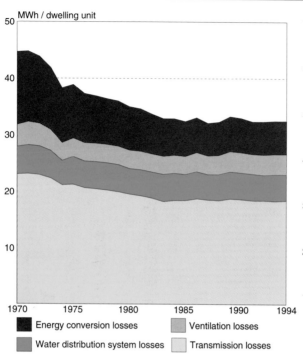

Figure 16. *Energy losses per dwelling unit in detached houses, 1970–1994. Energy use for heating purposes has been corrected to a statistically average climatic year.*

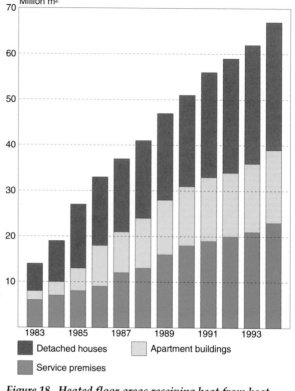

Figure 18. *Heated floor areas receiving heat from heat pumps, 1983–1994. (Heat pumps in district heating systems are not included.)*

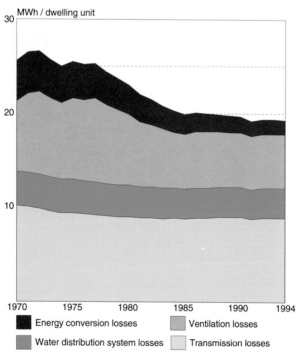

Figure 17. *Energy losses per dwelling unit in apartment buildings, 1970–1994. Energy use for heating purposes has been corrected to a statistically average climatic year.*

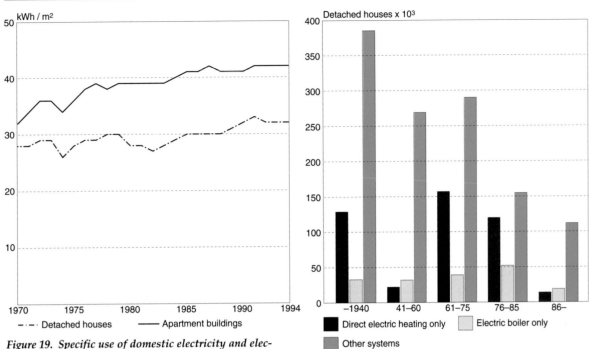

Figure 19. Specific use of domestic electricity and electricity for building services, kWh/m², year in detached houses and apartment buildings.

Figure 21. Number of detached houses, classified by type of heating system and year of completion.

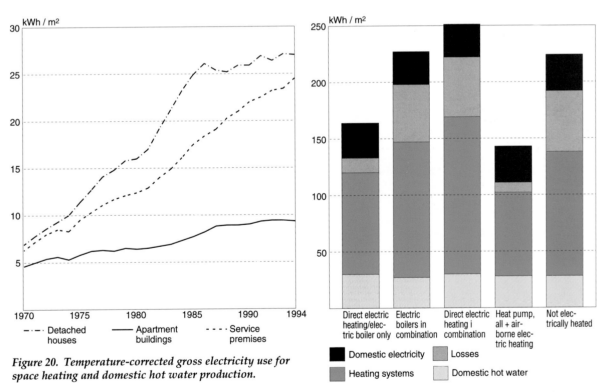

Figure 20. Temperature-corrected gross electricity use for space heating and domestic hot water production.

Figure 22. Specific energy use in detached houses, 1991, by type of heating system.

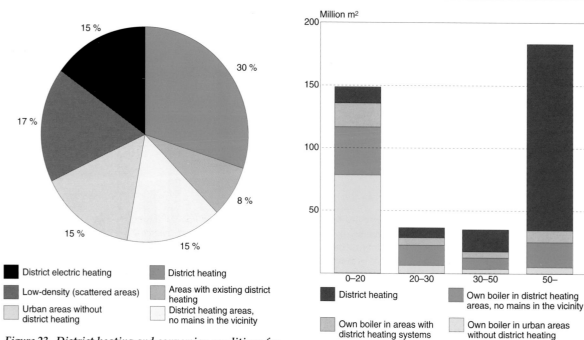

Figure 23. *District heating and conversion conditions for all heated floor area in the country's detached houses, apartment buildings and service premises.*

Figure 25. *Built environment siting in relation to district heating systems: columns indicate thermal load density.*

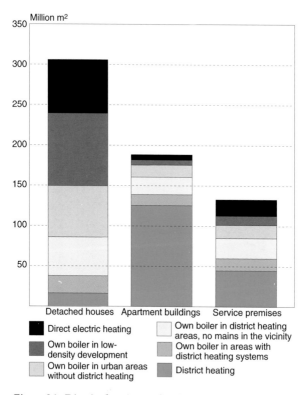

Figure 24. *District heating and conversion conditions in all types of buildings.*

Type of area	Present specific heating requirement, kWh/m², year	'Conservation level', kWh/m², year	Savings potential, kWh/m², year	Proportion with conservation measures, %
District heating	165	130	35	12
Own boiler				
Close to district heating network in				
densely built-up areas	167	131	36	19
sparsely built-up areas	151	122	29	13
In areas with district heating, no mains in the vicinity				
densely built-up areas	163	129	34	12
sparsely built-up areas	144	117	27	10
In urban areas without district heating				
densely built-up areas	161	129	32	10
sparsely built-up areas	146	119	27	11
Boilers in sparsely built-up areas	158	125	33	28
Direct electric heating etc.	147	128	19	14

Figure 26. Specific energy use for space heating of detached houses, apartment buildings and service premises, together with conservation level. The calculations are based on each building being thermally insulated to new building standards, windows being upgraded to triple-glazed windows and heat recovery systems being installed if the building has mechanical ventilation. At the same time, these savings would be somewhat offset by the fact that heat input from electrical equipment would be reduced as a result of replacing the equipment by the most efficient available on the market today, which would mean that more energy would be required from the radiators. The calculations have been performed individually for each building, with allowance for their age, type, equipment standard and whether improvements have already been applied.

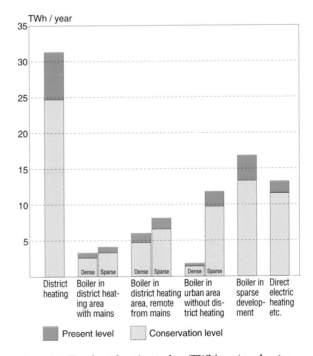

Figure 27. Total net heating today (TWh/year) and potential conservation level, classified by type of built environment with various heat supply conditions.

SOME EXPLANATIONS

Abbrevations

ASTM: American Society for Testing Materials

CEN: Comité Européen de Normalisation

IEA: International Energy Agency

IPCC: International Panel for Climatic Change

ISO: International Standards Organization

OECD: Organization for Economic Cooperation and Development

SAVE: EU development programme for more efficient use of energy.

THERMIE: EU development programme for energy-efficient technology within the areas of energy use, renewable energy sources, solid fuels and hydrocarbons.

Some prefixes

μ	micro	10^{-6}
m	milli	10^{-3}
k	kilo	10^{3}
M	mega	10^{6}
G	giga	10^{9}
T	tera	10^{12}

Some rules of thumb

1 TWh   is approximately the quantity of electricity used in Sweden in four days.

1 kW   is the approximate power of a cooker hotplate.

10 kW   is the approximate power of a domestic heating boiler.